The ART of Living Well

**Light Cooking and Eating
to Fit the Way We Live**

Rose Reisman

VIKING
CANADA

VIKING CANADA

Published by the Penguin Group

Penguin Books, a division of Pearson Canada, 10 Alcorn Avenue, Toronto, Ontario, Canada M4V 3B2

Penguin Books Ltd, 80 Strand, London WC2R 0RL, England

Penguin Putnam Inc., 375 Hudson Street, New York, New York 10014, U.S.A.

Penguin Books Australia Ltd, 250 Camberwell Road, Camberwell, Victoria 3124, Australia

Penguin Books India (P) Ltd, 11, Community Centre, Panchsheel Park, New Delhi – 110 017, India

Penguin Books (NZ) Ltd, cnr Rosedale and Airborne Roads, Albany, Auckland 1310, New Zealand

Penguin Books (South Africa) (Pty) Ltd, 24 Sturdee Avenue, Rosebank 2196, South Africa

Penguin Books Ltd, Registered Offices: 80 Strand, London WC2R 0RL, England

10 9 8 7 6 5 4 3 2 1

Colour inserts: Per Kristiansen

The nutrition label on page 91 is reprinted by permission of So Soya+ Inc., www.sosoya.com, telephone 416-293-6555.

Printed and bound in Canada on acid free paper.

National Library of Canada Cataloguing in Publication

Reisman, Rose, 1953–
    The art of living well : light cooking and eating to fit the way we live / Rose Reisman.

Includes bibliographical references and index.

ISBN 0-670-04347-8

1. Low-fat diet—Recipes. 2. Nutrition. I. Title.

RM237.7.R445 2002   641.5'638   C2002-903135-4

Visit Penguin Books' website at **www.penguin.ca**

I wake up most mornings with a joy and zest for life.
I owe all this to my treasured family, who love me
unconditionally and inspire me to live well.

My husband, Sam: after 26 years of marriage,
I still wake up each morning thrilled to be your partner.
I'll always love you.

Natalie: my wonderful, amazing, and self-disciplined
18-year-old daughter, who is starting her own journey in
the fall, at the University of Michigan.

David: my well-balanced, "all around" 16-year-old son,
who is so sweet he can give me a toothache!

Laura: my wild and wonderful 14-year-old "tempest,"
whose spirit will always be there.

Adam: my 10-year-old son, who, no matter how cool
he gets, will always be my baby.

My mother: my greatest fan.

My furry "children": Aspen, Meiko, and Misty, my
German shepherds and my ragdoll cat, who give me the
quiet moments in my day.

In memory of Monica Wright Roberts,
who inspired the modern breast cancer movement.
Her life force will live on forever.

Contents

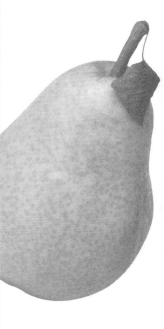

Acknowledgments

Thanks to Carol Seidman and Jay Hooper at the Canadian Breast Cancer Foundation, for your professional support of this project. Your expertise lends credibility to the support of breast cancer research, education, and awareness.

Thanks to Eva, Kate, and Mila, who assist me with my home, cooking school, and family. I couldn't do it without you.

Thanks to Lesleigh Landry, who helped in the testing, writing, and nutritional analysis of the recipes.

And thanks to the team at Viking Canada, the greatest publisher an author could ever wish for. Special thanks to Nicole de Montbrun and Andrea Crozier, for helping me formulate the idea for this book; Ed Carson, who has made all the business negotiations so easy and has endured my husband all the way; Tracy Bordian, thank you for overseeing the book so very well; and Mary Opper, for making the book look spectacular. You've all been a delight to work with.

Canadian Breast Cancer Foundation®

Dear Friend:

The Canadian Breast Cancer Foundation (CBCF) is delighted to be the recipient of generous support from the sales of Rose Reisman's newest book, *The Art of Living Well*. With your purchase of this exciting collection of outstanding recipes and culinary advice, we move that much closer to creating a future without breast cancer.

As the leading national volunteer-based organization dedicated to the fight against breast cancer, the Canadian Breast Cancer Foundation works collaboratively to fund, support, and advocate for

- relevant and innovative breast cancer research
- meaningful education and awareness programs
- early diagnosis and effective treatment
- a positive quality of life for those living with breast cancer

Since our inception in 1986, CBCF has allocated more than $21 million in grants for breast cancer projects and services. We thank you for your part in helping to eradicate breast cancer as a life-threatening disease, and we congratulate Rose Reisman and everyone who came up with the winning recipes for this project.

Carol Seidman, CFRE

CHIEF EXECUTIVE OFFICER
Canadian Breast Cancer Foundation

creating a future without breast cancer

Phone: 1-800-387-9816

Preface

As I write this book I am in my late forties. I have four children between the ages of 10 and 18—two girls and two boys—who are my greatest gifts in life. I have been successfully married for 26 years to Sam, my soulmate; and I enjoy the company of two German shepherds and a ragdoll cat. My life is hectic, never dull, and incredibly wonderful and fulfilling. I couldn't picture it any other way. But, like anyone's, my life has its ups and downs, and it does require lots of energy and patience.

I began my career as a teacher, but at the age of 30 went back to school, uncertain of what I wanted to be when I "grew up." While completing the second of two postgraduate degrees—a master's degree in fine arts in theatre administration and a master's in business administration—I had two small infants. By the time I completed the MBA, my fellow graduates were primed for interviews with large corporations, but I was not so quick to follow them. I remember my husband asking me if that was truly what I wanted to do. I knew if I went to work for a large corporation I would not see enough of my children, and I so loved being around them. But, as my mother would say, "All this education and then what?" I decided to take a part-time teaching position at a nearby college. I was now pregnant with my third child and the balance felt right.

It was at this time that I began experimenting in the kitchen. I found creating recipes so relaxing that I decided to write a cookbook. Everyone around me thought I was going through an early mid-life crisis! Unfazed, I began work on a deliciously high-fat dessert cookbook titled *Toronto's Dessert Scene,* in which I re-created recipes of well-known chefs. Unable to find a publisher, I produced the book myself. And the experience paid off: I sold more than 5000 books (a Canadian bestseller!). This success inspired me to write more books, all filled with recipes loaded with cream, butter, cheese, and other high-fat ingredients—after all, it was the addition of these fattening things that made my recipes so delicious.

And these ingredients weren't a problem for me, or so I thought. I comfortably managed my weight by eating small portions and exercising regularly. But just being slim and in shape doesn't guarantee good health. When I was in my mid-thirties, during a routine physical my doctor discovered I had extremely high cholesterol. Given my family history of heart disease, obesity, and diabetes, this finding was a signal for ill health to come. My doctor advised me to switch careers and stop writing cookbooks.

That's when I decided to take a detour instead and focus on healthy, lower-fat recipes. It wasn't an easy decision, because to me low-fat had always meant low in taste. Everything low-fat was poached, steamed, boiled, or grilled—with a squeeze of lemon juice or vinegar added for flavour. And desserts? Low-fat desserts meant fruit: sliced, poached, baked, or crumbled. I couldn't get excited about this type of cooking or this style of eating.

At the time, Anne Lindsay was in the forefront of light cooking in Canada. By studying her simple, straightforward recipes, I started to understand that you didn't have to remove all the fat to make food low-fat; all that was necessary was substituting lower-fat ingredients for high-fat ones. Inspired, I was determined to write the best-tasting low-fat cookbook ever. Titled *Rose Reisman Brings Home Light Cooking,* it had more than 175 lower-fat and lower-cholesterol recipes, ranging from appetizers to desserts.

Around that time, I had a close acquaintance who died from breast cancer, leaving three young children and a husband. Hers was not a rare situation. Approached by the Canadian Breast Cancer Foundation (CBCF) to help in raising funds, I suggested writing a cookbook and donating a portion of the proceeds to the cause. The CBCF was established in 1986 and is the largest charitable organization in Canada dedicated exclusively to supporting the advancement of breast cancer research, education, diagnosis, and treatment. This organization addresses the needs of Canadians from coast to coast and has chapters in British Columbia, Yukon, Alberta, and the Atlantic provinces. I will be touring Canada when this book is launched, not only to promote *The Art of Living Well,* but also to help raise more needed funds for the CBCF. See the CBCF website at www.cbcf.org for more information. *Light Cooking* sold more than 400,000 copies and was followed by *Light Pasta,* which sold 275,000. These two books raised over $700,000 for breast cancer research, education, and treatment. It was the most wonderful feeling: I was not only doing something I enjoyed but raising money for such a necessary cause. I am thrilled to once again donate a portion of the proceeds from this book to the CBCF.

More books followed, as did my light-cooking television show, *Lighten Up with Rose Reisman.* The response to the books and the show was great. I received numerous letters and e-mails from readers and viewers who were serving my meals throughout the week, and even for dinner parties. People were losing weight, getting healthy, eating great food—and enjoying the process. My message was being communicated: low-fat food doesn't mean deprivation or second best; it is the preferred, and delicious, alternative.

I now run a "light" cooking school in Toronto that offers courses in everything from appetizers to desserts, with specialties in sushi, vegetarian, ethnic foods, and even soy. My clients are of all ages and walks of life. My corporate groups are all on the bandwagon of helping their employees eat and live better. I love teaching my students all the benefits of eating in this way. It's not about dieting, but about a way of life.

Struggling with my own weight problems, learning how to adapt and change my eating while aging, writing a series of low-fat cookbooks, and dealing with a growing family—and obtaining the designation of registered nutritional consultant—have given me some expertise in the field. Now, I want to share with others what I have spent my life doing. *The Art of Living Well* is my guide to getting you well on your way.

In the following chapters, you'll find information you can use the rest of your life. You'll learn why we, as a nation, suffer so many illnesses because of our unhealthy lifestyle. We'll look at fad diets—what's in and what's not, and what they will do to and for you. You'll even learn about basic nutrition so that you can understand what those food manufacturers are telling you. A tour of the market and a translation of food labels are necessary if you're to be an enlightened shopper. These naturally will lead us to developing the perfect "light kitchen," where everything—ingredients, appliances—will lead you in the right direction. Knowing how to eat in any type of restaurant and what the better menu choices are will help you. "Hold the Mayo" discusses the pros and cons of popular restaurants and fast-food outlets. Because you bring your attitude to any lifetime change, there's a section that examines the stimuli that make us eat well or poorly and how we can reprogram them. Finally, there are loads of delicious and healthy recipes for you and your family. So read on, and start on the art of living well.

I have a passion for eating—and living—well. In fact, I've spent the greater part of my adult life practising and preaching the wonders of healthy eating and exercise. It's this particular passion that allows me to wake up most mornings feeling healthy, strong—both physically and mentally—and in control of my day. With four children, two dogs, a cat, and my husband (not necessarily in that order), that's quite a task.

Living Well

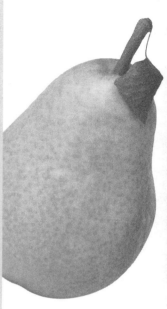

Enhancing Your Life

Of course, there's more to my life than what I feed myself and my family: I try to enjoy each day to the fullest, which includes fulfilling my duties to family, work, and social relationships. I want to feel positive about what I've accomplished that day. I take each day as it comes, hour by hour; it's the only way I can continue to grow and maximize the quality of my life.

My formula for healthy eating and living is not a science; neither is it something that can be learned overnight. It's a skill you need to practise over and over until you reach your level of "perfection." For our purposes, perfection means reaching a body weight that you feel comfortable with, achieving a level of physical fitness that makes you feel stronger, and eating in a way that you can maintain for the rest of your life. This is what I—and my family—aim for daily.

Eating as a Child

People always ask how I stay slim if I'm around food all the time. My first answer is that I'm always eating from my own cookbooks—light and healthy! And I also exercise regularly. But it wasn't always so.

Like most of us, I had to work at eating well. It took some time to unlearn the bad eating habits I learned as a child, coming from a family that indulged in the fattiest foods. Not surprisingly, my mother was extremely overweight and had high blood pressure. My father, who died at 57 of a massive coronary, had high blood pressure, high cholesterol, kidney problems, and ulcers. My grandmother, too, was obese and died from complications of diabetes. I can only assume their delicious but high-fat European fare served daily, coupled with a sedentary lifestyle, contributed to my family's poor health.

Fruits and vegetables were rare at our table, and whole-wheat products were unheard of. My family considered anything "light" and healthy as "bird food" and told me, "You'll never be strong and healthy unless you eat lots of *fleish* [Yiddish for meat]." One of my childhood indulgences—never discouraged by my parents—was eating the skin, along with the white slabs of greasy fat, from chickens and the fat from roasts. My family also believed that exercise tired you out and would lead to poor health! It was always better to relax.

At the age of nine, I was an overweight child. I remember the snide comments from friends and even teachers. My grade five teacher once observed that I would look "so pretty" if I was slimmer. My own father whispered to my mother that my "gruba touchas" (Yiddish for huge rear end) was spreading beyond control! And yet, my mother kept feeding me potato salad loaded with mayonnaise and latkes (potato pancakes) fried in oil. When I entered junior high school I noticed how all the slim girls wore the tightest jeans and shortest T-shirts. Why were they small and I so large? I had no idea it was because of the type of food I was eating. I just thought they were lucky and I wasn't—until I began to read the nutrition literature.

The connection between salami sandwiches and gaining weight was a revelation to me. I started taking salad and cottage cheese with fruit for lunch. My mother thought I was crazy but, after I lost 20 pounds, she changed her mind. For the first time, I felt attractive and good about myself. I got a part-time job and began dating—life seemed wonderful.

Eating as an Adult

As I got older, I read more and more on what healthy food was all about. It wasn't just about eating a restricted diet of cottage cheese and fruit, but about following the guidelines to healthy eating. It involved incorporating certain food groups: meat and alternatives, milk products, grains, and fruits and vegetables. It was about getting the right amount and type of protein, eating an appropriate amount of complex carbohydrates, and choosing lower-fat dairy products. It meant keeping saturated fat to a minimum and having poorer-quality (junk) foods only occasionally.

Over time, I also realized that aging was not ideal for weight maintenance. Every five to eight years my metabolism slowed down, which meant eating the same amount of food led to weight gain. Either I had to live with being heavier or I had to eat less—and/or exercise more. (There are always choices in life, though perhaps not the ones we want!) After the age of 30, unless I made some serious sacrifices, I could no longer weigh what I did at 21. Weighing five pounds more was fine, but even then I had to eat less. After 40, I realized that timing was crucial. Eating after eight o'clock at night could be deadly for weight control. Regular exercise was a must, not only for weight control, but also to delay the onslaught of sagging skin. Getting enough calcium and other vitamins and minerals was a must to feel energized and prevent myself from getting sick. I began studying the effects of certain foods on health. There were heart-healthy foods to prevent high cholesterol, high blood pressure, and heart disease; foods that could prevent certain kinds of cancer; and those that could ward off osteoporosis, obesity, and diabetes. As I began increasing my consumption of these foods, I not only felt better and had more energy, but I also became less susceptible to colds and flu. I even tolerated stress in my day more effectively.

It used to be that a woman in her late forties usually was overweight, was out of shape, and looked "middle-aged." Not today—not if you take care of yourself. In *my* late forties, I feel healthier and have more energy than I did in my twenties. And there's no doubt in my mind that this is due to my daily habits. Incorporating good food and exercise into each day are the lessons I teach my family, friends, students, and clients. The big-time payoff is feeling great, looking younger, and being healthy.

Why I Wrote This Book

After spending the last 14 years experimenting with and learning all about food, I have "digested" a lot of information. I have gone from a high-fat guru to, as some call me, the "Queen of Light." I can tell you how to adapt your favourite high-fat recipe to one that's lower in fat; I can explain to you why certain foods are healthy and some are not; I can teach you how to eat successfully in any type of restaurant; I can show you how to incorporate exercise into your regular schedule; I can give you the pros and cons of every new fad diet out there. And lots more!

I have found, and read, dozens of books focusing on cooking, shopping, food labels, nutrition, exercise, diets, specific foods, and more. What has been hard to come by is one comprehensive, easy-to-read book on all these topics that also included delicious, easy-to-prepare heart-healthy recipes. That's why I've written this book—truly one I have wanted at my fingertips and one that will help you find the answers to the art of eating and living well.

The students, clients, and corporate people I meet are too consumed with their work, family, or other obligations to do the reading and research I have done. They all tell me that they have books on cooking, nutrition, exercise, fad diets—but they rarely have the time to read all of this information. So they either get second-hand knowledge from friends or make ill-informed decisions often based on incorrect information. Lack of knowledge prevents people from making healthier choices and leading a healthy lifestyle. You don't have to become an expert in this field; you just need easy access to important information to become an educated consumer, empowered to make better decisions.

The recipes in this book are for people who have a busy life but still want to get delicious, healthy food on the table—on weekdays for the family and on weekends for entertaining. The most popular classes in my school were Speedy Weeknight Dinners and Entertaining Made Easy; they sold out every session. I created recipes that could be put together in less than 30 minutes, and that called for ingredients available in every supermarket across the country. My students found these dishes so delicious, healthy, and attractive that they would be thrilled to serve them for entertaining, as well as Monday to Friday fare.

Why not kill two birds with one stone? My weekends are filled with catering to my family's needs. I want to spend as little time in the kitchen as possible. But at the same time I don't want to be eating in restaurants on a regular basis, ordering in, or eating processed packaged foods all the time. Nothing is better than a homemade healthy meal that not only is delicious but can be made quickly.

Recently, I had a group of female gynecologists in for a business dinner, and one told me that she had studied the art of French cooking at the Cordon Bleu School in France. I felt as if I had to apologize for my cooking class that evening—everything I did was so simple. She laughed and said the last time she cooked in Cordon Bleu style was five years ago because a meal would take at least a day to prepare and another day to shop for!

From the 150 recipes in this book, you'll be able to get a meal on the table each night, and have a group over for dinner on the weekends, without spending the day slaving over the stove. I promise.

A Day in the Life

Conventional wisdom states that if you're around food all the time you'll ultimately tire of it. But that's just not the case, at least not for me. I am always tempted, especially if the food is delicious (which I like to think my recipes are). I honestly believe it would be much easier to watch my weight if I got out of the house and went to an office every day. Since that is not the case, I've had to develop strategies for my workplace. The task has not been easy—especially when I was testing my dessert cookbook, even if the recipes were low-fat! A calorie is a calorie, after all.

In the past, when testing recipes I would gain weight over several months. I assumed that this could not be avoided: I was eating too much, more often, and into the evening. I began to dread this cycle each time I wrote another book or did major entertaining. I decided that I needed to see a registered dietitian for answers. This is when I rediscovered Canada's Food Guide, which outlines the four basic food groups. With the help of a dietitian, I came to understand how many servings I could have daily and how the time of day at which I ate also played a large factor in keeping my weight at a constant level. (Even when I exercised, if I ate too much or too late in the evening, I would still gain weight. A three-mile walk will burn off only 250 calories—that's only one good bite of a rich dessert!)

Every mouthful of food, whether from testing recipes or from my children's plates, counted. So if I was going to be tasting throughout the day, I had to have some way to account for all food entering my mouth. My dietitian taught me how to add up these mouthfuls and fit them into the four food groups and their serving sizes. Once I began counting everything, I realized how quickly I could get to my serving size for the day. A few mouthfuls of pasta or rice could easily add up to a half-cup serving, which accounts for 1 grain portion. A few tastes of dessert would add a serving to the grains, fruit, and milk groups due to the flour, sugar, and dairy content.

This means that if you're a "picker" or "grazer," you have to count snacking or sampling foods. I honestly believe that this is where most people go off course. They subconsciously refuse to admit the "behind the scenes" eating, counting only what's on their plates. Then they are mystified when they gain weight. The minute, however, you begin to count in terms of the four food groups, the weight gain or loss makes sense. (I discuss the four food groups in detail in "The New Nutrition.")

When you eat is also a factor. You've probably heard how important it is to have breakfast. The reason is that your metabolism gets kick-started only when you begin eating. If you go long hours without eating, your metabolism isn't working at full capacity. If you're like me and are not an early morning eater, then by at least ten o'clock in the morning you should eat something to get your metabolism working. I always try to eat foods from at least three of the four food groups then. Doing so isn't as much work as it may seem—a bowl of cereal, milk, and some fruit will do it. Or try a peanut butter and banana sandwich with some yogourt. It's that easy.

Just combine at least three of the four food groups at each major meal and at least two of the food groups for your snacks. By doing this, you will reach your level of optimal nutrition—and feel satisfied and full after you eat. When you eat "junk" or food from only one of the four food groups, you do not get enough nutrition and are left dissatisfied and hungry. And when you're hungry, chances are you're not going to reach for the apple, but rather for the cookies or chocolates.

I enjoy lunch about three hours after breakfast. I include foods from three or all four of the food groups. Typically I have a large salad that has a grain, such as pasta or rice, and some protein in the form of chicken, fish, or beans. Other days I have a sandwich consisting of vegetables and chicken, and fruit for dessert. I always have some of my lower-fat desserts on hand, and not a day goes by that I don't have a slice or two to satisfy my sweet tooth. While I'm working I love to "graze." Watch out for the higher-fat foods, such as chips, chocolate, or too many nuts. I'll often have fruit, veggies and dip, dried fruit and a few nuts, or fruit-flavoured yogourt. And always lots of water or herbal tea.

I eat the majority of my calories during the day and only a small portion in the evening. At dinner, which I like to have before seven o'clock, I'll have a salad and soup, a vegetable dish, just a small amount of protein, and a small bowl of rice, pasta, or other grain. Late in the evening, I'll have some fruit, frozen yogourt, or a small piece of one of my low-fat desserts. I sleep great and wake filled with energy.

I try to lead my life with the word "moderation" in my mind most of the time. When asked if I have "do's" and "don'ts" in terms of nutrition, I try not to be black and white, but I do follow a few guidelines.

The *Do's*

Here are some of the things you should do:

- Eat within a couple of hours of waking.
- Try to eat foods from at least three of the four food groups at each meal, and foods from two groups at each snack.
- Get most of your calories from fruits, vegetables, and grains.

- Go ahead and enjoy some fat in your day.
- Drink at least six glasses of water or herbal tea daily.
- Eat soy products twice per week.
- Get some exercise at least four times per week.
- Learn basic nutrition and use your knowledge to assess food products.
- Have a well-stocked kitchen and good light recipes.
- Get your children eating well and "moving" from an early age.
- Go ahead and eat out, but make sure you know what to order.
- Control portion sizes.

The *Don'ts*

Here are some other guidelines to keep in mind:

- Don't go longer than two to three hours without food.
- Don't eat foods from just one food group.
- Don't go on fad diets, those that eliminate entire food groups.
- Don't eat a diet high in saturated fat, but don't eliminate fat from your diet.
- Don't take vitamins to replace healthy food.
- Don't eat processed or fast food on a regular basis.
- Don't have junk food at home.
- Don't give yourself excuses to binge.
- Don't eat a main meal, or snack on high-fat foods, late in the evening.
- Don't fret about one bad day.
- Don't weigh yourself continually.

Exercise

The other component to my day that leads to successful weight control is exercise. I don't believe you can feel good and be healthy without both components—eating well and exercising. The benefits of exercise are becoming increasingly clear each day:

- It improves your cardiovascular fitness and muscle strength, ultimately giving you increased energy.

- It can help reduce high blood pressure and high blood cholesterol, which can prevent heart disease and stroke.

- It helps to prevent the onset of diseases such as osteoporosis and even certain types of cancer.

- It helps bring about weight loss by burning calories and keeping your metabolism functioning efficiently, and helps maintain your ideal weight once you reach it.

- It makes you look better and younger, which in turn can boost your self-esteem.

There is no way around it: you need to "move" at least three times a week. This doesn't mean you have to become a marathon runner or join a gym; you just have to move. Exercise only works when you find the type that suits your lifestyle and that you can live with the rest of your life. You have so much to choose from: joining a gym, exercising at home, or just walking as often as possible; biking, running, swimming, racquet sports, hiking, and more. Don't choose an exercise that you hate because you won't stick with it. But do try to find an activity that gets your heart and muscles working. Before you begin any exercise program, always have a complete physical examination to assess your current fitness level and health. You may not want to run a marathon if your knees or back are in bad shape—perhaps swimming or biking is for you.

Exercise has been a way of life for me for over 20 years. It gives me the energy I need every day to carry out my responsibilities in a positive and effective manner. Even throughout my pregnancies I never stopped exercising. My claim to fame is running until the day I went into labour, and then running four days after! There is no question that my pregnancies and deliveries were easier because I exercised. I love exercise and use it not only to keep trim, but also to release stress. Most days I can wake at 5:30 in the morning, go to sleep at 11:30 at night, and stay fairly active throughout the day *because* of the exercise I get and the way I eat. Together, these practices give me tons of energy.

Health for the Rest of Your Life

That's the magic formula: the four food groups, the appropriate serving size, and exercise. This formula doesn't lose its effectiveness, unlike fad diets that seem to do wonders for a brief period and then backfire (you often gain back not only the weight you lost, but even more). Remember, when you begin, to give yourself time to adjust to these changes. They will enhance your health—and your life—every day from the time you start.

The State of the (Fat) Nation

With very little effort, we can have more nutritional information at our fingertips than we know what to do with. Hardly a day goes by in which we don't hear about startling new findings on diet, disease, exercise, and our health in general. Stores and restaurants emphasize healthy, lower-fat foods. We are told over and over again that eating certain foods leads to disease and ill health, while other foods can prevent disease and promote longevity.

So, if we are so well-informed about good health, why are illnesses and deaths due to poor diet and lifestyle more common than ever before? What we eat has been implicated in five of the ten leading causes of death in adult North Americans. Those five are—in order of deadliness—heart disease, stroke, cancer, diabetes, and osteoporosis.

There is no exact formula for preventing disease, but you can take definite steps to minimize risks. For instance, the stronger your immune system is, the stronger your body will be. And the best way to fortify your immune system is to consume healthy food, drink lots of water, exercise, and get adequate sleep. Let's look at the diseases that can be caused, or prevented, by the food we consume.

Heart Disease

My father died of a massive coronary when I was 16 years old. He never even made it to the hospital. He was a smoker, was overweight, had high cholesterol, had high blood pressure, and led an inactive life. His sister died only a few months later of the same disease, and his brother had the symptoms of early heart disease. But my uncle changed his diet and exercise, and just passed away last year at the age of 86! He lived 30 years beyond my dad and aunt by improving his lifestyle.

Heart disease and stroke are the number one cause of premature death in Canada, claiming the lives of more than 80,000 Canadians annually. These diseases cost the health-care system more than $20 billion a year in direct and indirect costs.

Risk Factors for Heart Disease

Two in three Canadians have one or more of the major risk factors for heart disease:

- High blood cholesterol: for every 1 percent reduction in blood cholesterol there's a 3 percent decline in the risk of heart attack.

- High triglycerides: the main form of fat found in both food and the body, triglycerides can increase the tendency of blood to clot.

- High blood pressure: limiting sodium, alcohol, and calories will decrease blood pressure.

- Smoking: 20 to 40 percent of the people who die from heart attacks are smokers. Smoking damages the lining of the arteries and produces free radicals in the body, increasing the bad cholesterol (LDL). Smoking also increases blood pressure and can cause blood clots.

- Diabetes: people who have diabetes have approximately three times a greater risk of getting heart disease than people who do not have diabetes.

- Failure to eat nutritiously.

- Lack of regular exercise: regular exercise reduces the risk of heart attack by 35 to 55 percent.

- Obesity: the extra stress that being overweight can put on your heart can lead to high blood pressure and diabetes. Having excess weight around your middle (waist, abdomen, and upper body) puts you at a greater risk than being generally overweight does.

- Stress: people suffering from stress often have higher blood cholesterol, higher blood pressure, and blood platelets that are more likely to clot. Constant stress can make a healthy lifestyle difficult—eating poorly, smoking, and drinking to cope can lead to heart disease.

Certain factors you can do little about:

- Heredity: you have an increased risk of heart attack if a parent died before the age of 55 of a heart attack.

- Age: 55 percent of all heart attacks occur after age 65.

- Sex: before age 55, men have a higher rate of heart attack than women. By the time a woman reaches age 60, she has the same chance as a man of having a heart attack.

Knowing that you have a higher risk should prompt you to lead a healthier lifestyle. We are not doomed by our genetics. They are only a piece in the puzzle that can be manipulated and redirected.

Preventing Heart Disease

Improving your eating and exercise regime will lessen the risk of and maybe even prevent illness:

- Eat a healthy diet including the antioxidant vitamins C and E, and beta carotene.

- Cut back on saturated fat: animal fat, such as that in meat and chicken, and higher-fat dairy products.

- Stop smoking.

- Exercise regularly.

- Lose weight and try to maintain your ideal body weight.

- Consider hormone therapy after menopause: it raises the good cholesterol (HDL) and lowers the risk of heart disease.

- Try drinking 4 to 6 ounces (125 to 175 mL) of red wine, which can increase your good cholesterol (HDL). Don't exceed these amounts.

- Consider taking half an aspirin tablet daily: it can lessen the risk of heart attack by one-third by reducing the ability of platelets in the blood to stick together and form clots (consult your doctor first).

High Cholesterol

There are two kinds of cholesterol: dietary cholesterol is found in foods; blood cholesterol is made by your liver. They are often called "good" and "bad" cholesterol, otherwise known as HDL (high-density lipoprotein) and LDL (low-density lipoprotein), respectively. The HDL takes excess cholesterol away from your body's cells to the liver for disposal and can decrease your risk of heart disease. The LDL takes the cholesterol to your body's cells. High levels of LDL in your blood can increase the risk of heart disease by building up plaque material on the artery walls.

Cholesterol levels are measured in milligrams of cholesterol per decilitres of blood (mg/dL). Levels of under 200 of total cholesterol and under 130 of LDL cholesterol are desirable, as is a protective level of HDL cholesterol of 60 or more. Your levels are considered borderline to high if your total cholesterol level is between 200 and 239 and your LDL cholesterol level is between 130 and 159. High cholesterol levels are a total cholesterol level of 240 or more and an LDL cholesterol level of 160 or more; if your HDL cholesterol level is 35 or less,[1] you are at risk for heart disease.

Factors Affecting Blood Cholesterol   A combination of factors, both those that you can control and those you can't, affect the amounts of LDL in your blood:

- Heredity: if one of your grandparents had a heart attack—before 55 years for men, and before 65 years for women—your risk of having a heart attack is higher.

- Diabetes: if uncontrolled, diabetes can raise your cholesterol levels.

- Body weight: excess weight, especially around the waist and stomach, often leads to a higher LDL cholesterol level.

- Lack of exercise: it can decrease the good cholesterol (HDL).

- Age: cholesterol increases with age.

- Sex: high cholesterol affects men approximately 10 years earlier than women.

Reducing Cholesterol   Here are some ways you can reduce your cholesterol levels:

- Substitute unsaturated fats for saturated fats: polyunsaturated and monounsaturated fats help lower blood cholesterol levels. Don't eat these fats uncontrollably, since a calorie is a calorie.

- Keep your fat intake to below 30 percent of your daily calories.

- Lose weight if you're overweight: excess body fat raises your total blood cholesterol and LDL cholesterol levels, and reduces HDL cholesterol.

- Exercise regularly: it helps raise your HDL cholesterol level.

- Eat foods high in soluble fibre, including legumes, beans, peas, sweet potatoes, apples, pears and other fruits, and vegetables. Soluble fibre causes the body to excrete bile, which sends more cholesterol to the liver and leads to lower blood cholesterol.

- Don't smoke: smoking raises your total cholesterol and reduces your HDL cholesterol levels.

- Drink in moderation: one to two drinks daily can increase your HDL cholesterol level.

If your cholesterol levels cannot be controlled by these lifestyle strategies, then your doctor will recommend medication.

High Blood Pressure (Hypertension)

More than 60 million North Americans—and one in five Canadian adults—have high blood pressure. It rates third as a leading risk factor contributing to death. But hypertension is one of the most common preventable risk factors for heart disease.

Blood pressure is indicated by two numbers, each referring to how many millimetres the pressure of the blood in your arteries can raise a column of mercury (Hg). The first number is the systolic pressure and represents the force of blood during a heartbeat. The second number, the diastolic, indicates the pressure between heartbeats.

Blood Pressure Levels

Category	Systolic (mm Hg)	Diastolic (mm Hg)
Optimal	Less than 120	Less than 80
Normal	Less than 130	Less than 85
High normal	130–139	85–89

Hypertension		
Mild	140–159	90–99
Moderate	160–179	100–109
Severe	180–209	110–119
Very severe	Greater than 210	Greater than 120

University of California at Berkeley, *The New Wellness Encyclopedia,* Houghton Mifflin Company, 1995, page 55.

Risk Factors for Hypertension   Some risk factors you can't change:

- Heredity: if high blood pressure is in your family history, your chances of developing it double.
- Race: African North Americans have the highest occurrence of hypertension.
- Age: the risk of hypertension increases with age.
- Pregnancy: a correlation between pregnancy and hypertension has been identified.

   As with heart disease, being in a higher-risk category for high blood presssure is not a reason to ignore taking steps to ensure good health.

Reducing Blood Pressure   Reducing your risk of or preventing high blood pressure by following these recommendations will be to your benefit:

- Exercise regularly: exercise can reduce mild hypertension.
- Keep your weight at a desirable level: obese people have a 20 percent greater chance of having high blood pressure. Losing as little as 8 to 10 pounds (3.6 to 4.5 kg) may lead to a meaningful drop in high blood pressure.

- Limit your alcohol consumption: more than two drinks daily can increase your chances of hypertension.
- Limit your sodium consumption: 1 teaspoon (2400 mg) of sodium daily is all you need to maintain good health. A lot of sodium is present in foods already, especially prepackaged, fast, canned, and preserved foods.
- Do not smoke.
- Follow the DASH (Dietary Approaches to Stop Hypertension) Diet,[2] aimed at lowering blood pressure almost as much as medications can: this diet is lower in total fat, saturated fat, and cholesterol; is high in vegetables and fruits, whole grains, and low-fat dairy products; is moderate in protein; and encourages the consumption of nuts, seeds, and legumes. It is a healthy way of eating whether or not you have high blood pressure.
- Make sure that you get enough vitamins and minerals, and fibre in your diet: it is important to consume foods that contain potassium, magnesium, and fibre.

If all else fails, your doctor will recommend hypertension-controlling medication, which you should not hesitate to take.

Cancer

I don't think there is a more chilling word in our language than "cancer." My mother, now 77, always asks, "If there is so much money raised for this disease, why hasn't it been cured yet?" Research is being done regularly, and millions of dollars are raised for it each year. Why is this disease so difficult to conquer?

The answer seems to lie in the fact that cancer is not just one disease. Rather, it is many different diseases that behave and react in different ways. One treatment will not affect the various kinds of cancer in the same way. Cancer is a disease in which abnormal cells grow out of control until a tumour forms. If the cells break away from the tumour, they can enter the body and settle in other areas, a process that is called metastasis. The genes in our body may become damaged by normal cell division or by exposure to cancer-causing agents in the environment and in the food we consume. Many studies are being done on specific cancers such as breast, prostate, ovarian, skin, and others. Some studies have had amazing results, while other types of cancers are still quite misunderstood.

Approximately 134,100 new cases of cancer and 65,300 deaths from cancer occurred in Canada in 2001. The most frequently diagnosed cancers continue to be breast cancer for women and prostate cancer for men. Lung cancer remains the leading cause of cancer death for both men and women.

Risk Factors for Cancer

The main risk factors for cancer are as follows:

- Lifestyle: Up to 70 percent of all cancers could be prevented if people made changes to their lifestyle.
- Diet: approximately 20 to 33 percent of all cancers are related to what you eat.
- Alcohol: a diet including excess alcohol has been linked to cancers of the breast, colon, mouth, stomach, pancreas, and prostate.
- Too little exercise: evidence indicates that exercise may prevent cancer of the colon and breast. Physical activity can reduce the risk of colon cancer by at least 20 to 30 percent.
- Weight gain: over half of North Americans are overweight. Avoiding weight gain may guard against cancer of the colon, kidney, uterus, and breast. Remember that being overweight also increases the risk of heart disease and diabetes.
- Smoking: smoking increases the risk of lung cancer, which kills over 40,000 Canadians each year.
- Sun exposure: excess exposure of unprotected skin to the sun causes skin cancer.

Lowering the Risk of Cancer

I have listed some measures that may reduce the risk of and even prevent cancer. Without a doubt, you'll feel better and be healthier if you follow these guidelines:

- Enjoy a variety of foods that give you all the necessary nutrients your body needs. Follow Canada's Food Guide. I'll discuss this in detail in "The New Nutrition."
- Emphasize grain products, vegetables, and fruits in your diet. Studies show that people who have the highest intakes of fruits and vegetables have the lowest rates of most cancers. Fruits and vegetables have large amounts of the antioxidant vitamins C and E, as well as folacin, carotenoids, and dietary fibre, all of which are important in preventing cancer. These substances help our body's defence system fight off free radicals that may be responsible for cancer growth.
- Choose lower-fat dairy products, lean meats, and foods prepared with a minimum of fat. Saturated fat, which is in animal fat, is a risk factor for prostate and colon cancer. Countries with high-fat diets have the highest rates of breast and prostate cancer, but direct links between diet and these cancers have not yet been established.

- Consume foods that contain omega-3 fatty acids, which may lower the risk of cancer and heart disease. These fats are found in canola oil, fattier fish, and flaxseed.

- Keep an ideal body weight by eating properly and exercising. Women who exercised at least four hours per week were found to have a nearly 60 percent lower risk of breast cancer. Women who had been exercising since their teens had the lowest incidence. Being overweight puts women at risk for uterine and postmenopausal breast cancer.

- Limit your consumption of salt, alcohol, and caffeine.

- Stop smoking.

- Increase your intake of soy products. They contain phytoestrogens called isoflavones that help fight against hormone-related cancers, such as breast, prostate, uterine, and ovarian cancers.

- Don't cook foods at a very high temperature, such as over a grill or open flame. Doing so can create compounds known to promote certain cancers.

- Avoid foods that contain certain nitrogen compounds (such as nitrates), moulds, and salt that is added to foods to preserve them. These additives can promote cancer.

- Drink green and black teas, which contain potent chemical antioxidants that might be able to stop cancer activity. Adding milk to the tea cancels its positive effects.

Breast Cancer

This year alone, 19,500 cases of breast cancer will be detected and more than 5000 women will die from this disease, making breast cancer the most common type of cancer among Canadian women.

Risk Factors for Breast Cancer   Dietary factors such as fat, fibre, fruits, vegetables, and alcohol have been studied over the years, but their relationship to breast cancer has not yet been fully determined. What is known, however, is that making dietary changes will improve your general health and may lower the risk of breast cancer. Here are some factors that are related to breast cancer:

- High-fat diet: in places where diets are low in fat, such as Asia, much lower rates of breast cancer have been noted. This could be because women who eat little fat and more fibre have lower levels of estrogen (see below).

- Charred saturated or animal fats: studies show that overcooking meat makes cancer-causing agents more common. Statistics show that women are four times more likely to develop breast cancer if they eat meats that are too well cooked.

- Estrogen: higher levels of estrogen increase the risk of breast cancer.

- Weight gain: increased body weight and fat accumulation can increase the risk of breast cancer. Gaining weight after menopause is also linked to a higher risk of breast cancer due to the increased level of estrogen, which is produced in fat cells.

- Alcohol: studies have shown that even having one, two, or three drinks daily can increase your chances of getting breast cancer. The more alcohol consumed, the higher the risk. Alcohol seems to make the breast cells more vulnerable to the effects of carcinogens; alcohol may prevent cells from repairing faulty genes; and alcohol may increase estrogen levels.

Lowering the Risk of Breast Cancer   The risk of breast cancer may be reduced by eating a healthy diet consisting of lower-fat foods, lots of fruits and vegetables, smaller amounts of saturated protein, little alcohol, and more soy. Keeping your weight in control and exercising may also reduce the risk. Follow these guidelines:

- Limit your meat intake to no more than 3 ounces (90 g) per day, a piece the size of a deck of cards.

- Try to consume three servings of fish per week, especially the higher-fat fish such as salmon and tuna. Studies show that eating foods containing omega-3 fatty acids, such as fatty fish, is associated with a lower risk of breast cancer.

- Introduce some soy to your diet. The countries that consume the largest amount of soy in their diets have lower amounts of breast cancer. The protective agents are known as isoflavones, which have an estrogen-like effect in the body, attaching to the estrogen receptors and blocking the ability of the woman's own estrogen to take that place, so breast cells have less contact with estrogen. There are now studies that say consuming an excess of soy may lead to a buildup of these estrogen-type isoflavones and may promote breast cancer, especially if it is genetic. The best advice is to include soy in your diet three times per week for a safe level.

- Eat more than two servings a day of fruits or vegetables. A diet rich in fruits and vegetables may lead to a decrease in breast cancer. Dark green vegetables are the most protective—spinach, Swiss chard, rapini, kale. These are sources of beta carotene, an antioxidant that may protect breast cells from the free radicals that cause normal cells to mutate into cancerous cells.

- Increase your intake of fibre. Consuming at least 20 grams of fibre daily can reduce your risk of breast cancer. Fibre may bind to the estrogen in the intestine and be excreted through the stool, thus reducing estrogen in your blood. High-fibre diets are also lower in fat and higher in fruits and vegetables, and both of these factors may play a part in lowering the risk of breast cancer.

- Include yogourt and fermented milk products in your diet. Fermented milk products have been shown to slow the growth of breast cancer cells.
- Drink tea. A study at Harvard University showed that drinking four or more cups of green, black, or oolong tea was related to a 30 percent reduced risk of breast cancer. The antioxidants in these teas destroy free radicals that contribute to cancer.

Prostate Cancer

After lung cancer, prostate cancer is the biggest cancer killer of North American men. By the age of 50, one in four men will develop the disease. The risk increases with age: one in two men will develop prostate cancer by the age of 70.

Lowering the Risk of Prostate Cancer   Following these guidelines may lower the risk of prostate cancer:

- Avoid a high-fat diet, especially one that contains animal fat. This type of fat may increase the hormones that cause prostate cancer.
- Eat lots of fruits and vegetables, particularly the cruciferous vegetables such as broccoli, cauliflower, and cabbage. They are rich in protective vitamins and phytochemicals.
- Have more selenium in your diet. This element is found in fish, whole grains, and Brazil nuts. If you take a selenium supplement, don't take more than 200 milligrams.
- Eat tomato-containing foods. Lycopene, an antioxidant found in red vegetables and fruits, may help prevent prostate cancer. Cooked tomatoes have more lycopene than fresh tomatoes. Watermelon and pink grapefruit are also good sources of lycopene.
- Eat soy-based foods, which may also reduce the risk of prostate cancer.

Colon Cancer (Colorectal Cancer)

Colon cancer affects the large intestine, in both men and women equally. Rectal cancer is more common in men.

Colorectal cancer is the third most common cancer and the second most common cause of cancer deaths in North America. Compared to people in other parts of the world, North Americans consume more red meat, fat, and refined carbohydrates. Studies show that these foods are correlated with an increased rate of colon cancer. The reason seems to be that vegetables contain anti-cancer agents such as beta carotene, vitamin C, and B vitamins.

Lowering the Risk of Colon Cancer   Following these guidelines may lower the risk of colon cancer:

- Eat a diet rich in dietary fibre, which may prevent colon and rectal cancer. Such a diet increases the size of your stools and dilutes the concentration of cancer-causing agents, speeding up the rate at which the feces leave the intestinal tract and thus allowing less time for carcinogens to develop.

- Reduce the amounts of total fat and saturated animal fat in your diet. Eating no more than 3 ounces (90 g) of red meat per day can lessen the risk.

- Eat more fish, especially fattier fish such as salmon and tuna. They contain omega-3 fatty acids, which may inhibit the growth of cancer cells.

- Try replacing refined flour products with whole-grain foods. A diet of refined sugars may increase the risk by increasing the blood insulin level, which has been linked to this type of cancer.

- Eat a diet rich in fruits and vegetables. Raw vegetables, including the cruciferous ones such as broccoli, cauliflower, and Brussels sprouts, seem to offer protection. Green leafy vegetables and tomatoes also might offer some protection. The substances that keep the bowel healthy are beta carotene, B vitamins, vitamin C, and antioxidants.

- Limit your alcohol intake to no more than two drinks per day. Alcohol, especially beer, may increase the risk.

Obesity—A National Epidemic

After smoking, obesity is the second largest cause of death in North America. Travel anywhere in North America and you'll find many adults and children who are overweight or obese. Often, the findings are worse outside of urban areas. People who are obese have increased risk of high blood pressure, high blood cholesterol, and diabetes. All of these conditions can increase the risk of heart disease and stroke.

The statistics are startling. Obesity in North America has increased 50 percent since 1991. Sadly, 25 percent of North American children are overweight and 80 percent of obese children become obese adults. Almost half of Canadian adults between the ages of 25 to 65 are overweight, and 29 percent are obese. Annual health-care costs are over $250 billion across North America.

Identifying Obesity

We are a nation of educated people who know the difference between high-fat and low-fat foods. We all know that fruits, vegetables, grains, and lower-fat dairy products are better for us than high-fat foods. More low-fat, light, low-cholesterol foods are available in stores than ever before. So what's going on? Before we examine this issue more closely, let's examine how to determine if someone is overweight.

Body Mass Index   The Body Mass Index, better known as the BMI, is a standard method of evaluating body weight in relation to height. The BMI is one way to determine if someone is over-weight, obese, underweight, or maintaining an ideal weight. To calculate your BMI, divide your weight in kilograms by the square of your height in metres.

A healthy BMI range is between 19 and 25. Between 25 to 29 is considered moderately overweight, and over 29 is obese.

Another way to find your BMI is to multiply your weight in pounds by 705, divide the result by your height in inches, and then divide again by your height. The result is your BMI.

For example, a woman weighs 150 pounds and her height is 5 feet 6 inches (66 inches):

$$150 \text{ lb} \times 705 = 105,750$$

$$105,750 \div 66 = 1602 \div 66 = 24 \text{ BMI}$$

This woman's BMI is in the healthy range.

The BMI may not be the best indicator of healthy weight. The index makes no allowance for different body builds and treats a large framed person in the same way that it treats a small framed person.

Other Methods of Evaluating Weight   Sports instructors, registered dietitians, and doctors often test for body fat. They use a device to pinch the excess fat in certain areas of the body. Men with more than 25 percent body fat and women with more than 30 percent body fat are obese.

Insurance companies often use weight-for-height tables. These tables vary widely and do not account for an important factor—a person's weight distribution. It's not just how much fat you have that counts; where the fat is on your body is important also.

Health Risks

In terms of weight distribution, people can be described as Apples or Pears. Women typically collect fat in their hips and buttocks, giving them a pear shape. Men generally collect weight around their bellies, giving them more of a round, apple shape. People with fat concentrated in the abdomen are more likely to develop many of the health problems related to obesity. To find out what shape you are, calculate your waist-to-hip ratio by dividing your waist measurement by your hip measurement. Women with a waist-to-hip ratio of more than 0.8 or men with a ratio of more than a 1.0 are Apples, and their fat distribution is a health risk. So take out your tape measures.

Being obese is a danger to one's health and is the precursor to many different serious diseases, but most obese people are also inactive and this can be a lethal combination. Only 20 percent of Canadians are considered active enough to benefit their health. The combination of obesity and inactivity costs the economy $3.1 billion each year and kills 21,000 Canadians per year prematurely. Canadians are among the biggest eaters in the world, consuming approximately 3000 calories per day, with one-third of these calories coming from fat.

Factors Contributing to Obesity

Obesity today is a major health concern and illness. The factors leading to obesity can be difficult to control but manageable if a person is given the right support.

Genetics   Obesity tends to run in families. My grandmother and mother were obese, and I inherited their genes. For people like me, healthy eating will always be a struggle, as our bodies are giving us contradictory messages, always wanting more food than what is healthy for us. But don't blame your genes and give in to this serious health problem. You must get the proper information about healthy eating to fight these genetic traits.

Environmental Factors   Often it's not only the genetic factors that lead to obesity but "inherited" lifestyle habits as well. Most obese families are not working toward a healthier lifestyle. They eat poorly and are inactive. They don't take the time to cook or shop for foods properly. It's easier to order in fast food, go to a fast-food establishment, or buy packaged or frozen meals. These foods are usually high in saturated fat, loaded with sodium, and full of empty calories. The more high-fat, salty foods you eat, the more you get used to having these in your diet.

Psychological Factors   We are a society that eats in response to negative emotions such as boredom, sadness, or anger. Most overweight people have no more psychological disturbance than people at a healthier weight, but for obese people eating is an emotional outlet. They often have to be taught to find other outlets for their emotions. A technique I teach my clients is to write out exactly what they're feeling and what is going on right at the moment they are eating out of control. Seeing a regular pattern to a problem often is the first step to managing and changing it. With the right support you can find alternative ways to deal with negative emotional feelings without resorting to food.

Other Causes   Certain illnesses, including hypothyroidism, Cushing's syndrome, depression, and certain neurological problems, can lead to overeating. Once again, having one of these illnesses does not give you licence to eat out of control. Certain drugs, such as steroids and some antidepressants, may also lead to excess weight gain. With the right information and professional support, you can minimize the weight gain.

Obesity in Children

Obesity rates in Canadian children between the ages of 7 and 13 have increased dramatically over the years. Studies have shown that children who increased their consumption of saturated fats or packaged food, along with sweetened soft drinks, iced tea, and fruit drinks, were more likely to become obese. Even sugar-sweetened drinks could lead to obesity because people may not compensate well for calories consumed in liquid form by eating fewer calories later.[3]

Obese children often become obese adults. Research indicates that today more Canadian children are overweight and obese than was the case in the past. In 1981, about 14 percent of girls and 18 percent of boys were obese. By 1991, 24 percent of girls and 26 percent of boys were obese or overweight. The weight gain is primarily due to lack of physical activity and the consumption of processed foods. In many families today, both parents are working and have little time for preparing home-cooked meals and shopping for healthier foods. The only way to feed the family is to buy prepared or packaged foods, loaded with saturated fat and excess salt.

Children today get little exercise. They are driven everywhere and sit in front of a computer or television, and exercise is not a large part of the school curriculum. My children's doctor told me that as long as children "move," they will not be overweight. Keeping your children active must be a major priority for you so that they can maintain a healthy body weight throughout their lives.

Battling Obesity

Obesity is now considered a national epidemic. Not taking action can lead to major health problems. You have to take a proactive, preventive approach that includes a calorie-reduced diet, exercise, and behavioural changes. Losing as little as 10 pounds (4.5 kg) can reduce your risk of high blood pressure, high cholesterol, and some serious diseases. Taking these steps can help you win the battle:

• Empower yourself to make better decisions concerning your weight.

• Be sure that your weight loss is gradual and safe. Fad diets never work in the long term.

- Exercise regularly. At least three times per week, slot 20 minutes of exercise into your day. You can even break up the 20 minutes into 5-minute intervals four times a day and get the same results.
- Reduce your intake of saturated fats and eat according to Canada's Food Guide (I discuss this in more detail in "The New Nutrition"). Often you will need a professional to assist and teach you in this area.
- When eating carbohydrates, choose those that have a lower glycemic index. These foods keep you full longer. (See "The New Nutrition" for more on the glycemic index.)
- Develop a regular schedule for eating throughout the day. Going long hours without food leads to uncontrollable bingeing. Include snacks in your day.
- Limit your alcohol intake, because alchohol contains a considerable number of calories and can stimulate your hunger.
- Avoid getting on the scale any more than once a week. Daily weight fluctuations from various causes, not food related, can lead to frustration. Too much sodium in your day can cause increased weight, as can water-weight from your menstrual cycle.
- If you fall off the wagon, try not to get frustrated and binge. Get back to eating better as quickly as possible. A few pounds gained back are easier to lose than a lot. Try to keep a check on yourself or allow a professional to monitor you.

Osteoporosis

More than 1.4 million Canadians have osteoporosis, a disease that affects bone mass and can lead to fractures—seven in ten fractures in people over the age of 45 are due to this disease.

One in four women over age 50, and over 50 percent over age 70 will develop osteoporosis. The risk is higher among people who do not do weight-bearing exercises, such as walking, running, stair climbing, and weight training. Surprisingly, a Canadian study indicated that osteoporosis affects almost as many men as women. Men often don't realize they have this condition.

Preventing Osteoporosis

To prevent the onset of this disease, everyone should eat a healthy diet and adopt the following practices:

- Exercise regularly. Weight-bearing exercise helps build stronger bones and slow down bone loss. But exercise does not guarantee the prevention of osteoporosis; many people also need medication, such as estrogen therapy, and supplements, such as calcium and vitamin D.

- Increase your intake of soy products. They contain isoflavones, a type of plant estrogen, which have been shown to preserve our bone structure. A daily intake of between 60 and 90 milligrams of isoflavones is required. Here are some recommended sources:

> 1/4 cup (50 mL) roasted soy nuts = 80 milligrams isoflavones
>
> 1/2 cup (125 mL) uncooked green soybeans = 70 milligrams isoflavones
>
> 4 ounces (125 g) tempeh = 60 milligrams isoflavones
>
> 4 ounces (125 g) tofu = 38 milligrams isoflavones
>
> 1 cup (250 mL) soy beverage = 27 milligrams isoflavones

- Eat enough protein-rich foods, such as poultry, fish, lean meat, tofu, and beans or lentils. The protein they provide is an important component of bone structure. Don't overdo the protein since too high an intake can cause your kidneys to excrete calcium and cause bone loss.
- Cut back on caffeine to no more than three cups of a caffeinated beverage daily. Coffee, tea, and cola-based drinks increase the amount of calcium your kidneys excrete through your urine.
- Ensure that your intake of vitamins and minerals that help in bone formation, such as vitamins A, C, and K, magnesium, and phosphorus, is adequate.

Diabetes

Diabetes is a condition in which the body either lacks insulin or cannot use it properly. The most common type of diabetes is Type 2, which affects over 90 percent of all people suffering from the disease. In Type 2 diabetics, the body produces an adequate amount of insulin but cannot use it properly, a situation known as insulin resistance. It usually affects people over the age of 40 and is associated with obesity, especially if the weight is centred on the abdomen. Type 2 diabetes is more prevalent in specific racial groups, such as people of Hispanic origin and African North Americans, as well as Aboriginal people.

Approximately 11 percent of Canadian women and men over the age of 65—more than 2 million Canadians—are afflicted with this disease, and it accounts for over 5000 deaths annually. Diabetes results in over $1 billion in direct and indirect costs annually in Canada. The disease can result in kidney failure, amputations, and blindness. Heart disease and stroke are common complications of diabetes.

Lowering the Risk of Diabetes

Findings now show a practical and easy way to prevent or delay diabetes. Studies announced at the National Institutes of Health[4] found that "commonsense" measures could lower diabetes risk dramatically. Even modest lifestyle changes—eating less fat, exercising two-and-a-half hours per week, and losing a moderate amount of weight—can cut the incidence of the disease by more than half among those at risk of Type 2 diabetes. The major factor in controlling Type 2 diabetes is diet, and the main advice given is to follow Canada's Food Guide. Take note of these important facts:

- Physical activity can reduce the risk of developing Type 2 diabetes by as much as 50 percent.

- High-carbohydrate, high-fibre diets have been found to reduce or eliminate the need for insulin. The Canadian Diabetes Association recommends 50 percent or more of one's diet be carbohydrates, less than 35 percent be fat, and the remainder be protein. Fibre foods are highly recommended.

- Carbohydrates such as breads, grains, beans, fruits, and vegetables are digested and converted to blood glucose. Although many people still believe that diabetics must have a diet low in carbohydrates, what is important is the type of carbohydrate and the amount eaten at each meal and snack. Proper carbohydrate distribution can be managed with the help of a registered dietitian. The best carbohydrates are those with a low glycemic index (see "The New Nutrition" page 63), as blood sugar control is improved if you eat low glycemic carbs.

- Good sources of soluble fibre, such as barley, oats, and legumes, are important to controlling insulin levels.

- A low-fat diet is crucial for the diabetic. High-fat diets promote obesity and can cause high cholesterol levels, which can lead to heart disease and stroke. Blood sugar levels are better controlled with a diet lower in saturated fat.

- Eating at least 30 grams of fibre daily allows a diabetic to better control blood sugar levels. Soluble fibre slows down the digestion of carbohydrates, so that they enter the bloodstream more slowly and keep the blood sugar level from rising as sharply. Controlling their blood sugar level allows diabetics to feel better by having fewer highs and lows in their energy level.

Immune System

The stronger your immune system, the less you get sick and the less you are prone to diseases in general. Eating well and exercising regularly, I haven't had a cold, virus, or infection in years.

Many factors can strengthen or depress your immune system:

- A healthy diet boosts your immune system. If your diet is deficient and, for example, lacks important components such as the zinc found in grains and meat, a supplement can help increase your immunity.

- A diet low in beta carotene, found in dark green or red fruits and vegetables, can depress the immune system.

- Vitamin C boosts immunity.

- Exercise boosts immunity.

- Sleep deprivation depresses the immune system.

- Extreme stress depresses the immune system.

- Smoking depresses the immune system.

Improving the State of the Nation

Many people play Russian roulette with their lives and say they believe in fate. This gives them the excuse to live an unhealthy lifestyle. They believe that taking preventive measures is a waste of time and that "the good die young."

There are no guarantees in life and frequently the good do die young. But, more often than not, when someone gets an illness it can be due to poor lifestyle habits. Why not take as many preventive measures as possible? You'll at least feel a lot better, improving the quality of your life as you are living it.

Diets:
The Good, the Bad,
and the So-So

The diet industry is one I'd like to have stocks in! Look at these the facts:

- North Americans spend close to $40 billion each year in this industry.
- Of this amount, $55 million is spent on weight-loss programs, their services, and their foods.
- More than 50 percent of women and 25 percent of men are now on a diet.
- Eight million men and women across North America are enrolled at commercial diet centres.
- Ninety-five percent of all dieters lose "the battle of the bulge."
- Over 2000 diet books are in print.

Many millions are spent on media campaigns targeting our body image. Twenty years ago a fashion model weighed 8 percent less than the average woman; today she weighs 23 percent less. Induced by the fashion industry and exploited by the media, the pervasive trend toward ultra-thinness is epidemic, leading to out-of-control dieting and, in some extreme cases, eating disorders.

Why Diets Don't Work

Hardly a day goes by without the appearance of an article or book introducing a new diet that promises impressive weight loss with little effort and few sacrifices. But if losing weight was that easy, North Americans wouldn't be getting fatter daily. There is a definite pattern: one loses weight initially on these diets, only to gain it all, and often more, back. The next new diet is waiting in line.

You must have noticed that every time you go on a diet it seems more difficult to lose weight than the time before. You will lose weight on any diet—5, 10, 20, maybe even 50 pounds (2.3 to 22.7 kg). Anyone can go on a diet and be successful…for a short time. But then, your old habits creep back, and slowly but surely your weight creeps back on—often even more of it. This cycle has been termed "yo-yo" dieting or on-and-off dieting, and it happens for a scientific reason.

When you diet, you lose lean muscle along with fat, especially if you're eating a low-calorie or unbalanced diet. The faster the weight loss, the higher the ratio of muscle tissue to fat that is lost. After you regain the weight, the fat returns but the lean muscle does not. Remember—the fat cells never disappear; they get smaller but will get larger again as you eat more food. The result is that your body learns to store the fat much more quickly and efficiently after each diet. You end up learning nothing, wasting time, and getting on the roller coaster ride of the diet game.

Why don't diets work? The reason is that they usually impose severe controls on what and when you eat. This is not a regime of daily eating that can be sustained forever. In contrast, any healthy eating plan has you eat in a way that you can sustain for the rest of your life. You won't have to think about it as a diet. It just becomes a way of life.

The answer is not in a book or in a diet. The answer is in you. You are your own nutrition control board. You have to switch your perspective from losing weight to eating healthy.

The following is a round-up of some of the more popular diet plans. Read these sections carefully and keep in mind that any diet that recommends eliminating an entire food group is not a healthy diet.

Low-Carbohydrate/High-Protein Diets

Today, many popular diets focus on low carbohydrates and high protein. Some forbid carbohydrates such as sugar, fruit, grains, milk, and even vegetables such as carrots, squash, sweet potatoes, and beets. What you can eat on these diets is all the meat, fish, and chicken your heart desires, regardless of the fat content. The Dr. Atkins protein diet[1] tops the list of these diets.

But what are the effects of omitting carbohydrates from your diet? When you don't eat carbs, your body lacks glucose, its only fuel source. On this diet, while you are burning fat your body survives by forming ketones through a process called ketosis, which gives you the fuel your body needs.

Eliminating carbohydrates from your diet has many disadvantages:

- Eating only protein, especially meat products full of saturated fat, can be damaging to your heart and increase cholesterol levels.
- Without carbohydrates, you lack energy.
- Your diet does not include the fibre that allows for proper elimination.
- You're lacking vitamins D, A, and C, beta carotene, and folate, especially if you're not a vegetable lover.
- Eating lots of protein without carbs can lead to excessive fluid loss.
- Once you go off the diet and begin eating carbohydrates again, you will gain weight back immediately unless you drastically cut back on the protein and fat—not easy for those who have enjoyed eating these foods in excess.

The only way this diet can be acceptable is if you stay on it for a short time and take the proper supplements. Often people need a kick-start to weight loss, and this diet may be the impetus. But if you remain on this kind of diet for very long, serious complications can occur:

- Ketosis will increase the blood level of uric acid, which is a risk factor for kidney stones and gout.
- Diets like the Dr. Atkins protein diet claim to lower blood cholesterol, but diets very high in saturated

fat are likely to boost blood cholesterol and increase the risk of heart disease. (Dr. Atkins recently suffered a heart attack!)

- These diets can lead to calcium loss and osteoporosis.

- Dr. Atkins suggests taking supplements on his diet, since it doesn't provide the daily nutrition you need. But no matter how many pills you take, you won't get enough fibre and the phyto-chemicals you need that are found in grains, fruits, and vegetables. You will also not benefit from the ability of these foods to lower cholesterol.

- For people with diabetes, these diets are especially risky because diabetics can develop kidney disease at a quicker pace than healthy individuals.

No long-term studies show that a high-protein/low-carbohydrate diet is more effective than other diets. Dr. Atkins blames the increase in obesity on excessive carbohydrate intake, which he claims causes insulin resistance and thus weight gain.

There is no evidence that this is the case. Fruits, vegetables, and grains are the mainstay of a healthy diet. Combining them with low-fat dairy products and small amounts of lean protein is all you need for good daily nutrition.

Moderate-Carbohydrate/Moderate-Protein Diets

With these diets you get a chance to have some carbohydrates, such as bread, fruits, and vegetables, but the portions are small. The theory is based on the idea that if you choose the right kind of carbs and watch your portion size, your pancreas will make less insulin, which is the sugar in your blood. It is believed that a lower insulin level causes your body to break down fat more easily, and thus you lose weight.

The Zone

This diet[2] is considered healthier and not as extreme as the Dr. Atkins diet since you eat lean protein and are allowed more carbohydrates. The "Zone" is the metabolic state in which the body works at peak efficiency. The diet promises you'll enjoy optimal body functions, freedom from hunger, and greater energy. The theory is that any food high in carbohydrates generates a rise in blood glucose, which leads to the production of more insulin, taking you out of the Zone and leading to the storage of calories in the form of fat. Author Barry Sears believes that the excess carbs in your diet not only make you fat but make you stay fat. This diet emphasizes fat as the biochemical key that prevents the accumulation of excess body fat. You use fat to lose fat. After that explanation, I still find the theory confusing.

The caloric composition of the Zone diet is 40 percent carbohydrates, 30 percent fat, and 30 percent protein. Canada's Food Guide (which I follow) recommends 70 percent carbs, 15 percent fat, and 15 percent protein. Quite a difference.

To know your portions in the Zone diet, you have to put your carbs, fat, and protein in blocks, or units of serving size. After computing your percentage of body fat and calculating your physical activity level, you can calculate your food blocks. It's easy—as long as you carry around your calculator and the book to keep referring to the appendix material! If you eat more blocks than your body requires, you'll gain weight. Any excess protein that can't be used by your body will be turned into fat, so you have to measure carefully.

The diet is low in the calcium department. Another major problem is that this diet has very specific requirements: the portions of carbs are small and your choices very limited. The carbs are restricted to those that have a low glycemic index, which means that the foods take longer to digest and lead to a slow rise in blood glucose, and keep you full longer than the high glycemic foods (see "The New Nutrition" page 63 for more on the glycemic index). You can forget potatoes, corn, all white-flour products, pasta, bananas, carrots, and fruit juices.

This diet has some positive features. The Zone does encourage you to eat proteins that are lower in fat, which is a real advantage over the Dr. Atkins protein diet. The Zone also promotes the use of healthy fats and oils, and so again is different from the diet recommended by Dr. Atkins, who doesn't differentiate among types of fats and doesn't discourage the consumption of saturated fats.

Sugar Busters

Sugar Busters[3] promotes a diet based on eating foods that lessen the amount of insulin your body produces—if you produce less insulin you won't store body fat.

This diet is not based firmly on good nutrition; it encourages eating plenty of red meat, pâté, bacon, and cheese. Food combining is an added component, since you are allowed to eat fruit before or after meals but never with a meal (see Food-Combining Diets, below).

This diet also limits portions of starchy carbohydrates and emphasizes low glycemic foods only. In other words, it includes no white rice, pasta, bread, potatoes, or corn. You can eat only whole-wheat grains, sweet potatoes, legumes, and some fruits and vegetables (all good things!). Starchy carbs can be eaten at only two of your three meals. Serving sizes are not specified, which means that many people will have portions too large for lifelong weight management.

You do not have to eat your carbs, protein, and fat in specific portions at each meal, so the calculations for this diet are easier than for the Zone diet. The positive aspect to the Sugar Busters diet is that it might induce you to eat more vegetables and leaner protein, as well as fewer carbohydrates.

The Carbohydrate Addict's Diet

Authors Drs. Rachael and Richard Heller[4] claim to have the lifelong solution to yo-yo dieting. Their book begins with a questionnaire designed to determine if you are a carbohydrate addict. If you are, then the assumption is that your carb eating is out of control. Their theory hangs on the premise that carbohydrate addictions are caused by the wrong amount of insulin in the blood. This blood insulin imbalance leads to weight-management problems, which in turn lead to obesity.

Although this diet doesn't cut out carbs (breads, fruits, and certain vegetables) entirely, it limits when you eat them and for how long. In other words, you can have one carb-rich carbohydrate meal—a Reward Meal—a day. This meal consists of 3 to 4 ounces (90 to 120 g) of protein, low-carbohydrate vegetables, and high-carb foods including dessert. The meal can last only 60 minutes. The other two meals in your day, called Complementary Meals, contain protein (only 3 to 4 oz/90 to 120 g), low-fat dairy products, and only low-carbohydrate vegetables. This combination causes you to produce less insulin, which means less hunger, fewer cravings, and a feeling of satisfaction. You do not have to weigh and measure food, but you are asked to mind your portions.

I don't like the idea of a reward meal—it makes me feel like a dog! I also think the restrictions associated with this diet are too severe: timing is limited, as is what you can eat. Presumably, having one misplaced carbohydrate food, such as a fruit, can throw the entire diet out the window. This style of eating can't be maintained for very long—and once you are off the diet, carbohydrate binge eating will kick in.

Food-Combining Diets

Food-combining diets have been around for decades. In the 1930s, Dr. William Hay wrote that starches should be eaten separately from proteins and that fruit should not be eaten with proteins or starches, but on its own. This was referred to as the "Hay System," a way of eating that promotes well-being and vitality through combining compatible foods.

Food combining is a style of eating that often places severe restrictions on when you eat and which foods you can eat together. The theory behind these diets is that your body cannot digest proteins and carbohydrates at the same time—the two food groups will sit in your stomach, ferment, cause indigestion, and lead to weight gain. Only if you eat carbs with vegetables, or protein with vegetables, can you digest your food properly, feel better, and lose weight. This theory has no proven support. The many people who do lose weight by food combining do so primarily because, since the diet is so restrictive, they're eating fewer calories. No cheese on your pizza; no meat sauce on noodles; no meat burritos or fajitas, sushi, or meat and potatoes. You can't eat fruit with any meal; fruit must be eaten on its own—and some fruits can't be eaten together.

The danger of this type of diet is that it limits calcium-rich foods and allows foods high in saturated fat, setting the stage for osteoporosis, high blood pressure, and heart disease.

Fit for Life

Food combining was made popular again by Harvey and Marilyn Diamond in the early 1980s with their book, *Fit for Life*.[5] The theory behind it is that your body uses certain enzymes to digest carbohydrates and starch, and others to break down proteins. If you eat these two food types together in a meal, the enzymes neutralize each other; the result is that you can't digest your food. The undigested food sits in your stomach, ferments, and forms toxins. This apparently leads to weight gain. Again, this theory has never been proven.

Dairy products are not allowed because they contain both proteins and carbohydrates; therefore, this diet is low in calcium.

Somersizing

Suzanne Somers,[6] the star of the 1970s sit-com *Three's Company,* believes in eating a variety of foods recommended by the U.S. food guide without measuring exact quantities. Somers credits weight loss to better digestion of foods by eating foods that are properly combined, believing that a mixed diet consisting of carbohydrates, proteins, and fat stays in the stomach too long. She calls any food with added sugar junk food or "funky food." Excess glucose comes from these foods and is transported to your fat cells, making you fat. With a higher amount of glucose produced, a greater amount of insulin is also produced to restore your blood sugar level. Her logic is that, if your body needs energy, the first place it will go to get it is the carbohydrate department; if there isn't enough there, then your body will go after the fat, which is the desired result.

Simple carbs that Somers calls funky foods are considered poor choices. The funky foods include all sugars, honey, maple syrup, molasses, beets, and carrots. The starches include white flour, pasta, couscous, white rice, corn, potatoes, sweet potatoes, and bananas.

You must separate foods: fruits must be eaten alone on an empty stomach; proteins and fats must be kept separate from carbohydrates. Proteins and fats are eaten with vegetables, and carbohydrates are eaten with vegetables but no fat. Other rules include waiting three hours between protein/fat meals and carbohydrate meals, and not skipping meals during the day. I know I would feel quite deprived on this diet.

Food combining is difficult to follow in the long term. If you're always the one cooking, then food combing may not present a problem. But if you want to eat out or at someone's home, separating and combining the components of carbohydrates, proteins, and fats is very difficult. Never eating fruit with a meal can be difficult. Waiting three hours before switching types of meals allows for no spontaneous eating. To me that's missing out on life's enjoyments.

Other Types of Diets

Eat Right for Your Type Diet

One of the authors of *Eat Right for Your Type*,[7] Peter D'Adamo, is a naturopath. He bases his diet on the theory that your blood type reflects your internal chemistry and determines the way you absorb nutrients. The foods that are incompatible with your blood type can interfere with your digestion, slow your metabolism, increase your insulin level, and cause you to retain water. The theory is based on how your ancestors ate.

Type O   This type came from ancestors who were hunters and gatherers. Type O people are best eating animal protein and limiting grains, legumes, and dairy products, which can add weight. The risk to Type O people of ulcers and arthritis increases if they eat incorrectly. Vigorous exercise is recommended for Type O people.

Type A   The ancestors of this type were cultivators, so Type A people do best on a vegetarian diet, limiting meat, wheat, and dairy products. The risk to Type A people of cancer and heart disease increases if they eat incorrectly. They should engage in gentle exercise, such as yoga or golf, and should meditate to relieve stress.

Type B   The ancestors of this type were nomads who ate a more varied diet. For Type B people, the foods to avoid are corn, lentils, peanuts, and most wheat products. This is the only blood type that does well with dairy products. The risk to Type B people of viruses that attack the nervous system increases if they eat incorrectly. They should engage in moderate exercise, such as walking or swimming.

Type AB   This group has most of the benefits and intolerances of Types A and B. Type AB people should avoid red meat, kidney and lima beans, seeds, corn, and most wheat products. They should practise calming exercises and relaxation techniques. Type AB people have the strongest immune system of all the blood types.

The problem with this diet is that each blood type has to eliminate most wheat products, which means no pasta, bread, cookies, bagels, crackers, or other all-purpose products. If you cut out all wheat products, you would certainly lose weight! You will not, however, get the needed nutrients and energy that wheat products supply. Also, most of the categories omit dairy products, which means that this diet could cause a lack of calcium and vitamin D.

I don't believe that the authors have evidence of what our ancestors ate and how their health was during those times. If you limit your calories through the reduction of carbohydrates and dairy products, naturally you'll lose weight. This is just another calorie-reduced diet.

Insulin Reduction Diet

Michel Montignac has argued that excess secretion of insulin, called hyperinsulinism, is the cause, not the result, of obesity.[8] His idea is that eating too many carbohydrates will cause the pancreas to produce excess insulin, which can lead to weight gain. He criticizes the Western diet consisting mainly of carbohydrates that increase insulin production—refined grains, potatoes, corn, and sugar. He believes that, by eating low glycemic carbohydrates, the obese will lose weight and reduce their risk of diabetes and heart disease.

The criticism of this diet is that it is masquerading as something new and innovative. Basically, this diet is a low-fat, low-calorie eating plan. That's fine, but then let's call it what it is and not something else. One danger is that most people don't enjoy eating only low glycemic carbs and so end up consuming most of their calories in animal protein, which can lead to disease.

Reversing Heart Disease Diet

Dr. Dean Ornish's program[9] claims to reverse heart disease. Lifestyle changes unblock the arteries so that blood flow to the heart increases. The program has several components:

- Techniques for managing stress more effectively
- A diet very low in fat and cholesterol

- Stopping addictions, such as smoking, drinking, or drugs
- Moderate exercise

The Reversal Diet   The Reversal Diet in Dr. Ornish's program is for people who have heart disease and want to begin reversing it. Carbohydrates make up about 75 percent of the diet and protein about 20 percent. The carbohydrates should be complex, such as fruits, vegetables, grains, and beans. Simple carbs such as sugar, honey, and alcohol are regarded as empty calories. Other features of this diet are as follows:

- No animal products except for egg whites and non-fat dairy products
- No added oils or other fats
- Less than 10 percent of calories from fat (most recommended diets suggest 30 percent)
- No more than 5 milligrams of cholesterol daily (healthy diets recommend 300 milligrams)
- No restriction of calories
- No caffeine or other stimulants

The Prevention Diet   The Prevention Diet in Dr. Ornish's program is for people who want to have good health and prevent heart disease.

If your cholesterol level is less than 150 and you're not taking cholesterol-lowering drugs, or if your ratio of total cholesterol to HDL (good cholesterol) is less than 3.0, then you should continue to eat as you have been eating. If your cholesterol level is higher, then gradually decrease the amount of saturated fat and cholesterol in your diet. Try eating no more than double what the Reversal Diet recommends.

No diet could be more restrictive and difficult than the Reversal Diet. Because it contains virtually no animal products, you're basically following a vegetarian diet. Forget about eating in a restaurant or eating out altogether. You may reverse heart disease, but it doesn't happen overnight, and that means a long time without any enjoyment when it comes to food. Not too many people want to live this life. To most people, food is comfort, enjoyment, and entertainment, which this diet removes.

The Prevention Diet is somewhat easier to follow, but it's still no walk in the park. Most North Americans have a higher cholesterol level than 150, so this diet won't pertain to them. Even if you double the amounts that the Reversal Diet recommends, the Prevention Diet is still fairly restrictive.

This is definitely a deprivation diet. It's not an easy diet to adhere to for a long period of time, and it would be months before this diet would result in any significant reversal of heart disease or lowering of cholesterol.

The Body Code

The Body Code[10] diet is based on Jay Cooper's theory that our human genetic type determines what we should eat. You answer a six-page questionnaire about your body shape, exercise tendencies, and preferred foods to identify your classification as a nurturer, communicator, warrior, or visionary genetic type. Each of these four types has a distinctive body shape that reveals where you hold your excess weight, describes your mind and personality type, and outlines the best foods to keep a healthy body weight and foods to avoid. Certain body types need different types of exercise to attain an ideal body weight and keep the body in strong muscular condition. The following is a brief profile of the four types:

The Warrior   Exercise should emphasize cardiovascular training and minimize strength training. This type craves meat and fatty foods, but should be on a plant-based diet.

The Nurturer   This type should emphasize cardio training with strength training for the upper body only. The Nurturer craves creamy and spicy foods, but should eat mostly fruits and vegetables.

The Communicator   Communicators enjoy a variety of exercise and crave carbohydrates and sweets, but should eat animal-based protein. Snacks should also include proteins.

The Visionary   Less cardio and more strength and flexibility training is recommended. This type should eat light protein and vegetables but little dairy.

The premise is that no matter what you eat, and how much or how little you exercise, you cannot change your basic Body Code. The elements over which we do have control are determined within a genetically programmed range. Although characterizing body types in this way might make sense, the problem is that the recommendations restrict certain types of food and limit your choices in terms of exercise. Depending on your genetic type, this diet is not always an easy or desirable one to follow.

Jenny Craig

This is one of the largest weight-management service companies in the world. The goal is to develop a healthy relationship with food, an active lifestyle, and a balanced approach to living. The diet is based on food packages acquired from the Jenny Craig company. There are breakfast, lunch, dinner, and snack items designed for the busy person. All the meals are low in fat, low in cholesterol, and high in fibre. They all offer nutritional balance, variety, and moderation. Once you reach your weight goal, the consultants teach you how to prepare your own meals.

I'm not a fan of packaged, ready-to-go meals. The only path to successful weight loss is learning how to prepare foods yourself from nutritious ingredients, and learning how to eat away from home. Even though the company helps you after you achieve weight loss, the transition is extreme.

Recommended Diets
Weight Watchers

Weight Watchers is one of the best-established weight-control programs in the world. At any given time, more than one million members participate in this program at more than 35,000 locations in 30 different countries. The Weight Watchers program claims to be a state-of-the-art, scientifically designed approach to weight control that promotes healthful eating, physical activity, group support, and weight maintenance management.

It's the ingenious Point system that makes this program so successful. Winning Points, termed "a self-discovery approach to weight loss," allows people to discover more about themselves in relation to weight loss, areas of dieting personality, satisfaction with meals, and eating patterns. Every food is allotted Points based on its calorie, fat, and fibre content. You choose what to eat daily, based on your weight, to stay within a Daily Points range. As long as you don't exceed your Points for the day, you can enjoy any food or beverage without guilt or weight gain. Points are also assigned to physical activity based on your current weight, the number of minutes the exercise is done, and the intensity level. You can actually swap Activity Points for Food Points.

People who participate in Weight Watchers have the freedom to enjoy special occasions and to eat out. No food is forbidden! The principles of portion control are reinforced to help members learn to achieve and maintain their ideal body weight.

I like this program because it meets the nutritional recommendations of many health organizations, and because it encourages members to eat a wide variety of foods in proper amounts to obtain healthy weight loss and/or maintenance. The group support provided by the meetings is at the heart of this diet plan. Participants can follow the example of role models and celebrate everyone's success. Weight Watchers seems to be the most balanced and commonsense way to diet. Students and clients of mine who have been members often keep their weight off and learn how to eat properly. I highly recommend this program.

Vegetarian Diet

It's confusing today when you hear people call themselves vegetarians, because often their diet might include fish, dairy, and even chicken. Then what is the definition of this diet? Let's look at some of the various categories:

Vegans   These are the most extreme vegetarians. They abstain from all foods of animal origin. This means that vegans eat no meat, fish, dairy products, or eggs.

Lactovegetarians   This group includes in their diet dairy products as protein sources. But depending on your choice of dairy products, a lactovegetarian diet is not necessarily low in fat.

Lacto-ovovegetarians   This group eats eggs as well as dairy foods.

Semi-vegetarians   Members of this group are not true vegetarians because they allow themselves some fish, chicken, and, occasionally, red meat in their diet.

Vegans run the greatest risk of vitamin deficiency. Vitamin B_{12} is found only in animal products. Vegans need supplements or fortified products. Vitamin D is found in animal products but also can be obtained from the sun. Iron, zinc, and calcium also are primarily found in animal products, but peas, lentils, and wheat products contain zinc. Broccoli, kale, and collard and mustard greens contain calcium, and beans, potatoes, dried fruit, and fortified cereals and breads supply iron.

Many grains and legumes are good, but not complete, sources of protein. They must be combined to make a complete protein. The only grain that is a complete, protein is quinoa, and the only bean is soy.

I think that everyone should be moving to a more plant-based diet and eating animal protein less often. A well-balanced vegetarian diet is an excellent way of eating. It's low in fat, calories, and cholesterol and gives you the essential vitamins and minerals you need. Excessive fat found in animal products is linked to heart disease, breast and colon cancer, and obesity.

If you want to become a vegetarian and you're concerned about eating the right foods, then it's best to include foods from at least three of the four food groups to ensure that you get the proper nutrients. The main nutrient that is missing from this diet if you cut out meat is vitamin B_{12}, which is only found in animal products. Also realize that being a vegetarian doesn't mean that your diet is low-fat or healthy. Plenty of vegetarian foods are loaded with oil, cheese or fat-based sauces. That's one of the reasons I wrote a book titled *Light Vegetarian Cooking*.

Okinawa Diet

If Oprah Winfrey can devote a show to this diet, we must be able to learn something from it! *The Okinawa Program*[11] claims to be a must-read for anyone interested in improving their diet and extending their life span—which I think is all of us.

A study conducted for more than 25 years found that the people of Okinawa, a collection of islands between Japan and Taiwan, are considered the world's healthiest people. They live active independent lives well into their nineties and hundreds. The diseases that afflict the Western world, such as heart disease, obesity, osteoporosis, certain cancers, and diseases that cause memory loss appear in Okinawa much less frequently than in North America.

Elderly Okinawans were found to have amazingly young, clean arteries, low cholesterol, healthy blood pressure, a low risk for hormone-dependent cancers and osteoporosis, and a low incidence of Alzheimer's disease. Their good health is believed to be the result of a low caloric intake; high consumption of soy, fruits and vegetables, fish, low glycemic foods, and high-fibre foods; the inclusion of good fats in their diet; moderate alcohol consumption; and a high level of exercise. Okinawans' excellent psycho-spiritual health is believed to be due to their positive attitudes, strong social networks, and devout spiritualism.

Authors Dr. Bradley Willcox and Dr. M. Suzuki believe that a low-fat diet, exercise, stress management, good family relationships, friends, and spiritual connectedness all play significant roles in our health. Conversely, they believe that genetics plays only a small part. Their proof? Once Okinawans adopt Western eating and lifestyle habits, they too fall prey to the illnesses that afflict our culture.

Can we benefit from what we know of Okinawan life? The Okinawan diet emphasizes fruits, vegetables, whole grains, soy products, and fatty fish rich in omega-3 fatty acids. Water and green tea are the main beverages. Okinawans exercise, not to burn calories, but rather to help connect the mind, body, and spirit, which they believe is a key to optimal aging. Their emotional and spiritual health is attained most likely by living at a slower pace than Westerners, thus minimizing stress. This way of eating and living should be a model for many of us, but our culture doesn't necessarily allow this slower-paced routine. The answer is in somehow finding a balance.

Diet Supplements
Diet Pills

Use of diet pills usually begins after frustrated dieters, just off another failed program, go back to their old habits and gain back the weight they lost. In desperation, they search for quick, no-pain appetite suppressants.

While it is possible to suppress your brain's appetite centres with medication, doing so isn't effective over the long term. Some of these medications, such as Fen-Phen or Redux, have proven to be dangerous (even causing some cases of heart disease when drugs were combined) and were eventually pulled from the market.

Other medications block the absorption of fat. In April 1999, the U.S. Food and Drug Administration approved Orlistat as a weight inhibitor for the treatment of obesity. This kind of medication includes digestive enzymes that break down dietary fat so that it can be absorbed. Taken before, during, or after a meal, Orlistat prevents digestion and up to 30 percent of the absorption of the fat in that meal, which passes through the intestinal tract until it is excreted. Orlistat is not a licence to eat unlimited fat. This drug has numerous drawbacks, including the fact that it is designed only for those who are seriously obese. The actual weight loss is minimal and, because the fat-soluble nutrients aren't absorbed, anyone taking Orlistat is prescribed additional supplements.

Meal Replacement Shakes

Having an occasional can of a meal-replacement beverage is fine when you know you can't eat a healthy meal, but long-term weight loss success requires permanent changes in how you eat. These meal substitutes are like dieting, which never works in the long term.

All liquid supplement drinks are made from water, sugar, milk and/or soy proteins, oils, artificial flavours, and vitamins and minerals. They contain approximately 200 calories per 8-ounce (250 mL) serving. Newer products on the market contain larger amounts of the currently popular antioxidant vitamins A, E, and C. Older beverages, such as Ultra Slim Fast™ or Carnation Instant Breakfast™, are losing sales. These products do not supply the benefits of a solid, well-balanced meal from the four food groups. Most meal-replacement beverages contain no fibre and, because you are depriving yourself of real food, will result in weight gain as you go back to your old eating habits.

The Diet Answer

We often get caught up in the fantasy of diets because of the promises they make. We are guaranteed instant results. We look at those pictures of "yesterday heavy" and "tomorrow thin" and expect our dreams to come true. We want an easy and effortless way to lose weight. Intelligent people with good common sense fall for this kind of marketing every day. And in the end these diets don't work.

The answer lies in continuous patience, hard work, and effort. There is no question that anyone can learn to live more healthily and, before you know it, doing so will become second nature. You'll wonder how you ever lived before because you'll feel better, healthier, and more energetic.

Before going on a specific diet plan, ask yourself a few questions:

- Is the diet healthy? A healthy diet doesn't drastically reduce or eliminate any one healthy food group. Diets that ban carbohydrates are too extreme.

- Does it promise weight loss that's too rapid? The weight loss should not exceed 2 pounds (1 kg) per week if you want to keep the weight off.

- Is it a starvation diet? The diet should never limit you to consuming fewer than 1200 calories daily.

- Does it include exercise? Exercise must be emphasized in any diet program. Remember that diets that ban carbohydrates will leave you feeling less energetic and more tired. Carbs are where your energy comes from.

- Do you have to buy special products? Don't go on diets for which you have to purchase packaged meals or drinks from specific locations. You shouldn't have to buy a number of herbal or other supplements. A once-a-day multivitamin is all you need if you're generally in good health.

- What happens after you've lost the weight? A maintenance program that's easy to follow should be included.

- Is it an easy diet for you to follow?

It's easy to identify—and avoid—extreme fad diets:

- Be careful about huge promises and claims. For instance, in the protein diet you can eat all the protein you want, but doing so can damage your kidneys and raise the level of bad cholesterol. Also beware of a diet that promises you a huge weight loss weekly.

- Be aware that in medical school, very little is taught about nutrition, exercise, or living well. Just because the book was written by a doctor, it doesn't make it any more credible.

- Beware of outlandish claims about a specific food. There are no magical fat-burning foods or any true secrets, except for one: to feel and look great, you need knowledge about how to eat and then you have to put it into practice.

- Avoid diets that eliminate food groups. Some food is definitely not as healthy as others but can still be consumed in moderation.

When a diet doesn't work, you can be affected physically and psychologically. Poor diets—which translate into poor nutrition—can lead to a breakdown of your immune system, making you more susceptible to illness. Your failure to successfully diet can also foster a negative relationship to food and encourage bad habits, such as binge eating when you fall off the wagon.

Most diets don't work in the long run because they restrict your food choices and rarely foster doable eating habits that can change your life. You're not developing new skills and strategies when you follow a fad diet. Fad diets also make it difficult for you to dine in restaurants, at friends' homes, and while travelling—or anywhere you don't have access to specific foods. The best "diet" is one that changes how you eat, a habit that is mastered over time and practised daily.

The New Nutrition

Before you can begin to understand how to eat properly to maintain an ideal body weight and feel your best, you must understand the basics of good nutrition. The best way to do that is to understand the four basic food groups, as outlined in Canada's Food Guide.[1] This guide was developed by Health Canada to help Canadians meet their daily nutritional needs and possibly prevent obesity and debilitating diseases such as heart disease, diabetes, and even cancer. Designed to meet the basic nutritional requirements of healthy children and adults (age 4 and up), this guide is a good start to improving and adjusting your eating habits to fit your age and activity level.

Whenever I lecture or give a demonstration, I invariably ask the audience if they can name the four food groups and how many servings of each group is allowed. Everyone has been exposed to this information, but few people, if any, can answer the question or know how they can incorporate the Food Guide's suggestions into their daily lives. (Naming the four food groups was one of the questions on the television program *Who Wants to be a Millionaire?* If I recall correctly, the contestant gave the wrong answer!)

After years of searching for a method of permanent weight control, I finally achieved my ideal weight by understanding and following the recommendations of Canada's Food Guide. When I ate the correct amounts from all four food groups—taking into account my size, age, and activity level—I felt great. I no longer craved junk foods. Nutritionally, I was pampering my body.

This guide is my food bible, and it should become yours too because it does much of the work for you. The foods selected are already lower in fat, high in fibre, and loaded with vitamins and minerals. Fat and sugar are kept to a minimum, and not one food group is eliminated. The best thing about this guide is that every food is allowed in moderation. You have to keep in mind, though, that permanent weight loss is not something that happens overnight or even in a few weeks. The time you take to understand what healthy eating involves and to practise it daily is the only guarantee of maintaining your ideal body weight for life.

The Food Guide is based on these key strategies:

- Try to incorporate a variety of foods from each of the four food groups into your diet. Doing so will prevent you getting bored from eating the same food over and over again and will ensure that you get the daily necessary nutrients.

- Make sure that the majority of the foods you eat are from the grains and the vegetables and fruit groups. (Forget about all-protein diets!)

- Always select lower-fat dairy foods and lower-fat lean meats. Keep foods with saturated fats to a minimum.

- Maintain an ideal body weight by eating healthily and exercising at least three times per week.
- Limit the salt, caffeine, and alcohol you consume.

The Food Guide's Four Food Groups

The four food groups—grains, fruits and vegetables, meat and alternatives, and dairy products—provide you with the 50 different nutrients you require each day. By eating from each food group and enjoying a variety of foods, you are certain to obtain these necessary nutrients.

Grains

Grains contain carbohydrates that provide you with energy, fibre, and vitamins and minerals. The vitamins include B vitamins, thiamin, riboflavin, niacin, vitamin E, and folic acid. The minerals are iron, zinc, and magnesium. When food shopping, always choose whole-wheat breads, rice, pasta, and cereal since these supply more nutrition than refined grain foods such as white bread, white rice, or egg pasta.

The Food Guide recommends 5 to 12 servings of grain products daily. To determine how many servings you need to maintain a healthy body weight, speak to a dietitian or your doctor. Naturally, the more active you are, the more servings you can have. If you're trying to lose weight, you'll need fewer servings, and if you're trying to gain weight, you'll need more. Here are several examples of 1 grain serving:

- 1 slice of bread
- 1 small roll
- 1/2 small bagel (about 1 oz/30 g)
- 1/2 cup (125 mL) rice, pasta, or other grain
- 3/4 cup (175 mL) cereal

As you see, the servings add up quickly. For example, a regular dinner of 3 cups (750 mL) cooked pasta is equal to approximately 6 servings in the grains section. One large bagel, which weighs about 8 ounces (240 g), is the equivalent of 8 servings in the grains group.

It's easy to understand why carbohydrates have been given a bad rap. If you eat too many carbohydrate servings, you can easily gain weight. What you put on your grains or breads can lead to weight gain too. Excess butter, cheese, or cream-based sauces give "innocent" grains their excess calories and fat.

Healthy Canada

CANADA'S Food Guide

TO HEALTHY EATING

Enjoy a variety of foods from each group every day.

Choose lower-fat foods more often.

Grain Products
Choose whole grain and enriched products more often.

Vegetables & Fruit
Choose dark green and orange vegetables and orange fruit more often.

Milk Products
Choose lower-fat milk products more often.

Meat & Alternatives
Choose leaner meats, poultry and fish, as well as dried peas, beans and lentils more often.

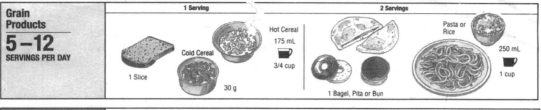

Grain Products

5–12 SERVINGS PER DAY

1 Serving

1 Slice

Cold Cereal
30 g

Hot Cereal
175 mL
3/4 cup

2 Servings

1 Bagel, Pita or Bun

Pasta or Rice
250 mL
1 cup

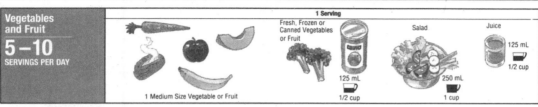

Vegetables and Fruit

5–10 SERVINGS PER DAY

1 Serving

1 Medium Size Vegetable or Fruit

Fresh, Frozen or Canned Vegetables or Fruit
125 mL
1/2 cup

Salad
250 mL
1 cup

Juice
125 mL
1/2 cup

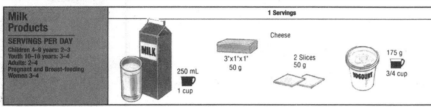

Milk Products

SERVINGS PER DAY
Children 4–9 years: 2–3
Youth 10–16 years: 3–4
Adults: 2–4
Pregnant and Breast-feeding Women 3–4

1 Servings

MILK
250 mL
1 cup

Cheese
3"x1"x1"
50 g

2 Slices
50 g

175 g
3/4 cup

Other Foods

Taste and enjoyment can also come from other foods and beverages that are not part of the 4 food groups. Some of these foods are higher in fat or Calories, so use these foods in moderation.

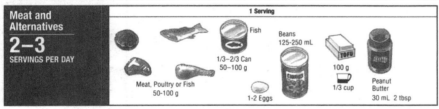

Meat and Alternatives

2–3 SERVINGS PER DAY

1 Serving

Meat, Poultry or Fish
50–100 g

Fish
1/3–2/3 Can
50–100 g

1-2 Eggs

Beans
125–250 mL

TOFU
100 g
1/3 cup

Peanut Butter
30 mL 2 tbsp

Different People Need Different Amounts of Food

The amount of food you need every day from the 4 food groups and other foods depends on your age, body size, activity level, whether you are male or female and if you are pregnant or breast-feeding. That's why the Food Guide gives a lower and higher number of servings for each food group. For example, young children can choose the lower number of servings, while male teenagers can go to the higher number. Most other people can choose servings somewhere in between.

Enjoy eating well, being active and feeling good about yourself. That's VITALIT

To avoid overindulgence in the grains category, take care to balance your diet by eating foods from the other food groups. If you eat only grains at a meal, you are not only missing important nutrients, but to compensate you're probably eating more food than you should. Eating foods from the different food groups at each meal—and even for snacks—is the way to avoid cravings and subsequent overeating.

Vegetables and Fruits

These miracle foods are loaded with vitamins, minerals, carbohydrates, and fibre. Some of the nutrients vegetables and fruits provide are vitamins A and C, iron, potassium, and beta carotene. They also supply antioxidants and phytochemicals, which protect the body's cells and may reduce the risk of cancer. Fruits and vegetables contain loads of fibre and water, which are good for your bowels. Furthermore, water and fibre may reduce the risk of colon cancer and intestinal disorders such as diverticulitis, a disease of the bowel in which tiny pouches develop in the wall of the colon; if these pouches become inflamed, stomach pain, fever, and diarrhea may result.

Vegetables and fruits, considered complex carbohydrates, should make up the largest portion of each meal. Daily requirements range from 5 to 10 servings. Let's take a look at what constitutes a serving size:

- 1 cup (250 mL) leafy green vegetables
- 1/2 cup (125 mL) cooked or raw chopped vegetables
- 1 medium fruit
- 1 cup (250 mL) berries
- 1/4 cup (50 mL) dried fruit
- 1/2 cup (125 mL) chopped canned fruit

It's always best to emphasize the dark green and orange and red vegetables and fruits in your diet to obtain maximum nutrition. Some examples are broccoli, sweet bell pepper, sweet potatoes, carrots, cantaloupe, strawberries, and tomatoes. They contain beta carotene, which the body converts to vitamin A, that acts as an antioxidant and may prevent some forms of cancer (see "The State of the (Fat) Nation").

Keep in mind that starchy vegetables such as potatoes and corn are higher in calories and should be counted in the grain category.

Milk Products

To be included in this group, foods must be a good source of calcium and vitamin D—as are milk, yogourt, and cheese—which explains why butter, cream cheese, and sour cream aren't and soy products are. (Any soy product fortified with calcium and vitamin D belongs in this group.) Foods within this category supply protein, fat, calcium, and vitamins A and D. Calcium is the greatest benefit from milk products. One glass of milk contains 300 milligrams of calcium, and the daily requirement of calcium is approximately 1500 milligrams. With the right combination of calcium-rich foods you can meet your calcium requirements without taking supplements. (But don't hesitate to take calcium supplements if you can't get the calcium required daily from foods.) The Food Guide calls for 2 to 4 servings from this category, with 1 serving being any of the following:

- 1 cup (250 mL) lower-fat milk
- 3/4 cup (175 mL) lower-fat yogourt
- 1-1/2 ounces (45 g) cheese

To maintain a healthy body weight, it's very important to understand your personal requirements and therefore the number of servings you should have.

Meat and Alternatives

This is the group that supplies most of our protein. It also supplies fat, some B vitamins, iron, zinc, and magnesium. Foods in this category include beef, poultry, fish, beans, soy products, and peanut butter. Health Canada recommends 2 to 3 servings daily, with 1 serving being any of the following:

- 3 ounces (90 g) of beef, poultry, or fish, which is a piece roughly the size of your palm
- 1/2 cup (125 mL) beans
- 2 tablespoons (30 mL) peanut butter

If you're eating leaner fish or beef, or the breast of chicken, then the serving size can be as much as 4 to 5 ounces (120 to 150 g), as these foods have much less fat.

Keep in mind that animal products contain saturated fat, which can cause your blood cholesterol level to rise. If you're looking for food sources that supply energy, it's better to consume carbohydrates and enjoy animal protein products in smaller amounts, or eat the non-animal or plant-based protein foods.

Foods That Don't Fit into the Food Groups

Foods that don't fall under any of the above categories should be eaten in moderation. These include oils, salad dressings, butter, margarine, snack foods, soft drinks, rich desserts, alcohol, tea, coffee, and condiments, such as honey, jams, and spreads. Many of these are loaded with fat and calories and lack nutritional value. But you needn't deprive yourself of these foods—I certainly don't! If you're eating regularly throughout the day, you can allow yourself small indulgences. Every day I have a treat or two, but always in moderation and never to replace the better-quality foods. Health problems arise when you're not getting the right nutrition. Avoid substituting poorer-quality foods (fried foods, sweets, junk food, and alcohol) for essential foods.

Problems with the Food Guide

The Food Guide is not perfect and certainly is not designed for Canadians who have serious health problems. If you do have an illness, you can adjust the recommendations in the Food Guide to your specific needs by consulting with your doctor or registered dietitian. Below are some of the Food Guide's shortcomings and suggestions for overcoming them.

Serving Sizes   Serving sizes are often unrealistic or confusing. For example, when the grain category says you can have between 5 and 12 servings daily, it is not always easy to determine how many servings you should actually consume. The number depends on your age, level of activity, and current health status. It's not practical to get out the measuring cups at each meal. When dining out, a plate of pasta can range from 4 to 8 servings of grains. You have to be able to "eyeball" serving sizes to suit your particular needs. This is mandatory is if you want to achieve an ideal body weight.

One answer to achieving the proper serving size is to keep a mental or written account during the day and then do some planning. For instance, if you know you are going to an Italian restaurant for dinner and will consume mostly grains (pasta, rice, bread), then for breakfast and lunch keep the grains to a minimum and enjoy more protein, dairy, and fruits and vegetables. The same applies for protein—if it's dinner at a steakhouse and you'll be consuming mostly protein, then keep your protein consumption during the day to a minimum and fill up on grains, dairy, and fruits and vegetables. This method works well and ultimately is the best way to achieve permanent weight control. It is the only technique that has worked for my husband and me.

Calorie Differences   Another drawback to the Food Guide is that it ignores the caloric differences of foods within the same category. For example, mangos, avocados, and watermelon have more calories than melons, berries, or apples. Different cuts and types of beef, chicken, and fish differ in fat and calories. A chicken breast has fewer calories and fat than dark meat. Flank steak is much lower in fat and calories than beef ribs or rib-eye steak. Certain white fish, such as sole and halibut, have fewer calories than salmon, sea bass, or mackerel. Cheeses vary greatly in the percentage of milk fat (MF) they contain. Hard cheeses, such as Cheddar or Swiss, are usually higher in fat than soft cheeses, such as cottage, ricotta, or goat cheese. Being aware of these differences helps you make better choices.

Nutritional Differences   Some grains have more vitamins, minerals, and protein than others. White-flour products are much less nutritious than whole-grain products. When flour is refined, the nutritious part of the grain is removed. This is often done so that the grain cooks faster. It's hard to avoid refined foods, since they are what is most often served in restaurants and fast-food establishments, and are most often found in packaged or processed foods.

The Food Guide doesn't specify which foods are high- or low-fibre, which are high- or low-fat, or which have a high or low glycemic index (see page 63). Eating a high-fibre, low-fat diet can make all the difference in the world to your health. Low glycemic foods keep you full longer than high glycemic foods and tend to be more nutritious. The Food Guide counts all cereals as the same, yet packaged cereals that contain marshmallows, chocolate, or food colouring are not as nutritious as whole-grain cereals that also contain much more fibre.

Different Needs   Keep in mind that everyone's needs are different and adjustments must be made according to your health, age, and present medical situation. Before determining your appropriate daily food values, be sure to take into consideration these factors.

Older adults   Nutritional needs change as you get older. After age 65 you don't absorb vitamin D and some B vitamins as well. An older woman needs more calcium and iron. Many older people no longer eat right and often don't eat enough. Speak to a nutritionist or your doctor to find out what nutrients you should be getting and what supplements you should take.

Children and teenagers   Kids today don't get proper nutrition because they eat too much fast food and have picky eating habits. Since kids are growing fast, they need to fuel their bodies even more than adults do.

Vegetarians and vegans Since vegetarians and vegans don't eat meat, they are missing vitamin B$_{12}$, which is found only in animal products. They also end up low in calcium and iron.

Despite its flaws, the Food Guide is still the best way to achieve permanent weight control. The problems outlined above can all be overcome, and the Food Guide is the most useful tool for healthy eating and weight maintenance.

Now that we understand the Food Guide and its four major food groups, let's take a look at the specific components that make up our food and how they can make a difference in weight management. I'll explain in the following sections the various aspects of calories, carbohydrates, the glycemic index, fibre, sugar, protein, fat, salt, water, caffeine, alcohol, and vitamins and minerals.

Calories

A calorie is the amount of energy food provides. To achieve an ideal weight you must take in only the number of calories your body needs—no more, no less. The specific number of calories you need daily depends on your age, activity level, sex, and body frame.

Once you understand the calorie and fat content of specific foods that you cook and that you eat in restaurants, you'll be well on your way toward your goals of weight loss and stability. If you're just starting to learn about calories and the fat content of different foods, some excellent calorie and fat guides are available in bookstores. Such books contain nutritional analyses of foods, as well as analyses of recipes from many well-known restaurants and fast-food establishments. Give yourself a couple of weeks to learn the calorie jargon.

Daily Calorie Requirements

The daily requirement for calories can be a confusing matter. Many different factors come into play.

Sedentary women and older adults require only 1600 to 1800 calories daily. If you're not moving, you're not burning those calories. Children, teenage girls, active women, and sedentary men require between 1800 and 2100 calories daily. Teenage boys, active men, and very active women require between 2700 and 3000 calories daily.[2]

Calories and the Food Guide   Now that you have some idea of how many calories you need daily to maintain a healthy body weight, you need to learn how to apply this knowledge to Canada's Food Guide. The following is a list of the four food groups that shows how different numbers of servings affect the calorie intake. This is an approximate calculation and varies according to the type and quality of food eaten. You'll find a good-quality calorie-counting book helpful.

Servings According to Daily Calorie Intake

	1500 Calories	2000 Calories	2600 Calories
Grains	6 servings	9 servings	12 servings
Vegetables and Fruits	6 servings	8 servings	10 servings
Milk Products	3 servings	3 servings	4 servings
Meat and Alternatives	2 servings	2–3 servings	3 servings

Remember that your activity level is a very important requirement in determining your calories, number of servings from each food group, and type of food. For example, fatty red meat has more calories than lean fish.

In my experience over the years, struggling with my own weight and dealing every day with people who have weight problems, I have concluded that there are three ways to achieve a lifetime of successful eating:

1. Eat a variety of foods from the four food groups. Experiment with different foods and try to incorporate them into your weekly diet.

2. Examine Canada's Food Guide and your ideal daily caloric intake, and eat moderate portions. Portion control is key in maintaining your weight. If you're eating properly during the day and combining the four food groups at each meal, you will be full and satisfied. The reason we eat more than we should is because we're not eating enough nutritious foods throughout the day to sustain our energy needs.

3. Consider the timing of your food intake. Many of us go without breakfast, have a light lunch, and then don't stop eating after six o'clock in the evening. Generally, at this time you're least active and you can't burn off those dinner calories as easily because your metabolism is slower

when you're inactive. So those calories get stored as fat. If you're not eating all day, you're not getting fuel or energy into your body, and the result will be fatigue and a low energy level.

People who do not eat breakfast and have small lunches should "graze" throughout the day. Eat only healthy snacks during the day and remember to incorporate foods from the four food groups.

Calories and Fat   The most frequent question I am asked is whether it's better to count calories or grams of fat when trying to lose weight. It's a very good question because both calories and fat affect weight loss and weight maintenance.

It's important to limit the amount of fat you eat because fat contains 9 calories per gram; protein and carbohydrates contain only 4 calories per gram. Fat-filled products add up quickly in terms of calories.

Many diet programs measure calories, grams of fat, or a combination of the two. For instance, when people go to a doctor or weight-loss clinic, they are given a diet that indicates how many calories to consume daily. These meal plans usually consist of foods that are low in fat.

Most popular, or fad, diets are based on reducing calories, not grams of fat. Diets that drastically cut down on carbs often allow you to eat foods that have loads of fat grams. Even a food-combining diet succeeds for a time, because it requires that you omit a lot of the carbs, dairy, and sugar from your diet—you're allowed to eat saturated fat protein until you feel full! These diets fail eventually because you can't live very long without certain food groups.

The healthiest and ultimately the most successful way of eating is watching both calories and fat in your diet. Because more and more low-fat or no-fat foods are available, we tend to choose them, falsely believing that we can consume as much of these foods as we want simply because they have little or no fat. As a result, we are fatter and unhealthier than ever. Many low- or no-fat foods have plenty of calories because, as the fat is reduced, sugar is added or servings are made larger. For instance, a low-fat muffin is usually three times the size of a healthy portion and has the same number of calories as a regular-fat regular-sized muffin; a much larger amount of sugar and flour makes up for the missing oil. Portion control is another problem. If you consume too much food (with the exception of certain fruits and vegetables), even food with little or no fat, you will take in too many calories during your day, and this will lead to weight gain.

Carbohydrates

Carbohydrates, protein, and fat make up the three major building blocks in our daily diet. Most health professionals state that the ideal daily diet is 55 percent carbohydrates, 15 percent protein, and less than 30 percent fat.[3] The best way to ensure these proportions is to look at your plate: plan to cover at least 50 percent of it with carbohydrate foods, with an emphasis on fruits and vegetables.

Simple carbohydrates are sugar-based foods that have calories and little or no nutrition. I like to call them empty-calorie foods. Complex carbohydrates are an excellent source of energy and important nutrients. They are the starches found in grains, vegetables, fruits, breads, and legumes. These foods are nutritionally better than simple carbs because complex carbs release glucose into the blood more slowly, which keeps you full longer. They make up a good part of a healthy low-fat diet and can reduce the risk of heart disease, stroke, diabetes, and some types of cancers.

It's best to try to stick to whole grains. They play a role in a heart-healthy, anti-cancer diet due to the fibre, vitamins, and phytochemicals they contain. They also help to control blood sugar and may help prevent Type 2 diabetes. Whole grains in the form of wheat, rice, barley, or rye come with the natural bran and germ. Refined grains, such as white rice and the grains found in bread or pasta, have the bran and germ removed during processing. The only way to know for sure if the product you buy is whole grain is to read the label. The first ingredient should be whole-wheat flour, oats, brown rice, or whole-rye flour.

The Carb Debate

Carbs are one of the most controversial foods around today. There was a time when we were told to consume lots of complex carbohydrates. Grains were the food that was supposed to keep us lean. Then in the 1970s, along came Dr. Atkins with a bestselling book on banning the carbs from your diet.[3] His philosophy was that carbohydrates were making America overweight. By the start of the 1990s, people were not losing but gaining weight on carbs, and we were becoming an obese society.

The truth is that carbohydrates were getting a bad reputation due to quality and portion size. The idea was that low-fibre, starchy carbs like potatoes, white bread, rice, and pasta led to high blood insulin levels, carbohydrate cravings, and weight gain. The healthier complex carbohydrates, such as brown rice, ancient grains, and fruits and vegetables, were not the culprits. Also, certain fad diets told us we could eat as many carbohydrates as we liked as long as we cut out the fat. Carbohydrates do contain calories, and taking in more calories than your body needs will always end in excess weight whether those calories come from carbs, fat, or protein.

Glycemic Index (GI)   The glycemic index was developed so that we could consume carbs of higher quality without gaining weight. Complex carbs all have different nutritional value. Some get converted to blood sugar quickly and some take longer. These complex carbs are classified in terms of their glycemic index, which is the ability of foods to cause a rise in blood sugar. Foods that have a low glycemic index raise blood sugar slowly and are ideal for keeping you full longer and achieving weight loss. Those with a high glycemic index raise your blood sugar quickly, leave you hungry sooner, and can contribute to weight gain.

These are foods with a high glycemic index:

- baked potato, carrots, corn, couscous, pasta, potato chips, white rice
- bananas, mango, pineapple, raisins, watermelon
- bagels, white bread and rolls, white-flour crackers, cakes, Cheerios, Corn Flakes, popcorn, rice cakes, pretzels
- chocolate, honey, sugar

Here are foods with a low glycemic index:

- beans, peas, peanuts, lentils, soybeans, sweet potatoes, barley, brown rice, bulgur
- apples, cherries, grapefruit, peaches, pears, plums
- milk, yogourt, soy milk
- oatmeal, All-Bran and Red River cereals

Realize that all these complex carbohydrates are still excellent nutritional foods, no matter what their glycemic index. Don't completely avoid those with a high glycemic index; just don't count on them to fill you up if you're looking for a sustained energy boost.

One of the reasons we are a carb-addicted society is that foods rich in carbs boost the brain's production of serotonin, which is a natural mood enhancer. When serotonin levels are high, one feels calm, peaceful, sleepy, and relaxed. When serotonin levels are low, one can feel tense, angry, and sleep deprived. I always find that if I'm stressed, anxious, or low, I crave carbs. The more bread, pasta, and potatoes I consume, the better my mood becomes.

Fibre

The hidden jewel found in carbohydrates is fibre. It has been shown to lower cholesterol, lessen the risk of heart disease, prevent bowel problems, reduce the risk of colon cancer, help people control Type 2 diabetes, and help in weight loss.

Fibre is of two types—soluble and insoluble. Soluble fibre is found in such foods as oats, barley, vegetables, fruit, brown rice, and oat bran. This type of fibre decreases blood cholesterol, which can decrease the risk of heart disease. Insoluble fibre is found in such foods as wheat and corn bran, and fruits and vegetables. This type of fibre helps promote regularity, which can decrease the risk of colon cancer.

New studies indicate that the more fibre you consume, the lower the risk of heart attack. With every 10 gram increase in fibre, the risk of heart attack can decrease by 20 percent. Most North Americans consume only about 11 grams of fibre daily. The National Cancer Institute recommends eating between 25 and 35 grams of fibre daily.

When you eat fibre, you'll feel fuller and more satisfied. The foods that contain soluble fibre have a low glycemic index (see page 63). Effective ways to increase your fibre are to increase your vegetable intake or reduce the amount of white refined grains in your diet. Start experimenting with whole grains. Increase your fibre intake slowly, or you may experience the side effects of feeling bloated, gassy, or crampy, or have diarrhea.

Let's take a look at how easy it is to get more fibre into your diet. Foods that are high in fibre have at least 4 grams of fibre per serving. Foods that contain 6 grams are very good sources of fibre.

Fibre and Chronic Disease   Lack of fibre in your diet can cause serious illnesses. We've already discussed the higher risk of colon cancer and Type 2 diabetes if the fibre in your diet is insufficient (see "The State of the (Fat) Nation").

Diverticulosis is an inflammation of the intestines. This disease is due to lack of fibre in the diet, which results in pressure in the colon when passing hard stools. A high-fibre diet alleviates this pressure by increasing the size and softness of the stools, and by speeding their passage through the colon. The longer the stools stay in the colon, the greater the chance of disease.

This disease has increased among North Americans since more refined and processed foods have been added to their diets. By increasing their intake of dietary fibre, people can greatly reduce their risk of disease and of complications and surgery related to it.

Let's summarize the benefits of fibre in your diet:

- Fibre reduces constipation.
- Insoluble fibre reduces the risk of diverticulosis.
- Colon cancer is rare among people who have high-fibre diets.
- Fibre reduces the risk of developing polyps, which may lead to precancerous conditions in the colon.
- Soluble fibre reduces the risk of heart disease, by helping lower the LDL (bad cholesterol).

Fibre Content of Foods

Fruits

Apple, pear, orange (1)   4 g

Dried apricots (1/3 cup/75 mL)   4 g

Raisins (2/3 cup/150 mL)   5 g

Banana   3 g

Grapefruit, raspberries, stewed prunes
(1/2 cup/125 mL)   2 g

Cantaloupe, orange juice (1 cup/250 mL)   1 g

Strawberries (1 cup/250 mL)   2 g

Blueberries (1 cup/250 mL)   4 g

Vegetables

Sweet potato (1 medium)   7 g

Baked potato with skin (1 medium)   5 g

Peas, carrots (1 cup/250 mL)   6 g

Spinach, cabbage (1/2 cup/125 mL boiled)   2 g

Corn on cob (1 medium)   6 g

Broccoli, asparagus (1 cup/250 mL)   4 g

Green beans (1/2 cup/125 mL)   4 g

Grains

Brown rice (1 cup/250 mL)   3 g

White rice (3/4 cup/175 mL)   1 g

Spaghetti (1 cup/250 mL)   2 g

Barley (1 cup/250 mL)   6 g

100% whole-wheat bread (1 slice)   6 g

White bread (1 slice)   1 g

All-Bran cereal (1/3 cup/75 mL)   9 g

Raisin Bran cereal (1/2 cup/125 mL)   4 g

Shredded Wheat cereal (2 pieces)   6 g

Oat bran, dry (1/3 cup/75 mL)   4 g

Beans

Kidney beans (1/2 cup/125 mL cooked)   6 g

Chickpeas (1/2 cup/125 mL cooked)   6 g

Lentils (1 cup/250 mL cooked)   7 g

Pinto beans (1/2 cup/125 mL cooked)   5.9 g

- Fibre reduces the risk of diabetes, as well as lessening its severity. Fibre can help reduce insulin requirements and improve glucose tolerance.
- Fibre lessens the likelihood of gallstones.
- Obesity is correlated with a low-fibre diet.

Sugar and Sweeteners

Sugar has to be my greatest weakness in the food department. When I have a craving, it's always for cookies, ice cream, cake, chocolate, or almost anything that contains sugar. Cravings are tied to my emotional state. When I'm happy, sad, excited, overwhelmed, or whatever, I crave sweets. They always seem to satisfy me—that is, until I get on the scale or try to fit into my jeans.

Some alarming statistics indicate that the average North American consumes about 120 pounds (55 kg) of sugar per year—approximately 40 teaspoons (200 mL) of sugar daily. All we need is 6 teaspoons (30 mL) daily.

Ongoing studies are attempting to prove a correlation between excess sugar in our diet and obesity, heart disease, high blood pressure, a rise in triglyceride levels, depression, mood swings, blood sugar problems, gallstones, kidney problems, and diabetes. To date, there is no direct proof that sugar causes these diseases, only that it may precipitate them.

Sugar comes in various forms: sucrose, glucose, lactose, maltose, molasses, honey, corn syrup, brown sugar, and more. None is more nutritious than the others, except for molasses, which contains B vitamins, calcium, potassium, and more. Fructose, a form of sugar that is not as refined, has twice the sweetness of sugar, so you use about half the amount. Contrary to what people believe, honey and brown sugar are not more nutritious than white sugar.

There is no reason to severely restrict your intake of sugar unless you have diabetes and are carbohydrate sensitive. If you are carbohydrate sensitive, consuming too many high glycemic carbs may trigger hunger and overeating. An empty carbohydrate with excess calories, sugar stimulates the release of insulin, the hormone that accounts for getting energy to our muscles. This causes the body to transform excess calories into fat. Insulin can trigger a reaction: if you are having a sugar low, better known as hypoglycemia, you crave more sugary foods, which can leave you feeling unwell and lead to mood swings. To prevent this, always combine the sugar you eat with foods high in fibre and/or protein to delay the entry of the sugar into the bloodstream.

After years of consuming an excess of sugary foods, one can develop a condition called insulin resistance. This means that the insulin your body manufactures is not carrying the sugar into your cells where it can either be used for energy or burned off. This condition can lead to the other illnesses, such as diabetes.

Over half the carbohydrates you consume daily are non-nutritious sugar carbs. Not surprisingly, foods such as candy, chewing gum, cakes, cereals, cookies, jams, chocolate, non-diet soft drinks, and artificial juices contain large amounts of sugar.

Sugar Content of Some Foods

Food	Sugar
Soft drink (12 oz)	8 tsp/40 g
Orange juice (6 oz)	6 tsp
Chocolate bar (3 oz)	21 tsp/105 g
Ice cream (1/2 cup/125 mL)	4 tsp/20 g
Sugar cereal (1/2 cup/125 mL)	2 tsp/10 g

"Hidden" sugar is present in foods such as potatoes, beets, carrots, corn, refined white-flour products, white rice, ketchup, barbecue sauces, and salad dressings. All these are examples of high glycemic foods.

Sugar Substitutes   There are many substitutes for refined sugar; some are healthier than sugar and others have side effects. What used to be known as an "artificial sweetener" is now called a sugar substitute or a low-calorie sweetener simply because the word "artificial" has a negative connotation.

Artificial sweeteners can be found in chewing gum, yogourt, beverages, cakes, chocolate bars, candies, and more. Such sweeteners have been around for decades but still haven't put an end to obesity. According to a commonly held theory, one possible reason is that people who use artificial sweeteners or eat artificially sweetened foods consume "missing calories" elsewhere, usually by eating higher-fat foods.

Regular use of sugar does not promote obesity, heart disease, or diabetes. The overuse of sugar leads to these problems, as does the overconsumption of fat. Here are some options for using alternatives to sugar:

- If you have diabetes, the best and most natural product to use is Splenda®, a calorie-free sweetener made from sucralose. The body cannot break down the sucralose and absorbs only 15 percent of it. You use it as you would sugar. So far, sucralose has not been associated with cancer or other illnesses.

- Saccharin®, which was used in soft drinks, jams, salad dressings, mouthwash, and toothpaste, was banned from Canada because it caused bladder cancer in rats. Neither a sugar nor a food, this sugar substitute is made from coal tar. It is 300 times sweeter than sugar.

- Cyclamate, which is used in Sweet'N'Low™ and Sugar Twin™, also causes bladder cancer in rats.

- Aspartame, better known as Nutrasweet™ or Equal™, is one of the most widely used sugar substitutes. It cannot be used in cooking because it loses its stability when heated. The FDA and the World Health Organization have concluded that this sweetener is safe. Aspartame is 180 times sweeter than sugar and has been known to cause such side effects as rashes, headaches, nausea, and mild depression.

- Stevia is a herbal extract that has been used as a calorie-free sweetener in South America and Japan. Under the U.S. Dietary Supplement Act of 1994, stevia can be sold as a "dietary supplement" in healthfood stores, on the Internet, or by mail order. It can't be labelled as a "sweetener," which is a food additive, or used in commercial food or beverages yet. Stevia can be used for cooking and is 300 times sweeter than sugar unless diluted.

- Evaporated cane juice is a minimally processed sweetener made from fresh, evaporated cane juice and is used like sugar.

- Organic sugar is harvested, clarified, evaporated, and crystallized within 24 hours. It retains most of the nutrients found in cane sugar. Refined sugar, on the other hand, loses most of these nutrients during processing. At least 90 percent of the natural sugar plant is stripped away during the refining process, which removes the fibre and protein of the sugar cane.

Evidence suggests that when you save calories by using artificial sweeteners, you tend to eat more calories elsewhere. Sweeteners can whet your appetite for more sweets. How often have you noticed someone in the coffee shop adding sweetener to his or her coffee while indulging in a muffin or croissant? The teaspoon of sugar has 16 calories and no fat, whereas the muffin or croissant has anywhere from 400 to 600 calories and 30 grams of fat!

The bottom line is that artificial sweeteners used in moderation and not as a major part of your diet are fine. Don't depend on them to eliminate excess calories from beverages, desserts, or your main meals. It never works, and you will make up those calories by bingeing on other foods. Most foods containing artificial sweeteners are usually of poor nutritional value. Their only benefit is that they don't cause tooth decay and they offer a sugar alternative to people with diabetes. The sugar derivatives, which are not artificial, are more nutritious than sugar but are not easily available and can be more expensive.

Protein

Much like carbohydrates, protein has lately been the focus of some controversial diets. For the longest time we have been told to have no more than a portion the size of the palm of your hand at any one meal. Then along came Dr. Atkins's *New Diet Revolution*,[4] which advocated eating as much protein as you wanted, but only if you omitted carbohydrates. Amazingly, Dr. Atkins was giving you permission to eat a 16-ounce (500 g) steak loaded with saturated fat, or a half pound (250 g) of greasy bacon. This is considered a healthy diet? I don't think so!

No wonder confusion about protein is pretty common today. First, let's make clear that meat contains saturated fat and cholesterol, which can cause heart disease and stroke. The excess fat can also lead to obesity, certain kinds of cancer, and other diseases. So should we eliminate meat altogether? Of course not: meat has protein and we need protein for good health. And, besides, meat is delicious.

Your body needs protein to build and maintain muscle and cell growth. Protein keeps your bones strong, produces enzymes to help digest your food, and allows your brain to function. Children who do not eat enough protein will not grow as tall—some may even experience hair loss, anemia, and digestion problems.

If you're following Canada's Food Guide, then you are receiving adequate protein from the dairy and the meat and alternatives food groups. Eat high-fat and saturated-fat protein in moderation, alternating it with other forms of protein such as fish, beans, and soy products that contain no saturated fat.

Meat, fish, dairy, poultry, cheese, eggs, and soy products are complete proteins; this means they contain all of the essential amino acids. An incomplete protein does not contain all of the essential amino acids. Foods that are incomplete proteins include grains, legumes, beans, nuts, and seeds. The good news is that you can make an incomplete protein complete by combining a grain with a legume or seed. For example, a piece of bread with some peanut butter equals a complete protein. Any grain combined with beans equals a complete protein.

Daily Protein Requirements

A 1-ounce (30 g) serving of a protein-rich food such as meat or chicken provides 7 grams of protein. A person needs between 6 and 9 ounces (180 to 270 g) of a protein source daily, which provide about 42 to 63 grams of protein.

- Children 1 to 9 years old need between 19 and 30 grams of protein daily.

- Males from 10 to 75 years old need between 38 and 55 grams of protein daily.

- Females from 10 to 75 years old need between 40 and 47 grams of protein daily.
- Pregnant women need between 50 and 68 grams of protein daily.

A simple way to calculate your protein requirement is to multiply your weight in kilograms by 1 gram of protein. For example, a person who weighs 69 kilograms needs 69 grams of protein daily. The average North American consumes between 90 and 120 grams of protein daily! The protein content of some foods is shown in the table on the next page.

It's easy to see how getting enough protein is usually not a problem. Our concern should be trying to cut back on consuming protein from animal sources due to the amount of saturated fat and cholesterol it contains.

Excess Protein   When I refer to consuming excess protein, I'm usually referring to animal protein such as meat, chicken, and cheese. Non-animal or plant proteins, such as beans or tofu, are not considered harmful to our health.

Protein Content of Animal-Based Products

Meat (3-oz/90 g serving)

Sirloin steak	26 g
Hamburger patty	21 g
Ham	19 g
Ground beef	24 g
Turkey or chicken breast	26 g
Tuna	30 g
Salmon	25 g
Lean white fish	21 g

High-Protein Sources Other than Meat

Tofu (1/2 cup/125 mL)	10 g
Soybeans (1/2 cup/125 mL)	10 g
Cottage cheese (1/2 cup/125 mL)	12 g
Cheddar cheese (1 oz/30 g)	7 g
Egg (1 large)	7 g
Lentils (1/2 cup/125 mL)	7 g
Milk (1/2 cup/125 mL)	4 g
Low-fat yogourt (1/2 cup/125 mL)	5 g
Pasta (1 cup/250 mL)	7 g
Brown rice (1 cup/250 mL)	5 g
100% Whole-wheat bread (1 slice)	3 g
Baked potato (1 medium)	8 g
Peanut butter (2 tbsp/25 mL)	10 g

Experts in the field say that too much protein leads to many health problems. Gary Null, author of *The Complete Guide to Health and Nutrition*,[5] believes that a long-term diet of excess protein can cause heart disease and kidney problems, and can result in phosphorus deficiency. Dr. Andrew Weil, author of *Natural Health, Natural Medicine*, believes that the metabolism of protein taxes the liver and kidneys, as well as the entire digestive system.[6] This can lead to fatigue and lack of energy. He also says that the diuretic effect of a high intake of protein leaches minerals, including calcium, out of the body and can lead to osteoporosis.

Lean protein is important for weight control. Boneless, skinless breast of turkey or chicken, egg whites, seafood, fish, beans, lentils, tofu, and 1% dairy products are some of the better protein choices. Consuming too much protein that is not lean increases the amount of saturated fat, cholesterol, and excess calories in your diet. Also, when you eat too much protein you don't leave yourself room for the lower-fat choices such as fruits, vegetables, and grains, which are needed for essential nutrition.

Adding up your daily protein grams is not an easy task. Just remember to include about 3 to 4 ounces (90 to 120 g) of protein at two of your main meals, and possibly at three meals if you're having lean protein. Snacks should include protein in the form of yogourt, a small amount of nuts, or milk or a soy beverage.

I beg you to forget about high-protein diets for many reasons. A high-protein diet doesn't allow you to burn fat efficiently. It increases your blood cholesterol simply because it promotes the consumption of higher-fat protein. This, over time, puts a tremendous strain on your kidneys and can lead to excessive fluid loss, constipation, and possibly kidney failure. You often end up losing water, not fat. The moment you begin to consume carbohydrates, your weight will increase due to water retention.

Fat

When you think of fat, what comes to mind? The texture of chocolate, the juiciness of a burger, the texture of salad dressings, and the creaminess of ice cream and cheese. Today we think of these as forbidden foods, or as special treats to be eaten only occasionally. We all know that high-fat foods are high in calories, fat, and cholesterol and can lead to obesity, certain types of cancers, and heart disease and stroke.

Let's take a look at some of the facts:

- In order for our bodies to have the amount of fat needed for protection, cushioning, and balance, we need about 1 tablespoon (15 mL) of fat daily.
- We are eating three to four times the amount of fat that we require daily.

- Nearly 50 percent of North Americans are overweight, over 25 percent are clinically obese (more than 40 1b/20 kg over their ideal weight), and 25 percent of children are overweight.

As a result, we've become a fat-phobic society, which has led to the creation of hundreds of reduced-fat food products. But we are not becoming a thin society. On the contrary, we are becoming an increasingly obese population. The problem could be that we are eating higher volumes of low-fat foods, which means we are taking in excess calories, or we are not satisfied with these low-fat foods and are bingeing on the higher-fat foods.

Cutting back on the fat, not cutting out the fat, is really the message. If you try to eliminate too much fat from your diet, you are endangering your health. Some of the problems that can occur are lack of energy and lack of skin elasticity. We all need fat in order for our cell walls to keep strong and to be able to absorb and metabolize essential vitamins and amino acids. Our bodies cannot make this fat, so we need to get it from the foods we eat.

Here are some more facts you should know about fat:

- Fat carries the fat-soluble vitamins A, D, E, and K, and supplies essential fatty acids.
- Fat cushions the internal organs and plays a role in body temperature control.
- Fat is a key element in the cells of the brain, spine, and nerves.
- Fat maintains healthy skin and hair.
- Low energy and a weak immune system are results of too little fat in one's diet.

Keep in mind that, at 9 calories per gram, fat has more calories per gram than protein or carbohydrates, at 4 calories per gram. Also, fat doesn't fill you up the same way that protein and carbs do, which means you're hungry soon after eating fat.

Remember that low-fat does not mean no-fat. Low- or no-fat products can still be loaded with calories. A calorie is a calorie. For example, low-fat cookies, baked potato chips, lower-fat hard cheeses, and light margarines are still filled with calories; they just don't have the same high-fat content.

Daily Fat Requirements

A healthy diet should contain a daily intake of between 25 and 30 percent fat. The typical North American diet exceeds that considerably, consisting of 40 percent or more fat. Remember to keep your fat to under 30 percent of your total daily calories and your saturated fat to below 10 percent of your total calories.

Different Types of Fat   All fats are not considered equal. In others words, a fat is not a fat.

Monounsaturated fat This fat is the healthiest type. It includes canola, olive, and peanut oils. Canola oil is considered the healthiest fat because it has the least amount of saturated fat. These fats are known to reduce blood cholesterol by increasing the good cholesterol (HDL).

Polyunsaturated fat This type of fat includes oils such as corn, safflower, soybean, sesame, and sunflower. They lower the total cholesterol and triglycerides (triglycerides are otherwise known as the stored fat). They also may reduce the risk of heart disease.

Saturated fat This fat increases blood cholesterol, the bad cholesterol (LDL), which increases the risk of heart disease and stroke. All animal fats found in meat, whole milk dairy products, and poultry are saturated fats, as are coconut and palm oils, which are the only vegetable sources of saturated fat. No more than 10 percent of your daily caloric intake should come from these fats.

Transfatty acid This is not natural fat. When unsaturated fat goes through hydrogenation, a manufacturing process that changes a liquid fat into a solid fat, it becomes a transfatty acid, which acts like a saturated fat. Transfatty acids are used to preserve food or to change its texture, for instance, to make spreadable margarine. They are found in processed and packaged foods. The oil used in fast-food restaurants is hydrogenated because it can be heated to a high temperature before it smokes. Therefore, the same oil can be used many times. Try to limit your intake of these foods.

Hydrogenated fat This fat, otherwise known as vegetable oil shortening, is among the worst types of fat. It is a highly saturated and artificial form of fat found mostly in processed foods, in which it is used as a preservative. Hydrogenated fat is related to the transfatty acids, which can increase the risk of heart disease and high cholesterol. Some examples of foods containing hydrogenated fats are breakfast cereals, granola bars, dips, chips, frozen dinners, ready-to-bake rolls, and frozen desserts.

Essential fatty acid One of the trendiest fats today are essential fatty acids, better known as EFAs. Many of us now know that EFAs are the reason that salmon has become so popular. The two major EFAs in the food we eat are omega-6 (linoleic acid) and omega-3 (linolenic acid). Studies show that these fats can help protect against diabetes, cancer, high blood pressure, allergies, and arthritis. Omega-6 is found in oils, nuts, and margarine and getting enough of it is easy. Omega-3 is not as common. Flaxseed oil is one of the best sources of omega-3. It is also found in fatty fish—such as salmon, tuna, mackerel, and eel—canola and soybean oils, and some leafy green vegetables.

Fat

Here's a breakdown of the various fats. Monosaturated fat is the healthiest, followed by polyunsaturated fat. Saturated fat is the least healthy.

Fat (per tbsp/15 mL)	Saturated (9 g)	Monounsaturated (g)	Polyunsaturated (g)
Butter	7.2	0.4	3.3
Margarine (corn)	2	4.5	4.4
Canola oil	1.0	8.2	4.1
Olive oil	1.8	9.9	1.1
Peanut oil	2.3	6.2	4.3
Safflower oil	1.2	1.6	10.1
Sesame oil	1.9	5.4	5.7
Sunflower oil	1.4	2.7	8.9
Soybean oil	2.0	3.2	7.9
Corn oil	1.7	3.3	8.0
Coconut oil	11.8	0.8	0.2
Palm oil	6.7	5.8	1.3

Before choosing an oil or fat, just remember to look for one that has the least amount of saturated fat and the most monounsaturated fats.

Where's the Fat?   The fat we can see and measure is not the only fat to worry about in our diet. It's important to measure fat intake if we want weight control, but what about those fats we can't see or easily count? To see where the fat is found in the foods we consume daily, check with a good calorie/fat guide. When looking at the analyses of different foods, check which foods contain larger amounts of saturated fat. You'll find more detail about each type of food you buy in "Don't Go to the Supermarket without Me"—and don't! In that chapter you'll find the leaner and healthier choices for all kinds of food products, organized by the aisles you'll find them in at the supermarket. Food counter books, which contain tables of nutritional analyses of all kinds of foods, can be very helpful.

   When making food choices, take a look at the percentage of fat in a specific food. If your calorie/fat guide doesn't break food down that way, here's the fat formula: multiply the total fat in grams by 9 (the number of calories per gram of fat) to get the number of calories in the fat. Then divide the number of fat calories by the total number of calories in the food, which will give you the percentage of fat in that food.

Here's an example to illustrate how the fat formula works: if one cookie is said to contain 150 calories and 10 grams of fat, and—as we know—every gram of fat has 9 calories, then the percentage of calories from fat in the cookie is

$$10 \text{ (grams of fat)} \times 9 \text{ (calories)} = 90 \div 150 \text{ (calories)} = 60\%$$

Sixty percent of the 150 calories in that cookie come from fat!

Even though you may be counting the fat in the butter, egg, and meat you eat, don't forget about the saturated fat in many foods that is easy to miss. We all know that fat is in butter, margarine, oils, sour cream, ice cream, cheese, peanut butter, sauces, and the visible fat on meat, but hidden fat is in many foods you may never have suspected. For instance, deli meat, store-bought baked goods, chocolate bars, pizza, quiche, marinated salads, fast food, and fried foods all have loads of hidden fat. So if you're wondering why you can't lose weight or lower your cholesterol levels even though you are cutting out the visible fats, take a closer look at those foods containing hidden fats that may be causing the problem.

Now that we understand the good, the bad, and the ugly facts about fat, we know that enjoying some fat, especially the heart-healthy kind, is necessary for good health. When considering the bad fats and their effects on our health, however, we must discuss the major impact of saturated fat on our cholesterol levels.

Fat, Cholesterol, and Heart Disease

We all are concerned about our cholesterol levels. This topic close to my heart, as my father died from a massive coronary due to high cholesterol levels. When I was 35, I learned that I had very high cholesterol levels, and this was the wake-up call for me to change my ways. I had been consuming too many of my calories in saturated fat and avoiding the heart-healthy foods. The only reason I kept weight off was because I exercised continually. Suddenly, I had to find out the ins and outs of cholesterol:

- The liver makes all the cholesterol you need for good health. Excess cholesterol from the food we eat is transported to the blood and over the years begins to clog the arteries.

- The daily amount of cholesterol appropriate for good health is 300 milligrams. Most people get much more. One egg (the yolk) has over 200 milligrams of cholesterol.

- According to the Heart and Stroke Foundation of Canada, over 8.3 million Canadians have higher cholesterol than normal.

- The foods that contain cholesterol are animal based because the animals those foods come from have livers. Therefore, cholesterol is found in all meat products, dairy (including cheese), and poultry (including eggs).
- Plant-based foods contain no cholesterol. The only vegetable oils that contain saturated fat are coconut and palm oils.
- No cholesterol doesn't mean calorie free.

Become familiar with the cholesterol levels of the various foods you consume. When looking at cholesterol charts like the one below, keep in mind that the acceptable daily amount is only 300 milligrams.

Cholesterol Levels of Some Common Foods

Food (3 oz/90 g unless stated)	Cholesterol (mg)
Skinless chicken breast	73
Ground beef, medium	79
Skinless turkey breast	59
Liver	415
White fish	62
Lobster	78
Shrimp	135
Egg yolk	200
Whole-fat milk (1 cup/250 mL)	35
Skim milk (1 cup/250 mL)	5
Cheddar cheese (1 oz/30 g)	31
Mozzarella (1 oz/30 g)	18
Butter (1 tbsp/15 mL)	31
Margarine, oil (1 tbsp/15 mL)	0
Grains, vegetables, nuts, fruits, beans	0

Lowering Fat and Cholesterol in Your Diet   Here are some ways to lower the amount of fat and cholesterol in your diet:

- Eat a more nutritious breakfast consisting of protein and carbohydrates. A healthy breakfast might include egg whites and toast, lower-fat cheese with bread, or peanut butter on toast. If you eat only carbohydrates (breads or cereals), your blood sugar will rise and you might store the extra calories as fat.

- Eat nutritious snacks between your main meals. Fruits, vegetables, lower-fat cheese and crackers, or fruit-flavoured yogourt are some good choices.

- Stop smoking—smoking decreases the good cholesterol (HDL).

- Try to lose excess weight, which can be associated with higher cholesterol levels.

- Exercise to increase your level of the good cholesterol (HDL).

- Reduce the amount of fatty meat in your diet and avoid the skin on meats. Avoid organ meats such as liver, kidney, heart, brains, and sweetbreads, which are very high in cholesterol.

- Substitute the white meat of chicken or turkey for the darker meat.

- Limit high-fat desserts and ice cream.

- Substitute vegetarian products or fish for meat in meals. Try adding beans and soy products to your repertoire, as they may lower bad cholesterol (LDL).

- Use the heart-healthy oils, such as canola, olive, peanut, and flaxseed.

- Avoid deli meats, which are loaded with fats and nitrates.

- Add more fibre to your diet by increasing the amount of fruits, vegetables, and grains.

- Avoid foods labelled "low fat," "cholesterol free," or "no fat." They usually have little nutritional value and, if eaten in excess, add up in calories.

- Avoid eating too many whole eggs. The yolk contains all the cholesterol. Try either egg whites, now sold in containers, or a substitute egg mixture that is additive-free.

- Read food labels and minimize your consumption of products that have hydrogenated oil, which is just another name for saturated fat.

- Eat more fish and seafood. The fattier fish, such as salmon, tuna, and swordfish, contain omega-3 fatty acids, which help to lower cholesterol and also help in the fight against cancer.

- Use lower-fat dairy products (2% MF or less). Use milk instead of cream. Use low-fat yogourt or low-fat sour cream instead of cream or high-fat sour cream.

- Use butter, light cream cheese, and other saturated fat spreads sparingly.

- Choose cheeses that have a stronger flavour so you eat less. Feta, goat, and Parmesan cheeses are very flavourful.

- Avoid deep-fried foods. Select foods that have been grilled, roasted, broiled, or baked instead. Often hydrogenated oils, which contain saturated fats, are used in restaurants.

- Use only nonstick pans and a vegetable cooking spray so that you lessen the likelihood of using excess saturated fat.

- Serve dressings or sauces beside—not on—your food, and never consume more than 2 table-spoons (25 mL). If lower-fat dressings are available, use them.

- Avoid using mayonnaise or butter on sandwiches. Instead, use mustard or a combination of Dijon mustard and low-fat yogourt or sour cream.

Your fat tastebuds You usually overeat high-fat foods because of the "mouth feel" of fat. It tastes good, smells wonderful, and feels good in your mouth. In order to change this feeling permanently, you must be willing to make lifetime dietary changes and try to reeducate your tastebuds. As you eat and cook lower-fat foods, over time you will lose the fat tastebuds. I actually find that if I eat too many high-fat foods, my body reacts negatively. I get bloated, have an unpleasant aftertaste in my mouth the next morning, and feel more sluggish. Give yourself at least six weeks of eating lower-fat, healthier foods to notice the difference. And do take note: When you reduce the fat in your foods, your tastebuds get used to food with less fat and are satisfied by them.

Salt

Sodium is a mineral that is essential for health. It helps conduct nerve signals, helps muscles contract, and maintains the fluid balance in the body. The problem is that we are a salt-addicted population.

Salt tastes great and preserves food, but excess salt leads to increased blood pressure. A silent killer, high blood pressure can lead to a stroke, which is the fourth highest cause of death in Canada. Excess salt is also linked to heart problems, kidney problems, and stomach cancer. Because salt causes the body to lose calcium through urine, salt is correlated with osteoporosis and other bone problems.

Daily Salt Requirements

Getting enough salt in our diet is rarely a problem. The average person gets approximately 2 teaspoons (10 mL) daily, which is 40 percent more than necessary. The amount of sodium ingested daily should be about 2400 milligrams, which is close to 1 teaspoon (5 mL).

When we think of salt, we tend to consider only table salt. But baking powder, baking soda, garlic salt, onion salt, and other seasonings all contribute to excess salt in your diet. Packaged, frozen, dried, processed, smoked, cured, canned, and preserved foods usually have large amounts of salt as well. Other foods to watch out for are processed meats and fish, pickled and marinated products, and fast and preserved foods.

Foods High in Sodium

Food	Sodium (mg)	Food	Sodium (mg)
Processed meats		**Snack foods**	
Salami (3 oz/90 g)	1900	Salted nuts (1 oz/30 g)	250
Hot dog (1)	639	Potato chips (1 oz/30 g)	135
Smoked turkey (3 oz/90 g)	916	Pretzels (1 oz/30 g)	500
Bacon (4 slices)	1020	Pizza (1 slice)	500
Canned food		Dill pickle (1)	800
Tuna (3 oz/90 g)	300	**Dairy products**	
Chicken soup (1 cup/250 mL)	1100	Cottage cheese (1/2 cup/250 mL)	500
Vegetable soup (1 cup/250 mL)	800	Processed cheese (1 slice)	175
Seasonings		Parmesan cheese (1 oz/30 g)	550
Table salt (1 tsp/5 mL)	2400		
Baking soda (1 tsp/5 mL)	1300		
Bouillon cube (1)	1100		
Soy sauce (1 tbsp/15 mL)	1100		

Reducing Salt   Taking these easy steps can help you lower your salt intake:

- Get rid of the salt shaker on the table and use herbs, spices, fresh garlic, onions, ginger, basil, dill, and pepper on your food instead.
- Minimize your consumption of condiments, processed foods, MSG, soy sauce, and deli meats.
- Read food labels carefully. Salt can be listed as sodium, sodium benzoate, sodium propionate, and sodium bicarbonate.
- Drain and rinse canned foods to remove the brine, which contains large amounts of salt.
- Do not salt the water used to cook pasta, rice, or other grains.
- Try using low-sodium soy sauce, bouillon cubes, and stock.

People who have high blood pressure should keep to a healthy diet. A diet called DASH (Dietary Approaches to Stop Hypertension) is rich in fruits, vegetables, and low-fat dairy products and is low in fat.[7] This diet is similar to Canada's Food Guide but is more specific about serving sizes and examples of specific foods.

Types of Salt   There are various types of salt, including kosher and sea salt. Kosher salt has about the same amount of sodium as table salt, whereas sea salt has more sodium. But both sea salt and kosher salt taste more intense and purer than table salt, so you tend to use less. Table salt contains iodine, which is a nutrient needed by the thyroid (other salts have no additives).

Water

Besides oxygen, water is the most important nutrient for our bodies. The body is between 60 percent and 70 percent water by weight.

Water performs essential daily functions in our bodies:

- It assists digestion and absorption of food and liquids.
- It is the primary component of blood, which transports nutrients, hormones, and waste from one part of our body to another.
- It is a regulator of body temperature. Sweating is one way our body regulates its internal temperature.
- It acts as a lubricant and a cushion to facilitate movement of our bodies.
- It is a regulator of blood pressure.

Daily Water Requirements

Through all the normal daily body functions, you lose about 8 to 10 cups (2 to 2.5 L) of water, which is why you're told to drink at least 6 to 8 cups (1.5 to 2 L) of water a day to keep hydrated.

To get the optimal effect, it's best to drink plain and simple H_2O. Other drinks such as juices, coffee, and soft drinks all count for some water, but the caffeinated drinks actually promote dehydration, while juices and soft drinks have excess calories due to the sugar they contain. If you can't break the habit of drinking caffeinated or sugared beverages, then for each one of these drinks have the same amount of water to keep your water intake up.

Symptoms of dehydration include headaches, light-headedness, dizziness, low energy, and increased heartrate. Once you feel thirsty, you're already dehydrated.

Increasing their water consumption is difficult for many people. Here are a few suggestions to make drinking more water a little easier:

- Always carry a bottle of water with you or keep a large bottle on your desk as you work.
- Don't try to drink a lot of water at once. Sip water throughout your day.
- Before each meal or snack, try to drink a cup of water, which also helps to satiate you.

Types of Water   One of the greatest confusions today seems to be about what type of water to drink. We've all been led to believe that bottled water is healthier for us than tap water. But then we hear evidence that bottled water is only as good as the source. Let's look at some of the various types of water we can consume.

Tap water This water, which originally comes from lakes, rivers, or reservoirs, has been treated to remove contaminants. The local government is supposed to continually check the safety of your water supply for contamination. Check the health records of your city. In some areas, people get their water from private wells. If you do, it is your responsibility to have the water checked. Installing a filtration system is a good way to guard against contaminants. Lead is a dangerous pollutant that can enter the water in your home from plumbing service lines, pipes, and brass faucets.

Bottled water There are two types of bottled water: filtered water, from which the minerals have been filtered out, and mineral water, which has minerals and comes from a natural spring. Bottled water is not necessarily safer than tap water. Bottled water can have a higher bacterial count than tap water and can be sold even if it does not meet the standards for tap water. To be safe, check to see if your bottled water manufacturer is backed by the International Bottled Water Association. Bottled water is also costly and bulky.

Distilled water Distilled water is the purest of waters, containing no sodium and no solid materials. It tastes of nothing, unlike mineral water, which tastes of the minerals it contains.

Home-filtered water To improve the taste of your water, a filtering pitcher will do just fine. Inexpensive home water filters might make tap water taste better but don't make it healthier. If you're trying to remove contaminants, you could consider installing a permanent water filter, although at a cost of more than $1000, it is an expensive alternative.

Home-distilled water For between $100 and $500 you can get a countertop distiller that boils water and condenses the vapour. Distilling reduces levels of chemicals in the water and can kill micro-organisms and remove chlorine and fluoride. Be sure your toothpaste contains fluoride if you drink distilled water.

Whatever type of water you choose to consume, just be sure to drink it throughout your day.

Caffeine

Caffeine is a natural stimulant found in many foods and beverages, including the obvious examples of coffee, tea, and chocolate. The controversy surrounding caffeine and its effects on our health continues, with many people citing its ill effects, others its benefits. The old adage about everything in moderation applies here: in moderation, caffeine won't harm your health. For our purposes, moderation can be defined as limiting coffee to 3 to 4 cups daily. Consuming caffeine in excess of this amount can bring on headaches, trembling, insomnia, indigestion, and an increased heartrate. Here are a few facts to counter some caffeine fiction:

- To date, caffeine has not been linked to heart disease or pancreatic cancer.
- Caffeine has not been linked to fibrocystic breast disease.
- Caffeine doesn't increase the risk for osteoporosis.
- Caffeine doesn't raise the risk of miscarriage and birth defects.

Caffeinated Beverages

Some examples of common teas are Orange Pekoe, English Breakfast, Earl Grey (all black teas), Chinese tea, and Japanese (usually green) tea—the colour depends on whether the tea leaves are fermented. All

Caffeine Content of Some Beverages and Chocolate

	Caffeine (mg)
Coffee (8 oz/250 mL)	
Drip	100–195
Decaf	3–6
Instant	80–120
Black tea (6 oz/175 mL), 3-minute brew	20–50
Cola (12 oz/375 mL)	30–50
Chocolate (1 oz/30 g), semi-sweet	5–35

real teas (not herbal infusions) contain antioxidants called polyphenols, which may prevent and stop cancer activity and lower bad cholesterol (LDL).[8] Green teas have less caffeine than black teas.

Most carbonated beverages or soft drinks are loaded with sugar, artificial colouring, artificial flavours, and caffeine. They are nothing more than empty calories. Chemically sweetened diet soft drinks may even be worse for you than the regular kind since they contain sugar substitutes, and the overall effects on human health of these substances are still unknown. Often these diet drinks whet your appetite, causing you to eat more. Try not to consume more than one a day.

Alcohol

Moderation is the key word when consuming alcohol. Small amounts of alcohol can reduce stress and actually reduce the risk of heart attack and stroke by increasing the good cholesterol (HDL); red wine especially has been shown to do so. Red wine contains bioflavonoids, the antioxidant agents that occur in grapes—unsweetened purple grape juice has the same properties. The recommended daily amount is 10 ounces (300 mL), or two glasses, of wine.

When drinking alcohol, be aware that it increases your appetite and speeds digestion, so you'll feel hungry sooner. Alcohol has been linked to rectal and liver cancer and to decreased bone density. High in empty calories, a 12-ounce (375 mL) beer contains 150 calories and 8 ounces (250 mL) of wine has

120 calories. One other thing: in most places where we drink alcohol—at bars, restaurants, or parties—we often eat salty, higher-fat foods, which in turn leads to more drinking.

Vitamins and Minerals

Ideally, all the nutrients you need daily should come from food, not supplements. A pill cannot supply all the necessary nutrients you need to strengthen your immune system—only a healthy diet can do that. If you keep to a low-fat diet rich in fruits, vegetables, and grains, you should get all the vitamins and minerals your body needs to fight disease and strengthen your immune system. Unfortunately, statistics show that less than 10 percent of North Americans get enough fruits and vegetables in their diet.

Vitamins and minerals are necessary for proper metabolic functioning. They can help prevent malnutrition, heart disease, and certain cancers. They also improve the quality of hair, nails, and skin. The body can't produce all the needed vitamins and minerals, so we obtain them from food. The fresher the foods, the more nutrients available.

Vitamins

There are 13 essential vitamins. These 13 are divided into two groups: fat-soluble and water-soluble vitamins. The fat-soluble vitamins are stored in your body and include vitamins A, E, D, and K. Since you can store these vitamins, you don't need to get a daily supply of them.

The water-soluble vitamins dissolve in water, so any extra is carried out of your body. Since they cannot be stored in your body for long, you need to get a fresh supply every day. Water-soluble vitamins include C and the B vitamins. Research done at the University of California at Berkeley[9] concluded that four specific vitamins should be taken regularly, even if your diet is healthy: the antioxidant vitamins E, C, and beta carotene, and the B vitamin folacin.

Daily Vitamin Requirements   You need 13 vitamins daily of which only 11 are listed in the table below with their recommended daily allowances (RDAs). The missing two—biotin and pantothenic acid—are not listed because you get these vitamins so easily from food even if you don't eat properly.

Vitamin RDAs for Adults

Vitamin	Men	Women
Fat soluble		
Vitamin A	5000 IU	4000 IU
Vitamin E	15 mg	15 mg
Vitamin K	80 mcg	65 mcg
Vitamin D	200 IU	200 IU
Water soluble		
Vitamin C	90 mg	75 mg
B vitamins		
Thiamin	1.5 mg	1.1 mg
Riboflavin	1.7 mg	1.3 mg
Niacin	19 mg	15 mg
Pyridoxine	2 mg	1.6 mg
Folic acid	200 mcg	180 mcg
Cobalamin	2 mcg	2 mcg

Pressman, Alan, *The Complete Idiot's Guide to Vitamins and Minerals,* Macmillan, 2000, page 5.

Minerals

Your body needs calcium, chloride, magnesium, phosphorus, potassium, sodium, sulfur, and other minerals, in very small amounts, for normal growth, health, and metabolism.

Daily Mineral Requirements   You need over 100 milligrams of each essential mineral daily, which you can easily get from food. In the table on page 87, all necessary minerals are listed except sulfur, which is so common in foods that no one is ever deficient in it.

Trace minerals Trace minerals include chromium, copper, iodine, iron, manganese, molybdenum, selenium, and zinc. You require less than 100 milligrams of each of copper, iron, and manganese daily.

Increasing Intake of Vitamins and Minerals

Here are some tips for increasing the vitamins and minerals in your diet:

- Whenever possible, use fresh food, not canned or processed. Frozen food is preferable to canned or processed, and can even have more nutrients than fresh, simply because frozen food may have been packaged when the nutrients were still at their prime.
- Always rinse canned foods well to eliminate the salt and chemicals that preserve the foods.
- Don't store cut vegetables in water because the vitamins will leach out.
- Try to eat your fruits and vegetables soon after you cut them. The longer they're exposed to oxygen, the greater the loss in nutrients.
- Try not to boil your vegetables: steaming or baking retains more of their nutrients.
- Eat the skin of fruits and vegetables. The skins contains fibre and other nutrients.

Mineral RDAs for Adults

Calcium	1000–1200 mg	Phosphorus	700 mg
Chloride	750 mg	Potassium	2000 mg
Fluoride	3.1–3.8 mg	Sodium	500 mg
Magnesium	320–420 mg		

Pressman, Alan, *The Complete Idiot's Guide to Vitamins and Minerals,* Macmillan, 2000, page 8.

Living with the New Nutrition

So there's the framework that living well is built on. The new nutrition makes full use of Canada's Food Guide. By letting the guide inform your decisions, you'll find it easy to choose high-quality foods from the four food groups. Each day you will receive the vitamins, minerals, and other nutrients your body needs to be fit and healthy. Rather than starving yourself of a food group or following a fad diet that you are bound to fail with, keep the following basic tips in mind:

- Keep your fat intake to a minimum, with as little saturated fat as you can live with.
- Eat carbohydrates that have a low glycemic index and contain plenty of fibre.
- Limit sugar, as it contains calories empty of nutrition and can contribute to weight gain.
- Keep your intake of protein to a minimum, and try to select leaner protein, such as chicken or turkey breast, or fish.
- Use a minimum of salt in your food.
- Keep your water intake high and caffeine intake low.

Now it's time to take the ideas of living well to the supermarket. Read on to the next chapter.

Don't Go to the Supermarket Without Me

I believe that one reason many Canadians eat poorly is that they don't have access to healthy foods in their homes. We have to buy these healthy foods regularly—and many people don't. Little wonder: food shopping can be an extremely confusing and time-consuming activity. There are hundreds of different items to choose from, yet we lack a handy manual to tell us which foods or brands are better than others. Therefore, often we fall prey to foods with alluring packages and promotions promising delicious fare and lower fat!

With today's hectic pace we don't give ourselves time to shop carefully. We purchase the products that are quickest to prepare and cook, and often overlook the healthier foods. Many people working full-time do their shopping in the evening when they're most exhausted and hate the chore. Rushed, they do little preplanning and shop for convenience rather than for healthy meals and snacks.

It's a well-known fact that people who shop when they're hungry tend to buy rich, fattening, and processed foods. Taking young children or teenagers with you to the supermarket might not always be a wise choice since their selections will be different from yours and your shopping basket will be soon filled with junk food.

Food Labels

Shopping for healthy ingredients today can be a humbling experience. We all see the food label, but most of us don't know what to look for on it. Often we are swayed by a product's claims. Never make a food choice based on a product label or marketing campaign. It is important to read between the lines and know what the terms on labels really mean. Remember, a food can be "light," "low in cholesterol," and contain "no fat," yet still be loaded with calories.

The Nutrition Label

In the United States, all food products must be labelled as specified under the Nutrition Labeling and Education Act of 1990. Currently no regulatory body governs nutritional food labelling in Canada, but most food products have a nutrition label that gives you some information about what you are consuming. This breakdown of nutrients is especially important for anyone on a restricted diet. It will soon be mandatory in Canada for all food products sold to display a nutrition label that provides information similar to that included in the sample label below. The nutrition information label shown is for So Soya, a soy protein product that is fat and cholesterol free and contains "up to 135 milligrams of isoflavones."

Nutrition Information

per 34 g serving (2/3 cup)

			Percentage of Recommended Daily Intake	
Energy	95 Cal/400 kJ			
Protein	18 g			
Fat	0.3 g		Calcium	10%
Polyunsaturates	0.1 g		Iron	24%
Monounsaturates	0.1 g		Zinc	20%
Saturates	0.1. g		Vitamin B_1	16%
Cholesterol	0 mg		Vitamin B_2	7%
Carbohydrate	10 g		Phosphorus	23%
Dietary fibre	6 g		Magnesium	43%
Sodium	3 mg			
Potassium	825 mg			

Standard Serving Sizes   In the United States, the FDA has set specific serving sizes that are suitable for the average person. This information enables the consumer to compare products based on the same amount of product.

Energy   Energy is the number of calories per serving.

Major Nutrients   The major nutrients contained in the food are listed in grams or milligrams, and also as a percentage of the total Recommended Daily Intake (RDI)—also referred to as the Daily Value (DV)—for someone consuming 2000 calories daily. The RDI is the amount you need of a given nutrient for the day. If you eat more or fewer than 2000 calories, you can make the appropriate adjustments.

Protein This is the number of grams of protein per serving.

Fat and cholesterol Ideally, the total amount of fat, the amount of saturated, polyunsaturated, and monounsaturated fat, and the number of calories from fat, as well as the cholesterol in grams, should be listed per serving. More often than not, however, only the total amount of fat and the amount of saturated fat and cholesterol are listed.

Carbohydrates, fibre, and sugar These can include simple and complex carbohydrates and the total fibre, including soluble and insoluble fibre.

Sodium The RDI for sodium is 2400 milligrams.

Potassium There is no RDI for potassium. To maintain good health, a daily amount of between 2 and 6 grams is recommended.

Vitamins and minerals Only the vitamins A and C and the minerals calcium and iron must be listed.

Where Do the Calories Come From?

When you look at a nutrition label, you can easily read the numbers beside the total fat and saturated fat; you might even see the calories from fat. But these numbers don't give you the true picture of where the fat in the food comes from. Let's look at an example:

Product X

Serving size	100 g		
Energy	102 calories	Fat	6 g
Protein	2 g	Carbohydrates	10 g

From the information above, it would appear that most of the calories come from the 10 grams of carbohydrates. But on closer examination, and by using some simple math, we find that isn't the case. What you need to know is that protein and carbohydrates have 4 calories per gram while fat has 9 calories per gram. The calories from protein, carbs, and fat are calculated as follows:

Protein = 2 g × 4 calories per g = 8 calories

Carbs = 10 g × 4 calories per g = 40 calories

Fat = 6 g × 9 calories per g = 54 calories

Since the total number of calories per serving is 102, more than half the calories come from fat.

Now, let's see what happens when you have to make a choice between two different products.

	Product 1	Product 2
Energy	200 calories	200 calories
Protein	8 g	10 g
Fat	5 g	12 g
Polyunsaturates	2 g	4 g
Monounsaturates	1 g	3 g
Saturates	2 g	5 g
Cholesterol	50 mg	100 mg
Carbohydrates	30 g	20 g
Sodium	400 mg	700 mg
Potassium	100 mg	100 mg

Because the energy and calories in these two products are identical, you might think that the products are identical and choose the one with the more appealing label or the lower price. But a closer examination of the fat content reveals the true nature of the foods. Product 1 has 5 grams of fat while Product 2 has 12 grams, of which 5 grams are the bad, or saturated, fat, much more than the 2 grams of saturated fat in Product 1. Remember, it's the saturated fat that clogs the arteries and can lead to health problems.

Apply the formula: multiply the fat grams by 9. Then divide by the total number of calories to get the percentage of fat for the product.

Product 1

5 g × 9 calories = 45

45 ÷ 200 calories = 23% of the calories comes from fat

Product 2

12 g × 9 calories = 198

198 ÷ 200 calories = 54% of the calories comes from fat

What a difference! By doing the fat calculation, you can truly determine which product is better for your health.

Labelling as a Second Language

Today, many product claims seem designed to confuse the consumer. Usually this confusion is intended to make a product look healthier and more appealing than it might in fact be. You might see products making claims such as "no fat", "no cholesterol," "lite," or "light"—and many others. Below are some interpretations of the most common food labelling claims.

Anything-free   There are lots of "free" labels: fat free, calorie free, cholesterol free, sodium free. What these terms indicate is that 1 serving contains such a small amount of the substance that it doesn't mean much in the nutritional picture and you don't have to be concerned. Here are what some common terms amount to:

Term	Amount (per 100 g serving)
Fat free	Less than 0.5 g
Calorie free	Less than 1 calorie
Sodium free	No more than 5 mg
Cholesterol free	No more than 3 mg

Light or Lite   These terms can be confusing and misleading. When "light" refers to a food product that has been altered, the term means that the food contains one-third fewer calories or half the fat of the regular product. "Lite" can be used to describe the taste, colour, or texture of the food in which *the fat or calories remain the same*—so "lite" olive oil may be light in taste, texture, or simply colour. "Light sodium" means a product contains half the amount of sodium used to make the regular product.

Low or Reduced   The word "low" on a label tells you that the product has a reduced level of a specific ingredient. Be aware that a product that may be low in fat may still be high in calories, or vice versa. "Reduced" compares the product to the regular product.

Term	Amount (per 100 g serving)
Low fat	3 g or less
Low (in) cholesterol	No more than 20 mg
Low calorie	15 calories or less
Low in saturated fat	No more than 2 g
Low sodium	Less than 40 mg; less than 50% of the sodium in the regular product
Fat reduced	At least 25% less fat than in the regular product
Calorie reduced	50% fewer calories than in the regular product

Source This word ensures that the food product provides a significant amount of a nutrient, say, fibre.

Term	Amount (per 100 g serving)
Source of fibre	2 g
High source of fibre	4 g
Very high source of fibre	6 g

Since the RDI for fibre is 25 to 35 grams, you can see that even a very high source of fibre provides only a part of what you need every day. Nutrient sources are defined as follows:

- A high source must provide 20 percent or more of the RDI for that nutrient.

- A good source contains between 10 and 19 percent of the RDI for a nutrient.

Other Terms   Here are some other terms you may see on product labels:

Fresh The food is raw, has never been frozen, has never been heated, and contains no preservatives.

Fortified or enriched A food must have a nutrient added to it so that at least 10 percent of the RDI is present. For example, if a food is fortified with iron, then 10 percent of the iron you need in your day is in 1 serving of this food.

Healthy This term is not used appropriately at all times. It means that a food is low in fat and saturated fat, and that a serving does not contain more than 480 milligrams of sodium or more than 60 milligrams of cholesterol.

Lean and extra lean These terms refer to the fat content of meat, fish, and chicken. Lean has fewer than 10 grams of fat, 4 grams of saturated fat, and 95 milligrams of cholesterol per 100 gram serving. Extra lean contains fewer than 5 grams of fat and 2 grams of saturated fat.

Natural or organic These terms are also used loosely. Used accurately and applied to meat or poultry, they refer to food that is minimally processed and free of artificial ingredients. For other foods, these terms have no legal definition. Fruits and vegetables bearing these designations have been grown with virtually no pesticides or chemicals.

100% pure fruit juice Fruit juice labelling can be misleading. To be 100 percent fruit juice, juice must contain nothing but the fruit. Juice labelled "pure fruit juice" can have only 10 to 34 percent fruit content. The rest is made up of water, sugar, colour, and flavouring. Fruit-flavoured drinks have only 10 percent real fruit juice or none at all. Read the labels carefully.

Ingredient List

When you are reading a food label, the order of the ingredients is worth paying attention to. The first ingredient listed has the most volume by weight. Therefore, if the first ingredient is a form of fat, you know that the product consists mainly of fat. If the label emphasizes whole-wheat flour, look at the order of the ingredients to see if sugar or fat is the first ingredient and the whole-wheat flour is buried toward the end of the list.

The ingredients in most food products are categorized and worded as follows:

Fat This can be listed as butter, lard, vegetable shortening, hydrogenated vegetable oil, or partially hydrogenated oil. "All vegetable oil" on the label does not mean no cholesterol or low in fat. The fat could be hydrogenated or saturated, for instance, as in the case of palm or coconut oil.

Sugar This can be listed as sucrose, glucose, dextrose, fructose, maltose, lactose, honey, corn syrup, or molasses. If a label says "no added sugar," the product may be high in natural sugar, for example, from fruit.

Sodium   This can be listed as salt, onion salt, celery salt, garlic salt, MSG, baking powder, baking soda, benzoate, sodium citrate, or sodium phosphate. MSG is also known as hydrolyzed vegetable protein and monosodium glutamate. Note that an ingredient like bouillon is high in sodium.

Flour Products   This listing can cause confusion. We know that the best flour is whole-wheat flour, but often the terms on labels are misleading. For instance, if just "wheat flour" is listed, it means that the white flour is mixed with some whole-wheat flour.

All-purpose flour This flour is made from hard and soft wheat and contains neither germ nor bran. All-purpose flour is called enriched flour because it contains five nutrients—thiamin, niacin, folate, riboflavin, and iron—that have been added after the processing to meet a specific standard. Bleached or unbleached all-purpose flour can be used interchangeably.

Cake or pastry flour This type of flour is used for tender pastries.

Wheat flour This term means that the flour is made from wheat. It is just white flour that has been refined and mixed with some whole-wheat flour.

Whole-grain flour The flour contains everything but the husk, but is not refined.

Whole-wheat flour This flour is the healthiest of all and contains the most fibre, since it is made from whole wheat kernels.

Food Additives   The topic of additives has to be one of the most confusing areas of all. We have been led to believe that if any food product has an additive, then it must be harmful to our health, and we often assume that if we can't pronounce the additive, it must be bad for our health. But some additives actually enhance the nutritional quality of a food. For example, vitamins and minerals are added to enrich foods such as grains, milk, juices, soy products, and other products.

The way to minimize additives is to eat fresh or minimally processed foods as much as possible. Processed foods always have the most additives.

Here are some of the most common food additives:

Better additives: Superfoods

Calcium propionate supplies some calcium, retarding spoilage from bacteria, breads in particular.

Beta carotene adds nutrition and a yellow/orange colour to foods such as margarine and cheeses. Remember that this nutrient is also a powerful antioxidant.

Monoglycerides and diglycerides keep the consistency of foods, such as margarine, ice cream, and breads, smooth or soft.

Vitamin E is an antioxidant added to oils.

Vitamins and minerals replace nutrients that are lost when food is processed.

Emulsifiers and stabilizers include lecithin, carrageenan, and guar gum. They are used to prevent foods such as peanut butter from separating, and improve the consistency and texture of products.

Citric acid/pH control agents prevent botulism in low-acid canned goods.

CAUTION: Questionable/undesirable additives

BHT and BHA in gum, active yeast, and processed foods are used to prevent spoilage. BHT and BHA can cause increased cholesterol, allergy reactions, liver and kidney damage, and the loss of vitamin D.

Sulfites, also known as sulfur dioxide, sodium sulfite, and sodium bisulfite, are used in vegetables at salad bars to make them look fresher and to prevent discoloration. They are also found in canned food, dehydrated foods, processed cookies and crackers, frozen shrimp, and wine. They can cause allergic reactions and worsen asthma in some people.

Nitrates/nitrites are found in deli smoked meats and preserved meats and are used to maintain colour, minimize bacteria, and enhance flavour. These additives have been connected to headaches, cancer, and birth defects.

Artificial colours, the reds, yellows, blues, and greens, are used to enhance colour and are usually found in lower-nutrient foods, such as candy and soft drinks. These additives are still under review.

Artificial sweeteners are used in soft drinks, yogourts, and ice creams and are sold in packages to sweeten beverages. I have discussed these in detail in the section on sugar substitutes (see "The New Nutrition," page 67). Depending on the sweetener, some artificial sweeteners used in moderation don't pose a serious health risk.

MSG (monosodium glutamate) is found in additives termed hydrolyzed or textured protein, sodium and calcium caseinate, yeast extract, autolyzed yeast, and gelatin. MSG is a very common additive that modifies the taste and aroma of food without adding colour or smell. It is found in canned soups and vegetables, sauces, snacks, frozen foods, and seasonings. MSG is most commonly known to be used in Asian food to enhance flavour and give a salty taste. Common side effects include headaches, a numb sensation in the neck and down the spine, and/or a tightness in the chest.

Getting Organized

Many of us lead highly structured lives, fitting in work, family, friendships, and social activities, but we tend to lack that structure in our daily routines. We eat whatever is around and go to fast-food restaurants for convenience. I'm shocked when I'm asked to examine someone's pantry, refrigerator, and freezer. Foods with little nutrition abound. These are the same foods that lead to obesity, high blood pressure, high cholesterol, diabetes, and certain cancers. How can we reach the goal of shopping and planning for healthy daily meals?

The answer lies in organization. The very aspect that gets you effectively through your work days can help you get the right foods in your life. Here are some steps you can take to become more organized about food:

- Plan your meals and groceries for the week or for two or three days in advance.

- Get on the Internet to order in groceries. You must pay a small surcharge, but it's worth it. You'll save valuable time, which you can spend selecting healthy foods.

- Always make a shopping list. Check your kitchen carefully before shopping, and make a detailed list so that you don't buy food you already have on hand and you don't forget items. Planning your shopping prevents having to run to the store several times during the week.

- Buy more than you think you'll need. You can always use the extra in the following days.

- Buy foods that you can refrigerate or freeze so that you have an ample supply in store. Be aware of expiry dates.

- Shop when you have the time, not when you're rushed.

- Keep a list of the food items you need to buy posted in the kitchen so that you won't get caught empty handed.

These are just some suggestions. Whatever works for you is fine. There is no perfect answer, just one that is well thought out.

I actually find shopping in today's stores an exhilarating experience. North American supermarkets are so high tech, fun, and beautiful to shop in. They are highly organized and offer so many choices. Most have fresh meat, fish, cheese, bakery, and take-out departments, so you never have to go to a specialty market.

I find shopping more organized if I weave my way up and down each aisle. That way I know I won't forget anything. I take my list with me, and always start on the outside aisles with the fresh produce. This is the healthiest section, and it gets me in the right frame of mind. The only aisle you might want to avoid is the snack section, with its candy, chocolate, and chips. Let's look at the various aisles and some of the better choices.

Vegetable and Fruit Section

In the past decade, enormous research has been done on diets rich in fruits and vegetables and how they may be responsible for lowering the risk of various cancers, high blood pressure, cholesterol levels, intestinal disorders such as constipation and diverticulosis, osteoporosis, and macular degeneration, which can cause blindness in the aged. These foods supply the majority of vitamins and minerals we need to live a healthy life. They supply antioxidants; vitamins C, K, and A; and beta carotene, folate, and potassium. Fruits and vegetables contain phytochemicals, which are health-promotimg compounds found in plants that help protect them, as well as protecting our bodies against disease. Some of the phytochemicals that have been identified are as follows:

- Flavonoids, also called bioflavonoids, give fruits and vegetables their bright colours and also provide powerful antioxidant protection.
- Lycopene is a phytochemical that has been in the press a lot lately. It is present in tomatoes and red fruits and vegetables, such as pink grapefruit and watermelon. The effect is best if the tomatoes are cooked.
- Lutein is found in orange, yellow, and dark green leafy vegetables. It may be responsible for preventing blindness in the elderly.
- Beta carotene is found in orange, red, yellow, and green vegetables and in orange fruits. Carrots, squash, sweet potatoes, cantaloupe, broccoli, green leafy vegetables, and tomatoes are good sources. The beta carotene is converted into essential vitamin A.

Vegetable Aisle

You should spend a lot of your time in this aisle. Be adventurous and try some new vegetables. In most supermarkets you'll find descriptions and nutritional facts about each vegetable, along with cooking instructions and even recipes. When selecting vegetables, go for those with an orange, red, or dark green colour. These have the most beta carotene, which is a dietary antioxidant.

Remember that you can eat a large variety and amount of vegetables with virtually no concern about calories or fat. Since they contain more calories, the starchier vegetables, such as potatoes, should be counted in your grains section.

I prefer fresh vegetables when in season, but frozen vegetables are wonderful as well, and sometimes even better! When fresh vegetables are picked, packed, and shipped, they begin to lose their nutrients immediately. They hold more of their nutrients if picked and frozen immediately, but the taste is always better when fresh.

Vegetables are great for salads, snacking, and stir-fries, and are a great addition to any grain dish. If want to skip the step of chopping, most supermarkets carry prewashed lettuces, stir-fry vegetables, and even peeled and chopped squash and pumpkin. There is no excuse for not using lots of vegetables!

Asparagus

Source of vitamins C and A, and iron; excellent source of folate

Buy firm asparagus with bright green stalks and tight, purple-tinted buds. It's best to trim the ends and store asparagus upright in 1 inch (2 cm) of water in a tall container. Refrigerate asparagus no more than a few days. Break the stem at the bottom near the woody end before cooking. Either steam or boil just until slightly tender and bright green. Immediately rinse with cold water.

Avocado

High in potassium, folate, fibre, phytoestrogens, and vitamin E

The Florida avocado is called the "alligator pear" and the California variety is called the Haas avocado. The Florida type is twice the size of the Haas avocado, is the sweeter, lighter, and moister of the two, and contains only half the fat and calories. The California type has a creamier flesh. Ripen avocados in a paper bag with an apple in a warm place until they yield to pressure. When ripe, avocados can be refrigerated for up to one week. Once it is sliced, an avocado will turn brown; you can sprinkle the cut surface with lemon juice to retard browning, but it's best not to slice avocados until just ready to serve.

CAUTION: One avocado has 30 grams of fat and 300 calories. Even though the fat is heart healthy, eat avocados in moderation.

Beans

Green beans

High in vitamin C and folate; source of vitamin A, potassium, riboflavin, and thiamin

Choose brightly coloured beans that are fresh. Canned beans are not good substitutes. Remove the string and cook in boiling water, or steam, for 3 minutes, or just until tender and bright green. Rinse with cold water to stop the cooking process. Before cooking, beans should be stored in an airtight bag in the refrigerator for up to 4 days. They are low in calories, having only 30 calories per cup (250 mL).

Fresh soybeans

Rich in calcium, iron, zinc, and many B vitamins; a complete protein, filled with cancer-fighting phytochemicals, namely isoflavones

Also known by their Japanese name, edamame, these beans are the new kid on the block. Fresh soybeans resemble sweet peas but are packed with more nutrition than any other bean or pea. They are usually available frozen. Boil them for 1 minute, drain, and sprinkle with sea salt.

Broccoli

Excellent source of vitamin C, folate, vitamin E, and beta carotene; source of calcium, iron, and potassium

SUPERFOOD: Broccoli is a nutritional powerhouse. One cup (250 mL) has more vitamin C than an orange. It is a member of the cruciferous vegetable family and is considered an antioxidant, or cancer-fighting agent. Raw broccoli has more nutrients than cooked; steam rather than boil broccoli in water to preserve those vitamins and minerals. One cup (250 mL) has only 45 calories. Broccoli should be firm, green, and not yellow. If some purple is evident, this is a mark of better quality. Store broccoli in the refrigerator in a plastic bag for up to 4 days.

Brussels Sprouts

Excellent source of dietary fibre, vitamin C, and folate; source of vitamin A, iron, and calcium

Many people find this vegetable bitter. Brussels sprouts must be purchased fresh and cooked carefully to bring out their delicate flavour. They are also part of the cruciferous family and are known as a cancer-fighting vegetable. Store in the refrigerator in a plastic bag for up to 3 days. Rinse well, trim the stems, and cut an X in the stem end so that it will cook evenly with the leaves. Cook until crisp in boiling water for about 10 minutes. If you overcook Brussels sprouts, the flavour will become bitter.

Cabbage

High in vitamin C, phytochemicals, potassium, fibre, folate, iron, and antioxidants

This is another member of the cruciferous vegetable family. When selecting red or green cabbages, choose ones with outer leaves that look fresh and crisp. Red cabbage is slightly sweeter than green cabbage. Wrapped in plastic, cabbages can be kept for up to one week in the refrigerator. I love using them raw in salads or cooked—sautéed, or in soups, stir-fries, or casseroles. To get rid of the smell when cooking cabbage, put a small potato, a piece of bread, some parsley, or a walnut into the cooking liquid to absorb the odour.

Carrots

Excellent source of beta carotene and vitamin A; source of dietary fibre, magnesium, potassium, vitamin C, and folate

Carrots contain beta carotene, which is a powerful antioxidant used to fight cancer. They are delicious either raw or cooked. Interestingly, they are one vegetable that actually has more nutrients when cooked rather than raw. They also become sweeter when cooked. The long narrow carrots have the best taste. Store in the refrigerator.

Cauliflower

Excellent source of vitamin C and folate; source of magnesium and potassium

This is a member of the cruciferous family of vegetables and is considered an antioxidant. It can be eaten raw or cooked. There are white, green, and purple varieties. Refrigerate for no more than 5 days.

Corn

Source of folate, potassium, thiamin, niacin, and magnesium; also contains the powerful antioxidant lutein

To choose the best corn, you don't need to peel away the husks. Just look for green husks that are moist and wrapped tightly around the corn. Keep wrapped in a plastic bag for up to 2 days, and refrigerate, which will help preserve the corn.

Cucumber (English or Common)

Source of magnesium, potassium, vitamins C and B$_6$, and folate

Cucumbers are usually eaten raw and should be stored unwashed in plastic bags for about one week. Cut cucumbers can be kept refrigerated for up to 5 days. Commercially produced cucumbers are often waxed to preserve their moisture content. Peel waxed cucumbers or just wash well. They are very low in calories and can be eaten in any amount you desire. Do not consider cucumbers as one of your dark green vegetables in terms of nutrients since only their skin is dark green.

Eggplant

Source of folate and potassium; contains phytochemicals

There are different varieties of eggplant, such as Italian, purple, and Japanese. The most common are the large purple and the thinner Italian types. Eggplants are a key ingredient in Italian, Indian, Middle

Eastern, and Asian dishes. Eggplants are very perishable, and it's best not to refrigerate them. If you are not using them right away, then store them in a cool, dark place. Always peel eggplant before eating and do not cut until just ready to cook or they will discolour. If you must cut eggplant early, then just squeeze some lemon juice over the cut surface to prevent discolouring. Salting is recommended to draw out the bitter juices, reduce the moisture content, and prevent the eggplant from absorbing too much oil when cooking. Eggplants are very low in calories, with only 22 calories per cup (250 mL). When served in restaurants, eggplant is typically deep-fried, which adds excessive calories and fat. Either bake or sauté eggplant in a small amount of oil.

Fennel

Source of potassium, magnesium, vitamin C, and folate

Fennel is usually available in cooler weather. It looks like fresh dillweed with a thick white bulb. It has a licorice flavour when eaten raw. Use the greens for seasoning and the bulb either raw in salads or steamed and added to pastas, in other vegetable dishes, or on its own.

Garlic

One of the most potent antioxidant foods available; contains a substance called allium that interferes with the formation of blood clots and may be responsible for garlic's ability to lower blood cholesterol and high blood pressure

SUPERFOOD: Garlic has been shown to have anti-cancer properties and to strengthen the immune system. The latest research also shows that eating garlic may reduce the risk of stomach, colon, and prostate cancer. The anti-cancer effects seem to be due to the presence of sulfur compounds that detoxify the liver, stimulate the immune system, and have a toxic effect on some cancer cells. You need about two or three cloves daily for maximum effects. If garlic upsets your stomach, then try the supplements made with aged garlic extract.

The most popular garlic is the California variety. Elephant garlic is not truly garlic but rather a member of the leek family.

Greens

The darker the green colour, the more nutritious the lettuce; the dark colour is a sign that beta carotene, vitamin C, folacin, and other phytochemicals are present.

SUPERFOOD: Not that long ago the main lettuce in supermarkets was iceberg. But today's markets offer many varieties of greens. Here's a summary of the most nutritious greens:

The most beta carotene: dandelion greens, spinach, broccoli rabe, kale, turnip and mustard greens

The most vitamin C: kale, broccoli rabe, turnip and mustard greens, watercress, collards

The most folacin: turnip and mustard greens, arugula, spinach, collards

The most calcium: turnip and dandelion greens, arugula, kale, watercress

The most iron: dandelion, turnip, and mustard greens, Swiss chard, kale

CAUTION: The least nutritious greens are Boston lettuce, iceberg lettuce, Bibb lettuce, and Belgian endive.

Romaine lettuce

The most nutritious lettuce and an excellent source of folate and vitamin A; high in vitamin C

Known as the main ingredient in the famous Caesar salad, romaine tastes slightly bitter and has a crunchy texture. Wash and dry romaine well, wrap in paper towels and refrigerate for up to one week.

Iceberg lettuce

High in folate; source of vitamin C

This pale green lettuce has fewer nutrients than the darker green varieties, but it's still a great choice for certain recipes that require a soft, flexible, inexpensive lettuce. This lettuce will keep longer than others—about two weeks if packed in a plastic bag in the refrigerator.

Leaf lettuce

High in vitamins A and C; source of calcium, iron, and potassium

This lettuce—either green or red—doesn't have a "head" like other lettuces. It is crisp and flavourful but more perishable than other lettuces. If washed and dried and wrapped in paper towels, leaf lettuce will keep for up to one week in the refrigerator.

Boston or Bibb lettuce

Excellent source of folate; source of vitamins A and C, magnesium, and potassium

These lettuce types have small, round, loosely formed heads and buttery soft leaves. It's best to wash these varieties carefully, wrap the leaves in paper towels, and refrigerate for up to one week.

Mesclun mix

If mix contains mustard greens, excellent source of vitamins C and E, and folate; source of calcium, iron, magnesium, potassium, and vitamin B_6

This is one of the trendiest lettuces in the supermarket today. It's a tasty mix of salad greens that comes to us from the south of France. It consists of baby greens, nasturtium leaves and blossoms, arugula, frisée, dandelion and mustard greens, and assorted loose leaf lettuce. Store mesclun in a plastic bag for no more than 5 days in the refrigerator. Do not wash before storing.

Belgian endive
Source of iron and folate

The leaves of endive grow in tapered bundles and are creamy white in the middle and yellow-green on the outside. Belgian endive has a slightly bitter taste and a crunchy bite. The leaves can be used for dipping, stuffing, and in salads. Store unwashed in paper towels for up to 2 days.

Chinese greens (nappa, bok choy)
High levels of beta carotene, vitamins C and A, and folate; source of calcium, iron, magnesium, and potassium

Bok choy has white stems, dark green flat leaves, and a bulbous base. These are great for salads or stir-fries and in soups and side dishes. Store unwashed in a perforated plastic bag for no more than 3 days.

Radicchio
Source of vitamins C and E, and folate

This red-leafed Italian chicory is bittersweet and often used in gourmet meals as a garnish. Store unwrapped in the refrigerator for up to one week. Remove the core and use the leaves in salads, with meats, cheese, nuts, or olives, or sautéed briefly.

Rapini (or broccoli rube)
Excellent source of vitamins A and C; high in calcium, iron, potassium, and magnesium

This bitter green can be fried, steamed, or braised and is related to the cabbage and turnip family. Wrap loosely in paper towels and keep in the refrigerator for a few days. Rapini should be cooked.

Spinach
Excellent source of folate, iron, magnesium, potassium, and riboflavin; high in calcium and vitamins E and B_6

Spinach will keep for up to 3 days in the refrigerator if wrapped loosely in paper towels. Eat raw in salads or sauté briefly as a side dish. The frozen variety is excellent for cooking purposes. Be sure to thaw and squeeze dry before using.

Swiss chard
Excellent source of beta carotene; high in potassium; source of vitamin C

Here you get two vegetables for the price of one. The ivory stalks can be cooked like asparagus, and the dark leaves can be steamed or stir-fried. The taste of Swiss chard is similar to beets with the texture of spinach. Wrap in plastic and store the leaves for up to 2 days and the stalks for 4 days in the refrigerator. It's best to cook this vegetable, since when eaten raw it has a bitter taste.

Collard greens

Excellent source of fibre, vitamins C and A, and folate; high in calcium and potassium; source of iron

This is called Old World cabbage, and it tastes like a combination of cabbage and kale. The intense green leaves are more nutritious than paler cabbages. Store in damp paper towels in a plastic bag and use within a few days. Wash well to rid of sand. Cook either slowly or quickly like spinach.

Kale

High in vitamins C and A; source of iron, vitamins E and B_6, calcium, potassium, magnesium, and folate

This vegetable has blue-green leaves and a thick centre stem. It tastes like a mild cabbage. Store unwashed in plastic bags for up to 4 days. Stir-fry and use as you would spinach. Decorative pink kale is used for garnish.

Jícama

High in vitamin C; source of potassium and folate

This vegetable looks like a brown turnip that has been flattened at both ends. The texture is crisp and the flavour is sweet. Choose the smaller ones, which are tastier. Place in a plastic bag for up to three weeks in the refrigerator. Eat it either raw or cooked. It is best when just peeled; otherwise cut and place in water to preserve.

Mushrooms

Very good source of pantothenic acid (a B vitamin); source of iron, potassium, zinc, niacin, folate, and selenium

There are many varieties of mushrooms that range widely in flavour, texture, and price. It is best to store most types of mushrooms in a paper bag, or place them in a single layer on a tray covered with a paper towel for up to 3 days. Do not wash before using, and never soak in water—water penetrates mushrooms and makes them soggy. Instead, wipe mushrooms with a damp paper towel or use a mushroom brush to remove any dirt.

Button These are small, white cultivated mushrooms, which have a mild taste when eaten raw and a more intense taste when cooked. Sauté on high heat to remove the excess moisture.

Brown These are brown and firmer than button mushrooms, with a meatier and more pronounced flavour. They should be cooked to enhance their flavour. They are also known as cremini mushrooms.

Chanterelle These mushrooms have a delicate, nutty flavour and a chewy texture. Most have been picked in the wild. The stronger the scent, the stronger the flavour.

Oyster This is my favourite variety of mushroom. They look like overgrown ears and either grow in the wild or are cultivated. They have a mild taste and a silky texture. They are very perishable and should be used right away. Never buy wet oyster mushrooms since this means they are spoiled.

Morel Gourmet chefs prize these mushrooms for their earthy, smoky, nutty flavour. They are found in the wild and have an unusual appearance. The cap resembles honeycombed brain matter. Refrigerate and use within 2 days.

Portobello These delicious mushrooms are a delight for vegetarians because they have a meat-like texture. Portobellos are large mushrooms that have a thick, brown cap with dark gills. They are wonderful grilled or sautéed.

Shiitake Gourmet chefs love these mushrooms because of their rich flavour and garlic aroma. They have a domed cap with edges that turn under. They are best when sautéed or braised.

Dried Dried mushrooms add an intense flavour to dishes. Many varieties are available, and dried mushrooms are affordable when you consider that you use only a small amount. You must soak them in boiling water until softened before using. I love them in soups, sauces, and Asian dishes. Use the soaking liquid in your recipe as the liquid ingredient.

Onion Family
Source of vitamin C, fibre, folate, and potassium

There are many varieties of onions. Dry onions should be stored in a dark, cool, ventilated place for up to two weeks. Once cut, keep refrigerated. Fresh onions—including green onions, scallions, and leeks—should be refrigerated.

To avoid tears when cutting onions, I like to use the larger varieties that I can peel more quickly and get more volume from. Other methods are to freeze for 10 minutes before chopping, rinse under cold water just before chopping, or buy frozen chopped onions. I have even seen goggles designed for onion chopping! I add onions to many of my dishes, raw or sautéed. Onions are very low in calories.

Spanish onions These are large-bulbed with yellow or white skin. Their taste is milder than regular onions. They add flavour without overpowering a dish. Sauté or eat raw.

Green onions Green onions have a white base that has not fully developed into a bulb, and long, straight green leaves. They can be used interchangeably with scallions, which are milder. Store in the refrigerator for up to 5 days. Eat either raw or sautéed.

Vidalia onions These are grown in Georgia and are a member of the sweet onion family. Others in this group include Maui and Walla Walla onions. These onions are mild and creamy. They are highly perishable due to their high moisture content. They are wonderful either raw or sautéed.

Pearl onions These onions are small, sweet, and tangy. Store in a cool, dark place for up to a month. To remove their skin, drop pearl onions in boiling water for 1 minute. Drain and run under cold water. They are perfect for stews and soups.

Shallots Shallots are a cross between the onion and garlic. Store them in a dark, cool place for up to a month. Slice off the roots, remove the papery skin, and use when you want the flavour of onion and garlic together.

Leeks
Supply more folate and iron than regular onions

Leeks look like large green onions with thick green tops and a white base. They must be cooked and cleaned well.

Chives Chives are referred to as a herb and are often used as a garnish.

Garlic A member of the onion family, garlic is used in cooking all over the world. Store in a dark, cool place and crush just before using. (See page 104 for more about the properties of garlic.)

Peas
Excellent source of folate and thiamin; high in iron, magnesium, and vitamin C

Green peas Fresh peas are always the best, but frozen peas are a fine substitute. Avoid the canned versions. If fresh, store for no more than 2 days in the refrigerator in a plastic bag. Boil until slightly tender and bright green, just a couple of minutes. Green peas have 60 calories per 1/2 cup (125 mL), more than other types of peas. They are a good source of fibre.

Snow peas This tender vegetable is a delicacy. You eat the pod and the peas within. Store unwashed in a plastic bag no more than 3 days. You can eat them raw or steam them just until bright green and slightly tender but still crisp, about 1 minute. They are wonderful in stir-fries, in salads, and on their own. They have 30 calories per 1/2 cup (125 mL).

Sugar snap peas These are the sweetest and crunchiest peas you can eat. They are a hybrid of the green pea and the snow pea. Like the snow pea, the entire sugar snap pea is edible. They are best eaten raw or only briefly cooked, otherwise they lose their natural sweetness. They keep for a few days in a bag in the refrigerator. They're great in salads, sautéed, or in stir-fries.

Peppers

Sweet bell peppers
High in vitamin C (three times the amount found in an orange); excellent source of vitamin A; rich in antioxidants; a source of fibre, folate, and potassium

These large peppers come in deep green, yellow, orange, red, and purple-black, and their colour may change as they ripen. The green peppers are picked earliest, and the ripest and sweetest are the red and purple. The skin of peppers should be smooth and shiny. Keep bell peppers in the refrigerator wrapped in plastic for up to 2 weeks. Remove the stem, cut the pepper in half, remove the seeds, and serve sliced peppers raw. They are also delicious when grilled or roasted.

Hot peppers
Excellent source of vitamins C and A, and antioxidants

There are many varieties of hot peppers, or chiles, including Anaheim, cherry, cubanelle, Fresno, habanero, jalapeño, Jamaican hot, poblano, serrano, and Thai. The general rule is the smaller the pepper, the hotter. Refrigerate hot peppers for up to two weeks. Eighty percent of the heat of a hot pepper comes from the ribs and seeds, which contain most of the capsaicin oil. This fiery substance can burn your skin for up to 12 hours. It's best to wear rubber gloves when working with hot peppers. Never rub your eyes or nose after working with them. If your mouth becomes inflamed, drink milk or eat a starchy substance like bread or rice.

Potatoes and Yams
Excellent source of potassium and fibre; high in vitamin C, iron, thiamin, niacin, vitamin B_6, and folate

There are many varieties of potatoes. Store them in a dark, cool, ventilated place away from direct light for up to two weeks. Yukon Gold potatoes can last up to two months. If there is any green on the potato, this means it was exposed to direct light. Just cut away the green and use the rest of the potato. As the skin of the potato contains half the fibre content, eat the skins.

Russet potatoes Known as Idaho baking potatoes, they are long and slightly rounded with coarse, brown skin. They have a low moisture and a high starch content. They are delicious when baked whole or sliced into wedges. Avoid potatoes that are soft, bruised, or wrinkled, have a greenish tinge, or are sprouting eyes.

Red potatoes These are boiling potatoes. They have a red, thin skin and a waxy texture. The flesh is white. Red potatoes are wonderful in potato salads and as oven-roasted potatoes.

New potatoes Small and young, these are recently harvested potatoes. They are best steamed or boiled.

Purple potatoes These potatoes are purple on the outside and blue on the inside. They are all-purpose potatoes.

Fingerlings These finger-shaped potatoes are sweet and crunchy and best cooked and eaten whole.

White potatoes These come in two varieties: the long whites are an all-purpose potato; the round variety is a boiling potato.

Yukon Gold potatoes These potatoes have golden-coloured skin and flesh. They have a moist, buttery, sweet flavour and make a wonderful mashed potato because of their natural creamy flavour and texture.

Sweet potatoes

Source of fibre, vitamins A, B_6, and E, folate, potassium, iron, and antioxidants, especially beta carotene

These are often called yams but are not the same. Sweet potatoes have a thick, rust-coloured skin and deep orange flesh. They are wonderful mashed, baked, or cooked as fries. Although they are higher in calories than white potatoes, sweet potatoes are loaded with fibre and potassium and are higher in nurients. They have a low glycemic index and satisfy you longer than the white varieties.

Yams

Excellent source of fibre and potassium; good source of vitamins C and B_6, folate, iron, and magnesium

Different from the sweet potato, yams have flesh that is either white, cream, or yellow. The taste is similar to a white potato but blander, and the texture is looser, coarser, and drier.

Sprouts

Bean sprouts
Contain folate and vitamin C

These are great in salads or cooked in stir-fries. The problem with bean sprouts is that they go bad quickly. I have found the answer to keeping them crisp for at least 3 to 4 days: place them in a bowl of cold water and keep in the refrigerator until ready to use.

Raw alfalfa sprouts CAUTION:
It's best to avoid these if you're elderly or have a weak immune system. Don't feed them to children, as raw alfalfa sprouts have been known to cause illness due to salmonella and E. coli bacteria. Washing them doesn't help because the bacteria grow as the sprouts germinate.

Squash

There are winter and summer squash. Winter varieties include acorn, buttercup, butternut, hubbard, pumpkin, spaghetti, and turban. The summer squash include yellow and green zucchini.

Winter squash
Good source of vitamins A and C, folate, and potassium; source of beta carotene and fibre

All winter squash have hard skins in dark, rich colours of green, orange, gold, or yellow. They should never be refrigerated until cut. Store in a cool, dark place from 1 to 3 months. Prick the skin, then bake for about an hour; slice open, remove the seeds, and eat the pulp.

Summer squash
High in folate; source of potassium, vitamin C, beta carotene, and fibre; high water content

Yellow or green zucchini must be stored in the refrigerator in a plastic bag for no more than 4 days. Do not peel the edible skin, as it contains the fibre. Zucchini can be eaten raw or cooked. The smaller the zucchini, the better the taste and texture. The larger ones should be used only for stuffing.

Tomatoes
Excellent source of vitamin C, beta carotene, potassium, folate, and vitamin E; high in lycopene (an antioxidant more powerful than beta carotene)

Smaller tomatoes have more nutrients than larger ones. There are many varieties to choose from. In general, tomatoes should not be refrigerated unless cut and should not be set in the sun. Store upside down on the stem. To ripen tomatoes quickly, place them in a paper bag.

Slicing tomatoes These are the common tomato. They are firm and juicy and are best used fresh.

Beefsteak/vine ripe tomatoes These are big, red, juicy tomatoes and are great eaten raw or cooked.

Hothouse tomatoes Grown in a controlled environment, these tend to be more flavourful than regular tomatoes.

Plum tomatoes This is my favourite tomato variety for salads and for cooking. They are the perfect cooking tomato: narrow and firm, with a thick, meaty wall and small seeds; they adapt well to heat and contain little liquid. They are also delicious raw.

Cherry tomatoes Either red or yellow, these small tomatoes are to be eaten fresh in salads or used as a garnish.

Teardrop tomatoes Smaller than cherry tomatoes, these are fairly new in the supermarkets. They have a pear-like shape, and are sweet and juicy. Serve whole in salads or for dipping.

Sun-dried tomatoes Sun-drying is an age-old Mediterranean tradition. Tomatoes are dried until reduced to a leathery texture. You can buy them dry or packed in oil; dry sun-dried tomatoes are healthier since they are not saturated in oil. Reconstitute dry sun-dried tomatoes in boiling water for about 15 minutes, then chop and use. They add an intense flavour to any dish. I buy them in bulk, freeze them, and use them as needed.

Tomatillo
Source of vitamin C, fibre, potassium, and niacin

The lemon-herb taste of tomatillos provides the base for salsas and green sauces. They look like small, green tomatoes but are surrounded by a parchment-like husk. Refrigerate tomatillos in a paper bag for up to a month. They can be eaten raw, but the flavour is enhanced and less acidic if they are cooked.

Fruit Aisle

The Food Guide suggests that you should consume between 5 and 10 servings of fruits and vegetables daily. This quantity is not a lot, considering that one fruit such as an apple or orange equals two servings. Most fruits are low in calories and fat and are loaded with fibre and nutrients. Frozen fruit is great for cooking or baking.

CAUTION: A high-calorie exception is coconut, which contains saturated fat. Dried fruit is extremely nutritious but should be eaten in moderation because, as a concentrated form of fruit, it is higher in calories. I usually avoid canned fruits due to the heavy, sugary syrups they are packed in. If you choose canned fruits, buy those with a label that reads "no added sugar," "packed in its own juice," or "unsweetened."

Apples
High in fibre (one-third of the fibre is in the skin); contain flavonoids, particularly quercetin, which can protect against certain forms of cancer

There are many different varieties of apples. Look for firm, smooth-skinned apples free of bruises and gouges. Store apples in a cool, dark place, or place them in a plastic bag in the refrigerator for up to six weeks. If using apples in cooking, cut them early and sprinkle with lemon juice to prevent browning.

Varieties of apples that are best for eating raw include Gala, McIntosh, and Red Delicious. Varieties of apples that are best cooked include Rome Beauty and Northern Spy. Varieties of apples that are good for eating and cooking include Braeburn, Cortland, Mutsu, Empire, Fuji, Golden Delicious, Granny Smith, Gravenstein, Spartan, Spy, and Jonagold.

Bananas
High in potassium; an excellent source of vitamins C and B_6, magnesium, and folate

Slightly green bananas will ripen at home. Never store bananas in the refrigerator, as this stops the ripening process—once they are ripe they can be refrigerated. Don't buy bruised bananas to eat because they are probably too ripe, but they can be perfect for baking. Freeze peeled overripe bananas for baking and cooking purposes.

Berries
There are many delicious varieties of berries, great for eating and cooking. Choose firm, plump, berries with good colour. Do not wash berries before storing. It's best to place them in a single layer on a paper towel in a moisture-proof container. They will last for 2 to 3 days in the refrigerator.

Blackberries
High in vitamin C, folate, and fibre; a source of potassium; contain flavonoids called anthocyanins, which can help prevent cancer and heart disease

These are sweet and juicy berries. Store in a single layer in the refrigerator for up to 3 days. Blackberries improve with cooking, as their flavour intensifies and their texture softens.

Blueberries

High in fibre and antioxidants; contain flavonoids called anthocyanins, which can help prevent cancer and heart disease

Both the large and small varieties are sweet and great for eating and baking. These can be refrigerated for up to two weeks and frozen for up to nine months for use in cooking.

Cranberries

Source of vitamin C and fibre

These are sold fresh during the fall, right in time for Thanksgiving. Store them in a plastic bag in the refrigerator for up to six weeks, or up to one year frozen. Cook these berries just until they pop. Longer cooking will result in mushy, bitter berries.

Strawberries

Number one in vitamin C; source of folate, potassium, and fibre; contain phytochemicals called flavonoids, which may reduce the risk of cancer and heart disease

Once picked strawberries don't ripen. Avoid those with green or white under the leaves. Eat these berries quickly since they don't last longer than 3 days. Wash strawberries gently and never soak them in water. Dry immediately with a paper towel.

Citrus Fruits

Oranges

Excellent source of fibre and vitamin C; high in folate; source of thiamin, potassium, and calcium; full of antioxidants

Look for oranges that feel firm. The colour of the rind doesn't make any difference. Store at room temperature for a few days, or refrigerate in plastic bags for up to two weeks. Orange zest freezes well for use in recipes. There are several varieties of orange, including the following:

Blood orange: The colour is red, purple, or burgundy. Blood oranges have a raspberry taste and are sweet and less acidic than regular oranges.

Clementine tangerine: These are sweet, juicy, and seedless.

Valencia orange: The flesh is sweet and juicy, and this type of orange contains few seeds.

Juice orange: These are best when squeezed.

Navel orange: Navel oranges are great for eating—sweet, juicy, and seedless.

Grapefruit

Excellent source of vitamin C; source of potassium and folate

There are three varieties—pink, yellow, and red. They should be heavy and firm. They can be kept at room temperature for up to 6 days, or up to six weeks in the refrigerator.

Lemons and limes

Loaded with vitamin C; rich in phytochemicals

Look for small to medium-sized fruit, which are the juiciest. Avoid lemons tinged with green on their peel, which aren't ripe enough. Limes need immediate refrigeration, whereas lemons can be stored at room temperature for a few days. Limes can be kept refrigerated in plastic bags for two weeks, and lemons longer. Freeze the juice for recipes.

Grapes

Source of vitamins C and B_6, potassium, and thiamin; contain important flavonoids, anthocyanins and quercetin, which can help prevent heart disease and cancer

Basic varieties include red grapes and green or white types. White grapes are sweeter than red. Wash grapes well before eating. They can be stored in the refrigerator for one week. Eat them frozen and unthawed for a great snack.

Kiwi

High in vitamin C, potassium, and folate; source of fibre, magnesium, and vitamin E

Buy the kiwi firm and let it ripen and soften at room temperature for one week before eating it. Ripe kiwis can be refrigerated for up to one week.

Mango

Excellent source of beta carotene and vitamins A and C; high source of vitamins E and B_6, and fibre; source of potassium, folate, thiamin, niacin, and riboflavin

Their peak season is from May to July. Florida mangos are picked hard and need a week at room temperature to ripen. Indonesian mangos, which are sweeter and have more flavour than Florida mangos, are increasingly available. They are small and all yellow. When ripe, a mango should give to slight pressure and have an intense smell. Ripe mangos can be refrigerated for up to 3 days.

Melons

If melons are picked before they reach maturity, they will never reach full flavour. Never buy melons that are rock hard. Except for the honeydew variety, a melon should not have a stem attached, as it means that the fruit was picked before ripe and won't ripen any further. Ripen at room temperature and, once cut, wrap and refrigerate for up to 5 days. You can quicken the ripening by putting the melon in a paper bag. A good melon should have a fruity scent and be heavy for its size. Pick melons that are symmetrical; the end should give to slight pressure. Avoid melons with lumps or soft spots, which indicate overripeness.

Cantaloupe
Excellent source of beta carotene and vitamin C; source of potassium, folate, fibre, vitamin B_6, and magnesium

Honeydew
High in vitamin C; source of potassium and thiamin

Watermelon
Source of vitamins C and B_6, potassium, and thiamin

Peaches
Source of potassium and fibre; contain antioxidant vitamins A, C, and E

There are many varieties of peaches, and white peaches have become very popular recently. All peaches are classified as clingstone or freestone; clingstones usually end up in cans. Peaches do not ripen after they have been picked. Select those with a creamy or yellow background colour that give to slight pressure. Refrigerate for up to a week.

Pears
Excellent source of fibre; source of vitamin C, folate, and potassium

Pears are one of the few fruits that have to ripen after being picked, so you can buy them at any stage. Ripen them more quickly by putting them in a paper bag. Store them in a plastic bag in the refrigerator for up to 5 days; this will not stop the ripening process. These are some varieties:

Anjou: This variety has white flesh and is great for eating and cooking.

Asian: Asian pears are apple-shaped and large, with white, crisp flesh.

Bartlett: Golden skinned, sweet, and juicy, Bartletts are good for eating and cooking.

Bosc: This variety is juicy and good for eating and cooking.

Pineapple

Excellent source of vitamin C; source of potassium, thiamin, and fibre; contains bromelain enzymes, which help reduce inflammation

Buy a large pineapple that is firm and has lots of colour. The stem should have a sweet aroma, but pulling a leaf out easily is not a sign of ripeness. Look for crisp, green leaves that show no yellowing or browning. Store a pineapple for up to 2 days at room temperature. Once cut, refrigerate for up to 3 days. Hawaiian pineapples are sweeter and juicier than Latin American varieties, which are picked while too green.

Dairy Products Aisle

On an outside aisle of the supermarket, you'll usually find the dairy products. According to the Food Guide, you should be consuming between 2 and 4 servings of dairy products a day. One serving of dairy equals 1 cup (250 mL) milk, 3/4 cup (175 mL) yogourt, 1-1/2 ounces (45 g) natural cheese, or 2 ounces (60 g) sliced processed cheese.

Always buy dairy products showing the latest expiry date so that they will stay fresh longer. All milk and dairy products are labelled with a milk fat (MF) or butter fat (BF) percentage. Naturally, the lower the number, the lower the fat content. What can be confusing is that 2% milk may contain only 2 percent fat by weight but 35 percent of its total calories may come from fat. (Remember the fat formula? See page 75.) About 23 percent of the total calories in 1% milk are from fat.

Other milk products you should include in your basket for lower-fat cooking are buttermilk and evaporated milk. Buttermilk has less fat than 1% milk and is great to use in sauces and desserts. Evaporated milk, either 1% or 2%, is also a terrific alternative to whole milk or cream when preparing sauces or desserts. However, I find the no-fat evaporated milk has too watery a consistency to be used in sauces.

A lower-fat diet should always minimize full-fat dairy products of any kind, such as cream cheese, whipping cream, cheese, and sour cream. Today there are always lower-fat alternatives. Avoid non-dairy creamers or fake whipped cream topping. They are made from hydrogenated vegetable fat, which is a form of saturated fat.

Milk

Milk is important for supplying calcium and vitamin D. To lower the risk of osteoporosis, these nutrients are a must in our diet, and one of the easiest ways to obtain them is through milk. One cup

(250 mL) of milk has 300 milligrams of calcium, and you only need three glasses per day to obtain your daily calcium intake. So drink up.

Varieties of milk range from homogenized 3% MF milk, to 2% MF, 1% MF, skim, and non-fat milk. I always avoid homogenized milk and select milk with 2% MF or less. For cooking purposes, I use either 1% or 2% milk. I find milk with a lower MF content too watery and thin and lacking in flavour.

Let's look at the fat and calories per 1 cup (250 mL) serving:

- Homogenized milk: 150 calories, 8 grams fat, 200 milligrams calcium
- 2% MF: 125 calories, 5 grams fat, 315 milligrams calcium
- 1% MF: 105 calories, 2 grams fat, 315 milligrams calcium
- Skim: 90 calories, 1 gram fat, 315 milligrams calcium

CAUTION: Homogenized milk has the least amount of calcium and is more fat saturated. This means that it can lead to weight gain, heart disease, and high cholesterol.

SUPERFOOD: **Buttermilk**   This milk sounds fattening, but it is actually skim milk with added lactic acid cultures that is allowed to develop until it is thick and creamy. Buttermilk adds great texture and a zesty flavour to baking and cooking. It's approximately equivalent to 1% milk in calories and fat.

CAUTION: **Heavy Cream**   This has 35% MF and is made from the fat that rises to the top of non-homogenized milk. Heavy cream is usually used for sauces and whipped for desserts. I avoid this high-fat milk product. For sauces, I always substitute evaporated milk.

Sour Cream   This is made from pasteurized, homogenized sweet cream. Lactic acid is added to the milk, and the mixture ferments until the proper flavour and texture is reached. Sour cream is great for sauces, dips, and toppings. The usual fat content is 14% MF, but you can now find sour cream with 0 to 5% MF, which is creamy and delicious, perfect for baking and cooking purposes.

Cheese

CAUTION: One of the toughest things when eating a lower-fat diet is resisting the world of cheese. For every advantage of this food there is a disadvantage. Cheese is high in protein but loaded with saturated fat and cholesterol, filled with calcium but also sodium. One ounce (30 g) of cheese, which equals 1 serving of dairy products, has approximately 100 calories and 9 grams of fat. When we should be having only between 2 and 4 servings of dairy products per day, 1 ounce is not very satisfying or filling. It's so easy to eat a chunk of cheese that might be 3 or 4 ounces (90 to 120 g)! Let's look at the varieties of cheeses:

- Very hard cheeses include Parmesan, Romano, and Asiago.
- Hard cheeses include Cheddar, Swiss, and Gruyère.
- Soft cheeses include brick, Havarti, Brie, mozzarella, blue, and Camembert.
- Unripened cheeses include cottage, cream, goat and feta, pot, and fresh ricotta.

The soft cheeses can be found in lower-fat forms. For example, cottage cheese can be found in forms containing 0.5 to 2% MF. Ricotta cheese can now be found that contains as little as 5% MF. The fat content of cream cheeses in Canada has been reduced to approximately 25% MF from the original 35% MF.

When selecting hard or natural cheeses such as mozzarella, Swiss, and Cheddar, try to select those lower in MF. Regular whole-fat cheeses can have anywhere from 24% MF to 35% MF. (Use the fat formula on page 75—1 ounce (30 g) of these cheeses gets 81 percent of its calories from fat!) The best-tasting lower-fat cheeses will have anywhere from 10% MF to 15% MF. They are also great to cook with. The lowest-fat cheeses, with less than 5% MF, usually have inferior taste and texture and are not good to cook with. I find that people who consume these cheeses always eat more since the cheeses are not satisfying.

Once opened, cheeses should be stored in the refrigerator wrapped in plastic. The hard cheeses keep the longest, and the unripened cheeses have the shortest shelf life. The harder cheeses last longer because they contain less water, which encourages bacteria growth.

I buy large blocks of hard cheese and freeze them for cooking purposes. They tend to crumble after they have been frozen, but are perfect for cooking. I allow them to semi-defrost, and then place them in the food processor to grate or chop them. This way, grated cheese is always on hand, ready to use. If you grate a lot of cheese, place it in a freezer bag and remove the amount that you need when cooking. This saves time and energy.

Yogourt

SUPERFOOD: This is a cultured milk with a thick consistency made by adding bacteria to milk and then allowing it to ferment until the desired flavour and texture is obtained. More nutritious than milk, yogourt contains more calcium, approximately 350 milligrams per cup (250 mL) (compared to 315 milligrams for 1% milk). This amount of yogourt provides one-third of the calcium you need daily. Yogourt is a good source of protein and has more B vitamins, phosphorus, and potassium than milk and is also more digestible. Fruit yogourts are less nutritious than plain yogourt since fruit yogourts contain less yogourt and more sugar. Lower-fat yogourts are good, but they are often loaded with sugar, so read the labels. The artificially sweetened ones are lower in calories but have chemical sweeteners that are unhealthy for you. Your best bet is to have low-fat plain yogourt and add your own fresh or dried fruit.

Eggs

Eggs are a good source of protein, iron, and vitamin A, but they do contain saturated fat and cholesterol. All the cholesterol is found in the yolk, which can have over 200 milligrams of cholesterol with 5 grams of fat. Since the recommended daily allowance for cholesterol is only 320 milligrams, many people restrict their weekly intake of eggs.

Egg whites are cholesterol free, and one egg white has only 15 calories. Substitute two egg whites for each whole egg in a recipe, or use an egg substitute. Read the label to ensure that the egg substitute doesn't contain food colouring and chemicals. Some egg substitutes available in stores today are made from 90 percent egg whites and 10 percent egg yolks. The colour is just like that of whole egg, the taste is great, and this product is more nutritious than eggs. The latest studies indicate that if you're healthy, eating one whole egg daily, or no more than six or seven per week, doesn't raise your cholesterol. Eating more than that adds unnecessary cholesterol to your diet. If you love eggs, try using one whole egg and two egg whites to give you two eggs, or try a commercial egg substitute that contains very little cholesterol.

These options are great news because eggs have important nutrients. They contain high-quality protein, vitamins A, D, B_{12}, and E, folate, and riboflavin.

To follow egg safety, buy AA- or A-graded eggs from refrigerated cases only. Get the eggs home quickly and place them in the coldest part of your refrigerator. Check the quality of the eggs before you buy them. Never buy cracked or leaking eggs, and never use a cracked egg because it can be contaminated with bacteria such as salmonella, which can cause food poisoning. It's safe to refrigerate eggs for as long as five weeks. Do not leave eggs out for longer than 2 hours at room temperature. Hard-cooked eggs can stay in the shell for a maximum of 10 days. You can freeze raw whole eggs (not in their shell), egg whites, or just the yolks. The best way to freeze whole eggs is to beat them first and then put them in a container with a tight lid. If you are freezing only the yolks then beat them first and add 1/4 teaspoon (1 mL) of salt or 1-1/2 teaspoons (7 mL) of sugar for every four egg yolks. I like to thaw frozen eggs overnight in the refrigerator or put the container under cool running water.

There has always been a debate about eating foods that contain raw eggs due to the possibility of salmonella poisoning. I did a television show at an egg factory, and officials there said that 1 in 20,000 eggs can be contaminated. Usually contamination occurs when eggs have been left out at room temperature for several hours, as is often the case in restaurants. I do eat foods containing raw eggs when I'm doing the cooking, but I would avoid serving raw eggs to people in poor health, the elderly, and pregnant women.

Don't be fooled by the colour difference between white and brown eggs. Brown eggs have the same nutritional value. Often I buy white and brown eggs and use the white ones for cooking and hard-cook the brown ones.

Designer Eggs   Omega-3 eggs, containing polyunsaturated fat, are produced by feeding laying hens a special diet containing 10 to 20 percent ground flaxseed, which is high in omega-3 fatty acids. These eggs are more heart healthy and help lower the bad (LDL) cholesterol. Three to four eggs supply the same amount of omega-3 fatty acids as a 3-ounce (90 g) serving of salmon, but they still contain cholesterol and fat.

Do these new eggs offer you better health? Let's first look at the benefits of omega-3 fatty acids:

- They are an important building block in all our cells.
- They help sustain normal blood pressure.
- They help promote normal blood clotting.
- They help keep our blood vessels flexible instead of stiff.

In addition to their benefits, these new eggs have some weaknesses:
- The total reduction in fat they provide is 25 percent, which is not that meaningful when an egg has 5 grams of fat to begin with.
- The reduction in cholesterol they provide is very small. A regular egg has 215 milligrams of cholesterol, and these new eggs have about 190 milligrams. That's not much of a difference
- The new eggs offer only 10 percent of the daily requirement of vitamin E.
- They can cost twice as much as regular eggs. You can always spend the money on flaxseed or fish and take an extra vitamin E supplement.

Grains and Cereals Aisle

According to the Food Guide you are allowed from 5 to 12 servings of grains, your complex carbohydrates, per day. This may sound like a lot, but remember that 1 serving is only 1/2 cup (125 mL). A plate of pasta, which might consist of 4 cups (1 L), equals 8 servings. Grain products include bread, crackers, cereals, rice, pasta, and other grains such as barley, kasha, millet, quinoa, and oats. Starchier vegetables, such as potatoes and sweet potatoes, should be counted as grain—half a regular potato equals 1 serving.

SUPERFOOD: Whole grains may cut the risk of heart disease, stroke, diabetes, colon cancer, and high blood pressure. The anti-cancer properties come from the antioxidants found in whole grains. Select whole-grain products, which are much healthier for you than white-flour carbohydrates. Whole-grain products are a source of fibre, vitamins, minerals, and phytochemicals, and are also a low-glycemic food, which means that you stay satisfied longer. Always look for the label "whole wheat," which means that 100 percent whole-wheat flour has been used. Be careful of the word "wheat" used alone on a product as it often refers to a combination of whole-wheat and white flour. Don't judge bread by the colour; often colour or caramel flavouring is added to the bread to make it look more like whole-wheat bread.

To determine if you are obtaining enough fibre in grain products, read the nutritional information. Each slice of bread should contain at least 2 grams of fibre. Cereals should contain at least 4 grams of fibre per serving.

CAUTION: Make sure your grain products contain no more than 6 grams of sugar per serving. If the first ingredient listed on the label is sugar, as is common in some breakfast cereals, the product is not very healthy. Also, always check the serving size. For example, in granola, the serving size is unusually small, about 1/4 cup (50 mL) because of the high number of calories and amount of fat in this type of cereal.

Cereals

Cold Cereals   Read the labels on the cereal boxes for the best health information. A healthy cereal should have less than 2 grams of fat per serving, less than 8 grams of sugar per serving, and more than 2 grams of fibre per 1-ounce (30 g) serving. Here are some tips for choosing a cold cereal:

- A healthier cereal will have the grain listed first, not the sugar.
- Look for a short ingredient list.
- Avoid the high-sugar and coloured cereals as they offer little nutrition.
- Look for brands with a high fibre content.
- Note the fat content and type of fat. For example, granola can be loaded with fat, often hydrogenated vegetable fat, which is saturated.
- Most cold cereals have excess sodium added.

Hot Cereals   These grain products contain fibre, B vitamins and vitamin E, iron, zinc, calcium, selenium, and magnesium. For even more nutrition, eat hot cereals with low-fat milk and fresh fruit. While hot cereals are often healthier than cold cereals, keep a few tips in mind:

- Avoid the sweetened types.
- Best choices are oatmeal, Cream of Wheat, and oat bran or oatmeal.
- Read the label and look for 2 grams of fat or less per serving.

Breads

High in complex carbohydrates; low-fat source of fibre, vitamins, and minerals

The more whole wheat a bread contains, the more fibre. To be whole-wheat bread, a bread must be made from 100 percent whole-wheat flour, not wheat flour or cracked wheat. Whole-wheat bread contains the fibre-rich bran and germ of the grain, both of which are eliminated through the refining process used to make white flour used in other breads.

An average piece of bread has only 70 calories and 1 gram of fat. Bread is not fattening—it's what you put on it that contributes the calories.

Pasta

High in protein and complex carbohydrates; virtually fat and sodium free; contains no cholesterol (except for egg pasta); good source of B vitamins and iron

Noodles or pasta have become a staple in the North American diet. I use them as a main dish, salad, or side dish.

A serving of 4 ounces (125 g) dry pasta is considered a main serving portion, and it contains approximately 400 calories and 2 grams of fat.

Pasta come in numerous shapes, sizes, and textures. The best rule is to serve finer and lighter sauces on thinner strands of pasta, such as spaghetti, fettuccine, or linguine, and heavier and more robust sauces over shapes like rigatoni, penne, and rotini.

Cooking pasta properly is very important: use lots of water with a couple of teaspoons of oil to prevent sticking. (I never salt the water since the sauce usually has salt.) Cook pasta at a rapid boil and never overcook—it should be "al dente" or firm to the bite. Immediately drain and serve, or rinse with cold water to stop the cooking process if serving later. To prevent sticking, it's best to add a few spoons of sauce immediately, or, when ready to eat, run pasta under hot water, mix with sauce, and serve immediately.

Pasta is available made from white and whole-grain flours, rice, buckwheat, and even beans (bean thread noodles).

Rice

Excellent source of complex carbohydrates; virtually fat and cholesterol free; contains fibre and is enriched with iron

Half the world's population uses rice as a staple; it is their main source of carbohydrates and there-fore their main source of energy. Many varieties of rice are available.

Most varieties of white rice require the same cooking time and a 1:1 ratio of liquid to rice. The liquid can be water, stock, or even tomato juice. If you like your rice softer, use up to 1-1/2 units of liquid. Follow this method to make perfect rice every time: bring liquid and rice to a boil, cover and simmer for 12 minutes, remove from the heat and keep covered for 10 minutes, and then fluff with a fork. Don't stir the rice while it's cooking.

Brown and wild rice require more liquid and more cooking time. Usually the amount of liquid is double the amount of rice, and cooking times vary between 25 and 35 minutes.

White Rice   These types of rice have been refined.

Basmati rice Basmati is a hulled, long-grain, aromatic rice imported from India. This rice has been aged for one year to develop its full flavour and is a must for Indian and Middle Eastern cuisines.

Jasmine rice This classic stir-fry rice is a hulled, long-grain, aromatic rice organically grown in Thailand and the United States.

Texmati rice This cross between basmati and long-grain American rice is grown in Texas and is fluffier and has a milder flavour and aroma than imported basmati.

Sushi rice This short-grain, sticky rice is used solely for sushi.

Brown Rice   Nutritionally better than refined white rice, brown rice still has the bran and germ, which make it richer in fibre, vitamins, and minerals. Medium-grain rice will yield a lighter, fluffier rice than the short-grain variety. The long-grain variety has a nutty flavour and cooks up fluffier and drier than other varieties. Brown rice must be cooked longer than white rice and with more liquid.

Other Grains

Wild Rice
High in protein; good source of B vitamins

This grain is not really rice at all but the seed of an aquatic grass. Closely related to the corn family, wild rice is indigenous to North America and known as a traditional staple for the Native peoples of the Minnesota area. Wild rice is high in B vitamins and is higher in protein and lower in calories than white rice. Wild rice must be cooked longer than white rice varieties and with more liquid.

Barley
Source of protein, fibre, and iron

This grain has a wonderful nutty flavour. Traditionally used in soups, today barley is often in side dishes, salads, main courses, and risottos. Scotch or pot barley, which is less refined than pearl barley and retains the bran, needs more time to cook than pearl barley, from which the hull, bran, and germ have been removed.

Buckwheat/Kasha
Good source of protein, fibre, and iron

Buckwheat flour is used in soba noodles. Kasha is roasted buckwheat kernels and is an excellent source of complex carbohydrates. In breakfast cereals, kasha supplies excellent nutrition and is low in fat. The kernel is cracked and sold in different sizes. You can use kasha the same way you would rice.

Cornmeal/Hominy
Complex carbohydrate; contains potassium and folic acid, and virtually no fat

There are two kinds of cornmeal, regular and stone ground. Stone-ground cornmeal has the oily germ and is higher in fibre and minerals than is regular cornmeal. Cornmeal is used for polenta dishes. Hominy is dried corn from which the hull and germ have been removed. It is cracked into flour for masa harina, which is used to make tortillas.

Couscous
Complex carbohydrate; contains folic acid, potassium, and virtually no fat

Couscous is tiny granules of semolina pasta. It's a wonderful dish that cooks in 5 minutes.

Millet
Good source of protein and iron; high in phosphorus and B vitamins

Millet, from which the hull has been removed, is cooked like couscous and is a wonderful grain to serve either warm or cold as a salad.

Quinoa
Complete protein source; high in calcium and iron

This is an ancient grain, pronounced *keen-wah*. It cooks quickly and is high in protein and minerals. Quinoa is the only grain that is a complete protein, and can be used during the Jewish holiday of

Passover. You should always refrigerate or freeze it to prevent it from going rancid. Use quinoa in place of rice, pasta, or other grains.

Wheatberries
High in fibre

This is the new grain on the block. Otherwise known as whole-wheat kernels, wheatberries take approximately 40 to 50 minutes to cook. Their texture is crunchy and their taste nut-like. You can reduce the cooking time by soaking wheatberries overnight. They are great as a breakfast cereal.

Bulgur
High in fibre; low in calories; source of protein and potassium

Bulgur is wheat that has been soaked, cooked, and dried. It is great in soups and is the grain traditionally used in tabbouleh.

Flaxseed
SUPERFOOD: Source of fibre and essential fatty acids

These are small whole-grain seeds that contain compounds called lignans, which are shown to have anti-cancer effects and may slow the growth of breast cancer. Try adding ground flaxseeds to cookie or cake mixes, or yogourt, or add the whole seeds to salads and casseroles.

Fats and Oils Aisle

Certain fats, such as monounsaturated and polyunsaturated fats, are actually good for you, helping to lower cholesterol. But in general, it's wise to limit your consumption of fat because of the calories. Remember, 1 tablespoon of any fat contains about 120 calories and 14 grams of fat! You can see how easily the calories and fat can add up and cause weight gain.

CAUTION: When a liquid oil is changed into a solid oil by a process called hydrogenation, trans-fatty acids are the result. The fat has become a saturated fat and causes the damage associated with that kind of fat.

When shopping, read the nutrition label and be sure the fat is either monounsaturated or polyunsaturated. Coconut and palm oil, even though vegetable fats, are considered saturated fats. The best oils for you are monounsaturated; use canola, olive, and peanut oils for most of your cooking needs. Polyunsaturated oils include corn, safflower, soybean, sesame, and cottonseed oils.

To add more distinct flavours to your dishes, use peanut, sesame, or olive oil. As olive and sesame oil do not tolerate high cooking temperatures, it's best to use these oils in salads or pasta dishes.

Olive Oil

Olive oil has been in the press a lot lately, especially it's role in the Mediterranean diet. The rates of heart attack and high cholesterol are lower in this part of the world than in North America. Studies have shown that this may be because of the protective agents in olive oil, which is a monounsaturated fat and considered heart healthy. There are many different types of olive oil, ranging in colour, flavour, and aroma. The best olive oil is dark green and "cold pressed," meaning the olives have been pressed only once and no heat has been used to extract the oil. Lighter olive oils have more of the flavour of the olive skins and seeds because more pressure was used to extract the oil.

Virgin Olive Oil   This is unrefined oil from the first pressing of the olives. The colour is dark green.

Extra-Virgin Oil   This oil has a medium colour and a very distinct olive flavour. This kind of olive oil is the most expensive, being cold pressed. Some studies indicate that extra-virgin olive oil helps prevent blood clots from forming and acts as an antioxidant to help protect against heart disease.

Extra-Light Oil   This oil has been refined to remove colour and flavour. Use it as you would other oils.

Light Oil   This oil is not calorie or fat reduced. Rather it is probably a mixture of pure olive oil and another polyunsaturated oil.

Vegetable Sprays

I use these to coat my pans and skillets because then I never use too much fat. These sprays contain few calories and do the trick. If you prefer not to use the store-bought cans, then purchase a pump and fill it with your own oil.

Solid Fats and Oils

Lard   *CAUTION:* I never keep this saturated, unhealthy fat in my home. I don't care if lard makes the flakiest pie crusts—use oil, or non-hydrogenated margarine or butter, instead. Saturated fat is responsible for heart disease and strokes, and high cholesterol, and is thought to promote certain types of cancer.

Vegetable Shortening   *CAUTION:* This form of oil has been hydrogenated to keep it in solid form. It's used in baking because it is cheaper than butter, margarine, or oil. Again I suggest tossing it out and using another type of oil, butter, or non-hydrogenated margarine.

Butter and Margarine   When purchasing butter, always select unsalted, which is healthier. If buying margarine, use one that is marked "non-hydrogenated," which means free of transfatty acids and not saturated. The softer the margarine, the less hydrogenated it is. Also look for a brand that has at least twice as much polyunsaturated as saturated fat.

Meat, Poultry, and Fish Section

Good sources of protein, iron, zinc, and B vitamins

Protein is essential in our diets since much of our body is made up of protein. It helps maintain blood pressure and water balance, and is needed to transport most substances, such as insulin, in and out of the body's cells. The amount of protein required in a day is between 50 and 80 grams— the amount contained in 7 to 11 ounces (210 to 330 g) of meat.

Allow about 1/4 to 1/3 pound (115 to 170 g) per serving of boneless meat or poultry. If the meat has some bone, then a serving is approximately 1/3 to 1/2 pound (170 to 230 g) per person. If you are buying meat that has many bony sections, such as ribs, shanks, or shoulder cuts, allow 3/4 to 1 pound (340 to 450 g) per person.

Meat and Poultry Aisle

During the past 20 years, meat consumption in North America has dropped 28 percent, mostly due to the press about saturated fat and cholesterol leading to heart disease and other diseases. But today meat is leaner than it's ever been. Certain lean cuts of meat can be as low in fat and cholesterol as chicken or fish.

Pork tenderloin is very low in fat, as are skinless turkey or chicken breast. Turkey breast only has 5 percent fat calories, even less than chicken at 8 percent fat calories. But if you decide to indulge in chicken or turkey bolognas or franks, then you are getting at least 70 percent fat calories. Remember to remove the skin and trim the fat from all meat—this will lessen the saturated fat by as much as half.

Always select lean and well-trimmed meat. One of the ways to recognize leaner meat is to look for a cut that is less marbled with fat. Classifications of meat describe its tenderness, juiciness, and flavour—AAA, AA, and A. Sometimes you'll also see meat classified as prime, choice, select, good, or standard. The difference is the amount of fat marbling. AAA and prime meat has the most fat and is the tastiest, but not the healthiest.

When meat is described as lean, it should contain no more than 10 percent fat when raw. Leaner cuts of meat can be tougher because there is little fat. Tenderize them by marinating in vinegar, wine, lemon juice, buttermilk, or yogourt for several hours. Flank steak becomes tender after just 2 hours of marinating.

Beef

Good source of B vitamins and iron

Select lean cuts marked sirloin, inside round, rump roast, sirloin tip, strip loin, flank, blade, tenderloin, chuck steaks, or roasts. The fattiest cuts are rib roasts, brisket, regular or medium ground beef, and short ribs.

Ground Beef   *CAUTION:* Be very careful when your choice is ground beef. Since it doesn't have visible fat that you can trim away, it is the third largest source of saturated fat for the average person (after cheese and milk). Ground beef can be labelled 80 percent lean, but that refers to the percentage of fat by weight—20 percent—which contributes 70 percent of the total calories. Cooking reduces the percentage of fat calories by only 10 percent. As you can see, lean ground beef is not really lean. Another safety factor to keep in mind is that ground meat can contain dangerous E. coli bacteria. Try replacing ground beef with ground turkey, chicken, or veal.

Lamb and Veal

Leaner cuts low in saturated fat and cholesterol; excellent source of protein; rich source of iron, zinc, and vitamin B$_{12}$; good source of B vitamins

Leg of lamb, veal roasts, veal cutlets, veal loin roasts, and veal chops are among the leanest cuts.

Pork

Excellent source of B vitamins, zinc, iron, and high-quality protein; fat less saturated than that in beef

Pork is 31 percent leaner than it was ten years ago, due to changes in breeding and feeding practices. The tenderloin, centre loin chop, lean ham, and loin and rib end roasts are your healthiest choices. The fattiest choices are ribs, loin blade, and shoulder. It's no longer necessary to cook fresh pork until it's well done; medium is fine. People contracted trichinosis from undercooked pork when production methods were not as clean. The disease is virtually eliminated from North America.

Poultry
Good source of B vitamins, but less iron than red meat

Poultry of all kinds is the leanest animal protein source as long as you remove the skin before eating. It has one-third the fat and calories of red meat. Try boneless and skinless chicken and turkey breast, Cornish hen, and ground chicken or turkey. Most supermarkets today are selling boneless chicken thighs—they are delicious, but be aware that the dark meat has slightly more calories and double the fat of the white meat.

Game Meats   Some game meats are very low in fat and calories—venison, ostrich, elk, and buffalo are good lean choices. A serving of 3-1/2 ounces (105 g) of any of these game meats has only 2 grams of fat (compared to 13 grams for a serving of beef the same size) and 135 calories (compared to 200 calories for beef). It's best to marinate these cuts and cook them on the rare side to make them more tender.

The Deli Section   *CAUTION:* Keep foods that contain nitrites and nitrates to a minimum. Examples are smoked meat, smoked fish, or deli meats such as hot dogs, corned beef, and salami. These foods often contain both nitrites and nitrates, which have been known to cause stomach cancer. Studies indicate that a diet that is high in vitamin C, including lots of fruits and vegetables, may block the cancer-causing agents in nitrites. Remember that the fat and salt content of smoked foods is enough reason to limit your intake.

Hot dogs CAUTION: Made from beef, chicken, veal, or pork, hot dogs are still one of the highest-fat meat choices. Even those labelled "lean" or "lite" are still loaded with fat, containing 9 to 12 grams of fat each, compared with 13 to 18 grams of fat for regular hot dogs. Hot dogs made with chicken or veal are not necessarily lower in fat because the manufacturers use the darker meat and often the chicken skin.

Cold cuts CAUTION: Traditional packaged cold cuts are loaded with fat and sodium. Many are made from dark meat, skin, and high-cholesterol organ meats. Brands advertise "80% fat free," but that is fat by weight—such a product gets 77 percent of its calories from fat and has as much sodium in 1 serving as your daily requirement! Look for cold cuts that have 1 gram of fat or less per serving. You're better off with fresh sliced turkey from the deli counter. Avoid cold cuts containing nitrates, colour, and additives.

Fish Aisle

Supplies B vitamins; excellent source of protein; good source of potassium; fat is polyunsaturated; higher-fat fish contains vitamins A and D

SUPERFOOD: One of the healthiest forms of protein is fish. It is low in sodium and contains less saturated fat than red meat or chicken. A 4-ounce (120 g) serving of a white fish has 146 calories, 2 grams of fat, and 54 milligrams of cholesterol; the same size serving of beef would have 250 calories, 10 grams of fat, and 102 milligrams of cholesterol.

Eat fish at least twice weekly to reap its benefits as a heart-healthy food. It contains omega-3 fatty acids, which can be responsible for lowering blood cholesterol, triglyceride levels, and the risk of heart disease. Fatty acids may play an important role in protecting the body from free radicals, preventing cancer, and slowing tumour growth. Some of the latest research also suggests that fatty acids help lessen depression by balancing the hormones affecting our moods.

Lean fish include cod, halibut, snapper, sole, mussels, squid, swordfish, and shellfish. Omega-3 is found in fattier fish, such as salmon, trout, mackerel, albacore tuna, sea bass, and sardines. The most popular fish in North America is canned tuna, but fresh fish offers more omega-3 fatty acids and tastes better. Avoid deep-fried fish, including Japanese tempura.

Here are some tips on buying fish:

- Fish should be shiny and not have a fishy odour.
- If the fish is whole, then the eyes should bulge and look clear. Cloudy eyes indicate that the fish is not fresh.
- Prewrapped fish you find in the supermarket is not always the freshest choice.
- If buying frozen fish, be sure it is clear of freezer burn and is vacuum sealed.
- If buying a whole fish, ask the fishmonger to "butterfly" it, removing the backbone and larger bones while still keeping the whole fish intact. You can just stuff and serve fish prepared in this way.
- If you get the fish home and it feels slimey or has a slight odour, rinse with cold water for a couple of minutes.
- Be sure the pieces of fish are similar in size and weight so that their cooking times will be the same.
- For ultimate freshness, cook the fish the day you buy it.

Canned Fish   Canned varieties, such as salmon, tuna, sardines, and anchovies, have similar nutrients to fresh but usually have double the calories and ten times the fat due to the oil they are packed in. If using canned fish, buy fish packed in water.

Shellfish
Low in calories; excellent source of protein and iron; have a significant amount of B vitamins and iron; contain zinc and copper

Shellfish include shrimp, clams, mussels, lobster, crab, and scallops. Shellfish can contain higher amounts of cholesterol and more sodium than other fish, but they are still more nutritious than meat or poultry because the fat is unsaturated.

A popular fish product called surimi is more commonly known as imitation crab. It is perfect for anyone with a shellfish allergy, since it is usually made from a mix of white fish, including Alaskan pollock, a deep-sea white fish. The skin and bones are removed, and the fish is ground, washed, and strained. The disadvantage of this product is that salt, sugar, and other flavours are added along with binders such as egg white or starch, so it's not the purest form of fish. It has no omega-3 fatty acids, but it has 75 percent less cholesterol than shellfish, is rich in protein, and has very little fat. It is already cooked and is great to use in salads.

Legumes Section

Rich in complex carbohydrates; high in fibre; low in fat; excellent source of plant protein; contain protein, calcium, iron, zinc, magnesium, and B vitamins

In this area of the supermarket you'll find canned and dried beans, peas, and lentils. Peanuts are also in the legume family. A legume is a seedpod that splits on two sides when ripe. These foods have lots of advantages:

- They are the only high-protein food that contains fibre.
- They can help lower cholesterol levels and aid in the fight against cancer, diabetes, and heart disease. Studies by the American Heart Association have shown that people who ate legumes at least four times per week had a 19 percent lower risk of coronary disease.[1]
- They are good for diabetics because legumes are digested slowly, thereby requiring less insulin than other carbohydrate-rich foods.

Most beans are considered incomplete proteins, except for the soybean, which is a complete protein. In order to get a complete protein, add any grain to any bean. Beans and rice make a complete protein, as do bread and peanut butter.

Some of the more common varieties of beans include chickpeas, red and white kidney beans, navy beans, lima beans, soybeans, black beans, black-eyed beans, split peas, and green, red, and brown lentils.

Canned Beans vs Dried Beans

There is nothing like the flavour of fresh-cooked beans. They are perfect in salads or added to a cooked dish at the last minute.

Canned beans are convenient to use. Just be sure to rinse and drain them well to get rid of the brine. Leftover beans can be stored in the refrigerator up to 3 days, or you can freeze them in tight containers for later use in soups, stews, or any dish that is cooked.

Dried beans have to cook, and this is a lengthy process. The traditional way is to soak the beans overnight, drain the water, and then cook them in fresh water until they are tender. The time required varies according to the bean. You can also try the quick-soak method: cover the beans with water, bring to a boil, cover with a lid, and cook for 1 minute. Leave the beans covered for 1 hour, drain and change the water, and cook the beans until tender.

Soy

SUPERFOOD: Soy is the only plant-based food that is a complete protein. It is considered one of the healthiest foods available.

Tofu
High in protein; contains B vitamins, zinc, iron, and calcium; contains isoflavones (responsible for pre-serving estrogen in the body)

Tofu or soybean curd is made from curdled soybean milk and is a main source of protein in Asian countries. A serving of 1/3 cup (75 mL) of tofu would replace a 3-ounce (90 g) serving of meat, fish, or chicken and contain no saturated fat, no cholesterol, and fewer calories.

Tofu comes in a variety of textures. The firm kind is wonderful as a substitute for meat or chicken and great in stir-fries or casseroles. This kind of tofu is the highest in protein, calcium, and fat. The medium- or- softer-textured types are great for dips and sauces; the silken tofu is great used in desserts, in milkshakes, and where a creamy milk texture is desired.

A daily intake of 25 grams of soy protein has health benefits:

- Soy protein can reduce high blood cholesterol levels by 10 to 15 percent, which may cut the chances of a heart attack.

- Studies show that soy can reduce the risk of cancer, including lung, colon, rectal, stomach, and prostate cancers.

- Soy products fortified with calcium help reduce the risk of osteoporosis.

- Research into soy's effect on people with diabetes has found less glucose in the urine of those who consumed soybeans. This is a positive development since people with diabetes have difficulty absorbing glucose.
- Soy foods may reduce the symptoms of menopause.

Other Soy Foods

If you do not enjoy tofu, a great variety of other soy products are available in the stores today that are as delicious as they are versatile.

Fresh soybeans (edamame) These are the newest trend in Japanese restaurants. Fresh soybeans look like lima beans but have a sweet, nutty flavour. Enjoy them as a snack or as part of a meal. Buy them frozen and boil them for a minute. Serve with sea or kosher salt.

Dried soybeans or canned soybeans These are great by themselves or added to soups or salads. The dried version must be soaked before being cooked, as with other beans.

Dried roasted soybeans Enjoy these as a snack, but remember that they are high in calories.

Soy flour It can replace up to one-third of the regular flour in recipes, and 1/4 cup (50 mL) of soy flour contains 190 calories and 9 grams of fat.

Soy milk A non-dairy beverage, soy milk is used in place of regular milk. Buy soy milk that is enriched with calcium and vitamin D. It comes in various flavours.

Soy cheese, yogourt, and sour cream These are all made from soy milk. Use them as you would the regular products.

Tempeh Tempeh is a chunky, fermented soybean cake made with rice or other grains. It can be marinated, grilled, or used in soups or casseroles.

Miso A fermented soybean paste, miso can be used in soups, dips, sauces, and marinades.

Ground soy Use this product in place of ground beef.

Soy burgers, hot dogs, and salami These are soy alternatives to the regular meat products.

Canned, Processed, and Frozen Foods Section

Fresh food always has better texture and taste than canned or frozen foods, but at times it's difficult to have fresh foods on hand. Canned, frozen, or processed foods can have excess fat, salt, and preservatives. Read the nutritional labels and look for products that have less then 15 grams of fat per serving, less than 400 calories per serving, and less than 800 milligrams of sodium per serving.

Surprisingly, frozen vegetables can be more nutritious than fresh ones, which may take days or even weeks to arrive on your shelves. When food is frozen, the nutrients are more potent since little time has elapsed between the picking and the freezing.

Canned food is a different matter. It has fewer nutrients, often salt and other additives are included to preserve the food, and the texture and taste of canned food are inferior. Having certain canned foods on hand makes cooking easier, more efficient, and less expensive. Acceptable canned products are canned tuna packed in water (not oil), canned soups (but avoid those that are cream based or have excess sodium), tomato sauces that contain ripe tomatoes, legumes, and fruit packed in its own juice.

Prepackaged or canned soups are often primarily made of water, which is why they are low in calories. They are usually loaded with sodium and, if cream based, with cholesterol and fat. Stick to vegetable- and stock-based soups that are low in sodium.

CAUTION: Packaged foods often contain excess sodium, fat, artificial colouring, and chemicals to preserve them. Today you can find more varieties than ever. Prepackaged lunch meals, often made up of processed cheese, meats, and cookies or a chocolate bar, are available. The serving size is small and the calories can exceed 400, with 25 grams of fat. Frozen meals are also loaded with fat, calories, sugar, flavour enhancers, starchy fillers, and sodium.

CAUTION: Manufacturers use transfatty acids in packaged foods to extend their shelf life and increase flavour. On packages of such foods as cookies, crackers, and cakes, transfatty acids will be called hydrogenated or partially hydrogenated vegetable oil, so beware.

Snack Aisle

CAUTION: This is the area you must avoid if you're hungry. Cookies, crackers, and potato and tortilla chips can contain hydrogenated vegetable fat or can be deep-fried and contain excess salt. Crackers can have as much fat as cookies.

Don't omit this area, just use it ever so carefully and always in moderation. Here are some of the better snack choices:

• popcorn (either home-popped or low-fat microwave varieties)

- pretzels

- baked tortilla chips

- fruit bars and lower-fat granola bars

- cookies such as animal crackers, digestive, or arrowroot, which don't have as much sugar and fat as other cookies

- low-fat crackers like Ry-Krisp, Melba toast, and rice cakes

- salsa, or home-made dips instead of commercial dips

Products with Hidden Sugar and Empty Calories

Name/Description	Quantity	Calories	Grams of Fat
Beverages			
Beer	12 oz/375 mL	150	0
Canned soft drink	8 oz/250 mL	100	0
Fruit juice, pure	8 oz/250 mL	150	0
Kool-Aid	8 oz/250 mL	100	0
Candy			
Fruit Roll-Up	1 roll	50	trace
Licorice Twizzlers, cherry	4 pieces	140	trace
Nibs candy	22 pieces	140	1
Cereals			
Granola, low-fat	1/2 cup/125 mL	210	3
Granola, regular	1/2 cup/125 mL	300	10
Kellogg's Corn Flakes	1 cup/250 mL	100	0
Kellogg's Rice Krispies	1 cup/250 mL	120	0

Beware of Hidden and Low-Fat Products

Name/Description	Quantity	Calories	Grams of Fat
Cakes			
Betty Crocker SuperMoist Yellow Cake	1/12 cake	270	13
Entenmann's Chocolate Cake	1/6 cake	500	20
Entenmann's Coffee Cake	1/10 cake	250	7
Entenmann's Fat-free Devil's Food Cake	1/6 cake	200	0
Entenmann's Pound Cake	1/6 cake	200	7
Pepperidge Farm Frozen Carrot Cake	1/8 cake	310	17
Sara Lee Frozen Cherry Cheesecake	1/4 cake	350	11
Sara Lee Frozen Chocolate Cake	1/4 cake	330	16
Weight Watchers Frozen Chocolate Cake	1 serving	200	6
Chips and popcorn			
Fritos, original	32 chips	160	10
Potato chips, baked	15 chips	120	2
Potato chips, regular	15 chips	150	10
Tortilla chips, regular	6 chips	140	6
Popcorn, air popped	1 cup/250 mL	31	0
Popcorn, oil popped	1 cup/250 mL	55	3
Cookies and bars			
Fig Newton	2	110	3
Granola bar, chocolate chip	1	150	5
Granola bar, low-fat chocolate chip	1	110	5

Name/Description	Quantity	Calories	Grams of Fat
Kellogg's Pop-Tart, blueberry	1	210	7
Kellogg's Pop-Tart, low-fat chocolate	1	190	3
Marshmallow Puff	1	90	4
Nabisco chocolate chip cookie	3	170	8
Oreo cookie, regular	3	180	8
Oreo cookie, fat-reduced	3	130	3
Snackwell cookie	2	110	2

Candy

Name/Description	Quantity	Calories	Grams of Fat
3 Musketeers bar	1	260	8
Hershey's Cookies 'n Cream bar	1	230	13
Chocolate-covered peanuts	10	210	13
Jelly beans	10 large	104	0
Fruit leather	1 large roll	73	1

Ice cream and frozen yogourt

Name/Description	Quantity	Calories	Grams of Fat
Baskin-Robbins ice cream, chocolate	1/2 cup/125 mL	150	10
Baskin-Robbins ice cream, jamoca almond fudge	1/2 cup/125 mL	150	8
Baskin-Robbins frozen yogourt	1/2 cup/125 mL	140	3
Ben and Jerry's ice cream, butter pecan	1/2 cup/125 mL	270	21
Ben and Jerry's sorbet, strawberry	1/2 cup/125 mL	110	0
Breyer's light ice cream	1/2 cup/125 mL	110	1
Häagen-Dazs ice cream, chocolate	1/2 cup/125 mL	282	19
Häagen-Dazs ice cream, cookie dough	1/2 cup/125 mL	298	19
Häagen-Dazs frozen yogourt, chocolate	1/2 cup/125 mL	160	3
Colombo frozen yogourt, non-fat chocolate	1/2 cup/125 mL	50	0

Name/Description	Quantity	Calories	Grams of Fat
Colombo frozen yogourt, French vanilla	1/2 cup/125 mL	100	0
Dairy Queen vanilla cone	1 medium	330	9
Dairy Queen chocolate-dipped vanilla cone	1 medium	490	24
Dairy Queen Chocolate Blizzard	1 medium	950	36

Donuts

Name/Description	Quantity	Calories	Grams of Fat
Dunkin' Donuts donut, chocolate	1	250	14
Dunkin' Donuts cookie, chocolate chunk	1	200	10
Dunkin' Donuts muffin, chocolate chip	1	400	16
Dunkin' Donuts muffin, low-fat blueberry	1	230	2

Packaged lunches

Name/Description	Quantity	Calories	Grams of Fat
Oscar Mayer Lunchables, bologna	1 pkg with drink	520	28
Oscar Mayer Lunchables, pizza	1 pkg	330	15

Frozen entrées

Name/Description	Quantity	Calories	Grams of Fat
Banquet Extra Helpings, chicken parmigiana	1 meal	650	33
Banquet Extra Helpings, fried chicken, all white meat	1 meal	820	44
Banquet Extra Helpings, Salisbury steak	1 meal	740	46
Chi Chi's beef burrito	1 meal	570	17
Healthy Choice beef macaroni	1 meal	210	2
Healthy Choice sesame chicken	1 meal	240	3
Old El Paso frozen burrito, bean and cheese	1	300	9
Weight Watchers chicken cordon bleu	1 entrée	230	4.5
Weight Watchers lasagna with meat sauce	1 entrée	270	7

Name/Description	Quantity	Calories	Grams of Fat
Fast food			
KFC crispy chicken breast	1	470	27
KFC crispy chicken quarter	1	560	36
KFC hot chicken wings	6	471	33
McDonald's Big Mac	1	560	31
McDonald's Chicken McNuggets	9 pieces	430	26
McDonald's Egg McMuffin	1	290	14
McDonald's french fries	1 large order	450	22
McDonald's Quarter Pounder with Cheese	1	530	30
Mrs. Field's Cookies brownie	1	420	20
Mrs. Field's Cookies chocolate chip cookie	1	240	12
Mrs. Field's Cookies peanut butter cookie	1	240	13
Pizza Hut personal pan pizza	1	630	24
Pizza Hut pepperoni pizza	1 slice	350	17
Pizza Hut cheese pizza	1 slice	300	14
Subway 6-inch sub, cold cuts	1	378	13
Subway 6-inch sub, turkey	1	289	4
Subway 6-inch sub, meatball	1	419	16
Taco Bell bacon cheeseburger burrito	1	570	31
Taco Bell bean burrito	1	380	12
Taco Bell chicken fajita wrap	1	470	22

Nuts

Great source of protein and unsaturated fat; significant source of vitamin E and fibre; contain calcium, zinc, magnesium, potassium, iron, and B vitamins

Nuts are high in nutrition. The greatest drawback is that they are loaded with calories and fat grams —approximately 160 calories and 16 grams of fat per ounce! Rather than having nuts as a snack, which allows you to overeat, toss a small amount into your recipes.

Herbs and Spices Aisle

In terms of healthier cooking, one of the best things you can do is reduce the amount of salt you use. Salt can lead to high blood pressure and other illnesses. The salt habit is not an easy one to break if you've been using salt as your main seasoning agent for years. One of the best ways to wean yourself off salt is to experiment with different herbs and spices.

Fresh vs Dried

I'm always asked whether I prefer fresh to dried herbs. There's no question that fresh herbs are always a wonderful taste experience, but you must remember to add fresh herbs only at the end of the cooking or as a garnish. If you add them during the cooking process, fresh herbs will lose most of their flavour and texture. For a more intense flavour, use dried herbs in cooking and fresh herbs as a garnish.

Dried herbs must be fresh. When shopping for them, buy small amounts that you'll use in a short time; otherwise they lose their intensity over time. How do you know when a herb is no longer flavourful? Easy—just smell it. If it has no fragrance or you even have trouble finding the scent, toss it out. Dried herbs that have lost their rich green colour and have turned grey, are past their prime.

A Directory of Herbs and Spices

Allspice I use this in baking, barbecuing, and jerk cooking.

Basil Basil is grown in a variety of flavours, from lemon basil to purple basil. Choose leaves that are fresh and fragrant. Wrap leaves in a slightly damp towel, place in a plastic bag, and refrigerate. Chop basil just before using it, or the leaves will turn black. I use basil to flavour tomato dishes, chicken, cheese, fish, pasta, stews, salads, and vegetables. The dried herb adds a more intense flavour to dishes.

Bay leaves The dried and fresh leaves can be used to flavour soups, roasts, poultry, tomato, and spaghetti sauces. Remove bay leaves from your dish before serving.

Caraway seeds These are commonly added to rye bread and cabbage dishes.

Chives Chives have a delicate onion flavour. They can be refrigerated for up to one week in a plastic bag. It's best to use scissors to cut chives, as a knife will bruise them. They are best with potatoes, vegetables, eggs, salads, sauces, fish, and soups—in other words, almost anything. I use whole or chopped chives to garnish dishes.

Cilantro, coriander, or Chinese parsley The fresh herb is commonly used in Mexican, Tex-Mex, Indian, Asian, and Thai cuisine. This is one of those herbs that you either love or hate because it has a very distinct flavour. If you find the flavour too intense, substitute parsley or basil. Wrap the leaves loosely in a plastic bag and place in the refrigerator. If you place the stems in a container of water in the refrigerator and change the water every few days, the coriander will last up to two weeks.

Coriander seed Coriander seed, which is not the same as the fresh herb, has a lemony flavour and is best used for foods that cook longer than one hour, such as roasts, or foods cooked for shorter times at high temperatures.

Chinese five spice This mix is used in many Chinese recipes. It is a combination of cinnamon, star anise, anise seed, ginger, and cloves.

Cinnamon Sold either in sticks or ground, cinnamon can be used in desserts, baked goods, and different ethnic cuisines. Keep it in an airtight container.

Cloves Cloves are used to sweeten desserts and also for pickling and barbecuing.

Cream of tartar Most often used to stabilize egg whites when beating them to the soft or firm stage, cream of tartar can also be used to reduce the discoloration of cooked vegetables.

Cumin This pungent spice is often added to Indian, Mexican, Asian, Middle Eastern, and Latin dishes. Use small amounts until you adapt to its taste.

Curry This common Indian spice is actually a blend of several spices, including pepper, turmeric, coriander, cumin, cardamom, ginger, nutmeg, fennel, cinnamon, cloves, and saffron.

Dill Dill has a very refreshing and slightly sweet taste. It's best used with fish or in potato salads, sour cream dips, salad dressings, and pickles. As a substitute for fresh dill, dried dill is fine if it is fresh and has a vibrant green colour.

Fennel seed This herb, which is used in Italian cooking, adds a licorice-like flavour to foods.

Garlic Garlic has a sweet, pungent flavour that adds intensity to food. It goes well with meat, fish, lamb, chicken, salads, dressings, sauces, vegetables, and almost anything but dessert! You can buy fresh garlic in the vegetable aisle, or you can buy powdered garlic or freshly chopped garlic preserved in oil. I always prefer the fresh garlic heads, but I do keep a jar of preserved garlic in the refrigerator for emergencies. Use twice as much preserved garlic as you would fresh, since the intensity of the jarred version is milder. The powder is good to use as a dry rub for meat, and it's best to use 1/4 teaspoon (1 mL) garlic powder to replace one garlic clove. Don't crush garlic and marinate it yourself for any longer than a couple of days. Bacteria can form and cause food poisoning. Crush extra garlic, freeze it in ice cube trays, put it into a small plastic bag, and use the frozen garlic as needed.

Ginger Powdered ginger is primarily used for baking, whereas the freshly grated root is used in Asian, Thai, and Indian cuisine. Fresh ginger should show no signs of cracking or withering, which indicate that the root is not fresh. Unpeeled ginger can be refrigerated for up to three weeks. Peeled ginger can be refrigerated for up to three months if stored in a tight container. I often grate a batch, freeze it in ice cube trays, and store in plastic bags.

Lemongrass This is a Southeast Asian herb that is also used in India and China. Lemongrass is becoming more common in supermarkets. Its lemony flavour is good in soups, sauces, and stir-fries. The greener the stalk, the fresher it is. It freezes very well, or you can wrap it in foil and refrigerate for up to two weeks. If you can't find lemongrass, you can always substitute lemon peel.

Mint This herb has a cool refreshing flavour. Choose mint with evenly coloured leaves and store in a glass of water, stems down. Cover with a plastic bag and refrigerate. Use mint for salads, lamb, fish, poultry, cucumbers, jellies, beverages, and desserts.

Nutmeg In Europe, nutmeg is commonly sprinkled on top of baked goods and cocoa. It is also used in baking and to flavour sauces for pasta, especially cream sauces.

Onion powder This is a great dry rub for meats you plan to roast or barbecue. Use 1/2 teaspoon (2 mL) of onion powder in place of 1/4 cup (50 mL) of freshly chopped onion.

Oregano This herb has a robust strong flavour. Look for fresh leaves with no spots, and keep fresh oregano refrigerated for a few days in a plastic bag. Oregano is best with tomatoes, meat dishes, tomato-based sauces, Greek dishes, and other Mediterranean cooking. The dried herb will give you a more intense flavour than the fresh herb and should be used during the cooking process. Fresh oregano is always best added at the end of the cooking or as a garnish.

Paprika This spice comes in hot and sweet varieties. Hungarian sweet paprika is the best spice for goulash, baked chicken, and adding colour and a sweet flavour. Also use paprika as a garnish.

Parsley This herb has a delicate celery-like flavour. Italian, or flat-leaf, parsley is stronger than the curly variety. Parsley is wonderful with all dishes because it enhances flavour and appearance. For a more intense flavour, substitute basil, dill, or coriander for parsley. Use parsley as a garnish.

Poppy seeds These tiny seeds are used in baking, either in cakes or as a topping for breads or rolls.

Peppercorns Peppercorns come in many varieties: black, white, green, pink, and Szechuan. Black pepper is the strongest and is picked before the berries are ripe. Often I buy a combination and grind them together. Freshly ground peppercorns give the best flavour.

Rosemary Rosemary adds a strong minty flavour to pork, lamb, chicken, fish, and vegetable dishes. Use it in moderation. Look for sprigs that are fresh and not drying out. Place them in a plastic bag and refrigerate.

Saffron This is one of the most expensive spices in the world because of the labour involved in harvesting it. Saffron is the red stigma of the flowering crocus, and each flower provides only three threads of saffron. It's used to flavour and colour Indian, Spanish, and northern European dishes. It gives the dish a rich golden colour, as in paella.

Sage The flavour of sage can best be described as aromatic and woodsy. This is a favourite herb for flavouring poultry, pork, and sausages.

Sesame seeds These are sprinkled on top of breads and rolls and are also used in Asian and Japanese cooking for flavour or as a garnish. The seeds taste better if toasted. Place sesame seeds in a frying pan; on a high heat, cook them just until slightly browned, approximately 2 minutes. Mixtures of white and black sesame seeds are sold that are beautiful to use in sushi dishes or as a garnish.

Tarragon This herb has a mild licorice flavour and is a favourite flavouring for poultry, fish, and many French dishes.

Thyme A spicy yet sweet flavour characterizes thyme. It is a great addition to poultry, pork, fish, marinades, soups, and roasts.

Vanilla Vanilla is found in either the whole bean or extract form. It is used to flavour desserts. Avoid artificial vanilla extract, which leaves an aftertaste.

Sauces and Condiments Aisle

Avoid sauces and dressings made with butter, cream, or excess oil. Read the labels carefully. The order of ingredients tells you the primary ingredients in the product. Choose lower-fat versions of salad dressings and mayonnaise. Also beware of high levels of sodium, such as those found in soy sauce and mustard.

Mayonnaise Choose the lighter brands and use mayonnaise sparingly. Add some Dijon mustard or wasabi for extra flavour. Mix with low-fat yogourt or sour cream to reduce the calories and fat. Avoid artificial mayonnaise.

Ketchup Ketchup is high in sodium and sugar.

Peanut butter Purchase peanut butter that is made from peanuts only. The other types often contain icing sugar and are hydrogenated, which means this naturally wonderful food becomes saturated. If the oil rises to the top, just mix firmly until blended. Do not pour the oil off, since it is the natural oil from the peanuts.

Salad dressings A single serving of regular Caesar salad (the kind on many restaurant menus) can contain as much as 600 calories and 35 grams of fat. In just 2 tablespoons (25 mL) of regular bottled salad dressing there are approximately 120 calories and 12 grams of fat! Use lower-fat varieties.

SUPERFOOD: Salsa Chopped tomatoes, onions, lemon, herbs, and hot peppers are combined in this low-fat condiment. It is great with baked tortilla chips, as a topping for potatoes or burgers, and even as a salad dressing.

Hold the Mayo: Restaurants and Fast-Food Outlets

In the past 20 years we have become a society that regularly dines away from our homes. The number of restaurants, fast-food places, and takeout establishments has grown at a rapid pace. Let's be honest: eating out can be a lot easier, more convenient, and sometimes even cheaper than preparing meals at home. One of the reasons why North Americans have become an obese society, though, is because we eat out so much. Eating in restaurants and fast-food outlets often means eating foods that are high in fat and low in nutrition. Usually, if the meals are inexpensive, then the quality of the food is inferior as well. Fattier and cheaper cuts of meat are used in these meals, and more fat and sodium are added for flavour. People love fried, salty foods because they taste so good, but they are not good for you.

Making the Right Choices When Dining Out

Believe it or not, you can indulge in lower-fat delicious food when eating out if you know how to make the right choices and choose restaurants that serve a variety of food. To do so, you need a little knowledge and a few techniques. You'll have to avoid restaurants that have a limited menu, such as the fish-and-chips restaurants or burgers-and-fries outlets, but even many of these may offer healthier choices.

Do you often overeat when eating out? You know you should stop eating when you're almost full, but you have the "clean off your plate" syndrome. You undo the button of your pants or unbuckle your belt. Sound familiar? Knowing when to stop eating is another challenge for many people. If leaving food on your plate seems wrong, why not ask to take the leftovers home?

Making healthy food choices when eating out requires some planning, discipline, and nutrition 101 information.

Planning

If you're going out for dinner, then plan your eating for the rest of the day accordingly. For example, when dinner out will be Italian food, skip the pasta and excess bread at lunch to avoid consuming too many carbohydrates. Before going to a steak house for dinner, eat little protein during the earlier part of the day.

Discipline

If you need to lose weight, then don't go to the restaurant with the idea that this is a special treat and you can stuff yourself until you can't move. Have something special at dinner, but don't overdo it, even if the occasion is a special one. Bingeing is never wise because soon, rather than later, you'll be bingeing even when it's not a special occasion. Eat lightly during the day when you know you'll want to eat large quantities later in the evening.

Nutrition 101

Be sure to have some nutrition ammunition at your side when you dine. Know that eating the entire contents of the bread basket will put you over the limit in the grains category of Canada's Food Guide. Order a lower-fat protein, such as fish or chicken breast, if you're watching your weight.

The good news is that many food establishments today are offering healthier choices of foods on their menu due to the public's increasing concern about health. If the restaurant doesn't offer healthier choices, then ask for some specific food items or dishes prepared in a certain way. Most restaurants will try to cater to you.

Six Rules for Dining Out

Rule #1

Before ordering your meal, ask the server exactly how it is prepared. Some of the cooking terms that indicate a lower fat and calorie content are grilled, steamed, poached, roasted, broiled, and baked. The menu won't always say whether the item is made with cream or butter. You may think that a soup described as a creamy vegetable soup is vegetable based and can't possibly be fattening. Think again! That soup could contain tons of oil, butter, or cream. Just ask! Naturally, it's best to stay away from the fried foods because of the excess oil they contain. Even a roasted or grilled dish can have lots of fat added to it. I always ask that as little fat as possible be used to prepare my meals.

Rule #2

Always ask if your meal comes with a sauce. Don't avoid sauce, but ask for it to be served on the side so that you can control the amount you eat. Most restaurants add much more sauce than necessary, and many sauces are made from butter, cream, oil, and cheese. Two tablespoons (25 mL) of sauce can add 15 grams of fat to your meal. Don't get extreme about avoiding sauces or dressings. Have some at your side, but control how much you eat.

Caesar salads are one of the greatest high-fat culprits and can contain over 600 calories and 38 grams of fat! I'll order Caesar salad in a restaurant but ask for the dressing on the side. Then I add no more than a couple of tablespoons. If the server tells you that the Caesar salad is already mixed, order another type of salad or a stock- or vegetable-based soup.

Rule #3

Try to remember what the leanest cuts of meats are and stick to them. Remember that chicken breast is leaner than the thigh; lean beef cuts, such as flank steak, fillet, tenderloin, and steaks with the fat removed, are lower in saturated fat then beef or pork ribs; game meats are lower in saturated fat and calories than other meats; and fish is always a great choice as long as it's not deep-fried.

Some types of fish are lean, but the fattier fish, such as salmon, sea bass, and tuna, have heart-healthy omega-3 fatty acids that actually help to lower the bad cholesterol (LDL) in your blood. People also get concerned about the amount of cholesterol in shellfish. The latest studies show that eating shellfish will not raise your cholesterol levels if you consume protein in moderation. It's best to have no more than 6 to 8 ounces (180 to 240 g) of protein per day.

Rule #4

Most restaurant and takeout foods have loads of sodium (salt) added to them to enhance their flavour and make you thirsty and keep coming back for more. Sodium is the leading cause of high blood pressure and can lead to heart attacks and strokes. Simply not adding salt at the table will not limit your sodium enough when you eat out because a large amount of salt is added to food prepared in restaurants. Stay away from marinated, pickled, smoked, cured, and canned foods if possible, which all contain large amounts of salt. Avoid bottled or prepared sauces, seasonings, and marinades.

Rule #5

Try to balance your meal when you eat out. For example, if you're having a pasta dinner that consists only of grains, then put the bread basket on someone else's table. Add vegetables and some protein to your pasta to make your meal nutritionally balanced. If you're having a steak for dinner, then avoid any appetizer with protein. Enjoy some bread or baked potato with your steak, and always have some vegetables.

Rule #6

This is the toughest rule of all: the moment you know you've eaten enough (you always know when that time has come), either ask the server to take away your plate, get up yourself and put it on an empty table, or ask the server to pack the leftovers for you to take home. Enjoy them the next day, not later that night! You know you hate the feeling of having overeaten, you know what you'll feel like the next morning, and you know what the scale will say the next day. So have some willpower!

Types of Restaurant Food: The Good and the Bad

Italian Food

Nothing satisfies my family more than a trip to the local Italian restaurant. What do we all love most? Naturally the pizza, fettuccine Alfredo, Caesar salad, and garlic bread. Many of the dishes you love are probably the worst for you in terms of fat and calories, but you can still indulge in some fabulous Italian fare if you choose carefully.

Higher-fat Italian Food

Caesar salad

1 dinner-plate-sized serving—up to 600 calories and 38 grams of fat

Traditionally, this salad contains between 1/4 and 1/3 cup (50 to 75 mL) of dressing. Ask for the dressing on the side and add no more than 2 or 3 tablespoons (25 to 45 mL). You'll reduce the calories and fat in the salad by at least half.

Garlic Bread

1 slice—up to 250 calories and 18 grams of fat

Garlic bread is usually saturated with oil, butter, and cheese. Ask for some focaccia bread instead and dip it in a little olive oil, which is usually supplied at your table.

Pizza

2 slices with cheese and pepperoni—600 calories and 30 grams of fat

The bread, tomato sauce, vegetables, and a modicum of cheese are fine; the sausage, salami, extra cheese, and extra-thick crust are not. If possible, ask for loads of vegetables and a moderate helping of cheese on a thin crust. This made-to-order pizza makes all the difference in the world.

Antipasto salad

6-ounce (180 g) serving to 520 calories and 26 grams of fat

These salads are usually loaded with smoked meats, oil-drenched olives and vegetables, and high-fat cheeses and sausages. Stay clear of these salads since most of the items in them are saturated with oil. Instead, try some roasted peppers or other grilled vegetables with a drizzle of olive oil.

Fried calamari

4 ounces (120 g)—200 calories and 10 grams of fat

These are absolutely delicious, but remember that they are deep-fried, which turns this lean seafood into a higher-fat choice. Four ounces (120 g) of plain calamari contain only 100 calories and 1 gram of fat. Ask for calamari sautéed or grilled.

Pasta

Pasta, a complex carbohydrate, is healthy and low in fat, depending what you put on it. Keep away from the cream sauces, as in fettuccine Alfredo, that are loaded with butter, cheese, and heavy cream. Order pasta served with a tomato, pesto, or stock-based sauce. Also avoid pasta dishes that include high-fat meats such as sausage or duck. Choose chicken, lean beef, and fish or seafood pasta dishes instead.

Tortellini, ravioli, manicotti, cannelloni:

1 cup (250 mL) tortellini—up to 260 calories and 6 grams of fat

Most of these pasta items are filled with cheese or higher-fat meats. If you really enjoy these dishes, then have an appetizer portion with tomato sauce rather than a sauce made with cream or butter.

Lasagna:

6-inch (15 cm) square—550 calories and 20 grams of fat

Lasagna is usually loaded with too much cheese and meat sauce. Go for a vegetable-based lasagna that has a tomato, not a cream, sauce. Have an appetizer portion of lasagna instead of a full meal.

Fettuccine Alfredo:

2-cup (500 mL) serving—700 calories and 58 grams of fat

This dish is better known as heart attack on a plate!

Chicken or veal Parmesan

12-ounce (360 g) serving—500 calories and 21 grams of fat

The problem with these dishes is that the meat is always breaded and fried. Ask the server if the cook can sauté, grill, or bake the meat and serve it with the tomato sauce and cheese. If that's not possible, order chicken cacciatore or meat served with a tomato or stock-based sauce.

Risotto

1-cup (250 mL) serving—525 calories and 10 grams of fat

This classic Italian dish is usually made with a lot of butter and cheese. Request that the risotto be made just with stock, no butter, and add the Parmesan cheese yourself. If the risotto can't be made this way, it's better to ask for a pasta or simpler rice dish.

Tiramisù

3-inch (8 cm) square—520 calories and 32 grams of fat

The only rich dessert that Italian cuisine is known for is tiramisù. This is dangerous territory. Tiramisù is made with mascarpone cheese, which can contain up to 45% MF. Share an order with the other people at your table or, better yet, have biscotti or an ice.

Lower-fat Italian Foods   I often start a meal at an Italian restaurant with a large salad, dressing on the side, or with a minestrone soup. Having these healthy foods first will start to fill you up so that you won't overdo it with the pasta and garlic bread. Here are some other good choices:

- Mussels marinara
- Grilled calamari
- Steamed clams or mussels
- Pastas with a tomato, pesto, or stock-based sauce
- Meat or fish in a tomato, wine, or stock-based sauce
- Thin-crust pizza with vegetables and minimal cheese
- Fruit sorbet, Italian ice

Chinese Food

Chinese cuisine has certainly come a long way. In North American restaurants, a Chinese meal used to be egg rolls, sweet and sour chicken balls, and fried rice. Those items were the least healthy for you because they were fried or deep-fried and contained an excess of sodium and fat, the latter often lard.

Fortunately, today Chinese cuisine includes a much wider range of healthier foods, among them many more vegetables. Stir-frying, which uses less oil than deep-frying, has become common and has reduced the fat and calories contained in Chinese food. You still have to make wise choices, however.

Higher-fat Chinese Food

Egg rolls

1 egg roll—170 calories and 6 grams of fat

These tasty morsels are always deep-fried. Most of the calories and taste come from the oil. The filling is usually healthy and consists of vegetables and meat. Ask for a baked egg roll, it available.

Egg drop soup

The egg in this dish makes it high in cholesterol and fat. Try another stock-based soup made without eggs.

Fried rice

2 cups (500 mL)—640 calories and 22 grams of fat

The rice is usually sautéed in lots of oil, or often in lard. The rice, vegetables, and meat are not fattening, but the excess fat is. Have either steamed rice or only a small portion of fried rice.

Sweet and sour dishes

Dinner-plate-sized serving—660 calories and 10 grams of fat

Any meat or fish in sweet and sour sauce has usually been deep-fried. Have a stir-fry instead.

Spareribs

6 ounces (180 g)—800 calories and 60 grams of fat

Spareribs win the prize for being the fattiest food in a Chinese restaurant. This cut of meat has the most fat and calories of any meat. Have one or two spareribs as an appetizer, but avoid having them as your main meal.

Watch out for MSG, an ingredient that causes unpleasant side effects in some people. Most Chinese restaurants today are omitting this flavour enhancer. Soy sauce is loaded with sodium. Use the lighter version of soy sauce or use soy sauce sparingly.

Lower-fat Chinese Food   Choose these healthy dishes when you go out for Chinese food:

- Hot and sour soup
- Chinese vegetable or wonton soup
- Stir-fried dishes made with a minimum of oil
- Chicken, seafood, vegetable, and tofu dishes
- Steamed fish or chicken
- Steamed white rice with some soy sauce and vegetables

Indian Food

Indian cuisine can be quite healthy because of the amount of complex carbohydrates—lentils, chickpeas, vegetables, and various breads—it contains. With the addition of yogourts, various spices, and chutneys, Indian meals can be low in fat and calories. But ghee, which is clarified butter, or coconut or palm oil, both of which contain saturated fat, are used to prepare many Indian dishes.

Higher-fat Indian Food

Coconut milk–based soups

1-cup (250 mL) serving—450 calories and 40 grams of fat

Coconut milk, a major ingredient in Indian cooking, contains saturated fat. One-quarter cup (50 mL) has 110 calories and 11 grams of fat. Ask instead for soups that are stock- or tomato-based.

Samosas

These are fried vegetable and meat turnovers. The fillings are usually potatoes, meat, and other vegetables. The deep-frying makes samosas a high-fat choice.

Curries

These too are usually made with coconut milk or cream, which both contain saturated fat. Ask for a curry made without these ingredients. Other choices are available.

Lower-fat Indian Food   Indian dishes can be healthy. Try these:

• Bean or lentil soups, which are usually stock- or tomato-based
• Tandoori chicken, beef, or fish dishes that are baked in a yogourt sauce
• Shish kebabs—meat, fish, and vegetables baked or grilled with spices
  and a marinade
• Rice pilafs and steamed rice
• Fruit and vegetable chutneys

French Food

Traditionally, this has always been a high-fat cuisine due to the use of butter, cream, and cheese. The traditional sauces are hollandaise, béchamel, and béarnaise. Today, however, French cuisine has become a nouvelle cuisine, one with a lighter and healthier approach to cooking. Lighter sauces are often wine- or tomato-based.

Higher-fat French Food

Quiche Lorraine

1 slice—up to 460 calories and 24 grams of fat

This pie consists of a buttery pie crust filled with a creamy custard containing cheese, meat such as ham or bacon, and vegetables.

French onion soup

1 cup (250 mL)—up to 460 calories and 40 grams of fat

This soup is delicious but, when topped with loads of cheese, becomes one that is high in saturated fat and calories.

Cream-based soup

1 cup (250 mL)—up to 350 calories and 29 grams of fat

Vichysoisse and other creamy soups contain heavy cream (35% MF) and butter, ingredients commonly used in French soups. Beware of puréed vegetable soups, which often contain these sources of saturated fat.

Fondue

Fondues are the crème de la crème of French cooking. If you're looking for foods with the highest calorie and fat content, then don't look any farther. Cheese and chocolate fondues head the list. Both are loaded with saturated fat. The foods that you dip in the fondues are fine, but the fondues themselves can kill you.

Duck, goose, and pâtés

1 ounce (30 g)—up to 180 calories and 17 grams of fat

These meats are high in fat and are often eaten with the skin, which is also high in saturated fat. Pâtés are made from meat, but cream or butter is added to give the pâté a smooth and creamy texture.

Gratin dishes

Gratins are prepared with lots of cheese and buttered breadcrumbs.

Lower-fat French Foods   These French dishes are good choices:

- Consommés made from meat, chicken, or fish stock
- Fish or chicken made with wine sauces not containing butter
- Poached or steamed fish dishes

Japanese Food

Japanese restaurants have been popping up all across North America, especially because people love sushi. Japanese cuisine generally involves a low-fat method of cooking emphasizing fish, vegetables, soy, and rice. The only negatives are the deep-fried dishes and the high amount of sodium used in Japanese sauces.

Higher-fat Japanese Food

Fish or vegetable tempura
Tempura is always deep-fried in a thick batter. Avoid dishes prepared this way.

Fried tofu (bean curd)
3-1/2 ounce (105 g) serving—270 calories and 22 grams of fat

When tofu is fried, its healthy benefits are outweighed by the excess fat used in the frying. Have tofu in another dish that is not fried. An equivalent serving of plain tofu contains only 75 calories and 4 grams of fat.

Avocado
1 avocado—300 calories and 30 grams of fat

Avocado—which is really a fruit, not a vegetable—is commonly used in Japanese salads and sushi dishes. Eat avocado in moderation.

Lower-fat Japanese Food

- Miso soup—a fish-based soup with soybean paste, tofu, and seaweed
- Sushi and sashimi—sashimi is raw fish minus the sushi rice
- Yakitori—shish kebabs of meat, chicken, or fish
- Shabu-shabu—sliced meat with noodles and vegetables
- Teriyaki dishes with meat, seafood, or tofu
- Steamed rice
- Tofu that has not been fried

When I go to a Japanese restaurant, before I order the main meal I always order a salad with the dressing on the side and a miso soup. These appetizers contain little fat and few calories, so you don't go overboard with the meal.

Mexican Food

With the amount of vegetables and complex carbohydrates in Mexican food, it should be healthy for you, but often many of the dishes contain excess fat, cheese, and sour cream or are deep-fried.

Higher-fat Mexican Foods

Tortilla chips, taco shells

1 ounce (30 g) of tortilla chips (about 8 chips)—150 calories and 8 grams of fat

1 taco shell—70 calories and 4 grams of fat

These are both deep-fried. Ask for the baked versions, but they may not be available.

Refried beans

These beans are often fried in lard. Opt for fresh or canned beans if you can.

Quesadillas, burritos, enchiladas

1 flour tortilla with cheese, sour cream, and fattier meats – over 400 calories and 20 grams of fat

These are the main dishes served as Mexican food in much of the United States and Canada. The problem with them is that often they are prepared with large quantities of cheese, sour cream, and higher-fat meats. Ask for the basic tortilla with fillings on the side so that you can make your own.

Guacamole

1/4 cup (50 mL)—240 calories and 24 grams of fat

This creamy avocado spread is fine if you don't eat too much of it. Avocado is higher in calories and fat than any other vegetable. The good news is that the fat is not a saturated fat. With 300 calories and 30 grams of fat per avocado, you have to eat this delight in moderation.

Taco salad

1 salad—over 600 calories and 30 grams of fat

These salads are served in a fried tortilla shell and are loaded with guacamole, sour cream, and cheese.

Lower-fat Mexican Food   Here are some choices that will help you avoid the fat in Mexican food:

- Baked tortilla chips served with salsa and lower-fat sour cream
- Fajitas, a soft taco, or a burrito made with chicken, beef, or seafood and lots of vegetables, with added salsa, low-fat sour cream, and a small amount of cheese
- Gazpacho—a tomato-based vegetable soup
- Vegetable-based burritos and enchiladas with small amounts of cheese
- Salads with the dressing on the side

Fast Food

This is currently one of the fastest growing businesses. People today are always in a rush and have no time to prepare food or even sit down for a meal. Fast-food restaurants serve us quickly, are inexpensive, and cater to North American tastebuds. Many of the foods they serve are high in fat and calories, but if you examine the menu carefully, you will find plenty of lower-fat healthier choices.

Higher-fat Fast Food

Burgers

Try to avoid burgers because the meat used in them is usually high-fat ground beef. Asking for the works—cheese, mayonnaise, and bacon—makes the burger a sky-high option in terms of calories and fat. Look what happens when you add cheese to a typical fast-food burger:

> Double burger with cheese—530 calories and 28 grams of fat
> Cheeseburger—320 calories and 14 grams of fat
> Chicken burger with cheese—530 calories and 25 grams of fat
> Quarter-pound burger with cheese—530 calories and 30 grams of fat

Mayonnaise-based sandwiches

2 tablespoons (25 mL) mayonnaise—200 calories and 22 grams of fat

Mayonnaise-based sandwiches include fish and chicken sandwiches and often double-decker beef burgers. The mayonnaise adds a considerable amount of saturated fat and lots of calories. Also watch out for tuna- and egg-salad sandwiches, which can be full of mayonnaise.

Fried chicken nuggets or fish fingers

6 nuggets or fingers—300 calories and 18 grams of fat

You can see that these foods are high in calories and fat. Grilled chicken breast is a much better option.

Pizza

1 slice thick-crust pizza with the works—350 calories and 17 grams of fat

Thick-crust pizzas covered with extra cheese and processed meats are loaded with fat and calories. A thin vegetarian pizza slice has only 186 calories and 7 grams of fat.

French fries

1 large order—450 calories and 22 grams of fat

These have to be among the fast foods highest in calories and fat. No one can ever have just a few french fries. Often the oil they are fried in is hydrogenated, and thus a form of saturated fat.

Nachos with cheese sauce

3 ounces (90 g) tortilla chips (about 20 chips) and 1/4 cup (50 mL) cheese sauce—500 calories and 34 grams of fat

These are doubly bad for you: the nachos are deep-fried tortilla chips, and the sauce is made from processed cheese and is loaded with saturated fat.

Hot dogs

1 regular-sized hot dog—150 calories and 15 grams of fat

Hot dogs are another not very nutritious food loaded with saturated fat. They contain poor-quality meat and nitrates, which are cancer-causing agents.

Sub sandwich

1 meatball or pizza sub—over 450 calories and over 20 grams of fat

Stick to the roasted turkey or chicken subs, and load them up with vegetables on a whole-wheat bun. This alternative has only 250 calories and 4 grams of fat.

Fried chicken

Quarter chicken (including the drumstick and thigh)—over 400 calories and 30 grams of fat

Avoid fried chicken completely, and instead have roasted or grilled chicken without the skin.

Fried chicken wings

4 wings—800 calories and 52 grams of fat

Avoid these completely too. The same quantity not fried contains 480 calories and 28 grams of fat. These are still not good nutritionally, but if you love wings, then those that are not fried are a better choice.

Lower-fat Fast Food   When you do eat fast food, choose these items:

- Bagel with light cream cheese or a small amount of peanut butter
- Grilled chicken with loads of vegetables and mustard or ketchup on a bun
- Thin-crust vegetable pizza
- Veggie burger that is not deep-fried
- Vegetable salad with lower-fat dressing
- Baked potato with vegetables, grated cheese, salsa, and light sour cream
- Fajitas and stir-fries
- Shish kebabs and rice
- Pastas with tomato sauce
- Frozen yogourt and low-fat ice cream

Delicatessen Food

These restaurants feature Eastern European fare. In the traditional diet of that part of the world, higher-fat foods indicated wealth. Forget about that today. Smoked meats, such as corned beef, pastrami, and salami, are not only loaded with saturated fat but also contain cancer-causing agents called nitrates. Kishke, a stuffed casing, is loaded with chicken fat and gravy, and latkes, or potato pancakes, are fried in tons of oil. No aspect of these foods is positive except that they are extremely tasty. My advice is to have the occasional deli sandwich, perhaps when you go to Carnegie Deli in New York City! Or better yet, try dishes such as lean roast beef or turkey breast sandwiches, chicken soup with some noodles, and rye or pumpernickel bread instead of challah, an egg-based bread.

Pickles are loaded with salt and olives contain a lot of calories and fat. A corned beef or pastrami sandwich made with 6 ounces (180 g) of meat contains 600 calories and 38 grams of fat. A similar sized roasted turkey or chicken sandwich contains only 350 calories and 8 grams of fat.

Buffet Food

I had an acquaintance who once called buffets "garbage up" dinners. And they can be. Most people don't make wise choices at buffets. They usually offer lots of healthy food items, but we all love the higher-fat dishes.

What attracts people to a buffet is not only the amount and variety of food, but the price. One single item on a menu can be double the price of the buffet!

At a buffet, try to start with the salad, crudités, and stock- or tomato-based soups. You'll begin to fill up. Then go back for the protein, vegetables, and grains. Leave a little room for dessert, selecting only one higher-fat item. Make the rest lower-fat choices, such as fruit or sorbet.

Higher-fat Buffet Food   Buffets offer lots of fat if that's what you're after:

- Salads made with mayonnaise and oils—pasta salads, potato salads, coleslaws, Caesar salads, marinated vegetables
- Pastas and main course items made with cream sauces
- Fried foods—vegetables or meats
- All the pastries at the dessert buffet

Lower-fat Buffet Food   Do yourself a favour and stick to these wise choices at buffets:

- Stock- or tomato-based soups
- Salads and vegetables with no more than 2 or 3 tablespoons (25 to 45 mL) of dressing, preferably one low in fat

- Fruits
- Fish, meat, or chicken, preferably grilled or baked without sauces unless tomato- or stock-based
- Pastas in tomato sauce
- Baked potatoes with a little cheese and lower-fat yogourt or sour cream
- Stir-fries
- White or whole-grain rice without oils or fat

Dining at Other People's Homes

Having a meal in someone's home can be difficult for many health-conscious people because they want to be a "good" guest. Don't worry about being so good; pay more attention to your eating habits and health. You can still stay on track when you eat at someone's home, but beware of the appetizers and alcohol at the beginning of the evening. The calories in them add up very quickly, often amounting to more calories than are in the upcoming dinner!

A selection of appetizers, which are often deep-fried or loaded with butter, oil, cheese, or cream, and two glasses of wine can contain over 1400 calories and 32 grams of fat! (Forget the meal!) You arrive at someone's home hungry, and you indulge in these tasty morsels and a few drinks. Alcohol causes the blood sugar level to rise quickly and produce more insulin, which will make you hungry sooner and leave you nutritionally deprived. Therefore, you tend to eat more rather than less. Once the meal comes, you feel you have to be a polite guest and eat what's on your plate.

The best solution is not to arrive starving. I always have a small but nutritious snack—maybe a salad or piece of bread with some protein or some fruit and yogourt—before I leave the house. Take another look at the foods that have a lower glycemic index (see page 63) for some good choices that will satisfy you for a longer time.

If the meal is loaded with fat, try to pick out the vegetables and protein and avoid the fatty sauces. If this is impossible, don't throw in the towel and clean your plate; eat most of the meal and get back on track tomorrow. By limiting the appetizers and alcohol, you can indulge more in the dinner and dessert.

Things to Remember When Dining Out

Keep these important points in mind when you dine out:

- In general, try to strike a balance between some of the higher-fat foods that you can't resist and the lower-fat foods that you know your body needs for health and a better body weight.

- Don't abandon your healthy style of eating when you go out for dinner. You must try to stick to it most of the time or you'll never control your food intake and weight.

- Above all, be assertive in restaurants. You're paying for the meal, so demand some concrete answers that will make it easier for you to eat healthily. Ask how the food is prepared and whether the cook can make certain foods the way you like them.

- Always pay attention to portion sizes because many restaurants serve portions that are big enough for four people. Wrap up what you don't want, and enjoy it the next day for lunch.

- If the situation really is impossible, enjoy the meal without stuffing yourself and get back on track the very next morning.

Holiday Eating

For many people, holidays are a problem, but they don't have to be. I meet so many people who gain between 5 and 10 pounds (2.3 and 4.5 kg) on their holidays either because they feel they don't have healthy choices or because they've already paid for the meals and feel they'd better get their money's worth! Is it really worth gaining the weight, which is so difficult to take off later? No. You'll feel great if you come home from a holiday having either lost weight or maintained it. All the rules of eating in a healthy way apply to holiday eating. Holidays are not an excuse to "garbage up" or for not exercising. Often people say that being on holiday means being on holiday from exercising too. Forget it! Exercise is just like brushing your teeth or taking a shower—part of your daily routine.

Eating When You Travel

No matter whether you travel by plane, bus, train, or car, most of the food available to you on the way is of poor quality. Be prepared, and either eat before you go or take along some easily carried food. I always pack fruit, vegetables, or some sandwiches prepared at home.

The Light Kitchen

Now—not tomorrow—is the time to transform your existing "higher-fat" kitchen to a healthy "light" kitchen. Learning how to lessen the fat in your cooking takes some knowledge of several aspects of cooking, including essential ingredients, various cooking terms, different methods of cooking, the cookware used, and techniques for lowering the fat. Once you're armed with this information, you can make any recipe light.

Once You Get Groceries Home

After the grocery shopping expedition we took in the last chapter, here are some tips on how to store your healthy food once you get it home.

In general I like to read the expiry date on products when one is displayed. The date refers to the date by which it's best to use the product for maximum freshness. I also like to use my senses of smell, sight, and taste to judge the quality. There are no hard and fast rules.

I like to wash all fruits and vegetables under running tap water just before eating them or preparing them for cooking. Washing with soap is not needed. If you want to remove dirt or wax more thoroughly, you can buy a fruit and vegetable wash, which works very well. For convenience, you can buy greens that have been prewashed and dried. They are either labelled "prewashed" or "triple-washed" and do not need to be washed. They are quite safe to eat.

Storing Staples

Baking powder and baking soda Both can be kept in the pantry unopened for up to eight months, and once opened for between three and six months. Baked goods that do not rise as usual may indicate that you should replace your supply of these ingredients.

Butter This can be kept in the refrigerator for up to three months and for up to nine months in the freezer. Margarine can be kept slightly longer.

Canned goods These can be kept for up to five years in the pantry, but once opened canned goods must be kept in the refrigerator for up to 5 days, or frozen in airtight containers if they are to be used later in cooking.

Cereal Keep unopened cereal in the pantry for up to one year; once opened, use cereal within six months.

Coffee Unopened packaged coffee will keep for up to two years; use coffee within a month once the package has been opened. Keep tightly covered. You can freeze coffee to lengthen its shelf life.

Condiments Most condiments, if unopened, can be kept in the pantry for a year or more. Opened condiments can be refrigerated for six months or longer.

Eggs It's best to keep eggs in the original container instead of in the egg container on the refrigerator door. Use eggs within three to five weeks. Leftover egg whites or yolks can be kept for up to 5 days. The whites can be frozen for up to a year. Four yolks can be beaten with 1/4 teaspoon (1 mL) salt or 1-1/2 teaspoons (7 mL) sugar and frozen for up to four months.

Flour White flour can be kept unopened in the pantry for up to one year and once opened for up to eight months. Whole-wheat flour is more delicate and can be stored for only for one month in the pantry but for up to eight months if refrigerated.

Jams and jellies If unopened, jams and jellies can be stored for one year in the pantry; once opened, refrigerate them for up to six months.

Meat Raw meat should be kept in the coldest part of the refrigerator for up to 2 or 3 days. Poultry keeps only 1 to 2 days, and fish or seafood for 2 days. Cooked meat can be kept for up to 4 days or in the freezer for up to four months if wrapped properly. Cold cuts can be kept for up to 5 days in the refrigerator and in the freezer for up to two months. Hot dogs can be kept for up to a week and frozen for two months or longer.

Pasta and rice Unopened, these grains can be kept in the pantry for up to two years; once opened, use within one year. Other grains, such as quinoa, millet, spelt, or bulgur, are more delicate. I store these grains frozen for up to one year and use them as needed.

Peanut butter This can stay in the pantry unopened for up to one year and in the refrigerator opened for up to three months. Replace peanut butter that has a rancid smell.

Sugar Store sugar in the pantry. It never spoils.

Vegetables Each vegetable has different storage requirements, but always store them in the vegetable crisper and use them within 5 to 7 days. Don't wash vegetables before storing. If you plan to store them in a plastic bag, make some holes in it first so that the vegetables can "breathe."

Vegetable oils Keep unopened oil in the pantry for up to eight months; once opened, keep oil in a dark, cool place for up to six months. Oils do not need to be refrigerated.

Stocking Your Light Kitchen

To start, you must have some essential ingredients, which make all the difference in the world. When you begin to cook dinner, how frustrating it is not to have the basic ingredients in your pantry, refrigerator, and freezer! Being organized is really the first step to creating a light kitchen.

The Light Pantry

Canned or Bottled Goods   Your pantry should include some basics, including condiments:

- beans of all varieties, especially chickpeas, white and red kidney beans, black beans, and soybeans
- canola and olive oil
- vegetable sprays
- lower-fat salad dressings
- lower-fat bottled sauces
- light coconut milk (never use regular coconut milk, which is high in saturated fat)
- tomato paste
- a variety of tomato-based pasta sauces
- tuna packed in water
- a variety of vinegars, such as balsamic, cider, and red wine vinegar
- condiments such as ketchup, sweet chili sauce, salsa, hot sauce, plum sauce, Dijon mustard, light mayonnaise, and low-sodium bouillon cubes or powder

Herbs and Spices   These are some of the more common dried herbs and spices to keep in your pantry: basil, oregano, bay leaves, thyme, rosemary, cumin, curry, pepper, cinnamon, dill, chili powder, sesame and poppy seeds, and paprika. I like to have fresh herbs on hand: Italian parsley, dill, coriander, and basil. Make sure you store them properly. (See "Don't Go to the Supermarket without Me" pages 142–145.)

Baking Products   Light desserts—and even savoury foods—are no-fuss if you have the following in your pantry:

- all-purpose flour
- baking powder and baking soda
- cornstarch
- white and brown sugar
- icing sugar
- unflavoured gelatin
- unsweetened cocoa

The Global Pantry   I like to think of my pantry as the "global" pantry—a cupboard in which I can always find an ingredient from world cuisines. Keeping a supply of some staple ingredients will allow you to prepare a variety of interesting dishes. You should be able to find these ingredients in most supermarkets.

Asian pantry   The more common ingredients are long-grain rice, sushi rice, soy sauce, sesame oil, rice wine vinegar, hoisin sauce, oyster sauce, fish sauce, plum sauce, hot chili sauce, black bean sauce, rice noodles, nori (seaweed), wasabi (Japanese horseradish), canned baby corn, canned water chestnuts, canned mandarin oranges, ginger, garlic, and sesame seeds.

Mediterranean pantry   A Mediterranean pantry should be stocked with canned tomatoes, tomato paste, black and green olives, roasted red peppers in water, anchovies, Dijon mustard, seasoned breadcrumbs, cornmeal, Arborio rice, sun-dried tomatoes, basil, oregano, bay leaves, a variety of canned beans, olive oil, and balsamic vinegar.

Mexican or Latin American pantry   Having on hand a variety of canned beans, as well as jalapeño peppers, baked tortilla chips, avocado, salsa, light sour cream, flour tortillas, rice, and lower-fat cheeses, will enable you to make some interesting and easy dishes.

Middle Eastern pantry   Healthy and interesting dishes are easy if you have available chickpeas, tahini (sesame paste), bulgur, couscous, brown rice, pitas, cumin, and fresh coriander.

North American pantry   Basic ingredients include different kinds of pastas, lower-fat cheeses, pasta sauce, lean meats, and condiments such as mustard, ketchup, sweet chili sauce, light mayonnaise, and low-fat sour cream.

Vegetarian pantry I love to prepare vegetarian meals occasionally for my family. You don't have to be a vegetarian to enjoy a meatless meal. Having a variety of grains, vegetables, sauces, and soy products in your pantry allows you to produce excellent vegetarian meals. Some useful ingredients for vegetarian cooking include firm and soft tofu; ground soy to substitute for meat products (the Yves brand is recommended); soy products such as bacon, hot dogs, hamburgers, and pepperoni slices; and soy milk, yogourt, cheese, sour cream, and cream cheese to substitute for dairy products.

Breads and Grains

Remember to keep basic breads and grains on hand:

- whole-wheat sliced bread (keep extra loaves in the freezer)
- flavoured tortillas, pitas, and sandwich buns, preferably whole-wheat products (keep extras in the freezer)
- cold cereals containing extra fibre, dried fruits, and little sugar
- hot cereals such as Cream of Wheat or oatmeal
- lower-fat granola and Grape Nuts cereal for baking
- rice: brown, white, and wild
- pasta of various varieties
- grains: barley, quinoa, millet, and wheatberries (buy these grains in bulk and freeze them)

Stocking Your Refrigerator and Freezer

Fresh Fruits and Vegetables   Keep fruits you enjoy on hand for easy nutritious eating: apples, bananas, grapes, oranges, grapefruit, lemons, pears, peaches, melons, berries, and so on.

Vegetables are great for salads, side dishes, snacks, and cooking, particularly in stir-fries. Some common ones to have around are asparagus, broccoli, cauliflower, carrots, celery, cucumbers, green beans, green onions, lettuce, mushrooms, onions, bell peppers, potatoes, sweet potatoes, and tomatoes.

Dairy   Keep these basic dairy products in your refrigerator:

- unsalted butter (freeze extra)
- non-hydrogenated, soft tub margarine

- lower-fat hard cheeses (freeze large blocks to grate for cooking)
- lower-fat cottage and ricotta cheeses
- light cream, goat, and feta cheeses
- lower-fat sour cream and yogourt
- eggs, large size
- containers of egg whites
- milk, 2% MF or lower

Meat and Alternatives   Have some of these meats and alternatives available in your freezer or refrigerator:

- lean ground beef, chicken, or turkey (in the freezer)
- boneless chicken breast, chicken legs and breasts with bone, and whole chickens (in the freezer)
- lean steaks (in the freezer)
- soy products: firm and soft tofu, ground soy to replace meat, soy cheese, soy hot dogs, and soy burgers and slices (in the refrigerator)

Frozen Foods   Make sure that your freezer contains these:

- frozen vegetables of your choice
- frozen yogourts or sorbets
- frozen cheese or vegetarian pizzas

Cookware

I'm asked constantly what type of cookware is the best. Many types of cookware are available today, and they range in quality and price. Choose cookware according to your needs: when my children were in their experimental cooking stages, I purchased inexpensive nonstick cookware; once the non-stick coating was damaged by metal utensils, I just bought another set, going through three sets a year. Now that the children are finished experimenting, I own a good-quality set that will last for years.

Let's look at some of the important aspects to consider when buying cookware:

- Purchase a good-quality set of nonstick frying pans, saucepans, and baking pans. They allow you to cook using only vegetable spray or a minimal amount of oil, water, or stock. Some of the better known brand name nonstick coatings are Teflon 2 and Silverstone, and some of the improved coatings are T-Fal and Silverstone Extra. These coatings are carbon-fluorine polymers that are inert, so nothing sticks to them and they don't react to acids in foods.

- Choose heavier pans that will last longer and conduct and retain the heat better. There are also no hot spots with heavier cookware. Some of the better brands of nonstick cookware include All-Clad, Lagostina, Cuisinart, and Calphalon, to name a few. Use regular cookware (not nonstick) for any type of cooking not requiring sautéing.

- To avoid scratching your nonstick cookware, don't use an abrasive cleaner or metal utensils. Once the pans have been scratched, they don't work as effectively and food cooked in them may be unhealthy (see Cookware Safety, below). Buy nonstick utensils that are sturdy, well designed, and useful.

- If you want to give food a grilled appearance, use a nonstick grill pan or an electric grill. You won't have to step outside in the winter to do the barbecuing, and food cooked in them is delicious and low in fat.

- Cast-iron pans have made a comeback. The most important thing to remember is to "season" your cast-iron pan before using it so it will cook better and last longer. Brush all surfaces of the pan generously with vegetable oil. Place the pan in a 350°F (175°C) oven for 2 hours. Wipe the pan again with vegetable oil and return to the oven, this time with the temperature at 200°F (100°C). Your pan is now seasoned, but will always require special care. After cooking, place your pan immediately in hot water and avoid using soap, if possible. Dry the pan and wipe it with a little oil.

Cookware Safety

Materials from your cookware can leach into your foods, especially if the cookware is scratched.[1] Keep these safety facts in mind:

- Stainless steel is safe for cooking and storing food and is the most popular type of cookware. Often it is coated with nonstick coatings.

- The connection between aluminum cookware and Alzheimer's disease is still unproven. Adults can consume at least 50 milligrams of aluminum daily without harm. Only 1 to 2 milligrams of the aluminum in your cookware would be absorbed.

- Copper cookware is coated with another metal to prevent the copper from coming in contact with the food. Do not use copper pots that do not have this coating.
- Nonstick coatings are chemically inert, which means that they pass through the body without breaking down or being absorbed.
- Certain glazes used on ceramics, especially those designed to be fired at low temperatures, may release lead and cadmium into food or liquids placed in them. North America has strict guidelines about using toxic materials.

Cooking Methods

The following is a listing of various cooking methods for lower-fat cooking. Take note that deep-frying is no longer in our cooking vocabulary, since food cooked this way becomes saturated in oil, fat, and excess calories. To see the difference in cooking methods: four fried chicken fingers can contain 200 calories and 11 grams of fat; baked they are approximately 100 calories and 1 gram of fat! So pay attention to the cooking methods you've been using and make some healthy changes.

Cooking in Liquid

Steaming　This method involves cooking food over boiling water—holding the food above the water to cook in the steam. It is one of the best methods for retaining nutrients. Steamed vegetables lose 50 percent fewer nutrients than boiled vegetables.

Boiling　To preserve the nutrients in foods, boil them in as little water as possible and add them when the water is boiling. Save the nutrient-rich water to use in soups.

Poaching　This is simmering a food in a liquid that is kept just below the boiling point. Eggs and fish are commonly poached.

Stewing　Stewing is a method used to cook tougher cuts of meat at a slow, gentle boil to make them more tender. This is a great way to cook inexpensive cuts of meat.

High-Heat Cooking

Even though barbecuing, grilling, sautéing, and broiling are low-fat forms of cooking, some health hazards result if meat gets crispy or charred. When smoke is created by burning fat, cancer-causing chemicals called polycyclic aromatic hydrocarbons (PAHs) are formed. When you plan to use these cooking methods, always choose leaner cuts of meat, fish, or chicken to reduce your exposure to these carcinogens.

Grilling or Barbecuing   This popular form of cooking is inherently low in fat and calories. I use either a barbecue or a nonstick grill pan that can be placed on the stove. Today virtually every food is being put on the grill.

To protect yourself from carcinogens, be sure you don't let your food catch fire; choose the leanest meats, fish, and poultry; barbecue slowly; raise the grill as far from the coals as possible; and don't let your food touch the flames.

Broiling   This is cooking at 500°F (250°C) for a short time. Sweet bell peppers are charred in this manner, and bread can be toasted. Toppings are browned for a few minutes under the broiler.

Frying and Sautéing   Frying uses excess oil, which translates into foods that are higher in fat and calories. For lower-fat cooking, this is not an appropriate method.

Sautéing requires a small amount of oil to cook foods. Using a nonstick frying pan and some vegetable spray, I sauté vegetables, meat, or fish. This method reduces the calories and fat considerably.

Cooking in the Oven

Baking and Roasting   This is a common method of cooking meats, fish, and some vegetables. To retain moisture, bake or roast at a higher temperature, between 375°F and 425°F (190° to 210°C), for a shorter period of time. Be sure to place a rack on the bottom of the roasting pan to prevent food from sitting in the released fat. Pouring about 1/2 cup (125 mL) of stock or water into the bottom of the pan will prevent the pan from burning and provide an instant gravy for meats and chicken. Keep in mind that fat drips into the liquid.

Microwaving   This is the best cooking method to preserve nutrients. I like to microwave vegetables and fish. A microwave is also great for heating and defrosting. Use the microwave to partially cook foods before you barbecue them. Place the thickest parts of the food toward the outside of the plate; when the food is almost done, let it sit for a few minutes to finish cooking.

The basic problem with this method is cooking food for too long. The key is to microwave on High for a short time. To be safe, microwave for less time than you think necessary, and then microwave for short periods as needed.

Nutrient Loss

No matter how you cook food, some nutrient loss will result. The amount of nutrients lost will depend on the freshness of the food, how it has been handled and stored before you obtained it, how long you cook it for, and the temperature at which it is cooked. Precut produce is convenient but contains lower levels of nutrients. Here are some ways to minimize nutrient loss:

- Cook the food for the shortest time possible. Microwaving, stir-frying, and steaming are the best methods. Baking or roasting at high temperatures increase the moisture of the food but lessen the nutrient value.
- Cook vegetables whole and unpeeled, or eat them raw. Most vegetables are more nutritious when eaten raw, except for carrots, which are more nutritious when cooked.
- Never soak fruits or vegetables in water.
- Boil vegetables in as little water as possible.

Light Cooking

Once you've made the commitment to change your way of eating, some simple but important practices will make the transition successful. It may take some time until you do them without thinking, but once you do you'll never turn back.

Cooking with Dairy

Milk   Milk containing either 1% or 2% MF is excellent for cooking and baking. I don't recommend using milk with less MF because watery milk won't give your food the desired texture.

Yogourt   Yogourt that contains 1% or 2% MF is excellent for cooking and baking. Avoid the higher-fat Balkan-style yogourts, which contain 4% MF or more. When adding yogourt to sauces, be sure that the sauce is not too hot or the yogourt will curdle.

Sour Cream   Sour cream containing anywhere from 1% to 5% MF is an excellent substitute for regular sour cream, which has 14% MF. Use low-fat sour cream for cooking or baking. As with yogourt, to prevent curdling add sour cream slowly to sauces that are not too hot.

Cheeses   If you want to cook with higher-fat cheese, such as Brie, Camembert, Parmesan, Asiago, blue, or Swiss, and no lower-fat substitutes are available, then keep the quantity to no more than 1 ounce (30 g) per person. Cook dishes that contain a lot of cheese only occasionally.

Hard cheeses   Cheddar, Swiss, mozzarella, and Parmesan cheeses usually contain between 28% and 35% MF. I like to cook with cheeses that contain between 9 and 15% MF, which is a saving of at least 50 percent in calories and fat. Some hard cheeses contain as little as 4% MF, but I think they lack flavour and texture. They melt poorly and give your foods a "plastic" taste.

Ricotta cheese   Now a staple in my home for cooking and baking, ricotta traditionally contains 10% MF, but an excellent 5% MF version is available. I would not recommend using ricotta that contains less fat because the cheese will be too dry. Be sure to find a smooth, creamy ricotta cheese that will give your cooking the best texture. You can add a couple of tablespoons of milk, yogourt, or sour cream to overly firm ricotta to make it smoother.

Goat and feta cheeses   These are great for cooking because of their distinct flavours and the fact that you need very little of them to achieve an intense taste. These cheeses are lower in fat than regular hard and soft cheeses. Goat and feta cheeses usually contain 15% MF, and today you can find delicious feta cheeses that contain as little as 10% MF.

Removing Fat from Meats

Trim all visible fat from beef, chicken, pork, and other meats before cooking them. With chicken, I leave the skin on all cuts except when a recipe calls for boneless breasts. The skin protects the chicken from losing moisture and flavour. The fat does not penetrate the meat, and you can season the meat under the skin. The trick is removing the skin before eating. Cooking chicken with the skin on will add only 1 gram of fat to your dish, and the food will be that much more flavourful.

Try to reduce the amount of animal fat protein in your diet. Take a pound (450 g) of cooked beef or chicken and toss it into a salad or pasta dish that serves four so that each person eats only about 4 ounces (120 g) of animal protein. In casseroles, meat sauces, or chili, try substituting cooked grains, such as rice or bulgur, or couscous, or cooked beans for at least 25 percent of the protein.

Removing Fat from Soups and Stocks

Removing and discarding fat from soups is easy if you chill the soup until the fat solidifies on top. If a recipe calls for cream, substitute milk or evaporated milk. To thicken soups without using cream, butter, egg yolks, or a butter-and-flour mixture (a roux), use cooked vegetables that are already puréed or purée the soup.

I always have a variety of stocks on hand to cook with. They add flavour and replace the cream, milk, butter, and oil in many recipes. You can use homemade stock, or you can buy stocks canned, in bouillon cubes, powdered, as concentrates, or in tetrapacks. If using powdered stock, add 1 teaspoon (5 mL) to 1 cup (250 mL) of boiling water. I wish I had the time to make my own stock for cooking, but I don't. I purchase stocks that contain no preservatives or MSG.

Using High-Fat Ingredients in Moderation

High-fat ingredients, such as those discussed below, should not be omitted from your cooking and baking. Use them in moderation to highlight a recipe.

Nuts   Use no more than 2 ounces (60 g) or 1/4 cup (50 mL) of nuts in your cooking or baking. This amount contains 400 calories and 40 grams of fat. Toasting your nuts gives them a better flavour. A great low-fat substitute is Grape Nuts cereal, low-fat granola, or a combination of both.

Chocolate   Use no more than 1/4 cup (50 mL) chocolate chips or a 2-ounce (60 g) square in a recipe. Use cocoa as a substitute for chocolate and just as a highlight. Cocoa has all the chocolate flavour without the cocoa butter. Instead of 1 ounce (30 g) of semi-sweet chocolate in a recipe, use 1-1/2 tablespoons (22 mL) of cocoa plus 2 tablespoons (25 mL) of sugar and 2 teaspoons (10 mL) of butter, margarine, or vegetable oil. Heat the mixture until the sugar melts.

Coconut   Coconut adds a great taste and texture to cooking and baking, but keep the amounts low since coconut contains saturated fat. Toasting the coconut gives it a better flavour.

Sugar   In any recipe, you can reduce the sugar by at least 25 percent without changing the texture or flavour significantly. Try adding a pinch of spice, such as cinnamon, nutmeg, allspice, or vanilla, or almond extract to heighten the flavour.

Reducing the Fat in Desserts

You can lessen the fat by as much as 50 percent in baked goods. The trick is to maintain the moisture that fat adds to cakes and other baking. For example, the amount of oil, butter, or margarine in a recipe can be brought down to one-half or one-third of that called for by substituting fruit or vegetables—such as puréed bananas, cooked dates or prunes, applesauce, grated carrots or zucchini—for the rest of the fat. I also like to use lower-fat yogourt, sour cream, or buttermilk to replace some of the fat.

Frostings or decorations for cakes are usually made with butter, lard, cream, or vegetable shortening. Low-fat substitutions include light cream cheese or ricotta cheese. Or use icing sugar and liquid as a glaze.

Beaten egg whites add volume and tenderness to cakes and desserts without the fat. I use them in cakes, cheesecakes, and mousse recipes in which whipping cream would traditionally be used.

Using Puréed or Grated Vegetables to Replace Fat

Use puréed or grated vegetables as wonderful replacements for the fat in all kinds of dishes:

- Cooked vegetables can be used to thicken puréed soups.
- Puréed peas can be substituted for avocado in guacamole.
- Puréed or grated sweet potatoes, carrots, or zucchini are great to use in cakes or muffins.
- Vegetables can replace some of the cheese and meat sauce in lasagnas and pizzas.

Making Lower-Fat Sauces

To make a sauce without using cream or butter, mix equal amounts of milk and any kind of stock. For every 1 cup (250 mL) of liquid, add 1 tablespoon (15 mL) of flour or 2 teaspoons (10 mL) of cornstarch and mix until smooth. Heat for approximately 3 minutes, stirring constantly, until the sauce is slightly thickened. To add variety, use such ingredients as sautéed mushrooms, shrimp, or cheese. For a thicker sauce, substitute a lower-fat evaporated milk for the milk.

Making Lower-Fat Salad Dressings

Don't feel you have to omit salad dressings or resort to using only lemon juice or vinegar. Use dressings in moderation and try not to add more than 2 tablespoons (25 mL) to your salad. Using a low-fat dressing is also good, but remember still to use smaller amounts.

The better choice for dressing is homemade, for two reasons: homemade dressing tastes better, and it's usually made with less fat than store-bought dressings. I often use orange juice concentrate, flavoured vinegars, a little water, and more intense oils, such as sesame or olive oil, so that I can reduce the amount of regular oil.

Ingredient Substitutions

Using lower-fat ingredients to replace high-fat foods will help lessen calories, fat, cholesterol, and sodium in your meals. With the right substitutions, you should have an excellent, rich dish with great taste and texture. Ingredient substitution is the basis for all my recipes.

Ingredient	Lower-Fat Substitution
Whole milk	Milk, 2% MF or less
Heavy cream	Evaporated milk, 2% MF
Sour cream	Sour cream, 5% MF or less; lower-fat yogourt
Mayonnaise	Lower-fat mayonnaise, yogourt, or sour cream
Butter	Nonhydrogenated margarine or canola or olive oil
1 whole egg	2 egg whites; an egg substitute
Cream cheese	Light cream cheese; ricotta cheese; lower-fat cottage cheese
Chocolate	Cocoa (see page 177)
Ice cream	Frozen sorbet; frozen yogourt
Salad dressings	Low-fat homemade; low-fat store-bought
Pesto sauce	Low-fat recipe; mix half pesto with half light cream cheese, yogourt, sour cream, or stock
Tortilla chips	Baked tortilla chips
Nuts (for cooking and baking)	Grape Nuts cereal; lower-fat granola; water chestnuts
Salt	Herbs or non-soldium seasoning
Ground meat	Ground soy

Having Your Cake and Eating It

By using simple substitutions, you can change virtually any recipe into a healthier, low-fat version with only a minimal loss—if any—in taste or texture. Below are examples of a cake and a pasta recipe that I've transformed into lower-in-fat recipes. Experiment with some of your favourite higher-fat recipes—if you substitute ingredients properly, you should not taste a difference in the results.

By comparing the nutritional analyses of the example recipes, it's easy to see how simple substitutions can make a shocking difference in terms of calories and fat. Use the suggested low-fat substitutions above to make the necessary changes to "enlighten" your favourite recipes.

Original Recipe

Light Version

Chocolate Cheesecake

Crust	Crust
2 cups/500 mL graham cracker crumbs	2 cups/500 mL graham cracker crumbs
2 tbsp/25 mL sugar	2 tbsp/25 mL sugar
1-1/2 tbsp/22 mL cocoa	1-1/2 tbsp/22 mL cocoa
1/4 cup/50 mL butter	1 tbsp/15 mL vegetable oil
	3 tbsp/45 mL water

Filling	Filling
24 oz/680 g cream cheese	2 cups/500 mL light ricotta cheese
	4 oz/120 g light cream cheese
1 cup/250 mL sugar	1 cup/250 mL sugar
3 tbsp/45 mL flour	2 tbsp/25 mL flour
3 eggs	2 eggs
1/4 cup/50 mL whipping cream	2 egg whites
6 oz/180 g melted semi-sweet chocolate	1/3 cup/75 mL light sour cream
	1/3 cup/75 mL cocoa

Original Recipe	Light Version

Nutritional analysis

Serves 10	Serves 10
Calories per serving 511	Calories per serving 380
Fat per serving 27 grams	Fat per serving 11 grams

Fettuccine with Creamy Mushroom Sauce

8 oz/240 g fettuccine	8 oz/240 g fettuccine
3 cups/750 mL sliced mushrooms	3 cups/750 mL sliced mushrooms
1/4 cup/50 mL butter	2 tsp/10 mL vegetable oil
1 cup/250 mL heavy cream	1/2 cup/125 mL chicken stock
	1/2 cup/125 mL evaporated milk
1/3 cup/75 mL Parmesan cheese	3 tbsp/45 mL Parmesan cheese

Nutritional analysis

Serves 4	Serves 4
Calories per serving 557	Calories per serving 275
Fat per serving 25 grams	Fat per serving 6 grams

Making the Change

From the day we're born, the environmental factors around us determine how we eat and live. With motivation and determination, however, we can change this direction.

The people I meet who struggle with weight control and exercise usually share four common character traits:

- Each is capable of exercising.
- Each is familiar with the basics of healthy eating.
- Each has good intentions about making the changes that will lead to a healthier life.
- Not one of them realizes that emotional issues play a significant role in the struggle.

It's no secret how hard these people initially have to work to get on the right track to a healthier way of eating, living, and thinking. Because they struggle, they soon have control over their lives, control that they never had previously.

Making the Change with Your Family

There's no question that our parents and siblings have a great deal of influence on how we eat and exercise. They are our primary role models. What they eat affects what we eat. If they are constantly on diets, then their behaviour sets the stage for us. Similarly, if they are eating regularly and healthily throughout the day, we will absorb these values. As we grow independent of our parents, ultimately we have to stop blaming them for our weight and lifestyle issues. We realize that they may be the reason we are the way we are today, but at some point we have to move forward and make our own positive lifestyle changes. Learn from the past and don't make the same mistakes your family did.

Children and Their Eating Habits

Getting children and teenagers to eat properly and regularly is a great challenge. Keeping your children fit and healthy is a difficult, but necessary task if you want them to achieve their maximum potential in school and after-school activities.

As a parent of four children, I feel responsibile for establishing lifelong patterns of healthy eating. My husband and I have always been our children's primary role models: if we don't eat well and exercise, why would they? The earlier they start, the easier it will be for them to lead healthy lives. But in today's fast-paced world this is not an easy task. Many obstacles stand in the way, for both parent and child:

- Fast-food establishments dominate every street corner.
- Huge portion sizes are served in restaurants and as takeout food.
- Junk food is advertised everywhere.
- Vending machines are packed with chocolate bars, chips, and soft drinks.
- Labels on food packages are misleading.
- Grocery foods are highly processed.
- Watching television, using the Internet, and playing computer games are taking the place of outdoor play and exercise.
- Famililes have less time to prepare and share homecooked meals.

The Health of Our Children

Good food and exercise are the building blocks for a healthy, strong, and emotionally stable child, but consider these statistics:

- Over 25 percent of children today are considered obese (obesity is defined as being 25 percent over one's ideal weight).
- The percentage of overweight children between the ages of 6 and 17 has doubled since 1970.
- Eighty percent of overweight children between the ages of 10 and 13 will be overweight or obese adults. Puberty is the worst time for children to be overweight, and being overweight then can cause a lifetime of struggling with weight issues. Self-esteem issues are at their highest during puberty.
- Health problems—including an increase of Type 2 diabetes and of levels of blood sugar, blood pressure, and cholesterol—are associated with children's weight problems.

Helping Kids Make the Change

After raising four children, I have found some necessary steps to improving their eating habits and helping them maintain a healthy relationship with food.

- Help children develop a healthy attitude to food from an early age. We are their role models, and what we do every day from their earliest years is crucial.

- Never use food to represent rewards, punishment, or comfort. Using food in this way removes the ability of children to listen to their own body signals of when and when not to eat.

- Don't make a difference between "good" and "bad" foods: this is the wrong message to be giving your children.

- Present a healthy variety of food choices to your children and allow them to decide how much to eat. Don't reward or punish your children for their eating habits.

- Try to keep your own diet worries to yourself. Be careful about constantly reinforcing slimness and body image. Commenting on your child's weight (by harping on "being overweight" or having the "perfect" body) sends the wrong message. Children need to understand that eating well is to ensure better health, not a perfect body.

- Reinforce exercise, but do not enforce it. Again, you are the best role model. If you're not moving, why should they?

If your children have been on a high-fat, high-sugar diet of highly processed foods for years, getting them to enjoy healthier fare is no easy task. But it's not impossible. The younger they are, the easier the transition. Here are some suggestions:

- Resist buying junk food at the grocery store. This will take some willpower, but you can do it! Enjoy these foods as treats when you occasionally go out.

- Lessen the amount of fast and processed foods your family eats, saving them for the rare occasion.

- Lessen your fat intake in home cooking.

- Teach your children how to read the labels on certain foods.

- Have your children order from the adult menu in restaurants if the child's menu consists of fast and processed foods.

- Have fruit, vegetables, and grains available to your children throughout their day. These foods will fill them so that they don't rely on fast food.

- Occasionally use meat substitutes, such as soy products—great in tomato sauces, chilis, and Tex-Mex dishes—in some of your children's favourite meals.

- Make sure your children move each day. This means limiting TV or computer time.

- Have your children take part in packing their own lunch bags.

- Involve your children from an early age in the kitchen and the shopping when possible.

- Allow children to serve themselves at the table. Try not to dictate what they should eat. All you should do is provide healthy choices and be a role model.

Power Snacking   Snacking is a national tradition. Adults and children snack while we work, watch television, or have friends over, or just because we're hungry. Snacking can be a healthy way of eating since it can prevent us from overeating at mealtime. Another way to describe this way of eating is "grazing." Studies show that grazing may help prevent weight issues, but you have to graze on the right kind of food. I call it power snacking: it satisfies cravings and keeps your energy levels high, so you avoid those blood sugar drops. Here's a list of some great power snacks:

- Homemade unbuttered popcorn, made in a microwave popcorn maker or in a paper bag. For the microwave bag method, toss a handful of popcorn into a paper sandwich bag, fold the top over, and microwave for 3 minutes on high. Add seasonings by spraying the popcorn first with vegetable spray.
- Sliced vegetables with a low-fat dip. You can eat bowls of them.
- Lower-calorie fruit such as melons, berries, oranges, grapefruits, and apples. Don't overdo it because fruit contains more calories and sugar than vegetables do. Watch the watermelon, pineapple, bananas, mangos, and grapes, which due to their sugar content have more calories than other fruits do.
- Cooked or steamed vegetables. These are filling and incredibly healthy. For a ratatouille type of dish, cook the vegetables in tomato sauce and add some canned beans and Parmesan cheese.
- Vegetable-based soups made with broth.
- A bowl of high-fibre cold cereal with low-fat milk and some berries.
- Certain packaged bars that are healthy and loaded with nutrition. The best bars to have are fruit or fig bars. Be careful of the granola-type bars that can be loaded with saturated or hydrogenated fat and sugar. Read the labels.
- Pretzels and baked tortilla chips that are not fried like potato chips or corn chips.
- Animal crackers, ginger snaps, graham crackers, and crackers made with non-hydrogenated fats. These are all good choices if your kids love commercial cookies, muffins, and cakes, of which most are loaded with fat, especially hydrogenated fat, and excess calories. Baking your own lower-fat versions is always the number one choice.
- Rice cakes in a variety of flavours, such as caramel, chocolate chip, apple cinnamon, and cheese. These are delicious low-fat snacks.

- Dried fruit, such as raisins, cranberries, apricots, and dates. Remember that they are a concentrated form of calories, nutrients, and energy, which means that they are not low in calories but are a healthier alternative to high-sugar and high-fat snacks. Add 2 tablespoons (25 mL) nuts to 1/4 cup (50 mL) diced dried fruit for a quick energy snack.

- Frozen yogourt, sorbet, milk-based frozen desserts, and frozen soy-based desserts. These are better choices than ice cream.

- Lower-fat yogourts, either plain or flavoured. Avoid the artificially sweetened ones. Serve with fresh fruit.

- One ounce (30 g) of lower-fat cheese or soy cheese with whole-wheat crackers. These make a good snack.

Fruits and Vegetables   For children or adults, there's not a healthier food group than fruits and vegetables, yet it's surprising how few fruits and vegetables children are eating. According to a Heart and Stroke Foundation study, only 20 percent of Canadian children aged 6 to 12 get the recommended daily minimum of 5 servings of fruits and vegetables.

Here are some recommendations for how to get your children to add more fruits and vegetables to their diet:

- Have washed and sliced fruits and vegetables out for easy eating access. Serve fruit-flavoured yogourt as a dipping sauce for fruit, and salad dressing for vegetables. For extra protein, serve sliced vegetables with peanut butter or light cream cheese.

- Add diced fruit to your breakfast choices, such as yogourt, pancakes, cereals, and muffin batters.

- Make smoothies with fresh or frozen fruit and milk, soy milk, or yogourt—a great snack or beverage.

- Prepare the makings for tacos, burritos, or tortillas, meals that allow children to add a variety of vegetables to their diet. Have shredded lettuce, diced tomatoes, onions, bell peppers, carrots, and other vegetables ready for these Tex-Mex meals.

- Add grated or diced vegetables to standard dishes such as tomato or spaghetti sauce, soups, chilis, pasta, stir-fries, and macaroni and cheese dishes.

- Make healthier french fries when your kids badger you for fries. Slice a potato into eight wedges. Brush them with a little oil or melted butter and sprinkle with your favourite seasonings. Bake at 375°F (190°C) for about 40 minutes until browned on all sides. Try this method with sweet potatoes as well.

- Make special healthy treats. For an unusual dessert, dip a banana in a lower-fat chocolate sauce or maple syrup and coat with chopped nuts or, better still, Grape Nuts cereal. Freeze. Try slicing your favourite fruit and dipping in a warmed lower-fat chocolate sauce as a fondue.

I hope that this information will give you enough ammunition to start your child on a lifetime of healthy eating.

Making the Change for Yourself

How often do we wish for more hours in our day? Many of us put ourselves last in terms of priorities. This is why so many North Americans lead an unhealthy lifestyle.

Changes in Your Activity Level

People can come up with any number of excuses for not exercising. Here are the most common ones, along with my suggestions for how to become more active:

- Being too busy is the number one excuse. We all have commitments to work, family, or school, but if you want to live a healthier lifestyle, then you have to find some time to exercise. The best times are either before you go to work in the morning, at lunch (if you can shower afterwards), or immediately after work.
- "I'm not athletic" or "Exercise isn't for me" are other frequently heard excuses. You don't have to be Arnold Schwarzenegger to walk around the block a few times.
- Boredom steps into the picture. So many people tire of exercise after a few weeks. When you do, it's time to alter your program so you don't get bored. Do something different in your workouts to keep your interest up. Most important, to do something you like.
- "Gyms are too expensive" or "It's too far to travel" are two other justifications for lack of exercise. In most cities today there is a gym on every corner, and some of them have great rates. Nothing is wrong with doing some exercise at home to a videotape or TV show, using an exercise machine, or getting outdoors.
- Fatigue seems like a great excuse. We believe that we don't have the extra energy to exercise. You've all heard it before, but exercise will give you more energy to do more in your day. That, I promise, is true.

The key is finding an exercise that you enjoy and that raises your heart rate. Getting support from your friends and family is important too. Finding the 20 to 30 minutes in your day, four times a week, is not always easy, but, once it becomes a priority, you'll be shocked at how easy it is and the excuses will fall away. Setting realistic goals and being flexible will lead to sustained success. An all-or-nothing attitude will always result in failure.

Keeping Motivated

The greatest problem in exercising regularly is keeping the motivation. Make a realistic plan that you can stick to and you'll avoid the risk of failure. In the beginning choose only those exercises that you enjoy so exercising doesn't become a chore.

- Initially plan short realistic goals so that you succeed. For example, if you begin jogging, don't plan to run a marathon in a short time. Try to increase your distance or speed over a period of six weeks.

- Make your exercise regimen enjoyable by either doing an exercise you like or having friends join you. Joining a club might be a perfect solution—there you'll be a part of a committed group doing exercise.

- Ensure success by doing a variety of exercises or cross training, rather than only doing one type of exercise. Variety will prevent boredom and injury.

- Don't get frustrated if you have to miss a few days of exercise, for whatever reason. Frustration will lead to failure and a discontinuation of exercise. Get back on the wagon, and try to let these minor lapses happen infrequently.

- Work exercise conveniently into your day. Plan to exercise in the morning, during a lunch break, right after work, or before you retire for the day. The best and most successful times are earlier in the day. As the day wears on, too many excuses will arise for not exercising.

- Keep your exercise program short and efficient. Consistency is what's important.

Obstacles to Making Healthy Changes

If your job is stressful and your work hours long, you probably have no time for a proper breakfast and don't take the time to pack a good lunch or snack. As a result, you are faced with a choice of either fast food or long hours without eating. Most jobs are sedentary and the work schedule doesn't include any free time for exercising.

The combination of both family and work is stressful and can lead to emotional eating.

If you're a stay-at-home parent, the refrigerator and your kids' leftover meals are hard to ignore. Boring jobs around the house can lead to emotional eating.

We all understand that adopting healthy changes will lead to a better quality of life, but we seem to procrastinate and fight these necessary changes. Why?

We have set ourselves up to believe that if we reach our goal of a healthier lifestyle, then we'll be happier and solve all our problems. Subconsciously we know this is probably not the case. Eating well, exercising regularly, and reaching an ideal weight doesn't mean we'll find the perfect job, get promoted, or have the perfect family. We also set up a cycle of blaming our weight problems for our lack of success.

Stress can prevent us from reaching our goal of a healthier lifestyle. Many of us resort to an unhealthy lifestyle when we are stressed. We all need a certain amount of stress in our lives: it can make us be more focused and work better. Unfortunately, few of us know how to manage stress or recognize when we are overstressed. Too much stress can negatively affect our health. Our blood pressure can rise, which can affect our heart functions and ultimately our immune system.

Overcoming the Obstacles

Analyze your current problems without using your weight and lifestyle issues as an excuse. Try to imagine your life if you were your ideal weight. Are you really experienced enough to get that job promotion? Would the "perfect" partner you're looking for truly be compatible with your personality?

Make your working and home environment more health friendly to encourage change. The night before you go to work, plan how you can eat in a healthy way the next day. This might include brown bagging your lunch and snacks or ensuring that you can have healthier choices at the available fast-food outlet or restaurant.

If your job is sedentary, try to find ways throughout the day to incorporate exercise. For instance, walk up stairs, park your car farther from your office, or use part of your lunch break to go for a brisk walk or get to the health club. There are always healthier alternatives around the corner. And, exercise doesn't have to be done all at one go—small intervals during the day will have the same effect. But none of this will be easy unless your change your mindset.

Don't be a martyr at the office or at home—what I mean by that is, don't work around the clock, leaving absolutely no time for yourself. You'll be no good to anyone if you're continually tired and unwell. Make yourself a priority. No one ever lost a job because he or she took a 20-minute break during the day to take a brisk walk, or took the time to eat a better meal or snack.

Examine your refrigerator and pantry and make necessary changes. Buy a proper set of running shoes and take them to work or put them beside the front door as a reminder to go for regular walks.

To better manage your stress level, try to recognize those aspects of your life that are affecting your health negatively. Search for friends, a support group, or a professional to help you deal with excess stress. This means realizing what is in your control and what is not. If something is not in your control, then plan strategies for yourself so that this external stressor will be deleted or diminished.

Before you can begin to practise the art of living well, you have to be ready. Proper nutrition and weight management are the starting points to feeling great physically and mentally and, most importantly, to feeling good about yourself. I believe that when one aspect of your life begins to turn for the better, others follow and life in general is more rewarding.

Many people make abusive lifestyle choices. They smoke, take drugs, overeat, don't exercise, work too hard, or drink excessively. That kind of lifestyle becomes a vicious cycle: we abuse ourselves because we don't feel well, and because we don't feel well we continue to smoke, drink, overeat, and so on.

Change isn't easy. Habits are formed over years and are difficult to break. Before you start on the path to healthier living, you have to be mentally prepared to make a lifelong commitment.

Questions to Ask Yourself

Are you truly ready? If not, you'll find a hundred and one excuses to backslide. You must have a well thought out plan and be motivated for all the right reasons—to improve your health so that you can live a long and happy life!

Why are you losing weight? If you're losing weight for the wrong reason, you'll never keep the weight off. Wrong reasons usually include trying to please someone other than yourself.

What will "the afterlife" be like? What will your life be like after you lose weight and start exercising? If you think all your problems will disappear, think again. You may still have some problems, but your life will be healthier and more fulfilling.

Why have you failed before? If you failed in the past, determine why. Maybe it was the rigid program or too many other personal factors going on in your life. Take these experiences and build positively on them before going forward.

Are you an emotional eater? If you are an emotional eater and are finding too many excuses not to improve your lifestyle, you should try speaking to a professional. A counselor can help you understand why you turn to food, and to recognize the signals that precipitate your emotional eating.

Do you think like a dieter? As a dieter, you're either off or on a new food plan. It means you deprive yourself of certain foods. Everything becomes black and white with no grey areas. To succeed, the word "moderation" must enter into the equation. You must be ready to stop thinking like a dieter.

Are you obsessed with forbidden foods? No foods should be forbidden. If you deprive yourself, you'll only binge at a later point. Try to keep your trigger foods to a minimum and indulge occasionally.

The Five Stages of Change

Psychologists believe you have to go through five stages if you are going to make permanent life changes.

1. Pre-contemplation: You're not yet thinking about changes, but subconsciously the ideas are formulating due to outside influences and pressures.

2. Contemplation: You are aware of your specific food or weight issue, but, for whatever reason, you are not ready to change things yet. Reasons vary depending on your particular circumstances.

3. Preparation: You've now acknowledged that you want to do something positive and begin a plan of action. You become empowered by reading and by listening and talking to people who can educate you in this new area of better health.

4. Action: You begin to put the information you gathered from the preparation stage into place. This stage will be successful only if you do this of your own accord. In other words, if your doctor tells you to lose weight because of your health, this stage will fail.

5. Maintenance: The newly acquired habits become a way of life. This is the stage we all hope to reach.

You can now realize why changing your dietary and exercise habits is difficult. Theoretically, change seems easy, but we are all creatures of habit. Changing our health habits—some of which we acquired when we were very young—takes time and we can't expect it to occur overnight. That's the reason that diets fail. We want success immediately, yet our habits take much longer to change. The art of living well has to be practised before it can be mastered.

Developing a Better Attitude to Food

Most of us have a love/hate relationship with food. Eating is a pleasurable activity, bringing together family, friends, and even work colleagues. But if you are struggling with your weight, eating out becomes an activity to dread. You begin to worry about what to eat or how you'll be able to avoid the nachos or crème brûlée. Eating out is especially difficult if you're trying to adhere to the latest fad diet that limits eating foods from some food groups. If you can't control the menu and feel unable to eat and enjoy yourself, you're setting yourself up for a dismal time.

We all need food to nourish our body, keep our bones strong, and even to keep our hair, nails, and skin looking healthy. Few of us make this important association when we sit down for a meal.

Food means different things to different people. Food is used for celebrations, fun, pleasure, comfort, romance, taste, and prosperity. For some people, food represents a great challenge in life. Their emotional state is tied to food, which helps them deal with stress—food becomes a coping mechanism. To those who have been plagued by weight issues all their lives, food represents a daily struggle. For those with food disorders, food represents fear. If they eat, they fear gaining weight; if they don't eat, they fear being found out.

What Works for Me…

…might work for you. I wasn't able to change my lifestyle until I understood what was preventing me from maintaining a healthy eating and exercising regimen. It was only when I made the connection that I could begin to work toward my goal.

- I know what I like. That means any food and exercise program must fit into my specific lifestyle. What's good for someone else may not be appropriate for me, so I've customized my lifelong plan. This also means that I've taken responsibility for my life. I can't blame others if I'm not living a healthy lifestyle.

- I try to be organized on a daily basis. This means that I preplan my shopping list to avoid running out of healthy ingredients in my kitchen. If I'm on the go, then I either brown bag some foods or ensure that I can order healthier foods at the places I'm visiting.

- Before I got to where I am now, I always used to remind myself why I was changing my lifestyle (to avoid diabetes or a stroke, which afflicted my parents at a relatively early age).

- I never get to a point where I'm famished: if I did, I'd eat more, and probably poorer-quality foods. Instead, I eat every two or three hours but always in a healthy way.

- Portion control is a key factor. I believe that the only reason people eat more than the ideal portion is because they are not eating enough food or the most nutritious food throughout their day.

- I always pay attention to Canada's Food Guide.

- I never think of food in terms of "good" or "bad." I believe that every food is acceptable, within moderation. I include chocolate in my diet a few times a week, but only in moderation. By eating everything—occasionally, and in small quantities—I never feel deprived.

- I am aware of the good and bad fats in my diet (unlike food, there definitely are bad fats!). I don't eliminate fat from my diet: fat is important if it's the right kind and eaten in moderation.

- Every day I remind myself that maintaining an ideal weight and exercising really has no beginning or end. When you begin, do what I did and start slowly, without looking for noticeable changes. The important thing is to keep it up. You'll begin to feel better and have more energy and self-esteem and a better body image. You'll even feel emotionally balanced.

- If I do eat poorly, I never feel as if I've gone "off the wagon"—if I did, I'd probably say, "What the heck!" and continue to binge. Instead, I tell myself that for the rest of the day I'll try to stay on a balanced diet.

- I never forget to move during the day. Exercise has become an integrated part of my day. Consistency is more important than intensity.

- Most of the time I avoid weighing myself. I believe that the scale can be my worst enemy. So many factors can tip the scale in the wrong direction. For example, a high-sodium meal can cause you to retain water and increase your weight. Your menstrual cycle can increase your weight. Airplane travel can promote water retention. So, once again, do as I do and don't weigh yourself more than once a week or once a month. I judge my weight by other factors, such as how I feel (I generally know when I'm up or down in weight) or how my clothes fit (fitted clothes with buttons and zippers will always reveal how I'm really doing).

Maintaining Success

When you finally reach your goals, the big question is this: where do you go from here? You've been so vigilant about exercise and food. How do you let loose enough so that you don't go back to square one? The toughest part is finding the discipline, inner strength, and willpower to make eating well and exercising a natural part of your life.

• Don't deprive yourself of any one food. But be sure that a trigger food (you know the ones: potato chips, cake, cookies—anything you love to indulge in) is one that you eat only occasionally, and sparingly.

• Don't think, "Now that I've lost weight and I'm exercising regularly, I can eat whatever I like, and whenever I like." If you do, the weight will return quickly and your fitness level will decline rapidly. Remember that your plan for healthy eating, and living, is a lifetime one.

• Pay close attention to the warning signs. If you start eating later in the evening or start going long hours without food, these are indications that old habits are returning. Stay aware and get yourself back in line quickly.

• Renew your commitment to healthy living daily. Tell yourself every day why you're eating well and exercising.

Being good to yourself and satisfying your needs gives you strength to help and support others. I believe in living in the moment and finding the happiness in my life. Doing so makes every problem and challenge easier to overcome and ultimately leads to "The Art of Living Well." Good luck, and enjoy!

Rose

Now that we are equipped with all the information on how to reach the goal of living well, let's get ready to cook. The 150 recipes that follow are delicious, healthy, and easy to prepare. I enjoy serving many of them during the week to my family, and use others for entertaining purposes. These recipes have been tested on my cooking-school students, friends, and family who have given them all a "thumbs up."

The recipes are grouped as Appetizers, Soups, Salads, Sandwiches and Wraps, Pasta and Grains, Vegetable Side Dishes, Soy, Chicken, Meat, Fish and Seafood, and—of course—incredible Desserts. You can enjoy any of these dishes for just about any meal you might plan.

Enjoy—and welcome to The Art of Living Well.

Recipes

Appetizers

Asparagus Prosciutto Cheese Tortilla Slices

The taste, texture, and appearance of this appetizer is wonderful. When you slice these tortillas into rolls, you see the green asparagus against the rosy prosciutto and white cheese spread. Using a coloured tortilla adds even more visual appeal.

6 medium-thick spears of asparagus 6
3/4 cup smooth 5% ricotta cheese 175 mL
1 oz light cream cheese, softened 30 g
1 tbsp light mayonnaise 15 mL
2 tbsp chopped green onions 25 mL
2 tbsp fresh lemon juice 25 mL
1/2 tsp minced garlic 2 mL
3 large flour tortillas 3
3 leaves soft leafy lettuce 3
2 oz sliced prosciutto 60 g

1. In a pot of boiling water, cook asparagus for 2 minutes, or until tender. Drain and rinse under cold running water. Drain well.
2. In a food processor, or in a bowl using an electric mixer, beat ricotta, cream cheese, mayonnaise, green onions, lemon juice, and garlic until smooth.
3. Spread cheese mixture evenly over tortillas. Place lettuce on top. Place prosciutto on top of lettuce. Place 2 spears of asparagus near bottom of each tortilla. Roll up tightly, wrap in plastic wrap, and chill (to get the best flavour).
4. Cut each tortilla on the diagonal into 6 pieces.

Makes 18 pieces.

NUTRITIONAL ANALYSIS
PER PIECE
66 calories
3.4 g protein
2.7 g fat, total
1.1 g fat, saturated
7.1 g carbohydrates
130 mg sodium
7 mg cholesterol
0.5 g fibre

TIPS
These can be made up to one day ahead if wrapped well in plastic wrap and chilled. If you don't combine dairy and meat, you can substitute smoked salmon for the prosciutto, or even leave it vegetarian.

Beef Hoisin Mini Meatballs

These are perfect appetizers for a dinner party. Meatballs are usually made from regular ground meat, which has three times the fat and calories of these—it's the fat that makes them taste so good. In my version, I compensate by using lean ground beef with the addition of a delicious hoisin sauce.

8 oz lean ground beef 250 g
3 tbsp dry breadcrumbs 45 mL
2 tbsp hoisin sauce 25 mL
1 tsp crushed garlic 5 mL
1 egg 1
2 tbsp minced green onions 25 mL

Sauce
1/3 cup hoisin sauce 75 mL
1/3 cup red currant jelly 75 mL
1 tsp crushed garlic 5 mL
1/2 tsp crushed fresh ginger 2 mL
2 tbsp water 25 mL
2 tbsp chopped green onions, as garnish
    25 mL
2 tbsp chopped coriander or parsley,
    as garnish 25 mL

1. In a bowl, combine beef, breadcrumbs, hoisin sauce, garlic, egg, and onion. Form into 20 to 24 small meatballs about 1 inch (2.5 cm) in diameter.
2. In a large nonstick frying pan sprayed with cooking spray, cook over medium-high heat, turning, for 3 minutes, or until browned on all sides.
3. To make sauce: In a bowl combine hoisin sauce, jelly, garlic, ginger, and water. Add to meatballs; cover and simmer on low heat for 10 minutes.
4. Garnish with green onions and coriander.

Makes 4 to 6 servings.

NUTRITIONAL ANALYSIS
PER 1/6-RECIPE SERVING
150 calories
8.1 g protein
4.2 g fat, total
1.5 g fat, saturated
19.2 g carbohydrates
321 mg sodium
52 mg cholesterol
0.6 g fibre

TIPS
For a lighter version, try ground chicken, turkey, pork, or veal. The red currant jelly gives the sauce the thickness it requires—you can find it in the jam section of your super-market.

Chicken–Onion Quesadillas

Quesadillas make a great appetizer or even a small meal. The combination of chicken, sautéed onions, and feta cheese make this outstanding. Select flavoured coloured tortillas, such as sun-dried tomato, pesto, or cheese.

8 oz skinless, boneless chicken breast 250 g
2 tsp vegetable oil 10 mL
2 cups sliced onions 500 mL
2 tsp minced garlic 10 mL
2 oz goat cheese or feta cheese 60 g
1/4 cup chopped fresh coriander 50 mL
1/4 cup chopped green onions 50 mL
1 tbsp grated Parmesan cheese 15 mL
6 medium flour tortillas 6
1/4 cup salsa 50 mL
2 tbsp low-fat sour cream 25 mL

Preheat grill or grill pan. Spray with cooking spray.

1. Grill chicken over medium-high heat, turning once, for 12 minutes, or until cooked through.
2. Meanwhile, in a saucepan sprayed with cooking spray, heat oil over medium-high heat. Cook onions and garlic for 10 minutes. Remove from heat. Stir in goat cheese, coriander, green onions, and Parmesan.
3. Thinly slice chicken; stir into filling.
4. Place tortillas flat on work surface. Spread chicken mixture evenly over half of each tortilla. Fold uncovered half of each tortilla over filling and press.
5. In a large nonstick frying or grill pan over medium-high heat, cook quesadillas for 3 minutes, or until golden. Turn and cook another minute. Cut each quesadilla into 4 wedges.
6. In a small bowl, stir together salsa and sour cream. Serve with quesadillas.

Italian Pizza Rolls

I featured these egg rolls in my book *Enlightened Home Cooking,* and they were a number one hit with the kids. All the fat and calories in traditional egg rolls comes from the deep-frying. Since these are baked, you can enjoy them without the guilt! I pack any leftovers for my children's lunches.

1 tsp vegetable oil 5 mL
1/4 cup finely chopped carrots 50 mL
1/4 cup finely chopped onions 50 mL
1 tsp minced garlic 5 mL
1/4 cup finely chopped sweet green peppers 50 mL
3 oz lean ground beef, chicken, or soy-based ground beef substitute 90 g
1/2 cup tomato pasta sauce 125 mL
1/2 cup shredded low-fat mozzarella cheese 125 mL
1 tbsp grated Parmesan cheese 15 mL
9 large egg roll wrappers (5-1/2 inches/13 cm square) 9

Preheat oven to 425°F (220°C). Spray a baking sheet with cooking spray.

1. In a nonstick frying pan sprayed with cooking spray, heat oil over medium heat; cook carrots, onions, and garlic, stirring occasionally, for 8 minutes, or until softened and browned. Stir in peppers; cook 2 minutes longer. Stir in beef; cook, stirring to break it up, for 2 minutes, or until no longer pink. Remove from heat.
2. Stir in tomato sauce, mozzarella, and Parmesan.
3. Put one wrapper on work surface with a corner pointing toward you, keeping rest of wrappers covered with a cloth to prevent them drying out. Put 2 tbsp (25 mL) filling in centre. Fold lower corner up over filling, fold in the two side corners, and roll the bundle away from you. Put on prepared pan. Repeat until all wrappers are filled.
4. Bake in centre of oven, for 15 to 18 minutes, or until golden, turning pizza rolls halfway through baking time.

Makes 9 servings.

NUTRITIONAL ANALYSIS
PER ROLL
126 calories
6.7 g protein
3 g fat, total
1.2 g fat, saturated
18 g carbohydrates
243 mg sodium
10 mg cholesterol
1.1 g fibre

TIPS
These can be made up in advance, frozen, and then baked. Using ground soy is a great way, not only to make these vegetarian, but to add soy to your family's diet.

Ricotta and Smoked Salmon Tortilla Bites

Whenever I entertain—either at home or in business—I always serve these delicious appetizers. The combination of a cheese spread with fresh dill and smoked salmon is always a hit. Traditionally these are made using whole-fat cream cheese, which has 35% MF. I bring the calories and fat right down by using 5% ricotta cheese instead.

3/4 cup smooth 5% ricotta cheese 175 mL
2 oz light cream cheese, softened 60 g
2 tbsp light mayonnaise or low-fat sour cream 25 mL
2 tsp fresh lemon juice 10 mL
2 tbsp chopped fresh dill (or 1/2 tsp/2 mL dried) 25 mL
2 tbsp chopped fresh chives or finely chopped green onions 25 mL
4 large flour tortillas 4
2 oz smoked salmon, chopped 60 g
4 lettuce leaves 4

1. In a food processor, or in a bowl using an electric mixer, beat ricotta, cream cheese, mayonnaise, and lemon juice until smooth. Stir in dill and chives.
2. Divide among tortillas, spreading evenly. Sprinkle evenly with smoked salmon. Top each tortilla with a lettuce leaf. Roll up tightly.
3. Wrap in plastic wrap and chill just until cold.
4. Cut each tortilla on the diagonal into 6 pieces.

Makes 24 pieces.

NUTRITIONAL ANALYSIS
PER PIECE
55 calories
2.5 g protein
2.1 g fat, total
0.8 g fat, saturated
6.6 g carbohydrates
127 mg sodium
4.2 mg cholesterol
0.4 g fibre

TIPS
You can make these up to a day in advance as long as you wrap them well. I love to use the coloured, flavoured tortillas for the beautiful colour contrast.

Seafood Potstickers with Peanut Sauce

These potstickers are addictive. Enjoy them as either an appetizer or a side dish.

Peanut Sauce

2 tbsp natural peanut butter 25 mL

2 tbsp water 25 mL

2 tbsp chopped fresh coriander 25 mL

1 tbsp honey 15 mL

1 tbsp rice wine vinegar 15 mL

2 tsp low-sodium soy sauce 10 mL

1 tsp sesame oil 5 mL

1/2 tsp minced garlic 2 mL

1/2 tsp minced fresh ginger 2 mL

Filling

8 oz shrimp, peeled, deveined, and
   diced 250 g

1 clove garlic, minced 1

1 green onion, chopped 1

2 tbsp chopped fresh coriander 25 mL

26 small egg roll wrappers
   (3 inches /8 cm square) 26

3/4 cup seafood or chicken stock 175 mL

1. To make peanut sauce: In a food processor, or in a bowl using a whisk, combine peanut butter, water, coriander, honey, vinegar, soy sauce, sesame oil, garlic, and ginger. Set aside 2 tbsp (25 mL).

2. To make filling: In a clean food processor, combine shrimp, garlic, green onion, coriander, and 2 tbsp (25 mL) of the reserved peanut sauce; pulse on and off until well mixed and shrimp is finely chopped.

3. Place 2 tsp (10 mL) filling in centre of each wrapper. Pull edges up, pleating and bunching. Press edges together to seal.

4. In a large nonstick frying pan sprayed with cooking spray, cook potstickers, flat-side down, over medium-high heat for 3 minutes, or until golden-brown on bottom.

5. Add stock; reduce heat to low. Cover and cook for 2 minutes or until cooked though. Remove from pan; discard any remaining stock. Serve with the remaining peanut sauce.

Makes 26 potstickers.

NUTRITIONAL ANALYSIS
PER POTSTICKER

41 calories

2.4 g protein

1 g fat, total

0.2 g fat, saturated

5.7 g carbohydrates

85 mg sodium

11 mg cholesterol

0.3 g fibre

TIPS

If you want to make these ahead, prepare them to step 3 (the step before you cook them); you can fill them up to a day in advance, and even freeze them before cooking. You can substitute "surimi" for the shrimp; this imitation crabmeat is made from a variety of white fish.

Seafood Satay

You can use fresh, firm fish if you don't want seafood. The light coconut peanut sauce is so creamy you'll never believe it's low in calories and fat—light coconut milk has 3 grams of fat per 1/4 cup (50 mL), compared to the 11 grams of fat per 1/4 cup (50 mL) of regular coconut milk.

1 lb shelled shrimp or scallops, or a combination 500 g

Sauce
1/4 cup light coconut milk 50 mL
2 tbsp natural peanut butter 25 mL
2 tsp low-sodium soy sauce 10 mL
2 tsp sesame oil 10 mL
2 tsp rice wine vinegar 10 mL
1 tsp honey 5 mL
1 tsp sesame seeds 5 mL
1 tsp minced garlic 5 mL
1/2 tsp minced fresh ginger 2 mL
1/8 tsp hot Asian chili sauce 0.5 mL

Sesame seeds and chopped coriander, as garnish

Preheat grill or grill pan. Spray with vegetable spray.

1. Thread shrimp on 8 short or 4 long skewers. If using wooden skewers, soak in water for 20 minutes before using.
2. To make sauce: In a blender or small food processor, combine coconut milk, peanut butter, soy sauce, sesame oil, rice wine vinegar, honey, sesame seeds, garlic, ginger, and hot Asian chili sauce; purée. Divide in half.
3. Brush skewers with half of sauce. Grill over medium-high heat for 5 minutes, turning once, or until seafood is just cooked though.
4. Serve with remaining sauce on the side. To garnish, sprinkle with additional sesame seeds and coriander.

Makes 4 servings.

NUTRITIONAL ANALYSIS
PER LONG SKEWER
173 calories
20 g protein
8.4 g fat, total
1.9 g fat, saturated
4.4 g carbohydrates
296 mg sodium
161 mg cholesterol
0.8 g fibre

TIPS
You can prepare kebabs and sauce up to a day in advance. Try using swordfish, tuna, halibut, haddock, or salmon; don't use a fish that will easily break apart when cooked.

Creamy Shrimp and Dill Spread

This is a creamy seafood dip that can be served with veggies, crackers, or flat bread. I often use it as a light spread in a sandwich. Smoked fish like trout or salmon would also be delicious.

4 oz shrimp, peeled and deveined 125 g

1/2 cup smooth 5% ricotta cheese 125 mL

2 oz light cream cheese, softened 60 g

1/4 cup chopped green onions 50 mL

3 tbsp finely chopped sweet peppers, any colour 45 mL

2 tbsp light mayonnaise 25 mL

2 tbsp chopped fresh dill 25 mL

2 tsp fresh lemon juice 10 mL

1/2 tsp minced garlic 2 mL

1/8 tsp freshly ground black pepper 0.5 mL

1. In a nonstick frying pan sprayed with cooking spray, cook shrimp over medium-high heat for 3 minutes, or until pink. Cool.
2. In a food processor, combine shrimp, ricotta, cream cheese, and green onions. Pulse on and off until shrimp is chopped and mixture combined.
3. Stir in sweet peppers, mayonnaise, dill, lemon juice, garlic, and black pepper.

Makes about 2/3 cup (150 mL).

NUTRITIONAL ANALYSIS
PER 1 TBSP (15 ML)
42 calories
3.6 g protein
2.4 g fat, total
1 g fat, saturated
1.5 g carbohydrates
74 mg sodium
21 mg cholesterol
0.1 g fibre

TIPS
This dip keeps well for a couple of days. If you don't have fresh dill, use either 1/2 tsp (2 mL) dried dill, or substitute fresh parsley or coriander. You can replace the shrimp with "surimi," an imitation crabmeat made from a variety of white fish.

Smoked Fish Pâté

Makes about 1-1/2 cups (375 mL).

NUTRITIONAL ANALYSIS
PER 1 TBSP (15 ML)
26 calories
2.2 g protein
1.5 g fat, total
0.6 g fat, saturated
0.8 g carbohydrates
120 mg sodium
7.2 mg cholesterol
0 g fibre

TIPS
You can spice up this spread by adding 1/2 tsp (2 mL) fresh minced jalapeño peppers or hot sauce. If I find prepackaged smoked fish at a reasonable price, I'll buy a few packages and freeze them for later use.

My cooking-school students all rated this as their favourite appetizer spread. I usually serve it with baked tortilla chips or celery sticks, or in a sandwich. You can now find prepackaged smoked fish in your local supermarket.

4 oz skinless boneless smoked fish (trout or salmon) 125 g
1-1/2 oz light cream cheese, softened 45 g
1/2 cup smooth 5% ricotta cheese 125 mL
1/4 cup low-fat sour cream 50 mL
2 tbsp light mayonnaise 25 mL
1 tbsp fresh lemon juice 15 mL
1/8 tsp freshly ground black pepper 0.5 mL
2 tbsp finely chopped chives or green onions 25 mL

1. In a food processor, combine smoked fish, cream cheese, ricotta, sour cream, mayonnaise, lemon juice, and pepper; purée until smooth. Stir in chives.

Smoked Salmon Sushi Pizza

My corporate clients vote this the number one best-tasting appetizer. For those who shy away from sushi because of concern about eating raw fish, this is the perfect solution. The key is cooking the sushi rice properly: I always use a water-to-rice ratio of one-to-one; never stir the rice, and keep it covered even when it's cooling—using a rice steamer is easy, since it's virtually foolproof.

2 cups sushi rice 500 mL
2 cups water 500 mL
1/4 cup rice wine vinegar 50 mL
1 tbsp granulated sugar 15 mL
16 thin slices English cucumber (skin on) 16
4 oz smoked salmon 125 g
1 tbsp light mayonnaise 15 mL
1/2 tsp wasabi (Japanese horseradish) 2 mL
1 sheet nori seaweed 1
1 tsp sesame seeds 5 mL
Low-sodium soy sauce and pickled ginger (optional)

1. In a saucepan, combine rice and water. Bring to a boil; boil for 1 minute. Reduce heat to low; cover and cook for 12 minutes. Remove from heat. Let stand covered for 10 minutes.
2. Meanwhile, in small saucepan, combine vinegar and sugar. Bring to a boil, stirring to dissolve sugar. Remove from heat.
3. Turn rice out into a large bowl. Stir in vinegar and sugar mixture. Cool just until the rice no longer feels hot. Do not let rice get cold or it will dry out.
4. Line an 8-inch square (2 L) baking dish with plastic wrap. Line bottom with cucumber slices. Lay smoked salmon over top. Combine mayonnaise and wasabi; spread over salmon. Top with half of rice; pat out firmly to even thickness, dipping your fingers in water to prevent the rice from sticking to your hands. Top with nori sheet. Top with remaining rice; pat out firmly to even thickness.
5. Invert and cut into 16 pieces. Sprinkle with sesame seeds. Serve immediately, or cover with plastic wrap and refrigerate until ready to use (within the same day). Serve at room temperature, with soy sauce, more wasabi, and pickled ginger, if desired.

Makes 16 servings.

NUTRITIONAL ANALYSIS
PER SERVING
97 calories
3.1 g protein
0.9 g fat, total
0.2 g fat, saturated
19 g carbohydrates
154 mg sodium
2 mg cholesterol
0.9 g fibre

TIPS
If you want to make the rice earlier in the day, cook and season it; when cool, place in a large plastic bag or a lunch bag, so it does not dry out. You can find rice wine vinegar already flavoured for sushi, so you don't have to add any sugar.

White Bean Hummous

The combination of white kidney beans and tahini (sesame seed paste) creates a creamy and buttery-tasting spread without any saturated fat. The beans are an excellent source of complex carbohydrates, fibre, and iron. I love this spread with baked homemade tortilla chips or as a spread for any sandwich.

1 cup canned white kidney beans, rinsed and drained 250 mL
3 tbsp chopped fresh parsley 45 mL
3 tbsp chopped green onions 45 mL
2 tbsp tahini 25 mL
2 tbsp water 25 mL
1 tbsp olive oil 15 mL
1 tbsp fresh lemon juice 15 mL
1/2 tsp dried oregano 2 mL
1/2 tsp minced garlic 2 mL
1/8 tsp each: salt and freshly ground black pepper 0.5 mL

1. In a food processor, combine beans, parsley, green onions, tahini, water, olive oil, lemon juice, oregano, garlic, salt, and pepper. Purée until smooth.

Makes about 3/4 cup (175 mL).

NUTRITIONAL ANALYSIS
PER 1 TBSP (15 ML)
48 calories
1.5 g protein
2.6 g fat, total
0.3 g fat, saturated
4.6 g carbohydrates
26 mg sodium
0 mg cholesterol
0.2 g fibre

TIP
Tahini can be purchased in your local supermarket in the ethnic section. If you don't have it, any nut butter will be fine.

Soups

Meatball and Egg Noodle Soup

Makes 4 to 6 servings.

NUTRITIONAL ANALYSIS
PER 1/6-RECIPE SERVING
212 calories
15 g protein
7.6 g fat, total
2.2 g fat, saturated
21 g carbohydrates
942 mg sodium
60 mg cholesterol
3 g fibre

TIP
This soup thickens quickly
due to the pasta; just
add more stock if too
thick. Try substituting rice
or another grain for the
noodles; remember to add
any cooking time required
for the grain.

Serve this soup as a meal if you like. The combination of miniature meatballs, pasta, and vegetables provides great nutrition. Try substituting ground chicken, pork, or veal for the ground beef.

Meatballs

8 oz lean ground beef 250 g

1/4 cup seasoned dry breadcrumbs 50 mL

2 tbsp barbecue sauce 25 mL

1 egg 1

1 tsp minced garlic 5 mL

1/2 tsp dried basil 2 mL

2 tsp vegetable oil 10 mL

1 cup chopped onions 250 mL

1-1/2 tsp minced garlic 7 mL

1/2 cup chopped sweet green peppers
   125 mL

1/2 cup chopped carrots 125 mL

3-1/2 cups beef or chicken stock 875 mL

1 19-oz/540 mL can tomatoes 1

2 tbsp tomato paste 25 mL

2 tsp chili powder 10 mL

1 tsp dried basil 5 mL

1 tsp granulated sugar 5 mL

1/2 tsp dried oregano 2 mL

1/4 tsp salt 1 mL

1 bay leaf 1

1 cup egg noodles 250 mL

2 tbsp grated Parmesan cheese,
   as garnish 25 mL

1. To make meatballs: In a bowl, stir together ground beef, breadcrumbs, barbecue sauce, egg, garlic, and basil. Form into 1-inch (2.5 cm) meatballs (about 24 meatballs). In a nonstick frying pan sprayed with cooking spray, cook meatballs over medium heat, turning occasionally, for 5 minutes, or until browned on all sides. Set aside.

2. In a large nonstick saucepan sprayed with cooking spray, heat oil over medium heat; cook onions and garlic for 5 minutes, or until browned. Stir in green peppers and carrots; cook for 3 minutes. Stir in stock, tomatoes, tomato paste, chili powder, basil, sugar, oregano, salt, bay leaf, and browned meatballs. Bring soup to a boil. Reduce heat to simmer; cover and cook for 15 minutes, occasionally breaking tomatoes with the back of a spoon, being careful not to break meatballs.

3. Stir in egg noodles; simmer for 5 minutes, or until noodles are tender; remove bay leaf. Serve sprinkled with Parmesan.

Creamy Cauliflower Purée with Smoked Salmon

A caterer served a soup like this at a party at my home one evening, and I fell in love with it. But the next morning I had a "food hangover" that told me the soup was filled with cream and butter. I created my own version without the fat, and it's outstanding.

2 tsp vegetable oil 10 mL
1 cup chopped onions 250 mL
2 tsp minced garlic 10 mL
4 cups chopped cauliflower (1/2 medium cauliflower) 1 L
4 cups chicken or vegetable stock 1 L
1 cup diced, peeled potatoes 250 mL
1 tsp Dijon mustard 5 mL
1/4 tsp each: salt and freshly ground black pepper 1 mL
2 oz smoked salmon, sliced 60 g
1/4 cup chopped fresh parsley, as garnish 50 mL

1. In a nonstick saucepan sprayed with cooking spray, heat oil over medium-high heat; add onions and garlic, and cook for 3 minutes.
2. Add cauliflower, stock, and potatoes. Bring to a boil. Reduce heat to simmer; cover and cook for 25 minutes, or until vegetables are tender.
3. In batches, purée soup in a blender or food processor. Return to saucepan. Add mustard, salt, and pepper.
4. Serve in bowls with slices of smoked salmon on top and parsley as garnish. Do not serve soup too hot, or the smoked salmon will cook.

Makes 4 to 6 servings.

NUTRITIONAL ANALYSIS
PER 1/6-RECIPE SERVING
106 calories
7.4 g protein
3.2 g fat, total
0.5 g fat, saturated
12 g carbohydrates
848 mg sodium
2.2 mg cholesterol
2.7 g fibre

TIPS
You can substitute prosciutto for the smoked salmon. If cauliflower is not your favourite vegetable, try broccoli; they are both part of the cruciferous vegetable family and help in the fight against cancer.

Old-Fashioned Split Pea Soup

Makes 6 servings.

NUTRITIONAL ANALYSIS
PER SERVING
167 calories
11 g protein
3 g fat, total
0.5 g fat, saturated
24 g carbohydrates
593 mg sodium
0 mg cholesterol
7.6 g fibre

TIPS
This soup can be prepared
a couple of days in
advance. If it becomes too
thick, just add more stock.
For a change, use yellow
split peas.

Nothing represents comfort food like split-pea soup. It's rich and filling (because the peas are high in fibre), a source of plant protein, and low in fat. For a complete meal, try adding some cooked ham, chicken, or low-fat sausage.

2 tsp vegetable oil 10 mL
1 cup chopped onions 250 mL
2/3 cup chopped carrots 150 mL
2 tsp minced garlic 10 mL
4 cups chicken stock 1 mL
1 cup chopped, peeled potatoes 250 mL
3/4 cup split peas 175 mL
1/4 tsp each: salt and freshly ground black pepper 1 mL

1. In a nonstick saucepan sprayed with cooking spray, heat oil over medium heat; add onions, carrots, and garlic, and cook for 5 minutes, or until softened.
2. Stir in stock, potatoes, split peas, salt, and pepper. Bring to a boil. Reduce heat to low; cover and cook for 40 minutes, or until peas are tender.
3. In batches, purée in a blender or food processor.

Pasta and Bean Soup (Fagioli)

This classic Italian soup is a medley of vegetables, beans, and pasta. Along with some Italian bread, it can be a wonderful lunch. This soup is a complete protein without any animal products—the beans and pasta combine to make a full protein.

2 tsp vegetable oil 10 mL

1/2 cup chopped onions 125 mL

1/3 cup chopped carrots 75 mL

1/3 cup chopped celery 75 mL

2 tsp minced garlic 10 mL

3-1/2 cups beef or chicken stock 875 mL

1 19-oz/540 mL can tomatoes 1

2 tsp granulated sugar 10 mL

1 tsp dried basil 5 mL

1/2 tsp dried oregano 2 mL

1/8 tsp each: salt and freshly ground black pepper 0.5 mL

3 cups canned red kidney beans, rinsed and drained 750 mL

1/2 cup elbow macaroni or small shell pasta 125 mL

3 tbsp grated Parmesan cheese, as garnish 45 mL

1/4 cup chopped fresh parsley, as garnish 50 mL

1. In a large nonstick saucepan sprayed with cooking spray, heat oil over medium heat; cook onions, carrots, celery, and garlic for 5 minutes.
2. Stir in stock, tomatoes, sugar, basil, oregano, salt, pepper, and 2 cups (500 mL) of the beans. Mash remaining 1 cup (250 mL) beans and stir into saucepan. Bring to a boil, crushing tomatoes with the back of a spoon. Reduce heat to simmer; cook for 15 minutes, stirring occasionally.
3. Stir in pasta; cook for 5 to 8 minutes, or until pasta is tender but firm. Serve sprinkled with Parmesan and parsley.

Makes 6 servings.

NUTRITIONAL ANALYSIS
PER SERVING
260 calories
14 g protein
3.6 g fat, total
0.6 g fat, saturated
43 g carbohydrates
638 mg sodium
2.5 mg cholesterol
13 g fibre

TIPS
Use any variety of beans you prefer, such as chickpeas, white kidney beans, or white navy beans. If you like the taste of freshly cooked beans instead of canned, use the quick soak and cook method: bring a pot of water to a boil, add 1-1/2 cups (375 mL) beans, and boil for 1 minute; let sit, covered, for 1 hour; replace water and simmer for 40 minutes, or until tender.

Southwestern Black Bean Gazpacho

Makes 6 to 8 servings.

NUTRITIONAL ANALYSIS
PER 1/8-RECIPE SERVING
121 calories
3.9 g protein
4.1 g fat, total
0.6 g fat, saturated
17 g carbohydrates
646 mg sodium
0.2 mg cholesterol
3.7 g fibre

TIPS
Great to serve on a hot summer day. If entertaining, serve in a champagne glass with a slice of lime. Try adding crumbled baked tortilla chips and a dollop of light sour cream as a garnish. This soup will last in the refrigerator for at least 4 days. Don't freeze it.

If it's time to try another version of gazpacho, then this is the one to try. Sautéed corn, sweet bell peppers, black beans, and coriander star in this version. The tomatoes add a nutritional powerhouse: they contain lycopene, which is an antioxidant more powerful than beta carotene.

1 cup canned corn, drained 250 mL
1 cup diced sweet red or yellow peppers 250 mL
1 cup diced sweet green peppers 250 mL
1/2 cup diced sweet onions 125 mL
1/2 cup chopped green onions 125 mL
4 large plum tomatoes, seeded and diced (approx. 2 cups/500 mL) 4
2 tsp minced garlic 10 mL
2 cups tomato juice 500 mL
1 cup chicken or vegetable stock 250 mL
1 cup canned black beans, rinsed and drained 250 mL
1/2 cup chopped fresh coriander 125 mL
1 tbsp olive oil 15 mL
1 tbsp balsamic vinegar 15 mL
1/2 tsp hot pepper sauce 2 mL
1/4 tsp each: salt and freshly ground black pepper 1 mL

1. In a nonstick frying pan sprayed with cooking spray, cook corn over medium heat, stirring often, for 8 minutes, or until slightly charred.
2. In a large bowl, stir together peppers, sweet and green onions, tomatoes, and garlic; set aside 1/2 cup (125 mL). In food processor, purée remaining vegetable mixture.
3. Return vegetable purée to bowl. Stir in charred corn, tomato juice, stock, black beans, coriander, olive oil, vinegar, hot pepper sauce, salt, pepper, and reserved vegetable mixture. Chill 1 to 2 hours.

Spinach Chickpea Soup

I find that most spinach soups have a somewhat bitter taste. This soup is the exception because the chickpeas and potatoes soften the flavour of the spinach and give the soup a creamy texture, without the use of butter or cream. Spinach is very low in calories, and is an excellent source of folate, iron, calcium, and potassium.

2 tsp vegetable oil 10 mL
1 cup chopped onions 250 mL
2 tsp minced garlic 10 mL
3 cups chicken or vegetable stock 750 mL
1-1/2 cups canned chickpeas, rinsed and drained 375 mL
1 cup peeled, diced potatoes 250 mL
Half 10-oz/300 g pkg frozen chopped spinach Half
1/4 tsp each: salt and freshly ground black pepper 1 mL
3 tbsp grated Parmesan cheese, as garnish 45 mL

1. In a nonstick saucepan sprayed with cooking spray, heat oil over medium-high heat; cook onions and garlic for 3 minutes. Stir in stock, chickpeas, potatoes, spinach, salt, and pepper. Bring to a boil. Reduce heat to medium-low; cover and cook for 15 minutes or until potato is tender.
2. In batches, purée soup in a blender or food processor. Serve sprinkled with Parmesan.

Makes 4 to 6 servings.

NUTRITIONAL ANALYSIS
PER 1/6-RECIPE SERVING
147 calories
7.9 g protein
4.4 g fat, total
0.6 g fat, saturated
19 g carbohydrates
681 mg sodium
3.1 mg cholesterol
4.1 g fibre

TIPS
When using frozen spinach, cut package in half while frozen so you can use the other half at a later time. This soup looks great with a dollop of light sour cream in the centre. Or mix 1/4 cup (50 mL) light sour cream with 1 tbsp (15 mL) water and spoon into a plastic bag; cut a hole in the corner of the bag and pipe sour cream in straight or concentric lines about 1/2 inch (1 cm) apart on top of soup; use a toothpick to pull through the lines.

White Bean and Chickpea Soup

Makes 4 servings.

NUTRITIONAL ANALYSIS
PER SERVING
212 calories
11 g protein
5.3 g fat, total
0.6 g fat, saturated
30 g carbohydrates
846 mg sodium
2.7 mg cholesterol
4.1 g fibre

TIPS
You can experiment with
other types of beans: white
navy beans, soybeans, or
red kidney beans are great
substitutes. This soup
freezes well.

The combination of white kidney beans and chickpeas makes this soup so rich tasting, you'll think it's loaded with butter or cream. Beans are a great source of complex carbohydrates, high in fibre, and low in fat.

2 tsp vegetable oil 10 mL
1 cup chopped onions 250 mL
1 cup chopped sweet red peppers 250 mL
2 tsp minced garlic 10 mL
2-1/2 cups chicken stock 625 mL
1 cup canned chickpeas, rinsed and drained 250 mL
1 cup canned white kidney beans, rinsed and drained 250 mL
1-1/2 tsp Dijon mustard 7 mL
1/2 tsp dried basil 2 mL
1/4 tsp hot chili sauce 1 mL
1/4 tsp salt 1 mL
1/2 cup low-fat milk 125 mL

1. In a nonstick saucepan sprayed with cooking spray, heat oil over medium heat; cook onions, red peppers, and garlic for 5 minutes, or until softened.
2. Stir in stock, chickpeas, kidney beans, mustard, basil, hot chili sauce, and salt. Bring to a boil. Reduce heat to low; cover and cook for 10 minutes.
3. In batches, purée soup in a blender or food processor. Return to saucepan. Whisk in milk. Heat over medium heat until heated through.

Sweet Onion Soup with Parmesan Cheese Croûtes

Croûtes are just larger versions of croutons. The caramelizing of the onions is what makes them so sweet in this soup. Traditional onion soups smothered in cheese can have over 600 calories and 30 grams of fat! You'll find that because this soup is so rich tasting, the small amount of cheese used is very satisfying.

2 tsp vegetable oil 10 mL
6 cups sliced Spanish onions 1.5 L
2 tsp packed brown sugar 10 mL
2 tsp minced garlic 10 mL
4-1/2 cups chicken or beef stock 1.125 L
1/2 cup dry white wine 125 mL
3/4 tsp dried thyme 4 mL
1/8 tsp salt 0.5 mL

Croûtes
6 thin slices baguette 6
1/4 cup shredded mozzarella cheese 50 mL
2 tsp grated Parmesan cheese 10 mL

Preheat oven to 425°F (220°C).

1. In a nonstick saucepan sprayed with cooking spray, heat oil over medium heat; cook onions for 10 minutes, or until softened but not browned. Stir in brown sugar and garlic; cook on low heat for 15 minutes longer, stirring often, or until golden brown. Do not burn.
2. Stir in stock, wine, thyme, and salt. Bring to a boil. Reduce heat to simmer; cover and cook for 10 minutes.
3. To make croûtes: Spray baguette slices on both sides with cooking spray, and place on baking sheet. Bake for 8 to 10 minutes, or until golden on top. Turn slices; sprinkle with mozzarella and Parmesan. Turn oven to broil and broil croûtes for 30 seconds, or until cheese melts.
4. Place one cheese croûte at the bottom of each of six soup bowls. Ladle soup on top.

Makes 6 servings.

NUTRITIONAL ANALYSIS
PER SERVING
172 calories
7.5 g protein
5.1 g fat, total
1.2 g fat, saturated
24 g carbohydrates
688 mg sodium
3.1 mg cholesterol
3.1 g fibre

TIPS
Any type of onion can be used, but if not sweet, you may need to increase the brown sugar. The croûtes can be made in advance and stored in an airtight container. The soup freezes well.

Sweet Red and Yellow Pepper Soup

Makes 6 servings.

NUTRITIONAL ANALYSIS
PER SERVING
114 calories
4.1 g protein
2.4 g fat, total
0.3 g fat, saturated
19 g carbohydrates
379 mg sodium
0 mg cholesterol
3.5 g fibre

TIP
If you find grilling or
broiling the sweet potatoes
difficult, try roasting them
at 425°F (220°C) for about
30 to 35 minutes, turning
occasionally—you'll have
greater control, as they
don't char as quickly.

I featured this soup in *Rose Reisman's Enlightened Home Cooking*, and it was rated as one of the most delicious soups, and the most beautiful soup because of its two-tone colour. The design is so simple, you'll catch a glimpse of the artistry used at upscale restaurants. The bell peppers are filled with an abundance of beta carotene, which helps in the fight against cancer.

2 sweet red peppers 2
2 sweet yellow peppers 2
2 tsp vegetable oil 10 mL
1-1/2 cups chopped onions 375 mL
1-1/4 cups chopped carrots 300 mL
1/2 cup chopped celery 125 mL
2 tsp minced garlic 10 mL
4 cups chicken or vegetable stock 1 L
1-1/2 cups diced, peeled potatoes 375 mL
1/4 tsp salt 1 mL
Freshly ground black pepper, to taste
1/4 cup chopped fresh coriander, basil, or dill, as garnish 50 mL

Preheat broiler or grill.

1. Under broiler or over medium-high heat on grill, cook peppers, turning occasionally, for 15 to 20 minutes, or until charred on all sides. Cool. Peel, stem, and core.
2. In a nonstick saucepan sprayed with cooking spray, heat oil over medium heat; cook onions, carrots, celery, and garlic, stirring occasionally, for 8 minutes, or until softened. Stir in stock and potatoes. Bring to a boil. Reduce heat to low; cover and cook for 20 to 25 minutes, or until carrots and potatoes are tender. Stir in salt.
3. In a blender or food processor, purée the red peppers until smooth. Add half of soup mixture to machine; process until smooth. Transfer to serving bowl. Season to taste with pepper. In a clean blender or food processor, purée yellow peppers until smooth. Add remaining soup mixture; process until smooth. Transfer to another serving bowl. Season to taste with pepper.
4. To serve, ladle some red pepper soup into one side of a bowl, while ladling some yellow pepper soup into the same bowl from the other side. Serve garnished with coriander.

Thai Coconut Chicken Soup

I have avoided ordering these soups in Thai restaurants, because of the high calories and saturated fat in the coconut milk. But thanks to food manufacturers, you can now find "light" coconut milk, which is 75% reduced in fat and calories.

4 oz skinless boneless chicken breast 125 g

1-1/2 cups light coconut milk 375 mL

1-1/2 cups chicken stock 375 mL

1/2 cup drained canned straw mushrooms 125 mL

2 tbsp oyster or fish sauce 25 mL

1 tbsp fresh lemon juice 15 mL

1/2 to 1 tsp hot Asian chili sauce 2 to 5 mL

1 tsp minced garlic 5 mL

1 tsp grated fresh ginger 5 mL

1 stalk lemongrass, sliced (or grated rind of 1 lemon) 1

1/2 cup chopped snow peas 125 mL

1/4 cup diced sweet red peppers 50 mL

1/4 cup chopped fresh coriander, as garnish 50 mL

Preheat grill or grill pan; spray with vegetable spray.

1. Grill chicken over medium-high heat for 6 minutes per side, or until cooked through. Dice.
2. In a saucepan, combine coconut milk, stock, mushrooms, oyster sauce, lemon juice, hot Asian chili sauce, garlic, ginger, and lemongrass. Bring to a simmer over medium-low heat; cook for 5 minutes. Stir in snow peas, red peppers, and chicken; cook for 1 minute. Serve garnished with coriander.

Makes 4 servings.

NUTRITIONAL ANALYSIS
PER SERVING
121 calories
10 g protein
5.6 g fat, total
4.3 g fat, saturated
7.6 g carbohydrates
456 mg sodium
16 mg cholesterol
2.1 g fibre

TIPS
This soup can be made in minutes. If you can't find straw mushrooms, you can sauté and add the same amount of your favourite mushrooms, sliced. Don't be concerned if you can't find lemongrass; I often use lemon rind instead, and it's delicious.

Fresh Plum Tomato Soup

NUTRITIONAL ANALYSIS
PER SERVING
108 calories
4.5 g protein
4.7 g fat, total
1.4 g fat, saturated
12 g carbohydrates
430 mg sodium
3.6 mg cholesterol
2.3 g fibre

TIPS
You can use ripe field tomatoes instead of plum tomatoes if desired, but seed them first. Don't use canned tomatoes in this soup. You can use any cheese you like, such as feta or mozzarella. This soup freezes well.

You'll never taste a fresher and tastier tomato soup than this one. Without butter or cream, this is so rich tasting you'll have trouble believing there are only about 100 calories per serving—and that's with the cheese! Tomatoes contain lycopene, a powerful antioxidant, which is known to help in the fight against prostate cancer.

2 tsp vegetable oil 10 mL
3/4 cup chopped sweet onions 175 mL
1-1/2 tsp minced garlic 7 mL
4 cups chopped plum tomatoes (about 8) 1 L
1 cup chicken or vegetable stock 250 mL
1-1/2 tbsp tomato paste 22 mL
2 tsp granulated sugar 10 mL
1/4 tsp each: salt and freshly ground black pepper 1 mL
1 oz goat cheese, as garnish 30 g
1/4 cup chopped fresh basil, as garnish 50 mL

1. In a nonstick saucepan sprayed with cooking spray, heat oil over medium heat; cook onions and garlic for 3 minutes. Stir in plum tomatoes, stock, tomato paste, sugar, salt, and pepper. Bring to a boil. Reduce heat to simmer; cover and cook for 15 minutes.
2. In batches, purée soup in a blender or food processor. Serve garnished with goat cheese and basil.

Creamy Wild Mushroom Soup

Anyone who doesn't love mushrooms will change their mind after trying this soup. The texture of this soup is smooth, and each mouthful is filled with the aroma and taste of whatever mushrooms you select. Mushroom soup in a restaurant is usually made with cream and butter, but this soup uses only a small amount of vegetable oil.

2 tsp vegetable oil 10 mL
1 cup chopped onions 250 mL
2 tsp minced garlic 10 mL
1/2 cup diced carrots 125 mL
6 cups diced wild mushrooms (about 12 oz/375 g) 1.5 L
3-1/2 cups chicken or vegetable stock 875 mL
1-1/2 cups chopped, peeled potatoes 375 mL
1/2 tsp each: dried rosemary and thyme 2 mL
1/2 tsp salt 2 mL
1/4 tsp freshly ground black pepper 1 mL
1/2 cup low-fat milk 125 mL
3 tbsp grated Parmesan cheese 45 mL
1/4 cup chopped fresh parsley, as garnish 50 mL

1. In a nonstick saucepan sprayed with cooking spray, heat oil over medium-high heat; cook onions and garlic for 5 minutes. Stir in carrots; cook for 3 minutes. Stir in mushrooms; cook for 10 minutes, or until mushroom liquid has evaporated and mushrooms are browned.
2. Stir in stock, potatoes, rosemary, thyme, salt, and pepper. Bring to a boil. Reduce heat to simmer; cover and cook for 15 minutes, or until potato and carrots are tender.
3. In batches, purée soup in a blender or food processor. Return to saucepan. Stir in milk and Parmesan. Serve garnished with parsley.

Makes 6 servings.

NUTRITIONAL ANALYSIS
PER SERVING
124 calories
7.1 g protein
3.5 g fat, total
0.8 g fat, saturated
16 g carbohydrates
542 mg sodium
3.7 mg cholesterol
2.1 g fibre

TIPS
I have often made this soup using a combination of portobello, brown, oyster, and regular button mushrooms; these are the most affordable. If your budget allows, the soup is sensational using porcinis, chanterelles, or shiitakes. This soup freezes well.

Yukon Gold Potato Soup

Makes 4 to 6 servings.

NUTRITIONAL ANALYSIS
PER 1/6-RECIPE SERVING
164 calories
7.3 g protein
3.4 g fat, total
0.7 g fat, saturated
26 g carbohydrates
752 mg sodium
2.5 mg cholesterol
2.6 g fibre

TIPS
If you want to peel and
cut your potatoes early in
the day, remember to cover
them with cold water to
prevent browning. This
soup freezes well.

The best potato ever developed was the Yukon Gold. It has a yellow colour, and tastes creamier and
sweeter than regular potatoes. I use them for any recipe calling for potatoes.

2 tsp vegetable oil 10 mL
1 cup chopped onions 250 mL
2 tsp minced garlic 10 mL
3 cups chicken or vegetable stock 750 mL
5 cups diced, peeled Yukon Gold potatoes
   (approx. 2 lb/1 kg or 4 medium potatoes) 1.25 L
1 tsp Dijon mustard 5 mL
1/2 tsp salt 2 mL
1/2 tsp dried basil 2 mL
1/4 tsp hot pepper sauce 1 mL
1/4 tsp freshly ground black pepper 1 mL
1/2 cup low-fat evaporated milk 125 mL
3 tbsp grated Parmesan cheese 45 mL
3 tbsp chopped fresh parsley, as garnish 45 mL

1. In a nonstick saucepan sprayed with cooking spray, heat oil over medium heat; cook onions and garlic
   for 5 minutes, or until onions are lightly browned.
2. Stir in stock, potatoes, mustard, salt, basil, hot pepper sauce, and pepper. Bring to a boil. Reduce heat
   to simmer; cover and cook for 15 minutes, or until potatoes are tender.
3. In batches, purée soup in a blender or food processor. Return to saucepan. Whisk in evaporated milk
   and Parmesan. Serve garnished with parsley.

Salads

Coleslaw with Dried Cranberries, Apricots, and Thai Dressing

NUTRITIONAL ANALYSIS
PER SERVING
65 calories
1.6 g protein
0.7 g fat, total
0.5 g fat, saturated
13 g carbohydrates
129 mg sodium
0 mg cholesterol
2.6 g fibre

TIP
Light coconut milk
has only 38 calories per
1/4 cup (50 mL), with
only 3 grams of fat; regular
coconut milk has more
than 100 calories per
1/4 cup (50 mL), with
11 grams of fat.

Now here's a coleslaw that will be the hit of your next get-together. Bright with the variety and colour of the vegetables and dried fruit, this sweet-flavoured Asian coleslaw is so fresh tasting that it even tastes great the next day.

3 cups thinly sliced green cabbage 750 mL
3 cups thinly sliced red cabbage 750 mL
1 cup sliced snow peas 250 mL
1 cup sliced sweet red peppers 250 mL
1/2 cup chopped green onions 125 mL
1/3 cup dried cranberries 75 mL
1/3 cup diced dried apricots 75 mL

Dressing
1/3 cup light coconut milk 75 mL
1/3 cup chopped fresh coriander 75 mL
2 tsp fish or oyster sauce 10 mL
2 tsp packed brown sugar 10 mL
1 tbsp fresh lemon juice 15 mL
1 tsp minced garlic 5 mL
1/2 tsp minced fresh ginger 2 mL
1/4 cup hot pepper sauce 1 mL

1. In a large bowl, stir together cabbages, snow peas, red peppers, green onions, cranberries, and apricots.
2. In a small bowl, whisk together coconut milk, coriander, fish sauce, brown sugar, lemon juice, garlic, ginger, and hot pepper sauce. Pour over cabbage mixture; toss to coat.

Asian Rice Noodle Salad with Coconut–Peanut Dressing

Rice noodles have a denser texture and creamier taste than wheat noodles. Combine them with a light coconut–peanut dressing and a variety of vegetables to make this great appetizer or main course.

8 oz medium-thick rice noodles,
   broken in half 250 g
1-1/2 cups chopped snow peas 375 mL
1-1/2 cups chopped sweet red peppers
   375 mL
1/2 cup chopped green onions 125 mL
1/3 cup chopped fresh coriander 75 mL
1/4 cup chopped peanuts 50 mL

Dressing
1/3 cup light coconut milk 75 mL
2 tbsp natural peanut butter 25 mL
1-1/2 tbsp low-sodium soy sauce 22 mL
1-1/2 tbsp rice wine vinegar 22 mL
2 tsp sesame oil 10 mL
2 tsp toasted sesame seeds 10 mL
1 tsp minced garlic 5 mL
2 tsp brown sugar 10 mL
1/2 tsp minced fresh ginger 2 mL
1/4 to 1/2 tsp hot Asian chili sauce 1 to 2 mL

1. In a large saucepan of boiling water, cook noodles for 3 to 5 minutes, or until tender. Drain. Rinse under cold running water. Drain.
2. In a large bowl, combine noodles, snow peas, red peppers, green onion, coriander, and peanuts.
3. In a small bowl using a whisk, or in a small food processor, beat coconut milk, peanut butter, soy sauce, vinegar, sesame oil, sesame seeds, garlic, brown sugar, ginger, and hot chili sauce until smooth. Pour over rice noodle mixture; toss to coat.

Makes 8 servings.

NUTRITIONAL ANALYSIS
PER SERVING
194 calories
5.8 g protein
6.5 g fat, total
1.3 g fat, saturated
28 g carbohydrates
116 mg sodium
0 mg cholesterol
2.2 g fibre

TIPS
You can always cook the noodles earlier in the day; just remember to rinse with cold water after cooking and rinse again with room temperature water just before tossing with other ingredients. Light coconut milk, which has 75% less fat and calories than regular coconut milk, is now available in most supermarkets.

Japanese Curly Noodle Salad
with Sesame Dressing

Makes 8 servings.

NUTRITIONAL ANALYSIS
PER SERVING
156 calories
4.3 g protein
5.2 g fat, total
0.6 g fat, saturated
23 g carbohydrates
348 mg sodium
0 mg cholesterol
4.2 g fibre

TIPS
You can substitute other vegetables of your choice, but be sure to keep the vibrant colours. Crushed garlic and ginger are available prepared in jars in the produce section of many supermarkets, if you don't have fresh on hand.

This is a quick and delicious Asian salad. If you want to serve it as a complete meal, just add some cooked chicken, meat, or seafood. The instant ramen noodles give the salad a crunchy, nut-like texture without the fat and calories.

1 3-oz/85 g package instant ramen noodles 1
6 cups thinly sliced nappa cabbage 1.5 L
1 cup thinly sliced carrots 250 mL
1 cup thinly sliced sweet red peppers 250 mL
1 cup chopped snow peas 250 mL
1/2 cup sliced water chestnuts 125 mL
1/4 cup chopped green onions 50 mL
1/4 cup sliced toasted almonds 50 mL
2 tsp sesame seeds 10 mL

Dressing
1/4 cup low-sodium soy sauce 50 mL
3 tbsp rice wine vinegar 45 mL
2 tbsp sesame oil 25 mL
4 tsp honey 20 mL
1-1/2 tsp crushed garlic 7 mL
1 tsp crushed fresh ginger 5 mL

1. Break the dry ramen noodles into small pieces. Discard seasoning packet. In a small nonstick frying pan, cook noodles over medium-high heat for 3 to 5 minutes, or until toasted.
2. Place noodles, cabbage, carrots, red peppers, snow peas, water chestnuts, green onions, almonds, and sesame seeds in a large bowl.
3. In a small bowl, whisk together soy sauce, vinegar, sesame oil, honey, garlic, and ginger. Pour over salad; toss to coat.

Mango Lettuce Salad with Feta and Olives, p. 237

Pesto-Stuffed Chicken Rolls, p. 299
Chicken Breasts with Olive, Feta, and Parsley Stuffing, p. 298

Tex-Mex Macaroni Salad with Charred Corn and Black Beans

This salad is delicious, either served at room temperature or chilled. This is the perfect salad to serve in a baked tortilla shell. Purchase a tortilla baking pan from a kitchen store, fit it with a large tortilla, and bake it at 400°F (200°C) for 10 minutes, or until crisp.

1-3/4 cups elbow macaroni 425 mL
1 cup drained canned corn 250 mL
1-1/2 cups chopped seeded plum tomatoes
   375 mL
1 cup canned black beans, rinsed and
   drained 250 mL
1/2 cup chopped green onions 125 mL
1/3 cup chopped fresh coriander 75 mL

Dressing
1/3 cup barbecue sauce 75 mL
2 tbsp cider vinegar 25 mL
1 tbsp molasses 15 mL
1/4 to 1/2 tsp hot pepper sauce 1 to 2 mL

1. In a pot of boiling water, cook macaroni for 8 to 10 minutes, or until tender but firm. Drain. Rinse. Place in a large bowl.
2. In a nonstick frying pan sprayed with cooking spray, cook corn over medium heat, stirring often, for 8 minutes, or until slightly charred. Add to macaroni, along with plum tomatoes, black beans, green onions, and coriander; toss to combine.
3. To make dressing: In a small bowl, whisk together barbecue sauce, cider vinegar, molasses, and hot pepper sauce. Pour over macaroni mixture; toss to coat.

Makes 8 servings.

NUTRITIONAL ANALYSIS
PER SERVING
229 calories
7.4 g protein
11 g fat, total
2.4 g fat, saturated
25 g carbohydrates
463 mg sodium
5 mg cholesterol
4.3 g fibre

TIPS
This salad can be mixed early in the day. If you don't have cider vinegar, substitute balsamic or raspberry vinegar. You can always use a fresh jalapeño pepper for some real heat: use about 1 tsp (5 mL) finely diced pepper without the seeds.

Curried Couscous, Chickpea, and Cranberry Salad

Makes 6 servings.

NUTRITIONAL ANALYSIS
PER SERVING
235 calories
6.2 g protein
3.2 g fat, total
0.7 g fat, saturated
45 g carbohydrates
204 mg sodium
0 mg cholesterol
3.7 g fibre

TIPS
If you don't have fresh basil, try either parsley or coriander. Always keep one container of orange juice concentrate in the freezer for cooking and baking purposes; you can remove the amount needed while still frozen.

This is a beautiful and delicious couscous salad. I love to serve it as part of a buffet meal. The sweet orange dressing goes so well with the dried cranberries, chickpeas, and basil.

1 cup chicken stock 250 mL
1 cup couscous 250 mL
1/2 tsp curry powder 2 mL
3/4 cup canned chickpeas, rinsed and
    drained 175 mL
1/3 cup dried cranberries 75 mL
1/4 cup chopped green onions 50 mL
1/4 cup diced sweet red peppers 50 mL
1/4 cup chopped fresh basil 50 mL

Dressing
1 tbsp olive oil 15 mL
2 tbsp thawed orange juice concentrate
    25 mL
2 tbsp fresh lemon juice 25 mL
2 tsp grated orange rind 10 mL
3 tbsp honey 45 mL
1 tsp minced garlic 5 mL

1. In a small saucepan, bring stock to a boil. Remove from heat. Stir in couscous and curry powder; cover and let stand for 5 minutes. Fluff with a fork. Transfer to a large bowl, and cool.
2. Stir chickpeas, cranberries, green onions, red peppers, and basil into cooled couscous.
3. To make dressing: In a small bowl, whisk together olive oil, orange juice concentrate, lemon juice, orange rind, honey, and garlic. Pour over couscous mixture; toss to coat.

Shrimp Couscous Salad with Chickpeas and Orange Dressing

This wonderful citrus-flavoured couscous dish is great as a side dish, as a main course, or served on a buffet table. The yogourt and orange juice concentrate make a delicious light-flavoured dressing.

1 cup chicken or fish stock 250 mL

1 cup couscous 250 mL

4 oz cooked, peeled shrimp, chopped 125 g

1/2 cup drained canned mandarin oranges
     125 mL

1/2 cup canned chickpeas, drained and
     rinsed 125 mL

1/3 cup chopped green onions 75 mL

1/4 cup raisins or dried cranberries 50 mL

Dressing

2 tbsp thawed orange juice concentrate
     25 mL

2 tbsp light yogourt (1% MF) 25 mL

2 tsp olive oil 10 mL

1 tsp minced garlic 5 mL

1/4 cup chopped fresh coriander or parsley,
     as garnish 50 mL

1. In a small saucepan, bring stock to a boil. Remove from heat. Stir in couscous; cover and let stand for 5 minutes. Fluff with a fork. Transfer to a large bowl, and cool.
2. Stir shrimp, mandarin oranges, chickpeas, green onions, and raisins into couscous.
3. To make dressing: In a small bowl, whisk together orange juice concentrate, yogourt, olive oil, and garlic. Pour over couscous mixture; toss to coat. Garnish with coriander.

Makes 6 servings.

NUTRITIONAL ANALYSIS
PER SERVING
208 calories
10 g protein
2.7 g fat, total
0.4 g fat, saturated
36 g carbohydrates
229 mg sodium
37 mg cholesterol
2.7 g fibre

TIPS
To cook the shrimp, sauté them in a nonstick frying pan sprayed with vegetable spray, just until they turn pink. Or microwave them with a little water in a bowl covered with plastic wrap, for about 1 minute, or until they turn pink.

Southwest Couscous Salad with Barbecue Dressing

Makes 4 to 6 servings.

NUTRITIONAL ANALYSIS
PER 1/6-RECIPE SERVING
172 calories
6.2 g protein
0.8 g fat, total
0.2 g fat, saturated
35 g carbohydrates
315 mg sodium
0 mg cholesterol
3.5 g fibre

TIPS
Use a basic, good-quality barbeque sauce in the dressing. The flavoured varieties will give the dressing a different taste. If the brand of couscous you're using seems to always clump, try adding 1 tsp (5 mL) of vegetable oil to your stock.

You've never tasted a couscous dish like this before. The Tex-Mex flavourings are wonderful with this grain. I love to serve this salad in a baked tortilla shell (see Tex-Mex Macaroni Salad, page 231).

1 cup chicken or vegetable stock 250 mL
1 cup couscous 250 mL
1/2 cup drained canned corn 125 mL
1/2 cup canned black beans, rinsed and
    drained 125 mL
1/2 cup chopped sweet red peppers 125 mL
1/2 cup chopped sweet green peppers
    125 mL
1/3 cup chopped green onions 75 mL

Dressing
3 tbsp barbecue sauce 45 mL
1 tbsp packed brown sugar 15 mL
2 tsp cider vinegar 10 mL
2 tsp molasses 10 mL
1 tsp minced garlic 5 mL

1/3 cup chopped fresh coriander,
    as garnish 75 mL

1. In a small saucepan, bring stock to a boil. Remove from heat. Stir in couscous; cover and let stand for 5 minutes. Fluff with a fork. Transfer to large bowl, and cool.
2. In a nonstick frying pan sprayed with cooking spray, cook corn over medium heat, stirring often, for 8 minutes, or until slightly charred.
3. Stir corn, black beans, red and green peppers, and green onions into couscous.
4. To make dressing: In a small bowl, whisk together barbecue sauce, brown sugar, vinegar, molasses, and garlic. Pour over couscous mixture; toss to coat. Garnish with coriander.

Quinoa Greek Salad

Quinoa, pronounced "keen-wah," is the most nutritious grain in town. It is a complete protein, which is beneficial for vegetarians. It also is high in calcium and iron. It is the only grain that is allowed on the Jewish holiday of Passover, because it is not actually considered a grain. You'll love this new version of a Greek salad.

2 cups chicken or vegetable stock 500 mL
1 cup quinoa 250 mL
1/2 cup diced sweet red peppers 125 mL
1/2 cup diced sweet green peppers 125 mL
1/2 cup diced English cucumber,
  skin on 125 mL
1/4 cup chopped green onions 50 mL
1/4 cup sliced black olives 50 mL
1/4 cup diced red onions 50 mL
3 oz light feta cheese, crumbled 90 g

Dressing
1/4 cup fresh lemon juice 50 mL
2 tbsp olive oil 25 mL
1 tsp minced garlic 5 mL
1/2 tsp dried basil 2 mL
1/2 tsp dried oregano (or 1/4 cup/50 mL
  fresh chopped) 2 mL
1/8 tsp freshly ground black pepper 0.5 mL

1. In a saucepan, bring stock to a boil. Stir in quinoa. Reduce heat to medium-low, cover and cook for 15 minutes, or until tender and liquid is absorbed. Transfer to large bowl, and cool.
2. Stir red and green peppers, cucumber, green onions, black olives, red onions, and feta into cooled quinoa.
3. To make dressing: In a small bowl, whisk together lemon juice, olive oil, garlic, basil, oregano, and pepper. Pour over quinoa mixture; toss to coat.

Makes 6 servings.

NUTRITIONAL ANALYSIS
PER SERVING
208 calories
7.6 g protein
9.1 g fat, total
1.8 g fat, saturated
24 g carbohydrates
437 mg sodium
3.4 mg cholesterol
2.5 g fibre

TIPS
Buy quinoa in bulk and keep it in the freezer. Some people like to rinse quinoa before cooking to rid it of a somewhat mineral taste. I don't bother if the quinoa is fresh. Toasting the quinoa in a nonstick frying pan for 2 minutes gives it a nutty flavour.

Mexican Salad with Avocado Dressing

This is a delicious lighter version of a Tex-Mex salad served in Mexican restaurants. It's a complete meal, including vegetables, cheese, and seafood. Often you will have this served in a deep-fried tortilla shell, which is loaded with fat and calories. Try a low-fat version by making your own baked tortilla shell (see page 231).

NUTRITIONAL ANALYSIS
PER SERVING
157 calories
6.6 g protein
6.9 g fat, total
1.8 g fat, saturated
21 g carbohydrates
229 mg sodium
7.1 mg cholesterol
4.1 g fibre

TIPS
I use just half an avocado, since they have the most calories and fat of any fruit or vegetable—one avocado has 30 grams of fat! The fat is monounsaturated and doesn't raise blood cholesterol. Remember to rub your avocado with lemon if cutting before you prepare the rest of the salad, to prevent it from discolouring.

1 large flour tortilla, cut in wedges 1
6 cups torn romaine lettuce 1.5 L
6 oz cooked, peeled shrimp, chopped
    (optional) 175 g
3/4 cup canned chickpeas, rinsed and
    drained 175 mL
1 cup sliced sweet red peppers 250 mL
3/4 cup sliced sweet onions 175 mL
1/2 cup shredded light Cheddar cheese
    125 mL
1/3 cup chopped fresh coriander 75 mL

Dressing
Half ripe avocado, chopped Half
1/4 cup low-fat sour cream 50 mL
1/4 cup water 50 mL
2 tbsp light mayonnaise 25 mL
2 tbsp fresh lemon juice 25 mL
1 tsp minced garlic 5 mL
1 tsp honey 5 mL
1/2 tsp minced jalapeño pepper
    (or 1/4 tsp/1 mL hot Asian chili sauce)
    2 mL

1/4 cup chopped green onions,
    as garnish 50 mL

Preheat oven to 400°F (200°C).

1. Place tortilla on a baking sheet. Spray tortilla with cooking spray. Bake for 5 minutes, or until crisp. Set aside to cool.
2. In a large bowl, toss together romaine, shrimp (if using), chickpeas, red peppers, onions, Cheddar, and coriander.
3. To make dressing: In a food processor, combine avocado, sour cream, water, mayonnaise, lemon juice, garlic, honey, and jalapeño; purée until smooth.
4. Pour dressing over romaine mixture; toss to coat. Crumble cooled tortilla wedges. Garnish with green onions and crumbled tortilla.

Mango Lettuce Salad with Feta and Olives

My favourite salads are those mixed with fruit, an intense cheese, and a sweet vinegar dressing. This one definitely fits the bill. Mangos contain an abundance of beta carotene, which may offer protection from many types of cancer, especially lung cancer.

4 cups torn, mixed salad greens 1 L
1 Belgian endive, sliced 1
1 small head radicchio, torn 1
1-1/2 cups diced ripe mango 375 mL
2 oz light feta cheese, crumbled 60 g
1/3 cup sliced black olives 75 mL

Dressing
2 tbsp balsamic vinegar 25 mL
2 tbsp olive oil 25 mL
1 tbsp honey 15 mL
2 tsp sesame oil 10 mL
1 tsp minced garlic 5 mL

1. In a bowl, toss together greens, endive, radicchio, mango, feta, and black olives.
2. To make dressing: In a small bowl, whisk together vinegar, olive oil, honey, sesame oil, and garlic. Pour over salad; toss to coat.

Makes 6 servings.

NUTRITIONAL ANALYSIS
PER SERVING
155 calories
3.3 g protein
9.1 g fat, total
1.7 g fat, saturated
15 g carbohydrates
210 mg sodium
3.4 mg cholesterol
2.4 g fibre

TIPS
You can substitute any variety of lettuces you wish, just keep the amounts the same. You can substitute ripe pears, peaches, strawberries, or blueberries for the mango. The sweetest mango is the Indonesian. It is smaller than the regular Florida variety, and yellow.

Roasted Sweet Peppers with Pine Nuts, Goat Cheese, and Basil

Makes 6 servings.

NUTRITIONAL ANALYSIS
PER SERVING
88 calories
2.7 g protein
4.9 g fat, total
1.3 g fat, saturated
8.3 g carbohydrates
20 mg sodium
2.2 mg cholesterol
2.5 g fibre

TIPS
If you're concerned about
the peppers burning, you
can roast them at 425°F
(220°C), turning
occasionally, for about
30 to 35 minutes until
completely charred. The
easiest way to peel the
peppers is to place them in
either a paper bag or a
bowl covered with plastic
wrap for about 15 minutes;
the steam allows for easier
peeling. A quicker method
is to run them under cold
water and peel at the same
time.

I can never make enough of this salad for company. Grilled sweet peppers are universally loved. In restaurants they are often marinated, which adds excess calories and fat. Here I use only 1 tablespoon (15 mL) of olive oil—and the results are outstanding. The red, yellow, and orange bell peppers contain an abundance of beta carotene and antioxidants, which help in the fight against cancer.

Dressing
1 tbsp olive oil 15 mL
1 tsp balsamic vinegar 5 mL

6 sweet peppers of various colours, cut in
   half, stemmed, and cored 6
1 oz goat cheese, crumbled 30 g
1/4 cup chopped fresh basil 50 mL
2 tbsp toasted pine nuts 25 mL

Preheat broiler.

1. To make dressing: In a small bowl, whisk together oil and vinegar. Set aside.
2. Broil peppers, turning occasionally, for 15 to 20 minutes, or until charred. Cool, peel, and slice thinly. Arrange on a platter.
3. Drizzle reserved dressing over peppers. Sprinkle with goat cheese, basil, and pine nuts.

Spinach and Oyster Mushroom Salad with Mandarin Oranges

Popeye was right. Spinach has to be one of the best vegetables to consume in terms of nutrition. It is loaded with iron and folate, as well as vitamins A and C. One cup has only 40 calories. Combined with sautéed mushrooms and a light mayonnaise dressing, it is outstanding.

1 tsp vegetable oil 5 mL
2 cups sliced oyster mushrooms 500 mL
8 cups torn spinach 2 L
1 cup drained canned mandarin oranges
   (11-oz/284 mL can) 250 mL
1/2 cup sliced water chestnuts 125 mL
1/2 cup sliced red onions 125 mL
1/3 cup toasted chopped pecans 75 mL

Dressing

2 tbsp olive oil 25 mL
2 tbsp light sour cream 25 mL
1 tbsp light mayonnaise 15 mL
1 tbsp balsamic vinegar 15 mL
2 tsp honey 10 mL
1/2 tsp minced garlic 2 mL

1. In a nonstick frying pan sprayed with vegetable spray, heat oil over medium-high heat; cook mushrooms for 5 minutes, or until browned. Set aside.
2. In a large bowl, combine spinach, mandarin oranges, water chestnuts, red onions, pecans, and warmed mushrooms.
3. In a small bowl, whisk together olive oil, sour cream, mayonnaise, vinegar, honey, and garlic. Pour over spinach mixture; toss to coat.

Makes 8 servings.

NUTRITIONAL ANALYSIS
PER SERVING
131 calories
2.6 g protein
8.5 g fat, total
1.1 g fat, saturated
11 g carbohydrates
55 mg sodium
1.9 mg cholesterol
1.9 g fibre

TIP
Supermarkets now carry baby spinach, which I find more tender and sweeter than regular spinach. Wash just before serving so the leaves don't wilt. Use a lettuce spinner or paper towels to dry.

Seared Sesame Tuna Niçoise Salad

Makes 6 servings.

NUTRITIONAL ANALYSIS
PER SERVING
244 calories
12 g protein
9 g fat, total
1.2 g fat, saturated
27 g carbohydrates
483 mg sodium
14 mg cholesterol
4.2 g fibre

TIPS
When selecting sweet
onions, the best varieties
are Vidalia, Walla Walla, or
Maui; they taste like sugar
and have no sharpness.
Remember, if using canned
tuna, select those packed in
water, not oil.

I was once served this type of salad in a restaurant, and it featured freshly seared tuna. What a difference! If raw tuna isn't your favourite, then either cook the tuna to medium or use canned tuna. Fresh tuna contains more omega-3 fatty acids than the canned variety.

1 lb mini potatoes, scrubbed, peel on (about 10) 500 g	**Dressing**
	2 tbsp olive oil 25 mL
8 oz green beans 250 g	2 tbsp balsamic vinegar 25 mL
3 plum tomatoes, sliced and seeded 3	1-1/2 tsp minced garlic 7 mL
1 cup sliced sweet onions 250 mL	1 tsp Dijon mustard 5 mL
1/3 cup sliced black olives 75 mL	1/2 tsp granulated sugar 2 mL
1/3 cup fresh chopped dill 75 mL	1/2 tsp salt 2 mL
4 cups leafy lettuce, torn 1 L	1/4 tsp freshly ground black pepper 1 mL
2 tbsp sesame seeds 25 mL	
8 oz fresh tuna 250 g	

1. Place potatoes in a saucepan and add cold water to cover. Bring to a boil. Reduce heat to medium-high; cook for approximately 15 minutes, or just until tender. Drain. Cool and cut into quarters.
2. Steam or blanch green beans just until barely tender. Rinse with cold water.
3. In a large bowl, combine potatoes, green beans, tomatoes, onions, olives, dill, and lettuce.
4. Place sesame seeds on a plate. Place tuna on top. Turn tuna to coat both sides in sesame seeds. In a nonstick frying pan sprayed with vegetable spray, cook tuna over medium-high heat for 2 minutes per side, or until desired doneness. Slice thinly. Add to salad.
5. To make dressing: In a small bowl, whisk together olive oil, vinegar, garlic, mustard, sugar, salt, and pepper. Drizzle over salad.

New Potato and Smoked Salmon Salad with Creamy Dill Dressing

You've never tasted a potato salad like this before. The smoked salmon, light dill dressing, and mini potatoes are a great combination. Most potato salads are loaded with fat and calories from the amount of mayonnaise used. In this version, the combination of light sour cream, mayonnaise, and olive oil bring the calories right down.

1-1/2 lb new mini potatoes, scrubbed, peel on 750 g
6 oz smoked salmon, chopped 175 g
1/2 cup chopped snow peas 125 mL
1/3 cup chopped green onions 75 mL

Dressing
1/2 cup light sour cream 125 mL
1/4 cup chopped fresh dill (or 1 tsp/5 mL dried) 50 mL
2 tbsp light mayonnaise 25 mL
2 tbsp olive oil 25 mL
1 tbsp fresh lemon juice 15 mL
2 tsp Dijon mustard 10 mL
1 tsp minced garlic 5 mL
1/4 tsp freshly ground black pepper 1 mL

1. Place potatoes in a saucepan and add cold water to cover. Bring to a boil. Reduce heat to medium-high; cook for approximately 15 minutes, or until tender when pierced with the tip of a knife. Drain. Cool.
2. Slice potatoes into 1/4-inch (5 mm) rounds. In a large bowl, combine potatoes, smoked salmon, snow peas, and green onions.
3. To make dressing: In a small bowl, whisk together sour cream, dill, mayonnaise, olive oil, lemon juice, mustard, garlic, and pepper. Pour over potato mixture; toss to coat.

Makes 8 servings.

NUTRITIONAL ANALYSIS
PER SERVING
179 calories
6.7 g protein
6.7 g fat, total
1.6 g fat, saturated
23 g carbohydrates
509 mg sodium
11 mg cholesterol
2.1 g fibre

TIPS
Make sure the potatoes are cool before adding the smoked salmon, or the salmon will cook. If mini potatoes are not available use a regular potato and cut into large cubes before cooking. This salad is great chilled, and can be prepared up to 1 day in advance.

Grilled Chicken Caesar Salad

Makes 6 servings.

NUTRITIONAL ANALYSIS
PER SERVING
164 calories
14 g protein
7.6 g fat, total
1.8 g fat, saturated
9.8 g carbohydrates
239 mg sodium
61 mg cholesterol
1.4 g fibre

TIPS
The statistics on consuming raw eggs are that 1 in 20,000 eggs may contain bacteria that can cause food poisoning. Food poisoning is often caused from using cracked eggs or eggs that have been left out at room temperature for several hours. Illness from raw eggs usually occurs outside the home, in restaurants or fast-food establishments, where food safety is not regularly practised. I would recommend that pregnant women, senior citizens, and those with a weak immune system avoid them. To eliminate the 1 egg in this recipe, increase your liquid ingredients by 3 tbsp (45 mL).

Consider this: a not-so-innocent traditional Caesar salad can have over 500 calories and 30 grams of fat per plate! The calories come from the excess oil, cheese, and eggs. My version is delicious, yet low in fat and calories. You don't need your salad to be swimming in dressing—there is just enough here. The large Italian croutons make this salad a standout.

8 oz boneless skinless chicken breast 250 g
2 cups 1-inch (2.5 cm) Italian bread cubes
   500 mL

Dressing

1 egg 1
3 tbsp grated Parmesan cheese 45 mL
3 anchovy fillets, minced 3

1 tbsp fresh lemon juice 15 mL
1 tsp Dijon mustard 5 mL
1-1/2 tsp minced garlic 7 mL
1/8 tsp freshly ground black pepper 0.5 mL
2 tbsp olive oil 25 mL

6 cups torn romaine lettuce 1.5 L

Preheat grill or grill pan; spray with vegetable spray. Preheat oven to 425°F (220°C).

1. Grill chicken over medium-high heat for 6 minutes per side, or until cooked through. Cut in strips.
2. Place bread cubes on a baking sheet. Spray cubes with vegetable spray. Bake for 8 to 10 minutes, or until golden.
3. To make dressing: In a small food processor, or in a bowl using a whisk, beat egg, Parmesan, anchovies, lemon juice, mustard, garlic, and pepper until smooth. Slowly add the olive oil, mixing until thickened.
4. In a bowl, toss together chicken, croutons, and romaine. Pour dressing over; toss to coat.

Goat Cheese Rounds over Caesar Greens

I have always loved this type of salad in restaurants, but never created it in my kitchen—until now. Here we go with my light version, which is beautiful, especially when entertaining. The key is to have the goat cheese as cold as possible so it doesn't melt when sautéing.

3 oz goat cheese, chilled 90 g

2 tbsp low-fat milk 25 mL

3 tbsp seasoned dry breadcrumbs 45 mL

Caesar Dressing

1 egg yolk 1

2 tbsp grated Parmesan cheese 25 mL

1 tbsp olive oil 15 mL

2 tsp fresh lemon juice 10 mL

2 tsp water 10 mL

1 tsp minced garlic 5 mL

2 anchovy fillets, minced 2

4 cups torn mixed salad greens 1 L

1. Divide goat cheese into four equal portions. Form each portion into a patty. Pour milk into a small bowl. Place breadcrumbs on a plate. Dip goat cheese patties in milk, then coat with breadcrumbs; place on a clean plate.
2. In a nonstick frying pan sprayed with cooking spray, cook goat cheese patties over medium-high heat for 3 minutes, turning once, or just until golden.
3. To make dressing: In a small food processor, or in a bowl using a whisk, beat together egg yolk, Parmesan, olive oil, lemon juice, water, garlic, and anchovies until smooth.
4. In a large bowl, toss greens with dressing. Divide among four plates. Place a warm goat cheese patty on top of each serving.

Makes 4 servings.

NUTRITIONAL ANALYSIS
PER SERVING
141 calories
7 g protein
9 g fat, total
2.2 g fat, saturated
10 g carbohydrates
336 mg sodium
50 mg cholesterol
1.6 g fibre

TIPS
Make sure not to sauté the cheese too long or it will begin to melt and the patties may break. Just sauté until browned on both sides. This salad makes a wonderful lunch along with some French bread.

Thai-Style Beef Salad with Orange–Sesame Dressing

Makes 6 servings.

NUTRITIONAL ANALYSIS
PER SERVING
166 calories
11 g protein
3.8 g fat, total
1 g fat, saturated
22 g carbohydrates
172 mg sodium
24 mg cholesterol
2.2 g fibre

TIPS
You can always substitute chicken, seafood, or firm tofu for the beef. The dressing is also delicious over other salads or as a marinade for chicken, pork, or fish.

The combination of tender beef, rice noodles, sweet vegetables, and orange Asian dressing makes this a delicious main course salad. Use a good-quality steak, making sure you don't overcook it. Thin vermicelli noodles give a lighter texture to this salad than a heavier pasta would.

8 oz boneless grilling steak 500 g
2 oz thin rice vermicelli 60 g
4 cups torn, mixed salad greens 1 L
1-1/2 cups chopped snow peas 375 mL
1 cup thinly sliced sweet red peppers 250 mL
1/2 cup sliced water chestnuts 125 mL
1/2 cup drained canned mandarin oranges
   125 mL
1/3 cup chopped sweet onions 75 mL
1/4 cup chopped green onions 50 mL

Dressing
2 tbsp thawed orange juice concentrate
   25 mL
1-1/2 tbsp packed brown sugar 22 mL
2 tbsp rice wine vinegar 25 mL
2 tbsp low-sodium soy sauce 25 mL
2 tsp sesame oil 10 mL
1 tsp minced garlic 5 mL
1/2 tsp minced fresh ginger 2 mL
1/2 tsp hot Asian chili sauce 2 mL
1/8 tsp salt 0.5 mL

1. In a nonstick frying or grill pan sprayed with cooking spray, cook steak over medium-high heat for 5 minutes, turning once, or until desired doneness. (Or cook over medium-high heat on the sprayed grill of a preheated barbecue.) Cool. Slice thinly.
2. Pour boiling water over rice noodles. Let stand 5 minutes. Drain.
3. In a large bowl, combine rice noodles, greens, snow peas, red peppers, water chestnuts, mandarin oranges, sweet onions, and green onions.
4. To make dressing: In a small bowl, whisk orange juice concentrate, brown sugar, vinegar, soy sauce, sesame oil, garlic, ginger, hot Asian chili sauce, and salt. Pour over rice noodle mixture; toss to coat. Place steak on top of salad.

Sandwiches and Wraps

Roasted Vegetarian Sandwich
with Brie Cheese

Makes 8 servings.

NUTRITIONAL ANALYSIS
PER 1/2 SANDWICH
187 calories
6 g protein
6 g fat, total
2.2 g fat, saturated
29 g carbohydrates
398 mg sodium
9 mg cholesterol
2.5 g fibre

TIPS
For the rolls, I like to
use either focaccia or
sourdough rolls. If using
store-bought pesto,
remember it is higher in
fat and calories than my
homemade version; use
a smaller amount or add
a little water to thin.

After tasting this sandwich you might decide to go vegetarian! The roasted vegetables, pesto, and Brie cheese are a sensational combination. And, yes, you can enjoy Brie cheese when you're eating light—just watch the amounts. Each sandwich only contains 1/2 oz (15 g) of Brie, which you'll find is enough.

Half large red onion, sliced Half
1 red bell pepper, cut in 8 wedges 1
1 large portobello mushroom, sliced thickly 1
1 zucchini, sliced in 3 lengthwise pieces 1
2 tbsp pesto sauce (from Pesto-Glazed Salmon, page 321)
    or store-bought 25 mL
2 tbsp light sour cream 25 mL
1 tbsp olive oil 15 mL
2 tsp balsamic vinegar 10 mL
1/2 tsp minced garlic 2 mL
4 large rolls (each approx. 3-1/2 oz/110 g), sliced lengthwise 4
2 oz Brie cheese, sliced thinly 60 g

Preheat oven to 450°F (230°C). Line a rimmed baking sheet with foil.

1. Place onion, pepper, mushroom, and zucchini on prepared baking sheet. Spray vegetables lightly with cooking spray. Roast vegetables, turning once, for 30 to 35 minutes, or until tender.
2. Meanwhile, in a small bowl, combine pesto and sour cream.
3. Once vegetables are roasted, cut into pieces that fit the shape of the bread. Toss with oil, vinegar, and garlic.
4. Spread pesto mixture over bread; top with vegetable mixture and Brie. Cut in half.

Goat Cheese and Tomato Salad Wraps

This is a great vegetarian wrap that is perfect as a complete meal or side dish. Tomatoes contain lycopene, which is known to help in the fight against prostate cancer.

3 oz goat cheese, crumbled 90 g

1-1/4 cups diced, seeded plum tomatoes 300 mL

1-1/4 cups diced English cucumber (skin on) 300 mL

1/2 cup chopped green onions 125 mL

2 tsp olive oil 10 mL

2 tsp balsamic vinegar 10 mL

1 tsp minced garlic 5 mL

4 large flour tortillas 4

1. In a bowl, stir together goat cheese, tomatoes, cucumber, green onions, oil, vinegar, and garlic.
2. Place a tortilla flat on work surface. Place one-quarter of goat cheese mixture in centre of tortilla. Roll bottom of tortilla up over filling tightly; fold in both sides and continue to roll. Repeat with remaining tortillas and filling. Cut in half.

Makes 8 servings.

NUTRITIONAL ANALYSIS
PER 1/2 WRAP
150 calories
6 g protein
5 g fat, total
2.8 g fat, saturated
20 g carbohydrates
209 mg sodium
6 mg cholesterol
1.6 g fibre

TIPS
You can substitute feta cheese for the goat cheese. Substitute another cheese if you like; just be sure it has a strong flavour to give the tortilla the best flavour. This tortilla would also be great if you added 4 oz (125 g) of diced cooked chicken or seafood.

Falafel with Creamy Tahini Lemon Dressing

Famous in Middle Eastern cuisine, falafels are meat-like fried chickpea balls served with a creamy oil-based tahini (sesame) sauce. This version is baked, with a light and creamy sauce.

1 19-oz/540 mL can chickpeas, rinsed and drained 1
1/4 cup chopped green onions 50 mL
1/4 cup chopped fresh coriander 50 mL
1/4 cup plain dry breadcrumbs 50 mL
2 tbsp tahini 25 mL
1 tbsp fresh lemon juice 15 mL
1-1/2 tsp minced garlic 7 mL
1/4 tsp baking powder 1 mL
1/4 tsp ground cumin 1 mL
1 egg 1
1/8 tsp freshly ground black pepper 0.5 mL

Creamy Tahini Lemon Dressing
1/3 cup vegetable stock 75 mL
1/3 cup smooth 5% ricotta or 2% cottage cheese 75 mL
2 tbsp tahini 25 mL
2 tbsp light mayonnaise 25 mL
2 tbsp olive oil 25 mL
1 tbsp fresh lemon juice 15 mL
1 tbsp low-sodium soy sauce 15 mL
1 tsp minced garlic 5 mL
1/4 cup chopped fresh coriander 50 mL

4 large pita breads, sliced in half 4
Tomato slices and lettuce leaves, as garnish (optional)

Preheat oven to 400°F (200°C). Spray a baking sheet with cooking spray.

1. In a food processor, combine chickpeas, green onions, coriander, breadcrumbs, tahini, lemon juice, garlic, baking powder, cumin, egg, and pepper. Pulse on and off until well mixed. Form into 16 balls of 2 tbsp (25 mL) each; flatten slightly. Place on prepared baking sheet.
2. Bake in centre of oven, turning once, for 15 to 20 minutes, or until golden.
3. To make dressing: In a food processor, combine stock, ricotta, tahini, mayonnaise, olive oil, lemon juice, soy sauce, and garlic; process until smooth. Stir in coriander. Divide in half; store half in refrigerator for later use as salad dressing, or as sauce over chicken or fish.
4. Place falafels in pita breads. Drizzle about 2 tbsp (25 mL) dressing over each. If desired, include tomato slices and lettuce inside pita.

California Roll Wraps

This recipe came to me one day when I couldn't decide if I wanted sushi or a wrap for lunch. What about a combination? It turned out great!

Sushi Rice

3/4 cup sushi rice 175 mL

3/4 cup water 175 mL

1 tbsp rice wine vinegar 15 mL

1-1/2 tsp granulated sugar 7 mL

6 oz imitation crabmeat (surimi), chopped 175 g

3/4 cup diced, peeled English cucumber 175 mL

1/2 cup diced avocado (half a medium avocado) 125 mL

1/3 cup chopped green onions 75 mL

2 tbsp chopped pickled ginger (optional) 25 mL

2 tbsp low-sodium soy sauce 25 mL

3-1/2 tbsp light mayonnaise 47 mL

3 tbsp light sour cream 45 mL

1/2 tsp wasabi (Japanese horseradish) 2 mL

6 large flour tortillas 6

Makes 12 servings.

NUTRITIONAL ANALYSIS
PER 1/2 WRAP
191 calories
5 g protein
5 g fat, total
1.4 g fat, saturated
30 g carbohydrates
460 mg sodium
5 mg cholesterol
0.8 g fibre

1. To make rice: In a saucepan, combine rice and water. Bring to a boil; boil for 1 minute. Reduce heat to low; cover and cook for 12 minutes. Remove from heat. Let stand covered for 10 minutes. Meanwhile, in a small saucepan, combine vinegar and sugar. Bring to a boil, stirring to dissolve sugar. Remove from heat.
2. Turn rice out into a large bowl. Stir in vinegar and sugar mixture. Cool.
3. In a bowl, stir together crabmeat, cucumber, avocado, green onions, ginger (if using), soy sauce, and cooled rice.
4. In a small bowl, combine mayonnaise, sour cream, and wasabi. Remove 2 tbsp (25 mL). Add remainder to crabmeat mixture.
5. Spread 2 tbsp (25 mL) reserved mayonnaise mixture thinly over tortillas.
6. Divide crab mixture evenly among tortillas, placing on bottom third of each tortilla. Roll once away from you, fold in both sides, and continue to roll. Cut in half to serve.

TIPS
Be sure to use sushi rice, which is available in most supermarkets. Cook it as directed in the recipe and you'll have perfect rice every time, or you can use a rice steamer. You can also find flavoured sushi vinegar, specially made for sushi with the sugar already added; if using this vinegar, omit the sugar in the recipe.

Shrimp Quesadillas with Feta, Dill, and Tomatoes

Makes 4 servings.

NUTRITIONAL ANALYSIS
PER QUESADILLA
307 calories
18 g protein
9.2 g fat, total
3.8 g fat, saturated
38 g carbohydrates
626 mg sodium
69 mg cholesterol
2.5 g fibre

TIPS
Serve these as appetizers
by slicing into wedges and
serving warm. You can
always substitute cooked
chicken for the shrimp.

Quesadillas are a versatile way to work with tortillas. Using a nonstick grill pan is an easy way to grill and warm the quesadillas until the cheese melts. The combination of plum tomatoes, feta cheese, and shrimp tastes great when heated.

4 oz diced, cooked shrimp 125 g
1/2 cup chopped, seeded plum tomatoes 125 mL
1/4 cup chopped green onions 50 mL
2 tbsp chopped fresh dill 25 mL
2 oz light feta cheese, crumbled 60 g
1/2 tsp minced garlic 2 mL
Freshly ground black pepper, to taste
4 large flour tortillas 4
1/2 cup shredded light mozzarella or Havarti cheese 125 mL

1. In a bowl, stir together shrimp, tomatoes, green onions, dill, feta, garlic, and pepper.
2. Place tortillas flat on work surface. Spread shrimp mixture evenly over half of each tortilla. Sprinkle evenly with mozzarella. Fold uncovered half of each tortilla over filling and press to seal.
3. In a large nonstick frying or grill pan over medium-high heat, cook quesadillas for 3 minutes or until golden. Turn and cook another minute.

Thai Shrimp Wrap with Rice and Peanut Sauce

10/10 everyone loved

You can achieve a Thai flavour by using readily available ingredients, such as natural peanut butter, fresh coriander, and fresh ginger. This wrap has shrimp, rice, and sweet vegetables tossed with a light Asian peanut dressing.

1 cup chicken or fish stock 250 mL

3/4 cup long-grain rice 175 mL

1 cup thinly sliced sweet peppers (red, green, yellow, or orange) 250 mL

1/2 cup thinly sliced carrots 125 mL

8 oz shrimp, peeled, deveined, and chopped 250 g

Peanut Sauce

3 tbsp natural peanut butter 45 mL

3 tbsp water 45 mL

2 tbsp each: low-sodium soy sauce, rice wine vinegar, and honey 25 mL

2 tsp sesame oil 10 mL

1 tsp minced garlic 5 mL

1/2 tsp minced fresh ginger 2 mL

1/4 tsp hot Asian chili sauce 1 mL

1/4 cup chopped fresh coriander 50 mL

6 large flour tortillas 6

Makes 12 servings.

NUTRITIONAL ANALYSIS
PER 1/2 WRAP
193 calories
8 g protein
5 g fat, total
1.1 g fat, saturated
28 g carbohydrates
351 mg sodium
27 mg cholesterol
1.8 g fibre

TIP
Always buy natural peanut butter that contains nothing but peanuts. The commercial brands often contain icing sugar and are hydrogenated, which means they are a form of saturated fat.

1. In a small saucepan, bring stock to a boil. Stir in rice. Reduce heat to low; cover and cook for 10 minutes. Remove from heat; cover and let stand for 10 minutes. Transfer to a bowl. Cool.

2. Meanwhile, in a large nonstick frying pan sprayed with cooking spray, cook peppers and carrots over medium-high heat for 3 minutes. Add shrimp; cook for 3 minutes, or until shrimp is pink. Cool.

3. To make sauce: In a small bowl, whisk together peanut butter, water, soy sauce, vinegar, honey, sesame oil, garlic, ginger, and hot Asian chili sauce until smooth.

4. Stir shrimp mixture, coriander, and sauce into rice.

5. Place a tortilla flat on work surface. Place 1/2 cup (125 mL) rice mixture in centre of tortilla. Roll bottom of tortilla up over filling tightly; fold in both sides and continue to roll. Repeat with remaining tortillas and filling. Cut in half.

Chicken and Caramelized Onion Sandwich

Makes 8 servings.

NUTRITIONAL ANALYSIS
PER 1/2 SANDWICH
252 calories
12 g protein
3.8 g fat, total
0.7 g fat, saturated
43 g carbohydrates
341 mg sodium
16 mg cholesterol
2.3 g fibre

TIPS
You can use a sweet onion,
such as Vidalia, Walla
Walla, or Maui, to intensify
the flavour. Leftover
chicken or turkey works
well if you have it on hand.

When the onions are sautéed slowly, you end up with caramelized onions that are impossible to resist. The sauce over the bread is a mixture of Dijon mustard and honey. It goes so well with the chicken and onions!

2 tsp vegetable oil 10 mL
4 cups thinly sliced onions 1 L
2 tbsp packed brown sugar 25 mL
2 tbsp cider vinegar 25 mL
1-1/2 tsp minced garlic 7 mL
8 oz skinless boneless chicken breast 250 g
1/4 cup honey 50 mL
1 tbsp Dijon mustard 15 mL
4 large rolls (each approx. 3-1/2 oz/110 g) 4
Lettuce

Preheat grill or grill pan. Spray with cooking spray.

1. In a nonstick frying pan sprayed with cooking spray, heat oil over medium-high heat; cook onions for 5 minutes. Stir in brown sugar, vinegar, and garlic; cook on low heat, stirring occasionally, for 10 minutes, or until onions are tender.
2. Grill chicken over medium-high heat for 12 minutes, turning once, until cooked through. Slice thinly.
3. In a small bowl, stir together honey and mustard.
4. Slice rolls in half; spread cut sides with honey mixture. Fill with chicken and onions, and line with lettuce. Cut in half.

Creamy Dijon Chicken Salad in a Pita

I tend to avoid chicken salad in restaurants because it is loaded with mayonnaise, which gives this innocent-seeming salad an abundance of calories and fat. For this recipe, I use lots of diced vegetables with a light sour cream–Dijon mayonnaise dressing. You'll never believe it's low in calories and fat.

6 oz skinless boneless chicken breast 175 g
1 cup diced plum tomatoes 250 mL
3/4 cup diced sweet green peppers 175 mL
1/3 cup chopped green onions 75 mL
3 tbsp chopped black olives 45 mL
2 oz light feta cheese, crumbled 60 g
1/4 cup light sour cream 50 mL
2 tbsp light mayonnaise 25 mL
1 tbsp fresh lemon juice 15 mL
2 tsp dried tarragon 10 mL
1 tsp Dijon mustard 5 mL
1 tsp minced garlic 5 mL
1/8 tsp freshly ground black pepper 0.5 mL
2 large pita breads 2
Lettuce

Preheat grill or grill pan. Spray with cooking spray.

1. Grill chicken over medium-high heat for 12 minutes, turning once, until cooked through. Cool and chop.
2. In a bowl, stir together chicken, tomatoes, green peppers, green onions, olives, and feta. In another bowl, stir together sour cream, mayonnaise, lemon juice, tarragon, mustard, garlic, and pepper; pour over chicken mixture and toss to coat.
3. Cut pita breads in half and line pockets with lettuce leaves. Divide filling among pitas, about 3/4 cup (175 mL) per half. Serve immediately.

Makes 4 servings.

NUTRITIONAL ANALYSIS
PER 1/2 PITA
240 calories
17 g protein
8 g fat, total
2.6 g fat, saturated
25 g carbohydrates
532 mg sodium
37 mg cholesterol
2 g fibre

TIP
You can always substitute tortillas for pita breads— just wrap the filling—or use your favourite roll.

Beef Fajitas with Sweet Peppers, Coriander, and Cheese

Makes 6 servings.

NUTRITIONAL ANALYSIS
PER 1/2 FAJITA
231 calories
15 g protein
7 g fat, total
2.3 g fat, saturated
26 g carbohydrates
314 mg sodium
29 mg cholesterol
2.4 g fibre

TIPS
I like to serve this as a
"make-it-yourself" fajita
buffet. People love to have
the ingredients out before
them to make their own
versions. You can use
seafood, chicken, or tofu
in place of the beef.

Fajitas are my favourite type of Tex-Mex food. These ones are creamy and rich tasting, without the excess fat of regular fajitas loaded with too much cheese, sour cream, guacamole, and beef. In my version, you get plenty of vegetables along some light cheese and sour cream. Easy to make, and the whole family loves them.

8 oz boneless grilling steak 250 g
2 tsp vegetable oil 10 mL
1-1/2 cups thinly sliced onions 375 mL
1-1/2 tsp minced garlic 7 mL
1-1/2 cups sweet red pepper strips 375 mL
1/4 cup chopped fresh coriander or parsley 50 mL
3 tbsp chopped green onions 45 mL
6 small flour tortillas 6
1/2 cup shredded light Cheddar cheese 125 mL
1/3 cup salsa 75 mL
1/4 cup light sour cream 50 mL

Preheat oven to 425°F (220°C). Spray a baking sheet with cooking spray.

1. In a nonstick frying pan sprayed with cooking spray, cook beef over medium-high heat for 5 minutes, turning once, or until desired doneness. Remove beef from frying pan. Slice thinly.
2. Respray pan. Add oil to pan; cook onions and garlic for 4 minutes, or until browned. Reduce heat to medium. Stir in red pepper strips; cook for 5 minutes, or until softened. Remove from heat. Stir in coriander, green onions, and cooked beef.
3. Divide mixture evenly among tortillas, placing in centre of each torilla. Top with Cheddar, salsa, and sour cream. Roll bottom of tortilla up over filling tightly; fold in both sides and continue to roll.
4. Place on prepared baking sheet. Bake in centre of oven for 5 minutes, or until heated through and the cheese is melted.

Grilled Steak and Mashed Potato Wrap

I call this a comfort wrap. What could be better than mashed potatoes with sautéed onions and tender steak rolled together in a tortilla?

8 oz boneless grilling steak 250 g
1 tsp vegetable oil 5 mL
3/4 cup chopped onions 175 mL
1 tsp minced garlic 5 mL
1 lb medium Yukon Gold potatoes 500 g
3 tbsp each: light sour cream and chicken stock 45 mL
1/4 tsp salt 1 mL
1/8 tsp freshly ground black pepper 0.5 mL
1 tbsp barbecue sauce 15 mL
4 large flour tortillas 4

Preheat grill or grill pan. Spray with cooking spray.

1. Grill steak over medium-high heat for 8 minutes, turning once, or until medium-rare. Transfer to plate, cover with foil, and set aside until potatoes are cooked.
2. In a nonstick frying pan sprayed with cooking spray, heat oil over medium-high heat; cook onions and garlic for 5 minutes, or until browned. Set aside.
3. Peel and quarter potatoes. Place in a saucepan and cover with cold water. Bring to a boil. Reduce heat to medium-high; cook for 15 to 20 minutes, or until potatoes are tender when pierced with the tip of a knife. Drain.
4. Mash potatoes with sour cream, stock, salt, and pepper. Stir in onion mixture.
5. Thinly slice steak and pour barbecue sauce over top.
6. Place a tortilla flat on work surface. Place one-quarter of warm potato mixture in centre of tortilla; top with one-quarter of steak. Roll bottom of tortilla up over filling tightly; fold in both sides and continue to roll. Repeat with remaining tortillas, potatoes, and steak. Cut in half. Serve warm.

Makes 8 servings.

NUTRITIONAL ANALYSIS
PER 1/2 WRAP
206 calories
11 g protein
4.9 g fat, total
1.9 g fat, saturated
30 g carbohydrates
283 mg sodium
19 mg cholesterol
2.2 g fibre

TIP
Yukon Gold potatoes have the creamiest and sweetest flavour of all potatoes. If unavailable, use regular white potatoes.

Muffaletta (Smoked Salmon, Pesto, and Cheese Sandwich)

No, this is not an Italian sandwich! Its origin is in New Orleans, and it is traditionally made with loads of oil, olives, and often smoked meats or cheese. My adaptation is delicious, and beautiful to look at and serve. Roasted peppers with a creamy pesto–cheese filling, highlighted with smoked salmon, make this an outstanding sandwich.

2 sweet peppers, any colour 2
1 whole round Italian bread or round sourdough bread, about 675 g 1
2 tbsp pesto sauce (from Pesto-Glazed Salmon, page 321) or store-bought 25 mL
1/2 cup smooth 5% ricotta cheese 125 mL
2 oz light cream cheese, softened 60 g
2 oz light feta cheese, crumbed 60 g
4 oz smoked salmon or grilled chicken 125 g
2 cups shredded lettuce 500 mL
2 plum tomatoes, sliced 2
1/3 cup diced red onions 75 mL
1/4 cup chopped black olives 50 mL

Preheat oven to 425°F (220°C).

1. Place peppers on baking sheet. Bake for 25 to 30 minutes, or until charred on both sides. Cool. Peel, stem, and core. Slice thinly.
2. Slice bread in half horizontally. Remove inner part of bread, leaving 1-inch (2.5 cm) crust all around. Spread inside surfaces of bread halves with pesto.
3. In a food processor or blender, purée ricotta with cream cheese until smooth. Stir in feta.
4. Spread cheese mixture onto bottom half of loaf. Layer with roasted peppers, salmon, lettuce, tomatoes, onions, and olives. Top with top half of bread. Serve immediately or wrap tightly in plastic wrap and chill until serving.

Makes 8 servings.

NUTRITIONAL ANALYSIS
PER 1/8 LOAF
244 calories
12 g protein
6.2 g fat, total
2.5 g fat, saturated
35 g carbohydrates
767 mg sodium
13 mg cholesterol
2.2 g fibre

TIPS
You can use ready-made roasted sweet bell peppers in a jar packed in water if you don't want to roast your own. If a round bread is not available, use a loaf-style bread.

Pasta and Grains

Bruschetta Pasta with Goat Cheese and Fresh Basil

Makes 4 to 6 servings.

NUTRITIONAL ANALYSIS
PER 1/6-RECIPE SERVING
262 calories
9.7 g protein
9.7 g fat, total
2.8 g fat, saturated
34 g carbohydrates
269 mg sodium
9.1 mg cholesterol
2.2 g fibre

TIPS
If served warm, the cheese
will melt over the pasta.
This pasta dish is also
delicious served at room
temperature or chilled.
You can substitute feta or
a milder cheese such as
mozzarella for the goat
cheese.

If you love bruschetta, then you'll love this version over pasta. Fresh chopped plum tomatoes, sweet onions, olives, goat cheese, and fresh basil make this a wonderful light pasta. Tomatoes contain lycopene, a powerful antioxidant that is showing promise in the fight against prostate and breast cancer, as well as lowering cholesterol levels.

3 cups chopped plum tomatoes 750 mL
1/2 cup diced sweet onions 125 mL
1/4 cup sliced black olives 50 mL
3 tbsp grated Parmesan cheese 45 mL
2 tbsp olive oil 25 mL
1-1/2 tbsp balsamic vinegar 22 mL
1-1/2 tsp minced garlic 7 mL
1 tsp Dijon mustard 5 mL
1 tsp hot chili flakes 5 mL
2 oz goat cheese, crumbled 60 g
4 anchovy fillets, diced 4
8 oz rigatoni 250 g
1/2 cup chopped fresh basil 125 mL

1. In a large bowl, stir together tomatoes, onions, olives, Parmesan, olive oil, vinegar, garlic, mustard, chili flakes, goat cheese, and anchovies.
2. In a large pot of boiling water, cook rigatoni for 6 to 8 minutes, or until tender but firm. Drain. Add tomato mixture; toss to coat. Toss with fresh basil. Serve warm.

Old-Fashioned Baked Macaroni and Cheese Casserole

Comfort food without the fat and calories, and my children's favourite pasta dish—when they prefer this to any of the boxed versions, you know their tastebuds are healthier!

3 tbsp all-purpose flour 45 mL

1-1/3 cups chicken or vegetable stock
   325 mL

1-1/4 cups low-fat milk 300 mL

1-1/4 cups shredded light Cheddar cheese
   300 mL

2 tbsp grated Parmesan cheese 25 mL

1 tsp Dijon mustard 5 mL

12 oz elbow macaroni (approx. 2-1/2
   cups/625 mL) 375 g

Topping

1/3 cup seasoned dry breadcrumbs 75 mL

3 tbsp grated Parmesan cheese 45 mL

1 tsp vegetable oil 5 mL

Preheat oven to 450°F (230°C). Spray an 8-cup (2 L) casserole dish with cooking spray.

1. In a saucepan, whisk flour, stock, and milk until smooth. Place over medium heat; cook, whisking, for 3 minutes, or until hot and thickened. Stir in Cheddar, Parmesan, and mustard; cook 1 minute longer, or until cheese melts. Remove from heat.

2. In a large pot of boiling water, cook macaroni for 8 to 10 minutes, or until tender but firm. Drain. Toss with cheese sauce. Pour into prepared casserole dish.

3. To make topping: In a small bowl, stir together breadcrumbs, Parmesan, and oil. Sprinkle over casserole.

4. Bake in centre of oven for 10 minutes, or until top is golden.

Makes 8 servings.

NUTRITIONAL ANALYSIS
PER SERVING
257 calories
14 g protein
4.5 g fat, total
2 g fat, saturated
40 g carbohydrates
480 mg sodium
8.4 mg cholesterol
1.3 g fibre

TIPS
I often make this recipe and freeze individual servings in plastic containers—they're perfect for the children's lunches. Feel free to add some vegetables such as green peas, diced bell peppers, or carrots.

Creamy Tuna Dressing over Pasta Niçoise

Makes 6 servings.

NUTRITIONAL ANALYSIS
PER SERVING
329 calories
14 g protein
9 g fat, total
0.8 g fat, saturated
48 g carbohydrates
285 mg sodium
7.8 mg cholesterol
2.4 g fibre

TIPS
Always buy tuna packed in
water, not oil; oil-packed
tuna has double the
calories and six times the
fat. You can substitute
either penne or farfalle,
which is the butterfly-
shaped pasta, for the
rotini.

This tuna sauce is not only delicious over pasta, but great as a sauce over cooked beef or chicken. You can keep it refrigerated for up to 3 days.

Sauce

1 can (170 g) water-packed flaked tuna, drained 1

3/4 cup chicken stock 175 mL

2 tbsp light mayonnaise 25 mL

2 tbsp vegetable oil 25 mL

1 tbsp fresh lemon juice 15 mL

1 tbsp drained capers 15 mL

1-1/2 tsp minced garlic 7 mL

1/4 tsp freshly ground black pepper 1 mL

12 oz rotini (approx. 4 cups/1 kg) 375 g

1-1/2 cups chopped plum tomatoes 375 mL

1-1/4 cups chopped English cucumber (skin on) 300 mL

1/2 cup chopped sweet onions 125 mL

1/3 cup sliced black olives 75 mL

1/3 cup chopped green onions 75 mL

1/3 cup fresh chopped dill 75 mL

1. Place tuna, stock, mayonnaise, oil, lemon juice, capers, garlic, and pepper in food processor; purée until smooth.

2. In a large pot of boiling water, cook rotini for 8 to 10 minutes, or until tender but firm. Drain. Rinse under cold running water; drain. Transfer to a large serving bowl.

3. Add tomatoes, cucumbers, onions, olives, green onions, dill, and tuna sauce; toss well. Serve at room temperature or chilled.

Pasta with Chicken, Tomatoes, Peppers, and Beans

Serve this pasta salad at room temperature to bring out all the flavours. It is a complete meal with the chicken and beans, or it can be served as a side dish. Using half an avocado adds a rich flavour to the salad. Avocado contains 300 calories with 30 grams of heart-healthy fat, so eat in moderation.

8 oz boneless skinless chicken breast 250 g

12 oz rotini or penne (approx. 4 cups/ 1 kg) 375 g

3 cups diced plum tomatoes 750 mL

1 cup diced sweet onions 250 mL

1 cup diced sweet yellow or red peppers 250 mL

1 cup canned black beans, drained and rinsed 250 mL

Half ripe avocado, diced Half

1/2 cup chopped fresh coriander 125 mL

1/4 cup fresh lemon juice 50 mL

3 tbsp olive oil 45 mL

2 tsp minced garlic 10 mL

1/2 to 1 tsp hot pepper sauce 2 to 5 mL

1/4 tsp salt 1 mL

1/8 tsp freshly ground black pepper 0.5 mL

Preheat grill or grill pan sprayed with vegetable spray.

1. Grill chicken over medium-high heat for 6 minutes per side, or until cooked through. Slice thinly.
2. In a large pot of boiling water, cook pasta for 8 to 10 minutes, or until tender but firm. Drain. Rinse under cold running water; drain.
3. In a large bowl, stir together pasta, chicken, tomatoes, onions, peppers, black beans, avocado, coriander, lemon juice, olive oil, garlic, hot pepper sauce, salt, and pepper.

Makes 6 to 8 servings.

NUTRITIONAL ANALYSIS
PER 1/8-RECIPE SERVING
311 calories
15 g protein
8.3 g fat, total
1.2 g fat, saturated
44 g carbohydrates
235 mg sodium
16 mg cholesterol
4.7 g fibre

TIPS
For some extra heat, omit the pepper sauce and add 1 tsp (5 mL) minced jalapeño pepper. The sweet onion should be the Vidalia, Walla Walla, or Maui variety.

Creamy Baked Beefaroni

Makes 8 to 10 servings.

NUTRITIONAL ANALYSIS
PER 1/10-RECIPE SERVING
338 calories
21 g protein
8.7 g fat, total
3.3 g fat, saturated
44 g carbohydrates
507 mg sodium
21 mg cholesterol
2.5 g fibre

TIPS
I love to freeze any
leftovers for an extra meal
or lunch for the kids. Use
your favourite tomato
sauce or make your own.

This is a recipe I created for *Rose Reisman's Enlightened Home Cooking*. It has become a weekly staple in our home, and sure beats the boxed version! Lately I've been substituting ground soy for the ground beef, which allows my family to get more soy protein in their diet. It's also great for vegetarians or for those who are kosher.

Meat Sauce
1 tsp vegetable oil 5 mL
1 cup chopped onions 250 mL
2 tsp minced garlic 10 mL
12 oz lean ground beef 375 g
1-3/4 cups tomato pasta sauce 425 mL
1/2 cup beef or chicken stock 125 mL

Cheese Sauce
1-1/2 tbsp margarine or butter 22 mL
1/4 cup all-purpose flour 50 mL
2 cups low-fat milk 500 mL
1-3/4 cups beef or chicken stock 425 mL
1 cup shredded light Cheddar cheese 250 mL

1 lb penne 500 g
1/2 cup shredded light mozzarella cheese
   125 mL
2 tbsp grated Parmesan cheese 25 mL

Preheat oven to 450°F (230°C). Spray a 13 x 9-inch (3 L) baking dish with cooking spray.

1. To make meat sauce: In a nonstick saucepan sprayed with cooking spray, heat oil over medium heat; cook onions and garlic for 4 minutes, or until softened. Stir in beef; cook, stirring to break it up, for 4 minutes, or until no longer pink. Stir in tomato sauce and stock. Cover and cook for 10 minutes, or until thickened. Set aside.
2. To make cheese sauce: In a nonstick saucepan, melt margarine over medium-low heat; cook flour for 1 minute, stirring. Gradually whisk in milk and stock. Increase heat to medium; cook, stirring constantly, until mixture begins to boil. Reduce heat to low and cook, stirring occasionally, for 5 minutes, or until thickened. Stir in Cheddar. Remove from heat. Stir cheese sauce into meat sauce.
3. In a large pot of boiling water, cook penne for 8 to 10 minutes, or until tender but firm. Drain.
4. Toss pasta with sauce. Pour into prepared baking dish. Sprinkle with mozzarella and Parmesan. Bake in centre of oven for 10 minutes, or until bubbly.

Thai Mussels in Coconut Sauce, p. 329

Roasted Vegetarian Sandwich with Brie Cheese, p. 246

Calzone with Chicken and Cheese

My pizza-delivery bills rose after my kids discovered calzones—a new twist on pizza, with dough folded over a pizza filling. Now I make my own. Most supermarkets sell fresh pizza dough in the refrigerator section. Have fun with the fillings and get creative.

1-3/4 lb store-bought pizza dough 875 g
3/4 cup tomato pasta sauce 175 mL
4 oz cooked boneless skinless chicken breast, chopped 125 g
3/4 cup diced sweet red peppers 175 mL
1/4 cup diced onions 50 mL
3/4 cup shredded light mozzarella cheese 175 mL
1 oz light feta cheese, crumbled 30 g

Preheat oven to 400°F (200°C). Spray a baking sheet with cooking spray.

1. Divide pizza dough in half. On a floured surface, roll out each half to a large circle, about 1/4-inch (5 mm) thick.
2. Spread tomato sauce over half of each piece of dough; top evenly with chicken, red peppers, onions, mozzarella, and feta. Fold unfilled half of dough up over filling and press to close. Place on prepared baking sheet.
3. Bake in centre of oven for 30 minutes, or until golden brown. Cut each calzone in half or thirds.

Makes 4 to 6 servings.

NUTRITIONAL ANALYSIS
PER 1/6-RECIPE SERVING
480 calories
24 g protein
10 g fat, total
2.2 g fat, saturated
73 g carbohydrates
933 mg sodium
26 mg cholesterol
5 g fibre

TIPS
Rolling the dough out can be tricky. Sprinkle a little flour over top and be patient. The dough initially will keep springing back, but over a few minutes it will begin to flatten. Use any vegetables the kids love. I keep away from preserved meat such as pepperoni because of the high fat and sodium content.

Layered Tortilla, Bean, Tomato, and Cheese Pie

Makes 8 servings.

NUTRITIONAL ANALYSIS
PER SERVING
298 calories
14 g protein
7.3 g fat, total
2.7 g fat, saturated
44 g carbohydrates
681 mg sodium
11 mg cholesterol
5.8 g fibre

TIPS
Mashing the beans gives
the tortilla pie a better
texture. Be sure to cook the
sauce so that it thickens, or
it will be too loose.

This is one of the most beautiful and delicious recipes to serve. A variety of coloured tortillas looks amazing when sliced, exposing the tomato sauce, vegetables, and cheese. I often prepare a couple of these and freeze them, then bake them.

1 cup drained canned corn 250 mL
2 tsp vegetable oil 10 mL
1/2 cup chopped onions 125 mL
2 tsp minced garlic 10 mL
1 cup chopped sweet red peppers 250 mL
1/2 cup chopped sweet green peppers 125 mL
1-1/2 cups tomato pasta sauce 375 mL
1-1/2 tsp dried basil 7 mL
1 tsp each: chili powder and ground cumin 5 mL
1-1/2 cups canned black beans, rinsed and drained 375 mL
1-1/2 cups canned white kidney beans, rinsed and drained 375 mL
1 cup shredded light mozzarella cheese 250 mL
1/2 cup shredded light Cheddar cheese 125 mL
2 tbsp grated Parmesan cheese 25 mL
5 large (10-inch/25 cm) flour tortillas 5

Preheat oven to 350°F (180°C). Spray a 9-inch (2.5 L) springform pan with cooking spray.

1. In a nonstick saucepan sprayed with cooking spray, cook corn over medium heat, stirring often, for 8 minutes, or until slightly charred. Set aside. Add oil to pan and cook onions and garlic for 4 minutes, stirring occasionally. Stir in red and green peppers; cook for 3 minutes, stirring occasionally. Stir in tomato sauce, charred corn, basil, chili powder, and cumin; cover and cook, stirring occasionally, for 6 to 8 minutes, until slightly thickened. Remove from heat.
2. In a bowl, combine black beans and white kidney beans. Mash roughly and stir into vegetable mixture.
3. In a small bowl, combine mozzarella, Cheddar, and Parmesan cheeses.
4. Place a tortilla in prepared springform pan. Spread with one-quarter of the vegetable–bean sauce. Sprinkle with one-quarter of the cheese mixture. Repeat layers three times, leaving a little cheese for the topping. Top with final tortilla; sprinkle with remaining cheese. Cover pan tightly with foil.
5. Bake for 20 minutes, or until heated through and cheese has melted. Cut into 8 wedges with a sharp knife.

Vidalia Onion Risotto

Once you've tried Vidalia onions, you'll never want a regular onion again. Vidalias are so sweet that you can enjoy them raw—I don't even cry when I chop them! This risotto beats all others in flavour and texture, without the use of butter or excess fat.

3 to 3-1/2 cups chicken or vegetable stock 750 to 875 mL
2 tsp vegetable oil 10 mL
2 cups diced Vidalia onion (about 1 large), or other sweet onion 500 mL
1-1/2 tsp minced garlic 7 mL
1 tsp dried oregano 5 mL
1 cup Arborio rice 250 mL
2 oz light feta cheese, crumbled 60 g
3 tbsp grated Parmesan cheese 45 mL
1/4 cup chopped fresh parsley 50 mL

1. In a saucepan, bring stock to a boil. Reduce heat to maintain simmer.
2. In a nonstick saucepan sprayed with vegetable spray, heat oil over medium heat; cook onion, garlic, and oregano, stirring often, for 10 minutes, or until golden and soft.
3. Stir in rice; cook, stirring, for 1 minute. Add 1/2 cup (125 mL) simmering stock; cook, stirring, until liquid is absorbed. Continue to cook, adding stock 1/2 cup (125 mL) at a time, stirring constantly and making sure all liquid is absorbed before making next addition, for about 18 minutes, or until rice is tender but slightly firm at the centre. Adjust heat as necessary to maintain slow, bubbling simmer. Remove from heat.
4. Stir in feta, Parmesan, and parsley. Serve immediately.

Makes 4 servings.

NUTRITIONAL ANALYSIS
PER SERVING
320 calories
14 g protein
7.5 g fat, total
2.8 g fat, saturated
49 g carbohydrates
800 mg sodium
8.8 mg cholesterol
3.1 g fibre

TIPS
Risotto is a dish that must be served immediately for the best flavour. If you do reheat it, then add more stock and simmer for a few minutes until the extra stock is absorbed.

Chicken and Hoisin Fried Rice

Makes 4 servings.

NUTRITIONAL ANALYSIS
PER SERVING
254 calories
18 g protein
5.1 g fat, total
0.6 g fat, saturated
34 g carbohydrates
708 mg sodium
33 mg cholesterol
3.1 g fibre

TIP
Substitute cooked beef, pork, shrimp, or firm tofu for the chicken. I freeze remainders of this rice in small containers for the kids' lunches. Add other vegetables of your choice.

My children feel this is better than any fried rice they've eaten in Chinese restaurants. Traditional fried rice is often made with lard or excess amounts of oil, adding greatly to the fat and calories. This version calls for only 1 tablespoon (15 mL) of vegetable oil, and the hoisin sauce adds moisture.

1 cup long-grain rice 250 mL
8 oz skinless boneless chicken breast 250 g
1/3 cup chicken stock 75 mL
3 tbsp low-sodium soy sauce 45 mL
3 tbsp hoisin sauce 45 mL
2/3 cup chopped carrots 150 mL
1 tbsp vegetable oil 15 mL
1 cup chopped sweet red peppers 250 mL
1 cup chopped snow peas 250 mL
1-1/2 tsp minced garlic 7 mL
1 tsp minced fresh ginger 5 mL
2 green onions, chopped, as garnish 2

Preheat grill or grill pan sprayed with vegetable spray.

1. In a saucepan, bring 1-1/4 cups (300 mL) water to a boil. Stir in rice. Cover; reduce heat to low and cook for 12 minutes. Remove from heat. Let stand, covered, for 10 minutes. Transfer to bowl. Cool.
2. Grill chicken over medium-high heat for 6 minutes per side, or until cooked through. Dice.
3. In a small bowl, whisk together stock, soy sauce, and hoisin sauce. Set aside.
4. In a pot of boiling water, cook carrots for 4 minutes, or until tender-crisp. Drain.
5. In a nonstick wok or large frying pan sprayed with vegetable spray, heat oil over high heat; cook red peppers, snow peas, garlic, ginger, and carrots for 2 minutes, stirring constantly. Add rice; cook, stirring, for 2 minutes longer. Add stock mixture and chicken; cook for 1 minute longer, or until heated through. Serve garnished with green onions.

Beef Risotto with Prosciutto and Oyster Mushrooms

I created a recipe similar to this, using chicken, for *Sensational Light Pasta and Grains*. Tender beefsteak with oyster mushrooms goes beautifully with creamy risotto.

4 oz beef tenderloin steak 125 g
3 to 3-1/2 cups chicken stock 750 to 875 mL
2 tsp vegetable oil 10 mL
1-1/2 cups chopped leeks 375 mL
1-1/2 tsp minced garlic 7 mL
3 cups sliced oyster mushrooms 750 mL
1 cup Arborio rice 250 mL
1/2 cup dry white wine 125 mL
1-1/2 oz prosciutto, cut in thin strips 45 g
2 tbsp grated Parmesan cheese 25 mL

1. In a nonstick frying pan sprayed with cooking spray, or on a preheated barbecue, cook beef over medium-high heat for 5 minutes, turning once, or until cooked medium. Cool slightly. Cube.
2. In a saucepan, bring stock to a boil. Reduce heat to maintain simmer.
3. In a nonstick saucepan sprayed with cooking spray, heat oil over medium-high heat; cook leeks and garlic for 3 minutes, or until softened. Stir in mushrooms; cook, stirring occasionally, for 5 to 8 minutes, or until vegetables are tender.
4. Stir in rice; cook, stirring, for 1 minute. Add wine; cook for 1 minute, or until liquid is absorbed. Add 1/2 cup (125 mL) simmering stock; cook, stirring, until liquid is absorbed. Continue to cook, adding stock 1/2 cup (125 mL) at a time, stirring constantly and making sure all liquid is absorbed before making next addition, for about 18 minutes, or until rice is tender but slightly firm at the centre. Adjust heat as necessary to maintain slow, bubbling simmer. Remove from heat.
5. Stir in beef, prosciutto, and Parmesan. Serve immediately.

Makes 4 servings.

NUTRITIONAL ANALYSIS
PER SERVING
372 calories
22 g protein
9.8 g fat, total
2.9 g fat, saturated
49 g carbohydrates
790 mg sodium
30 mg cholesterol
3.3 g fibre

TIP
Risotto in restaurants includes lots of butter, cream, and cheese, which makes it a high-fat and caloric dish. As you see from this recipe, you can reduce the fat and calories and still make a delicious risotto.

Rose's Famous Light Fettuccine Alfredo

Makes 6 servings.

NUTRITIONAL ANALYSIS
PER SERVING
233 calories
12 g protein
4.1 g fat, total
1.7 g fat, saturated
37 g carbohydrates
411 mg sodium
8.4 mg cholesterol
1.7 g fibre

TIP
I like to add some chopped
fresh herbs such as basil,
dill, or parsley, and even
some diced smoked
salmon, prosciutto, or
cooked vegetables.

As I came to the end of editing this book, I realized that I had forgotten one of the most delicious and simplest recipes from my repertoire. I was reminded not only by my children and husband (who enjoy this pasta weekly), but also by my cousin, Jewel Gold. She asked me if I had a low-fat fettuccine Alfredo recipe for her family. When I gave her this recipe, she told me that it didn't appear in any of my books. Well, thanks to Jewel, here it is!

12 oz fettuccine 375 g
1 cup cold chicken or vegetable stock 250 mL
1 cup 2% evaporated milk 250 mL
1 tsp Dijon mustard 5 mL
1/2 tsp freshly ground black pepper 2 mL
3 tbsp all-purpose flour 45 mL
1 tsp crushed garlic 5 mL
6 tbsp grated Parmesan cheese 85 mL

1. In a large pot of boiling water, cook fettuccine for 8 to 10 minutes, or until tender but firm. Drain.
2. In a medium saucepan, combine stock, evaporated milk, mustard, pepper, flour, and garlic. Whisk until smooth, off heat. Place over medium heat and simmer for 4 to 5 minutes, just until thickened, whisking constantly. Remove from heat and add 4 tbsp (60 mL) of the cheese. Pour over pasta and sprinkle with remaining 2 tbsp (25 mL) of cheese. Serve immediately.

Vegetable Side Dishes

Asparagus with Caesar Dressing

Makes 4 servings.

NUTRITIONAL ANALYSIS
PER SERVING
76 calories
4.1 g protein
4.4 g fat, total
0.9 g fat, saturated
5 g carbohydrates
130 mg sodium
2.9 mg cholesterol
1.7 g fibre

TIP
If preparing the asparagus early in the day, be sure to rinse with very cold water after cooking to prevent browning. Then you can reheat by rinsing in hot water. These are also great served at room temperature.

Asparagus is always a delicious and elegant vegetable to serve, and it is a source of vitamins C and A, iron, and an excellent source of folate. The Caesar dressing is sensational over top. Try thinly slicing some fresh Parmesan, using a cheese slicer or sharp knife, to use as a garnish.

1 lb asparagus, trimmed 500 g
1 tbsp grated Parmesan cheese 15 mL
1 tbsp olive oil 15 mL
2 tsp fresh lemon juice 10 mL
2 tsp water 10 mL
2 anchovy fillets, chopped 2
1 tsp crushed garlic 5 mL
1/2 tsp Dijon mustard 2 mL

1. Steam or microwave asparagus until tender but still green, approximately 3 minutes. Place on a serving dish.
2. In a small bowl, mix 1/2 tbsp (7 mL) of the Parmesan, the olive oil, lemon juice, water, anchovies, garlic, and mustard. Pour over asparagus.
3. Sprinkle with the remaining 1/2 tbsp (7 mL) Parmesan.

Green Beans with Coconut Sauce

The combination of light coconut milk, peanut butter, sautéed vegetables, and fresh coriander add a whole new dimension to green beans, which are high in vitamin C and folate.

1/3 cup light coconut milk 75 mL
1-1/2 tbsp natural peanut butter 22 mL
1 tbsp fresh lemon juice 15 mL
2 tsp low-sodium soy sauce 10 mL
1 tsp sesame oil 5 mL
1 tsp honey 5 mL
1/2 tsp minced fresh ginger 2 mL
1-1/2 lb green beans 750 g
2 tsp vegetable oil 10 mL
1 cup chopped onions 250 mL
1/3 cup diced sweet red peppers 75 mL
1 tsp minced garlic 5 mL
3 tbsp chopped fresh coriander, as garnish 45 mL

1. In a bowl, whisk together coconut milk, peanut butter, lemon juice, soy sauce, sesame oil, honey, and ginger. Set aside.
2. Blanch or steam green beans for 2 minutes, or until tender-crisp.
3. In a nonstick frying pan sprayed with cooking spray, heat oil over medium-high heat; cook onions, peppers, and garlic for 5 minutes.
4. Drain green beans; add to frying pan. Stir in coconut milk mixture; cook for 1 minute, or until heated through. Serve garnished with fresh coriander.

Makes 6 servings.

NUTRITIONAL ANALYSIS
PER SERVING
118 calories
3.6 g protein
5.3 g fat, total
1.2 g fat, saturated
14 g carbohydrates
74 mg sodium
0 mg cholesterol
4.6 g fibre

TIP
Be sure not to overcook the beans or they'll lose their bright green colour and crispy texture. If you want to cook them earlier in the day, rinse with cold water after cooking until they are no longer warm. When ready to serve, rinse with boiling water, then pour sauce over them.

Mushroom and Cheese Phyllo Strudel

If you love mushrooms, you'll get your fill in this strudel—6 cups of meaty oyster mushrooms, mixed with cheese, black olives, and dill are wonderful in this roll. You can use any variety of mushrooms you like.

2 tsp vegetable oil 10 mL
1 cup chopped onions 250 mL
2 tsp minced garlic 10 mL
6 cups sliced oyster mushrooms (about 1 lb/500 g) 1.5 L
1/4 cup vegetable stock 50 mL
1 tsp dried thyme 5 mL
3/4 cup smooth 5% ricotta cheese 175 mL
2 oz goat cheese 60 g
1/3 cup low-fat milk 75 mL
1/3 cup chopped fresh dill 75 mL
1/4 cup sliced black olives 50 mL
2 tbsp grated Parmesan cheese 25 mL
1/8 tsp each: salt and freshly ground black pepper 0.5 mL
6 sheets phyllo pastry 6

Preheat oven to 375°F (190°C). Spray baking sheet with cooking spray.

1. In a large nonstick frying pan sprayed with cooking spray, heat oil over medium-high heat; cook onions and garlic for 4 minutes, or until softened. Stir in mushrooms, stock, and thyme; cook, stirring often, for 8 to 10 minutes, or until mushrooms are browned and liquid is absorbed. Transfer to bowl. Cool for 5 minutes.

2. Stir ricotta, goat cheese, milk, dill, black olives, Parmesan, salt, and pepper into cooled mushroom mixture.

3. Layer two sheets of phyllo, keeping remaining phyllo covered with a cloth to prevent drying out. Spray phyllo with cooking spray. Layer two more sheets of phyllo on top. Spray with cooking spray. Layer two more sheets of phyllo on top. Spread filling over surface of phyllo, leaving a 2-inch (5 cm) border uncovered along the edges. Starting from the long end, roll several times. Tuck in short ends and continue to roll.

4. Place on prepared baking sheet. Spray strudel with cooking spray. Bake in centre of oven for 25 to 30 minutes, or until golden.

Stuffed Portobello Mushrooms

Portobello mushrooms have a meaty flavour and texture, and are perfect for vegetarian diets. They are excellent grilled, sautéed, or stuffed as in this recipe. Brie cheese is high in calories, so I only use it in small amounts, but a little goes a long way.

1/2 cup smooth 5% ricotta cheese 125 mL
1/4 cup chopped rehydrated sun-dried
  tomatoes 50 mL
2 oz diced Brie cheese 60 g
2 tbsp minced green onions 25 mL
4 tsp fresh lemon juice 20 mL
1 tbsp grated Parmesan cheese 15 mL
1 tsp Dijon mustard 5 mL
1/2 tsp minced garlic 2 mL
1/8 tsp freshly ground black pepper 0.5 mL
4 portobello mushroom caps 4

Topping
2 tbsp seasoned dry breadcrumbs 25 mL
2 tsp grated Parmesan cheese 10 mL
1-1/2 tsp water 7 mL

Preheat oven to 425°F (220°C). Spray a baking sheet with vegetable spray.

1. In a bowl, stir together ricotta, sun-dried tomatoes, Brie, green onions, lemon juice, Parmesan, mustard, garlic, and pepper.
2. Wipe mushroom caps. Place cup side up on prepared baking sheet. Divide stuffing among caps.
3. To make topping: In a small bowl, stir together breadcrumbs, Parmesan, and water. Sprinkle evenly over mushroom caps.
4. Bake in centre of oven for 12 to 15 minutes, or until browned and heated through. Slice in half.

Makes 8 servings.

NUTRITIONAL ANALYSIS
PER SERVING
82 calories
6 g protein
3.7 g fat, total
2.2 g fat, saturated
6 g carbohydrates
198 mg sodium
13 mg cholesterol
2.1 g fibre

TIPS
You can use jumbo mushrooms if you don't want to use portobellos. Buy your sun-dried tomatoes in bulk and store them in the freezer; reconstitute them as you need by soaking in boiling water for 15 minutes, draining, and chopping.

Bean, Roasted Garlic, and Potato Purée

Makes 4 to 6 servings.

NUTRITIONAL ANALYSIS
PER 1/6-RECIPE SERVING
155 calories
4.8 g protein
3.6 g fat, total
0.6 g fat, saturated
26 g carbohydrates
114 mg sodium
1.6 mg cholesterol
1.8 g fibre

TIPS
Roasted garlic is wonderful
as a side vegetable or as
a spread over bread or
crackers. I often use my
toaster oven to roast garlic.
Never mash potatoes in a
food processor or they will
become sticky.

These are the healthiest "mashed potatoes" ever. Potatoes are an excellent source of potassium and fibre, and are high in vitamin C, iron, and folate. Combined with beans, which are an excellent source of fibre and plant protein, the dish becomes a nutritional powerhouse. Roasting garlic is easy, and produces a sweet flavour.

1 head garlic 1
1 lb Yukon Gold potatoes, peeled and quartered 500 g
1 tsp vegetable oil 5 mL
1 cup chopped onions 250 mL
1 cup canned white kidney beans, rinsed and drained 250 mL
1/4 cup low-fat evaporated milk 50 mL
1 tbsp olive oil 15 mL
1/4 tsp each: salt and freshly ground black pepper 1 mL

Preheat oven to 450°F (230°C).

1. Cut top 1/2 inch (1 cm) from head of garlic to slightly expose cloves. Wrap in foil. Bake for 20 minutes.
2. In a saucepan, cover potatoes with cold water. Bring to a boil; cook for 15 minutes, or until tender.
3. Meanwhile, in a nonstick frying pan sprayed with vegetable spray, heat oil over medium-high heat; cook onions for 5 minutes, or until golden.
4. Drain potatoes, and return to saucepan. Squeeze garlic flesh out of skins into pot with potatoes. Add onions to potatoes. Mash.
5. In a food processor, combine beans, evaporated milk, olive oil, salt, and pepper; purée. Stir into mashed potatoes. If desired, return potato mixture to stovetop and heat gently.

Cheddar Cheese Potato Skins

Every time you eat these in restaurants, keep in mind they are usually fried and contain loads of fat and calories. My baked version is crispy and light, using a small amount of light cheese. I love these as a side vegetable dish, appetizer, or light lunch.

2 baking potatoes 2
1-1/2 tbsp olive oil 22 mL
1 tbsp chopped fresh parsley 15 mL
1-1/2 tsp minced garlic 7 mL
1/8 tsp chili powder 0.5 mL
1/8 tsp each: salt and freshly ground black pepper 0.5 mL
1/3 cup shredded light Cheddar cheese 75 mL
1 tbsp grated Parmesan cheese 15 mL

Preheat oven to 425°F (220°C).

1. Bake potatoes for 1 hour, or until tender. (Or pierce skins and microwave on High for 8 to 10 minutes.) Cool. Slice in half lengthwise. Carefully remove pulp, leaving skin intact. Reserve pulp for another use. Place skins on prepared baking sheet.
2. In a small bowl, stir together olive oil, parsley, garlic, chili powder, salt, and pepper. Spread or brush over inner surface of potato skins. Sprinkle with Cheddar and Parmesan.
3. Bake in centre of oven for 20 minutes, or until crisp.

Makes 4 servings.

NUTRITIONAL ANALYSIS
PER SERVING
156 calories
4.9 g protein
6.3 g fat, total
1.4 g fat, saturated
20 g carbohydrates
170 mg sodium
3.2 mg cholesterol
3.5 g fibre

TIPS
You can make these up to a day in advance and bake just before serving. Try different cheeses and seasonings if you like.

Potato Parmesan with Tomato Sauce and Cheese

Makes 6 servings.

NUTRITIONAL ANALYSIS
PER SERVING
175 calories
8.1 g protein
3.4 g fat, total
1.8 g fat, saturated
28 g carbohydrates
465 mg sodium
43 mg cholesterol
2.8 g fibre

TIPS
The potatoes can be prepared early in the day and baked just before serving. They are even delicious the next day reheated. You can substitute parsley or even fresh coriander for the dill.

We've all had veal or chicken Parmesan—here's a great vegetarian version. This is wonderful served as an appetizer, a vegetable side dish, or a vegetarian main course. Eat the potato skins, since this is where a lot of the fibre is contained.

3 medium potatoes, scrubbed, peel on (about 1-1/2 lb/750 g)	3
1 egg	1
3 tbsp low-fat milk or water	45 mL
3/4 cup seasoned dry breadcrumbs	175 mL
2 tbsp chopped fresh dill (or 1/2 tsp/2 mL dried)	25 mL
2 tbsp grated Parmesan cheese	25 mL
1/2 cup tomato pasta sauce	125 mL
1/3 cup shredded part-skim mozzarella cheese	75 mL

Preheat oven to 375°F (190°C). Spray a baking sheet with cooking spray.

1. In a saucepan, cover potatoes with cold water. Bring to a boil; cook for 20 to 25 minutes, or until just tender when pierced with a fork. Drain. When cool enough to handle, cut into 1/2-inch (1 cm) round slices.
2. In a small bowl, whisk together egg and milk. On a plate, stir together breadcrumbs, dill, and 1 tbsp (15 mL) of the Parmesan. Dip potato slices in egg wash, coat with crumb mixture, and place in a single layer on prepared baking sheet.
3. Bake in centre of oven, turning halfway, for 15 minutes, or until golden and tender when pierced with a fork. Top each slice with some tomato sauce. Sprinkle with mozzarella and the remaining 1 tbsp (15 mL) Parmesan. Bake for 5 minutes longer.

Potato Wedge Fries

These are the best and healthiest French fries you'll ever eat. Forget the regular fast-food fries that are deep-fried and can contain over 20 grams of fat for a small serving. Experiment and use any seasonings you like.

3 large baking potatoes 3
2 tbsp olive oil 25 mL
1 tsp minced garlic 5 mL
2 tbsp grated Parmesan cheese 25 mL
1/4 tsp chili powder 1 mL

Preheat oven to 375°F (190°C). Spray a rimmed baking sheet with cooking spray.

1. Scrub potatoes and cut lengthwise into 8 wedges. Put on prepared baking sheet.
2. In a small bowl, combine oil and garlic. In another small bowl, combine Parmesan and chili powder. Brush potato wedges with half of oil mixture, then sprinkle with half of Parmesan mixture.
3. Bake for 20 minutes. Turn the wedges; brush with remaining oil mixture and sprinkle with remaining Parmesan mixture. Bake for another 20 minutes, or just until potatoes are tender and crisp.

Makes 6 servings.

NUTRITIONAL ANALYSIS
PER SERVING
156 calories
3 g protein
5.3 g fat, total
1 g fat, saturated
24 g carbohydrates
47 mg sodium
1.6 mg cholesterol
2.3 g fibre

TIP
You can cut the potatoes early in the day, as long as you keep them in cold water so they won't turn brown.

Rosti Potatoes with Caramelized Onions

Makes 6 servings.

NUTRITIONAL ANALYSIS
PER SERVING
146 calories
4.4 g protein
4.5 g fat, total
2 g fat, saturated
22 g carbohydrates
275 mg sodium
9.7 mg cholesterol
2.2 g fibre

TIP
When sautéing, be sure
not to use too high a heat
or you'll burn the potatoes
and they won't cook
thoroughly.

This recipe was inspired by the Mövenpick Swiss restaurant chain, where "rosti" is grated potatoes sautéed in oil. I took the idea, made a filling of cheese and sautéed onions, and used only 2 teaspoons (10 mL) of butter to brown. They are amazing!

2 tsp vegetable oil 10 mL
1-1/2 cups finely diced sweet onions 375 mL
1 tsp minced garlic 5 mL
1/4 cup shredded light Cheddar cheese 50 mL
1 tbsp grated Parmesan cheese 15 mL
3 medium Yukon Gold potatoes 3
1/2 tsp salt 2 mL
1/8 tsp freshly ground black pepper 0.5 mL
2 tsp butter or margarine 10 mL
1/3 cup low-fat sour cream 75 mL

1. In a nonstick frying pan sprayed with cooking spray, heat oil over high heat; cook onions and garlic for 2 minutes. Reduce heat to medium-low; cook for 10 minutes, or until soft and golden. Transfer to bowl; stir in Cheddar and Parmesan.
2. Peel potatoes. Coarsely grate. In a bowl, toss with salt and pepper.
3. In a 9- or 10-inch (23 or 25 cm) nonstick frying pan sprayed with cooking spray, melt butter over medium-low heat; add half of potatoes, spreading them over bottom of pan and pressing flat. Top with onion mixture. Sprinkle evenly with remaining potatoes, and press firmly. Cook for 8 minutes, or until browned underneath. Slide out onto a dinner plate and flip back carefully or invert into pan. Cook another 8 minutes, or until other side is golden. Cut into wedges. Serve with sour cream.

Scalloped Potato Mushroom Casserole

I love scalloped potatoes, but most recipes are filled with fat and calories from the excess butter and cheese used. This dish uses Yukon Gold potatoes, which are creamy and more buttery tasting than regular white potatoes. The oyster mushrooms give the dish a wonderful taste and texture, and the evaporated milk gives a creamy consistency without the use of heavy cream.

2 lb Yukon Gold potatoes 1 kg

2 tsp vegetable oil 10 mL

1 cup chopped onions 250 mL

2 tsp minced garlic 10 mL

3 cups sliced oyster mushrooms 750 mL

1/2 tsp dried thyme 2 mL

1/4 tsp each: salt and freshly ground
   black pepper 1 mL

1-1/4 cups vegetable or chicken stock
   300 mL

1 cup low-fat evaporated milk 250 mL

2 tbsp all-purpose flour 25 mL

1 tsp Dijon mustard 5 mL

1/2 cup shredded light Cheddar or
   Swiss cheese 125 mL

2 tbsp grated Parmesan cheese 25 mL

1/4 cup seasoned dry breadcrumbs 50 mL

2 tsp water 10 mL

1/2 tsp minced garlic 2 mL

1/4 tsp chili powder 1 mL

Preheat oven to 350°F (180°C). Spray a 13- x 9-inch (3L) baking dish with cooking spray.

1. Peel potatoes and place in a saucepan. Add cold water to cover. Bring to a boil; cook for 8 to 10 minutes, or until easily pierced with the tip of a sharp knife. Drain. Slice into 1/4-inch-thick (5 mm) rounds. Place in prepared baking dish.
2. In a large nonstick frying pan sprayed with cooking spray, heat oil over medium-high heat; cook onions and garlic for 3 minutes, or until softened. Stir in mushrooms, thyme, salt, and pepper; cook for 8 minutes, or until mushrooms are browned and dry. In a bowl, whisk together stock, evaporated milk, flour, and mustard; stir into mushroom mixture. Cook, stirring, for 4 minutes, or until slightly thickened. Pour over potatoes.
3. In a bowl, stir together Cheddar and Parmesan cheeses; sprinkle over casserole.
4. In another bowl, stir together breadcrumbs, water, garlic, and chili powder; sprinkle over casserole. Bake, covered, for 20 minutes. Turn oven to broil; broil for 2 minutes, or until topping is golden.

Makes 6 to 8 servings.

NUTRITIONAL ANALYSIS
PER 1/8 RECIPE SERVING
202 calories
9.4 g protein
4.5 g fat, total
2.2 g fat, saturated
31 g carbohydrates
321 mg sodium
12 mg cholesterol
3.1 g fibre

TIPS
This dish can be prepared early in the day, brought to room temperature, and then baked. If you want a strong cheese, use Swiss cheese instead of Cheddar.

Sweet Potato and Carrot Casserole with Molasses and Pecans

Makes 6 servings.

NUTRITIONAL ANALYSIS
PER SERVING
233 calories
2.2 g protein
4.9 g fat, total
0.6 g fat, saturated
45 g carbohydrates
62 mg sodium
0 mg cholesterol
5.3 g fibre

TIPS
A great dish to prepare up to a day in advance and heat just before serving. To toast the nuts, heat them in a frying pan and toast until just browned, approximately 3 minutes; be careful not to burn them.

I adapted this recipe from my first low-fat cookbook *Rose Reisman's Light Cooking*. It's not only a great vegetable side dish, but a great dish to serve during the Jewish holiday of Passover. If you can find fresh sweet pineapple, use it instead of the canned. You're getting a double blast of beta carotene from the sweet potatoes and carrots.

1 lb sweet potatoes, peeled and cut in 1/2-inch (1 cm) cubes 500 g
1 lb carrots, thinly sliced widthwise 500 g
1-1/4 cups fresh or drained canned pineapple chunks 300 mL
1/2 cup dried cranberries 125 mL
1/3 cup packed brown sugar 75 mL
3 tbsp thawed orange juice concentrate 45 mL
1 tbsp margarine or butter 15 mL
2 tbsp molasses 25 mL
1-1/2 tsp cinnamon 7 mL
3 tbsp chopped toasted pecans 45 mL

Preheat oven to 350°F (180°C). Spray a 9-inch (2.5 L) square baking dish with cooking spray.

1. In a saucepan, combine sweet potatoes and carrots with cold water to cover. Bring to a boil. Cook for 8 to 10 minutes, or until tender. Drain.
2. In a bowl, toss sweet potatoes and carrots with pineapple and cranberries. Place in prepared baking dish.
3. In a small saucepan, combine brown sugar, orange juice concentrate, margarine, molasses, and cinnamon; cook, stirring, over medium heat for 1 minute, or until melted and smooth.
4. Pour sauce over vegetables. Bake covered for 15 minutes, or until heated through. Toss, then sprinkle with pecans.

Snow Peas with Sesame Sauce

Snow peas are a delicacy. They are sweet, tender, and elegant to serve. They are high in vitamins C and A, and are a source of iron, vitamin E, and folate. Even though nuts are high in calories and fat, I use them sparingly to highlight this dish.

1 tbsp honey 15 mL
1 tbsp rice wine vinegar 15 mL
1 tbsp sesame oil 15 mL
1 tbsp low-sodium soy sauce 15 mL
1/2 tsp minced garlic 2 mL
1 tsp vegetable oil 5 mL
1 lb snow peas, trimmed 500 g
2 tbsp chopped toasted cashews 25 mL
1 tbsp toasted sesame seeds 15 mL

1. In a small bowl, combine honey, vinegar, sesame oil, soy sauce, and garlic. Set aside.
2. In a large nonstick frying pan sprayed with cooking spray, heat oil over medium-high heat; cook snow peas for 3 minutes, or until tender-crisp. Pour sauce over peas; cook until heated through. Serve immediately, sprinkled with cashews and sesame seeds.

Makes 6 servings.

NUTRITIONAL ANALYSIS
PER SERVING
100 calories
2.8 g protein
5.3 g fat, total
0.8 g fat, saturated
10 g carbohydrates
93 mg sodium
0 mg cholesterol
2.2 g fibre

TIPS
Be sure not to overcook the snow peas or they will loose their crispness and bright green colour. For a special treat, try substituting sugar snap peas.

Roasted Vegetable Couscous Strudel

Makes 8 servings.

NUTRITIONAL ANALYSIS
PER SERVING
155 calories
5 g protein
4.3 g fat, total
1.5 g fat, saturated
24 g carbohydrates
128 mg sodium
3.3 mg cholesterol
2.2 g fibre

TIP
If your couscous tends to
stick together or clump, try
adding 1 tsp (5 mL) of
oil to the cooking liquid.
Fluff immediately after
letting the couscous sit for
5 minutes.

Roasted vegetables are delicious at any time. Mixing them with couscous and rolling in phyllo is outstanding. Use any vegetables of your choice.

Half large sweet onion, thickly sliced Half
2 carrots, cut into 1/2-inch (1 cm) chunks 2
Half large sweet red or yellow pepper, cut in chunks Half
1 plum tomato, quartered 1
1 tbsp olive oil 15 mL
1 tbsp balsamic vinegar 15 mL
8 large cloves garlic (skin on) 8
1 cup vegetable or chicken stock 250 mL
3/4 cup couscous 175 mL
1/2 tsp dried basil 2 mL
2 oz goat cheese, crumbled 60 g
1/4 tsp freshly ground black pepper 1 mL
5 sheets phyllo pastry 5

Preheat oven to 425°F (220°C). Spray a baking sheet with cooking spray.

1. In a bowl, toss onions, carrots, peppers, tomatoes, olive oil, vinegar, and garlic. Spread over prepared baking sheet. Bake, stirring occasionally, for 30 minutes, or until tender.

2. Squeeze garlic out of skins into a bowl. Cool vegetables. Chop coarsely, and put in bowl with garlic.

3. In a small saucepan, bring stock to a boil. Stir in couscous and basil. Remove from heat. Cover and let stand for 5 minutes, or until liquid is absorbed. Fluff with a fork. Stir into vegetable mixture, along with goat cheese and pepper.

4. Layer two sheets of phyllo, keeping remaining phyllo covered with a cloth to prevent drying out. Spray phyllo with cooking spray. Layer two more sheets of phyllo on top. Spray with cooking spray. Put last phyllo sheet on top.

5. Leaving a 2-inch (5 cm) border uncovered along the edges, place filling along long end of phyllo rectangle. Roll phyllo up and over filling to completely enclose it, fold short ends in, and continue to roll up strudel.

6. Place on prepared baking sheet. Spray strudel with cooking spray. Bake for 20 to 25 minutes, or until golden.

Soy

Polenta with Tofu Stew

Makes 6 servings.

NUTRITIONAL ANALYSIS
PER SERVING
243 calories
13 g protein
4.3 g fat, total
0.8 g fat, saturated
38 g carbohydrates
918 mg sodium
0 mg cholesterol
5.8 g fibre

TIP
If you make your polenta
well before serving, it will
turn firm instead of being
soft and smooth. Don't
worry, all you have to do is
add more stock or water
and whisk over a gentle
heat until smooth again.

This stew is has a meaty taste because of the firm tofu, mushrooms, and potatoes. The soft polenta gives a mashed-potato texture, but is more flavourful than potatoes. For a meatier texture, use oyster or portobello mushrooms.

8 oz firm tofu, cubed 250 g
2 tsp vegetable oil 10 mL
1 cup diced onions 250 mL
2 tsp minced garlic 10 mL
1-1/2 cups chopped mushrooms 375 mL
2 cups vegetable or chicken stock 500 mL
1-1/2 cups diced, peeled potatoes 375 mL
1 cup tomato pasta sauce 250 mL
1 cup diced carrots 250 mL
2 bay leaves 2
1-1/2 tsp dried basil 7 mL
1/4 tsp each: salt and freshly ground
   black pepper 1 mL
1 tbsp tomato paste 15 mL
2 tsp packed brown sugar 10 mL

Polenta
3-1/2 cups vegetable or chicken stock
   875 mL
1 cup cornmeal 250 mL

1. In a large nonstick frying pan sprayed with cooking spray, cook tofu over medium-high heat, stirring occasionally, for 5 minutes, or until brown on all sides. Remove from pan.
2. Respray pan; add oil and cook onions and garlic over medium-high heat for 3 minutes, or until browned. Stir in mushrooms; cook for 5 minutes, or just until browned. Add stock, potatoes, tomato sauce, carrots, bay leaves, basil, salt, pepper, tomato paste, and brown sugar. Bring to a boil. Stir in cooked tofu. Reduce heat to low, cover and cook for 20 minutes, or until potato is tender.
3. To make polenta: In a deep saucepan over medium-high heat, bring stock to a boil. Reduce heat to low; gradually whisk in cornmeal. Cook, stirring constantly, for 5 minutes, just until creamy and smooth.
4. Pour polenta onto a serving platter; pour stew over top.

Tofu Stir-Fry with Sweet and Sour Sauce, Snow Peas, and Red Peppers

I adapted this recipe from one that used chicken or pork. Firm tofu is great with a sweet and sour sauce. I like to serve this over a pilaf of rice, a bed of couscous, or a plate of thick rice noodles.

Sauce

1 cup vegetable or chicken stock 250 mL

1/3 cup packed brown sugar 75 mL

1/3 cup sweet chili sauce 75 mL

2 tbsp rice wine vinegar 25 mL

4 tsp cornstarch 20 mL

1 tbsp low-sodium soy sauce 15 mL

2 tsp sesame oil 10 mL

2 tsp minced garlic 10 mL

1-1/2 tsp minced fresh ginger 7 mL

12 oz extra-firm tofu, cubed 375 g

1 tsp vegetable oil 5 mL

1-1/2 chopped cups snow peas or sugar snap
  peas 375 mL

1-1/4 cups sweet red pepper strips 300 mL

3/4 cup sweet green pepper strips 175 mL

1/2 cup chopped green onions, as garnish
  125 mL

1. To make sauce: In a small bowl, whisk together stock, brown sugar, chili sauce, vinegar, cornstarch, soy sauce, sesame oil, garlic, and ginger; set aside.

2. In a nonstick wok or frying pan sprayed with cooking spray, cook tofu over medium-high heat for 5 minutes, or until browned on all sides. Remove from wok.

3. Add oil to wok. Cook snow peas and red and green peppers, stirring constantly, for 3 minutes, or until tender-crisp. Stir sauce again and add to wok along with cooked tofu. Cook for 1 minute, or until thickened. Serve garnished with green onions.

Makes 4 servings.

NUTRITIONAL ANALYSIS
PER SERVING
311 calories
16 g protein
11 g fat, total
1.6 g fat, saturated
37 g carbohydrates
991 mg sodium
0 mg cholesterol
3.9 g fibre

TIPS
Be sure to use the sweet chili sauce, not the hot! You can substitute ketchup, but you may have to add some extra brown sugar; taste and adjust. It's best not to stir-fry until you're actually ready to eat, or you'll overcook the vegetables.

Three-Cheese Ground Soy Lasagna

Makes 8 servings.

NUTRITIONAL ANALYSIS
PER SERVING
327 calories
26 g protein
9.2 g fat, total
5.2 g fat, saturated
35 g carbohydrates
693 mg sodium
30 mg cholesterol
5.4 g fibre

TIP
If you want a spicier
flavour, try the Mexican-
flavoured ground soy or
add 1 tsp (5 mL) of hot
pepper sauce.

This lasagna is so fabulous, nobody will ever suspect there's no meat in it. The ground soy tastes like ground beef or chicken with all the healthy components of soy, which is known to help in the fight against heart disease and cancer.

9 lasagna noodles 9
1 tsp vegetable oil 5 mL
1 cup diced onions 250 mL
2 tsp minced garlic 10 mL
3 cups tomato pasta sauce 750 mL
1-1/2 tsp dried basil 7 mL
12 oz soy-based ground beef substitute 375 g
2 cups smooth 5% ricotta cheese 500 mL
1 cup shredded low-fat mozzarella cheese 250 mL
1/3 cup low fat-milk 75 mL
1/4 cup grated Parmesan cheese 50 mL

Preheat oven to 350°F (180°C). Spray a 13- x 9-inch (3 L) baking dish with cooking spray.

1. In a large pot of boiling water, cook lasagna noodles for 12 to 14 minutes, or until tender. Drain. Rinse under cold running water; drain. Set aside.
2. To make the sauce: In a nonstick saucepan sprayed with cooking spray, heat oil over medium-high heat; cook onions and garlic for 5 minutes, or until browned. Stir in tomato sauce and basil. Bring to a boil. Reduce heat to simmer; cover and cook for 12 to 15 minutes, or until slightly thickened. Stir in ground soy; simmer for 3 minutes. Set aside.
3. To make cheese mixture: In a bowl, stir together ricotta, mozzarella, milk, and 3 tbsp (45 mL) of the Parmesan.
4. Spread 1/4 cup (50 mL) of the tomato sauce over the bottom of prepared baking dish.
   Top with three noodles. Spread half of cheese mixture over noodles. Top with one-third of tomato sauce. Top with three noodles. Spread remaining cheese mixture over noodles. Top with one-third of tomato sauce. Top with remaining noodles. Spread remaining tomato sauce over top. Sprinkle with the remaining Parmesan. Cover pan tightly with foil.
5. Bake in centre of oven for 20 to 25 minutes, or until hot.

Ground Soy Macaroni and Corn Chili

This is my replacement for "ski-hill" chili. The kids love it too. The soy-based beef subtstitute gives this chili a milder flavour. It is perfect served in a bowl, over a large bun, or even in a large, hollowed-out loaf of bread, for a dramatic presentation!

1-1/2 tsp vegetable oil 7 mL

1 cup chopped onions 250 mL

1/2 cup finely chopped carrots 125 mL

3/4 cup drained canned corn 175 mL

1 tsp minced garlic 5 mL

8 oz soy-based ground beef substitute 250 g

1 19-oz/540 mL can tomatoes, crushed 1

2 cups vegetable or chicken stock 500 mL

1-1/2 cups diced, peeled potatoes 375 mL

3/4 cup canned red kidney beans, rinsed and drained 175 mL

2 tbsp tomato paste 25 mL

1-1/2 tsp chili powder 7 mL

1-1/2 tsp dried oregano 7 mL

1-1/2 tsp dried basil 7 mL

1/4 tsp each: salt and freshly ground black pepper 1 mL

1/3 cup elbow macaroni 75 mL

2 tbsp grated Parmesan cheese 25 mL

1. In a large nonstick saucepan sprayed with cooking spray, heat oil over medium heat; cook onions, carrots, corn, and garlic, stirring occasionally, for 8 minutes, or until softened and corn begins to brown. Add ground soy, tomatoes, stock, potatoes, beans, tomato paste, chili powder, oregano, basil, salt, and pepper; bring to a boil. Reduce heat to low; cover and simmer for 25 to 30 minutes, or until potatoes are tender.
2. Bring chili to a boil and add macaroni; cook for 5 minutes, or until pasta is tender but firm. Serve sprinkled with Parmesan.

Makes 8 servings.

NUTRITIONAL ANALYSIS
PER SERVING
165 calories
12 g protein
2.3 g fat, total
0.5 g fat, saturated
24 g carbohydrates
658 mg sodium
1.2 mg cholesterol
5.6 g fibre

TIP
You can always substitute other small-shaped pasta, or another grain that cooks in a few minutes, for the macaroni.

Oriental Soy Bundles in Lettuce

This resembles the dish served in Chinese restaurants as Rainbow, which is usually a mixture of ground pork, vegetables, sauce, and lots of fat, stir-fried and served in lettuce leaves. I have made the traditional dish so much healthier and tastier that I serve this at least twice a week in my home.

Sauce
1/4 cup hoisin sauce 50 mL
2 tbsp rice wine vinegar 25 mL
2 tsp minced garlic 10 mL
1-1/2 tsp minced fresh ginger 7 mL
1 tbsp brown sugar 15 mL
2 tsp sesame oil 10 mL

1 tsp vegetable oil 5 mL
1/3 cup finely chopped carrots 75 mL
3/4 cup finely chopped sweet red or
   green peppers 175 mL
3/4 cup finely chopped mushrooms 175 mL
12 oz soy-based ground beef substitute 375 g
1/2 cup chopped, drained canned
   water chestnuts 125 mL
2 green onions, chopped 2
2 tbsp hoisin sauce 25 mL
1 tbsp water 15 mL
8 large leaves iceberg lettuce 8

1. To make sauce: In a small bowl, whisk together hoisin, vinegar, garlic, ginger, brown sugar, and sesame oil. Set aside.
2. In a nonstick frying pan sprayed with cooking spray, heat vegetable oil over medium heat; cook carrots for 3 minutes. Stir in peppers and mushrooms; cook for 3 minutes, or until vegetables are softened. Stir in ground soy, water chestnuts, and green onions. Stir in reserved sauce; cook for 2 minutes, or until heated through. Remove from heat.
3. In a small bowl, stir together hoisin sauce and water. Spread on lettuce leaves. Divide soy mixture among lettuce leaves. Serve open or rolled up.

Potstickers with Coconut Sauce

I adapted this recipe from *Sensationally Light Pasta and Grains,* in which it contained ground beef. I made it to satisfy my daughter, who claims to be vegetarian (but chicken fingers don't count!). These are so tender and delicious with the light coconut sauce, you'll never believe you are getting a light but extremely nutritious dish.

6 oz soy-based ground beef substitute 175 g
1/4 cup finely chopped green onions 50 mL
1 tbsp oyster sauce 15 mL
2 tsp rice wine vinegar 10 mL
1 tsp sesame oil 5 mL
1 tsp minced garlic 5 mL
1/2 tsp minced fresh ginger 5 mL
20 (approx.) small (3-inch/8 cm) egg roll
  wrappers 20

Sauce

1/3 cup light coconut milk 75 mL
1/4 cup chopped green onions 50 mL
3 tbsp water 45 mL
2 tbsp chopped fresh coriander 25 mL
1 tbsp rice wine vinegar 15 mL
1 tbsp oyster sauce 15 mL

1. In a bowl, combine ground soy, green onions, oyster sauce, vinegar, sesame oil, garlic, and ginger. Place 2 tsp (10 mL) filling in centre of each wrapper. Pull edges up, pleating and bunching. Press edges together to seal.
2. To make sauce: In another bowl, whisk together coconut milk, green onions, water, coriander, vinegar, and oyster sauce.
3. In a large nonstick frying pan sprayed with cooking spray, cook potstickers, flat-side down, over medium-high heat for 3 minutes, or until golden brown on bottom. Add sauce; reduce heat to low. Cover and cook for 3 minutes. Serve with any sauce remaining in the pan.

Makes 4 to 6 servings.

NUTRITIONAL ANALYSIS
PER 3 POTSTICKERS
110 calories
8 g protein
1.6 g fat, total
0.8 g fat, saturated
45.1 g carbohydrates
290 mg sodium
19 mg cholesterol
2 g fibre

TIP
Ground soy can be found in the produce section of your supermarket. A major company that produces vegetarian soy products—including soy ground beef, hot dogs, hamburgers, chili, bacon, salami, and more—is called Yves.

"Sloppy Joes"

Makes 8 servings.

NUTRITIONAL ANALYSIS
PER SERVING
165 calories
14 g protein
2.8 g fat, total
0.7 g fat, saturated
21 g carbohydrates
550 mg sodium
1.8 mg cholesterol
4.5 g fibre

TIP
This Sloppy Joe mixture is great served over rice or pasta as well. I sometimes serve a bowl of it with some baked tortilla chips as an appetizer.

I don't think I'll ever go back to using ground beef in this recipe again. The ground soy is outstanding. I buy multiple packages and freeze them so it's always on hand.

2 tsp vegetable oil 10 mL
1/2 cup chopped onions 125 mL
2 tsp minced garlic 10 mL
1/4 cup each: chopped sweet red peppers and
    chopped sweet green peppers 50 mL
2 cups tomato pasta sauce 500 mL
1 tsp dried basil 5 mL
1 tsp granulated sugar 5 mL
1/2 tsp dried oregano 2 mL
12 oz soy-based ground beef substitute 375 g
4 hamburger buns 4
3 tbsp grated Parmesan cheese 45 mL

1. In a nonstick saucepan sprayed with cooking spray, heat oil over medium-high heat; cook onions, garlic, and red and green peppers for 5 minutes. Stir in tomato sauce, basil, sugar, and oregano. Bring to a boil. Reduce heat to simmer; cook, covered, for 15 minutes. Stir in ground soy; simmer for 2 minutes.
2. Split and toast buns.
3. Ladle soy mixture over buns. Sprinkle with Parmesan.

Chicken

Chicken Bruschetta

Makes 4 servings.

NUTRITIONAL ANALYSIS
PER SERVING
367 calories
36 g protein
11 g fat, total
2.6 g fat, saturated
31 g carbohydrates
982 mg sodium
123 mg cholesterol
2.4 g fibre

TIP
If you have only field
tomatoes, be sure to seed
them, since they have too
much water. You can
replace the basil with fresh
parsley or even coriander.

I've always loved bruschetta in Italian restaurants, so I adapted the topping for chicken. It's outstanding and dramatic looking. The trick is not to overcook the tomato topping. If you prepared the chicken early in the day, then pop it in the oven to warm before adding the bruschetta topping.

4 skinless boneless chicken breasts (1 lb/500 g) 4
1/4 cup all-purpose flour 50 mL
1 egg 1
2 tbsp low-fat milk 25 mL
1 cup seasoned dry breadcrumbs 250 mL
2 tsp vegetable oil 10 mL
1-1/2 cups diced plum tomatoes 375 mL
1/4 cup chopped green onions 50 mL
1 tbsp olive oil 15 mL
1 tsp minced garlic 5 mL
3 tbsp grated Parmesan cheese 45 mL
1/4 cup chopped fresh basil, as garnish 50 mL

Preheat oven to 425°F (220°C). Spray a baking sheet with vegetable spray.

1. Between two sheets of waxed paper, pound chicken breasts to an even 1/2-inch (1 cm) thickness.
2. Place flour on a plate. In a shallow bowl, beat egg with milk. Place breadcrumbs on a separate plate.
3. In a large nonstick frying pan sprayed with vegetable spray, heat oil over medium-high heat. Coat each pounded chicken breast in flour, dip in egg mixture, then coat in breadcrumbs. Cook for 3 minutes per side, or until browned and almost cooked through. Transfer to prepared baking sheet.
4. In a bowl, stir together tomatoes, green onions, olive oil, and garlic. Spoon over chicken breasts. Sprinkle with Parmesan. Bake in centre of oven for 5 minutes, or until chicken is cooked through and tomato topping is hot. Serve garnished with basil.

Chicken and Eggplant Parmesan

Eggplant, a healthy vegetable, is often loaded with fat and calories from the amount of oil used in frying or sautéing. In this recipe I bake the breadcrumb-coated eggplant, and it turns out great.

1 whole egg 1
1 egg white 1
1 tbsp water or low-fat milk 15 mL
3/4 cup seasoned dry breadcrumbs 175 mL
3 tbsp chopped fresh parsley 45 mL
1 tbsp grated Parmesan cheese 15 mL
1 tsp minced garlic 5 mL
4 crosswise slices of eggplant, skin on, approximately
   1/2-inch (1 cm) thick 4
4 skinless boneless chicken breasts (1 lb/500 g) 4
2 tsp vegetable oil 10 mL
1/2 cup tomato pasta sauce 125 mL
1/3 cup shredded light mozzarella cheese 75 mL

Preheat oven to 425°F (220°C). Spray a baking sheet with cooking spray.

1. In small a bowl, whisk together whole egg, egg white, and water. On a plate, stir together breadcrumbs, parsley, Parmesan, and garlic. Dip eggplant in egg wash, then coat with breadcrumb mixture. Place eggplant slices on prepared baking sheet. Reserve remaining egg wash and breadcrumb mixture for chicken. Bake eggplant, turning once, for 20 minutes, or until tender.

2. Between two sheets of waxed paper, pound chicken breasts to an even 1/4-inch (5 mm) thickness. In a large nonstick frying pan sprayed with cooking spray, heat oil over medium-high heat. Dip chicken in remaining egg wash, then coat with remaining breadcrumb mixture. Cook, turning once, for 4 minutes, or until golden brown and almost cooked through.

3. Spread 1 tbsp (15 mL) tomato sauce on each eggplant slice on baking sheet. Place one chicken breast on top of each eggplant slice. Spread another 1 tbsp (15 mL) tomato sauce on top of each breast. Sprinkle with mozzarella. Bake for 5 minutes, or until cheese is golden and chicken is cooked through.

Makes 4 servings.

NUTRITIONAL ANALYSIS
PER SERVING
312 calories
37 g protein
8.4 g fat, total
2.8 g fat, saturated
22 g carbohydrates
895 mg sodium
129 mg cholesterol
2.7 g fibre

TIPS
You can cook the eggplant and chicken early in the day; bring to room temperature before baking with cheese and tomato sauce. Eggplant should be bought when it's young. If overripe it will be bitter (this is when you should salt it). If the eggplant skin doesn't spring back, then it's too old.

Chicken with Orange–Soy Salsa

Makes 6 servings.

NUTRITIONAL ANALYSIS
PER SERVING
293 calories
31 g protein
7.7 g fat, total
1.6 g fat, saturated
25 g carbohydrates
424 mg sodium
126 mg cholesterol
0.6 g fibre

TIPS
For extra spice, use a hot
salsa. I keep a can of orange
juice concentrate in the
freezer for cooking and
baking purposes. You can
measure it while it is still
frozen.

Boneless chicken thighs are the best invention since sliced bread! Supermarkets never used to sell them, and the effort to bone them was too great. Dark meat chicken may have more calories but the texture is like butter. Have a smaller portion than you would the white meat.

2 lb skinless boneless chicken thighs 1 kg
3 tbsp all-purpose flour 45 mL
2 tsp vegetable oil 10 mL
1/2 cup salsa 125 mL
1/3 cup honey 75 mL
3 tbsp thawed orange juice concentrate 45 mL
2 tbsp low-sodium soy sauce 25 mL
2 tsp cornstarch 10 mL
1 tsp Dijon mustard 5 mL
1 tsp minced garlic 5 mL
1 tsp minced fresh ginger 5 mL
Parsley, as garnish

Preheat oven to 425°F (220°C).

1. Dust chicken thighs with flour. In a large nonstick frying pan sprayed with cooking spray, heat oil over medium-high heat; in batches, cook chicken until browned on all sides, about 5 minutes per batch. Transfer to a 13 x 9-inch baking dish.
2. In a bowl, stir together salsa, honey, orange juice concentrate, soy sauce, cornstarch, mustard, garlic, and ginger; pour over chicken.
3. Bake, uncovered, in centre of oven for 18 to 20 minutes, or until chicken is cooked through. Garnish with parsley.

Green Beans with Coconut Sauce, p. 271

Honey Nut–Coated Salmon, p. 320

Chicken, Red Pepper, and Snow Pea Stir-Fry

A standard yet delicious stir-fry. My family prefers this one to all the others. Dusting the chicken with flour keeps the moisture in. You can always substitute steak, pork, or firm tofu. Be sure not to overcook your vegetables or meat. Serve over rice or rice noodles.

Sauce

1 cup chicken stock 250 mL

2 tbsp low-sodium soy sauce 25 mL

3 tbsp hoisin sauce 45 mL

4 tsp cornstarch 20 mL

1 tbsp brown sugar 15 mL

1 tsp sesame oil 5 mL

1-1/2 tsp crushed garlic 7 mL

1 tsp minced fresh ginger 5 mL

8 oz boneless skinless chicken breasts,
  cut in 1-inch (2.5 cm) cubes 250 g

2 tbsp all-purpose flour 25 mL

2 tsp vegetable oil 10 mL

1-1/2 cups thinly sliced sweet red peppers
  375 mL

1-1/2 cups snow peas, cut in half 375 mL

1/2 cup sliced water chestnuts 125 mL

1/4 cup coarsely chopped cashews,
  as garnish 50 mL

1 large green onion, chopped, as garnish 1

1. To make sauce: In a small bowl, whisk together stock, soy sauce, hoisin sauce, cornstarch, brown sugar, sesame oil, garlic, and ginger.
2. Dust chicken with flour. In a nonstick wok or frying pan sprayed with vegetable spray, cook chicken for 3 minutes, or until browned on all sides but not cooked through. Remove from pan.
3. Respray pan; add oil and sauté red peppers and snow peas, stirring, for 2 minutes, or until vegetables are tender-crisp. Stir sauce; add to wok along with chicken and water chestnuts; cook for 2 minutes, or until chicken is cooked through and sauce has thickened. Serve garnished with cashews and green onions.

Makes 4 servings.

NUTRITIONAL ANALYSIS
PER SERVING
247 calories
17 g protein
10 g fat, total
1.4 g fat, saturated
20 g carbohydrates
703 mg sodium
33 mg cholesterol
2.8 g fibre

TIP
I often make larger quantities of this sauce and either refrigerate it for a few days or freeze it, for use in a stir-fry or as a sauce over chicken, fish, or meat.

Chicken and Asian Coconut Sauce over Rice

Makes 4 to 6 servings.

NUTRITIONAL ANALYSIS
PER 1/6-RECIPE SERVING
401 calories
21 g protein
7.2 g fat, total
2.6 g fat, saturated
63 g carbohydrates
762 mg sodium
33 mg cholesterol
2 g fibre

TIPS
Light coconut milk is the
greatest product introduced
to supermarkets in the last
couple of years. It is 75%
reduced in fat and calories
with only 38 calories and
3 grams of fat per 1/4 cup
(50 mL). Replace the
chicken with pork if
desired.

This dish reminds me of a Thai stir-fry, with the flavours of coconut milk, fish sauce, coriander, and ginger. The coconut milk and oyster sauce penetrate the chicken and make it incredibly moist. Be sure not to overcook the peppers.

2 cups basmati rice 500 mL
2 cups chicken stock 500 mL
2 tsp vegetable oil 10 mL
1 cup chopped onions 250 mL
1-1/2 tsp minced garlic 7 mL
1 tsp minced fresh ginger 5 mL
1 cup thinly sliced sweet red peppers 250 mL
3/4 cup thinly sliced sweet green peppers 175 mL
3 skinless boneless chicken breasts (12 oz/375 g), cut in
   1-inch (2.5 cm) cubes 3
2 tbsp all-purpose flour 25 mL
2 tsp vegetable oil 10 mL
1 cup light coconut milk 250 mL
2 tbsp fish sauce or oyster sauce 25 mL
1/4 to 1/2 tsp hot Asian chili sauce 1 to 2 mL
1/3 cup chopped fresh coriander, as garnish 75 mL

1. In a saucepan, combine rice and stock. Bring to a boil. Reduce heat to medium-low; cover and cook for 12 minutes. Remove from heat. Let stand covered for 10 minutes. Fluff with a fork.
2. In a large nonstick frying pan sprayed with cooking spray, heat oil over medium-high heat; cook onions, garlic, and ginger for 5 minutes, or until onions are browned. Add red and green peppers; cook for 5 minutes, or until peppers are softened. Transfer mixture to a bowl.
3. Dust chicken with flour. Respray frying pan with cooking spray. Add oil and heat over medium-high heat; cook chicken for 3 minutes, or until browned on all sides. Stir in coconut milk, fish sauce, and hot Asian chili sauce. Bring to a boil. Reduce heat to simmer; cover and cook for 2 minutes, or until chicken is cooked through. Stir in onion mixture.
4. Serve chicken over rice, garnished with coriander.

Mediterranean Chicken with Tomatoes and Olives

Mediterranean flavours are wonderful with chicken breasts. Dusting the chicken with flour helps keep in moisture without using excess fat.

6 skinless boneless chicken breasts (1-1/2 lb/750 g) 6
1/4 cup all-purpose flour 50 mL
2 tsp vegetable oil 10 mL
1/2 cup chopped onions 125 mL
1 tsp minced garlic 5 mL
1 cup chopped plum tomatoes 250 mL
1/2 cup seasoned dry breadcrumbs 125 mL
1/4 cup diced black olives 50 mL
2 tbsp chopped fresh parsley 25 mL
4 tsp water 20 mL
1 tbsp grated Parmesan cheese 15 mL
2 tsp vegetable oil 10 mL
1/2 tsp dried basil 2 mL
1/8 tsp each: salt and freshly ground black pepper 0.5 mL
 Chopped fresh parsley, as garnish

Preheat oven to 425°F (220°C).

1. Dust chicken breasts with flour. In a large nonstick frying pan sprayed with cooking spray, heat oil over medium-high heat; in batches, cook chicken until browned on both sides. Transfer to a 9-inch square baking dish.
2. Respray frying pan with cooking spray; cook onions and garlic over medium heat for 3 minutes, or until onions are browned.
3. In a small bowl, stir together onion mixture, tomatoes, breadcrumbs, olives, parsley, water, Parmesan, oil, basil, salt, and pepper. Spoon over chicken.
4. Bake, uncovered, in centre of oven for 10 minutes, or until chicken is cooked through and topping is hot. Serve garnished with fresh parsley.

Makes 6 servings.

NUTRITIONAL ANALYSIS
PER SERVING
229 calories
29 g protein
6.3 g fat, total
0.9 g fat, saturated
14 g carbohydrates
456 mg sodium
67 mg cholesterol
1.2 g fibre

TIP
The topping and chicken can be made up to 1 day in advance. Don't cook the chicken all the way through. Bake an extra 5 to 10 minutes if chilled.

Chicken Breasts with Olive, Feta, and Parsley Stuffing

Makes 4 servings.

NUTRITIONAL ANALYSIS
PER SERVING
254 calories
33 g protein
8.2 g fat, total
2.3 g fat, saturated
12 g carbohydrates
710 mg sodium
124 mg cholesterol
0.8 g fibre

TIP
You can prepare and sauté
these rolled chicken breasts
up to a day in advance.
Bake just before serving.
Bake an extra 5 to 10
minutes if chilled.

Stuffing these boneless breasts with this savoury filling is delicious. The trick to enjoying olives is to have them in moderation. They contain monounsaturated heart-healthy fat, but can have excess calories if eaten in large quantities.

4 skinless boneless chicken breasts (1 lb/500 g) 4
2 oz light feta cheese, crumbled 60 g
3 tbsp chopped fresh parsley 45 mL
2 tbsp chopped black olives 25 mL
1/2 tsp dried basil 2 mL
1 egg 1
2 tbsp water or low-fat milk 25 mL
1/2 cup seasoned dry breadcrumbs 125 mL
2 tsp vegetable oil 10 mL

Preheat oven to 425°F (220°C). Spray a baking sheet with vegetable spray.

1. Between two sheets of waxed paper, pound chicken breasts to an even 1/2-inch (1 cm) thickness.
2. In a bowl, stir together feta, parsley, olives, and basil. Divide mixture among chicken breasts, placing near end of each. Roll up; secure edges with toothpicks or small skewers.
3. In a shallow bowl, whisk egg with water. Place breadcrumbs on a plate.
4. In a large nonstick frying pan sprayed with vegetable spray, heat oil over medium-high heat. Dip each chicken roll in egg wash, then coat in breadcrumbs. Cook, turning occasionally, for 3 minutes, or until well browned on all sides. Transfer to prepared baking sheet.
5. Bake for 12 to 14 minutes, or until chicken is cooked through. Remove toothpicks before serving. Serve whole or sliced crosswise into medallions.

Pesto-Stuffed Chicken Rolls

Rolling and stuffing boneless chicken breasts creates a delicious, elegant, and simple dish. I always serve them when entertaining. Serve them whole, sliced in half, or cut into medallions.

4 skinless boneless chicken breasts (1 lb/500 g) 4
1 oz light cream cheese, softened 30 g
1 tbsp store-bought or homemade pesto 15 mL
2 tbsp chopped roasted red peppers 25 mL
1 egg 1
2 tbsp water or low-fat milk 25 mL
1/2 cup seasoned dry breadcrumbs 125 mL
2 tsp vegetable oil 10 mL

Preheat oven to 425°F (220°C). Spray a baking sheet with vegetable spray.

1. Between two sheets of waxed paper, pound chicken breasts to an even 1/2-inch (1 cm) thickness.
2. In a small bowl, stir together cream cheese and pesto until smooth. Divide among chicken breasts, spreading thinly over surface. Sprinkle with red peppers. Starting at short end, roll up chicken breasts. Secure edges with toothpicks or small skewers.
3. In a shallow bowl, whisk egg with water. Place breadcrumbs on a plate.
4. In a large nonstick frying pan sprayed with vegetable spray, heat oil over medium-high heat. Dip each chicken roll in egg wash, then coat in breadcrumbs. Cook, turning occasionally, for 3 minutes, or until well browned on all sides. Transfer to prepared baking sheet.
5. Bake for 12 to 14 minutes, or until chicken is cooked through. Remove toothpicks before serving. Serve whole or sliced crosswise into medallions.

Makes 4 servings.

NUTRITIONAL ANALYSIS
PER SERVING
242 calories
31 g protein
7.8 g fat, total
1.9 g fat, saturated
12 g carbohydrates
569 mg sodium
123 mg cholesterol
0.8 g fibre

TIP
Making your own lower-fat pesto (see Pesto-Glazed Salmon, page 321, for the recipe) is always preferable, nutritionally and in terms of fat, but 1 tbsp (15 mL) of the store-bought version is fine.

Prosciutto-Stuffed Chicken Breasts with Mushroom Sauce

Makes 4 servings.

NUTRITIONAL ANALYSIS
PER SERVING
268 calories
36 g protein
10 g fat, total
3.2 g fat, saturated
8.4 g carbohydrates
474 mg sodium
86 mg cholesterol
1.1 g fibre

TIPS
If using regular mush-
rooms, sauté on a higher
heat so the excess liquid
evaporates, otherwise the
mushrooms will have a
rubbery texture. The
thinner you pound the
chicken, the easier it is
to roll the breasts.

Boneless chicken breasts taste great with a thin slice of fresh prosciutto, cheese, and a creamy mushroom sauce. The oyster mushrooms have a firmer, meatier texture than regular, and no excess moisture.

4 skinless boneless chicken breasts
  (1 lb/500 g) 4
1/3 cup shredded light mozzarella or Havarti
  cheese 75 mL
1 tbsp grated Parmesan cheese 15 mL
4 thin slices prosciutto (1-1/2 oz/45 g) 4
2 tbsp all-purpose flour 25 mL
2 tsp vegetable oil 10 mL

Mushroom Sauce
1 tsp vegetable oil 5 mL
2 cups chopped oyster mushrooms 500 mL
1/2 cup chicken stock 125 mL
1/3 cup low-fat evaporated milk 75 mL
1/2 tsp Dijon mustard 2 mL
1 tsp all-purpose flour 5 mL

1/4 cup chopped fresh parsley,
  as garnish 50 mL

Preheat oven to 400°F (200°C). Spray a baking sheet with vegetable spray.

1. Between two sheets of waxed paper, pound chicken breasts to an even 1/2-inch (1 cm) thickness.
2. In a small bowl, stir together mozzarella and Parmesan. Place a slice of prosciutto on each chicken breast. Divide cheese mixture among breasts, placing near short end. Roll up; secure edges with toothpicks or small skewers. Dust with flour.
3. In a nonstick frying pan sprayed with vegetable spray, heat oil over medium-high heat; cook chicken rolls, turning occasionally, for 3 minutes, or until golden on all sides.
4. Transfer to prepared baking sheet. Bake for 12 to 14 minutes, or until chicken is cooked through.
5. To make sauce: In a nonstick saucepan sprayed with vegetable spray, heat oil over medium heat; cook mushrooms for 5 minutes, or until browned. In a bowl, whisk together chicken stock, evaporated milk, mustard, and flour; stir into mushrooms. Cook for 2 minutes, or until simmering and thickened. Remove from heat.
6. Remove toothpicks from chicken rolls. Serve whole or sliced crosswise into medallions. Pour sauce over and garnish with parsley.

Roast Chicken with Pine Nuts and Cranberry Stuffing

This is a traditional bread stuffing with a twist—the flavours of savoury olives and sweet dried cranberries with fresh parsley. I like to triple the recipe and use it for a turkey. You could use other dried fruit such as diced apricots, dates, or prunes.

Makes 6 servings.

NUTRITIONAL ANALYSIS
PER SERVING
430 calories
29 g protein
14 g fat, total
2.7 g fat, saturated
47 g carbohydrates
696 mg sodium
72 mg cholesterol
3.9 g fibre

Bread Stuffing
2 tsp vegetable oil 10 mL
1 cup chopped onions 250 mL
1 cup chopped sweet red, green, or yellow
    peppers 250 mL
4 cups Italian bread cut in 1-inch (2.5 cm)
    cubes 1 L
3/4 cup chopped fresh parsley 175 mL
1/2 cup chopped green onions 125 mL
1/3 cup sliced black olives 75 mL
1/3 cup dried cranberries 75 mL
1/4 cup water 50 mL
2 tbsp toasted pine nuts 25 mL
2 tsp minced garlic 10 mL
1 tsp dried rosemary 5 mL
1/4 tsp each: salt and freshly ground black
    pepper 1 mL

3 lb roasting chicken 1.5 kg
1/2 cup chicken stock 125 mL

Preheat oven to 375°F (190°C).

Cranberry Sauce
1 cup canned whole cranberry sauce
    250 mL
3 tbsp low-sodium soy sauce 45 mL
2 tbsp thawed orange juice concentrate
    25 mL
1 tbsp sesame oil 15 mL
1 tbsp fresh lemon juice 15 mL
2 tsp brown sugar 10 mL
1-1/2 tsp minced garlic 7 mL
1 tsp minced fresh ginger 5 mL

TIPS
The cranberry sauce is unusual and delicious with the chicken and bread stuffing. Be sure to buy canned whole cranberry sauce not the jellied version. If using a meat thermometer, the internal temperature must reach 180°F (90°C) for the chicken to be done.

1. To make stuffing: In a nonstick saucepan sprayed with cooking spray, heat oil over medium-high heat; cook onions and peppers for 5 minutes, or until softened. Remove from heat. Stir in bread, parsley, green onions, olives, dried cranberries, water, pine nuts, garlic, rosemary, salt, and pepper. Transfer to food processor. Pulse on and off just until mixed. Transfer to bowl. If mixture seems dry, add a little more water. Cool.

2. Stuff bread mixture loosely into chicken; place remaining stuffing in a casserole dish. Place chicken on rack in a roasting pan. Spray chicken with cooking spray and rub with garlic, if desired. Pour stock into pan. Bake in centre of oven, basting with juices every 15 minutes, for 60 to 70 minutes, or until juices run clear when thickest part of thigh is skewered. Add more stock for basting if necessary. Cover casserole dish of extra stuffing and place in oven for last 1/2 hour of cooking time.
3. Tent chicken with foil and let it rest while making the sauce.
4. In a saucepan, combine cranberry sauce, soy sauce, orange juice concentrate, sesame oil, lemon juice, brown sugar, garlic, and ginger. Bring to a boil, stirring. Reduce heat and simmer for 4 minutes.
5. Remove and discard chicken skin before serving. Discard any pan juices. Carve chicken and serve with stuffing and sauce.

Maple-Glazed Cornish Hens with Orzo

Cornish hens are an elegant entrée for a dinner. I'll often make them when entertaining, and serve every guest half a hen. Orzo, a rice-shaped pasta, is delicious with the maple–orange glaze and dried fruit. If you have fresh pineapple on hand, use it.

Glaze

1/4 cup maple syrup 50 mL
1/4 cup thawed orange juice concentrate
 50 mL
1 tbsp honey 15 mL
1 tbsp low-sodium soy sauce 15 mL
2 tsp sesame oil 10 mL
1-1/2 tsp Dijon mustard 7 mL
1 tsp minced garlic 5 mL

2 Cornish hens, each 1-1/2 lb (750 g) 2
1/2 cup chicken stock 125 mL

Preheat oven to 400°F (200°C).

Orzo Stuffing

1/2 cup orzo 125 mL
1/3 cup diced dried apricots 75 mL
1/3 cup dried cranberries 75 mL
1/3 cup chopped green onions 75 mL
1/3 cup drained canned or fresh diced
 pineapple, or pineapple tidbits 75 mL

Makes 4 servings.

NUTRITIONAL ANALYSIS
PER SERVING
412 calories
30 g protein
7.1 g fat, total
1.5 g fat, saturated
57 g carbohydrates
240 mg sodium
117 mg cholesterol
2.5 g fibre

TIP
It takes willpower to remove the skin and not eat it. But remember that the 1 oz (30 g) of skin adds 11 grams of fat to your meal! I keep the skin on while cooking so that the hens don't dry out.

1. To make glaze: In a bowl, whisk together maple syrup, orange juice concentrate, honey, soy sauce, sesame oil, mustard, and garlic. Remove 2 tbsp (25 mL) of glaze to use in orzo mixture. Divide remaining glaze in half.

2. To make stuffing: In a saucepan of boiling water, cook orzo for 8 to 10 minutes, or until tender but firm. Drain. In a bowl, toss orzo with reserved 2 tbsp (25 mL) glaze, apricots, cranberries, green onions, and pineapple.

3. Stuff Cornish hens loosely with orzo stuffing; place remaining stuffing in a casserole dish. Place hens on rack in a roasting pan. Pour stock in pan; bake, basting occasionally with half the glaze, for 50 minutes, or until cooked through (internal temperature must register 180°F/90°C on a meat thermometer). If stock evaporates, add more. Cover casserole dish of extra stuffing and place in oven for last 1/2 hour of cooking time.

4. Tent hens with foil while you heat sauce. In a small saucepan, bring remaining half of glaze to simmer; serve with hens. Remove and discard hen skin before serving. Discard any pan juices.

Turkey Fingers with Plum Sauce

I'm sure you have enough recipes for chicken fingers. How about trying boneless turkey breast? It's moister and leaner than boneless chicken. Most supermarkets now sell it prepackaged in small quantities. You can always substitute good old boneless chicken breast.

Makes 6 servings.

NUTRITIONAL ANALYSIS
PER SERVING
221 calories
24 g protein
4.6 g fat, total
2.5 g fat, saturated
21 g carbohydrates
292 mg sodium
90 mg cholesterol
1.2 g fibre

TIP
Instead of Plum Dipping Sauce, try Honey Mustard Dipping Sauce: In a small bowl, stir together 1/4 cup (50 mL) honey and 1 tsp (5 mL) Dijon mustard.

1 lb boneless turkey breast 500 g
1 egg 1
2 tbsp water 25 mL
1 cup plain dry breadcrumbs 250 mL
1/4 cup unsweetened coconut 50 mL
3 tbsp finely chopped fresh parsley 45 mL
1/4 tsp chili powder 1 mL

Plum Dipping Sauce
1/3 cup plum sauce 75 mL
2 tbsp thawed orange juice concentrate 25 mL
1 tsp low-sodium soy sauce 5 mL

Preheat oven to 425°F (220°C). Spray a baking sheet with cooking spray.

1. Cut turkey into strips 1/2 inch x 1/2 inch x the width of the breast.
2. In a shallow bowl, whisk egg with water. On a plate, stir together breadcrumbs, coconut, parsley, and chili powder. Dip turkey strips in egg wash, then into breadcrumb mixture. Place on prepared baking sheet.
3. Bake in centre of oven for 12 minutes, turning halfway, until cooked through.
4. To make sauce: In a bowl, stir together plum sauce, orange juice concentrate, and soy sauce.
5. Serve turkey fingers with dipping sauce.

Meat

Black Bean Beef Tenderloin

Makes 4 servings.

NUTRITIONAL ANALYSIS
PER SERVING
271 calories
24 g protein
11 g fat, total
3.6 g fat, saturated
19 g carbohydrates
321 mg sodium
70 mg cholesterol
0.4 g fibre

TIP
You can precut the
tenderloin into 4 equal
pieces, and then cook or
barbecue the tenderloin
to the desired doneness,
with no need to complete
in the oven.

A one-pound piece of beef tenderloin is beautiful to serve. You can cut the slices as thick as you like. Beef tenderloin has one of the lowest fat contents for a high-quality meat. It has a butter-like texture, which the black bean sauce enhances.

1/4 cup packed brown sugar 50 mL
1/4 cup ketchup or sweet chili sauce 50 mL
3 tbsp black bean sauce 45 mL
1 tbsp rice wine vinegar 15 mL
2 tsp sesame oil 10 mL
1 tsp minced garlic 5 mL
1 tsp minced fresh ginger 5 mL
1 1-lb (500 g) piece beef tenderloin 1

Preheat oven to 400°F (200°C).

1. In a bowl, whisk together brown sugar, ketchup, black bean sauce, vinegar, sesame oil, garlic, and ginger.
2. In a nonstick frying pan sprayed with cooking spray and set over medium-high heat, cook tenderloin for 4 minutes, or until browned on all sides. Transfer to a shallow baking dish. Pour half of sauce over beef.
3. Bake in centre of oven for 15 to 20 minutes, or until desired doneness (135°F/57°C on meat thermometer for medium-rare). Serve with remaining sauce.

Standing Rib Roast with Caramelized Onions

Similar to rack of lamb, this standing rib roast should be saved for special occasions. It is higher in calories and fat than other cuts, but is outstanding. Serving it with caramelized onions sends this roast over the top!

1/2 cup seasoned dry breadcrumbs 125 mL
3 tbsp water 45 mL
2 tsp vegetable oil 10 mL
1 tsp minced garlic 5 mL
4 lb beef rib roast (with bones) 2 kg
3/4 cup beef or chicken stock 175 mL
1/3 cup red wine 75 mL
2 tsp vegetable oil 10 mL
3 large peeled, sliced sweet onions 3
2 tbsp packed brown sugar 25 mL
1 tbsp balsamic vinegar 15 mL
2 tsp minced garlic 10 mL

Preheat oven to 400°F (200°C).

1. In a bowl, stir together breadcrumbs, water, oil, and garlic.
2. In a large nonstick frying pan sprayed with cooking spray and set over medium-high heat, cook beef for 5 minutes, or until browned on all sides.
3. Place beef on rack in a roasting pan, bone side down. Pour stock and wine into roasting pan. Roast in centre of oven for 40 minutes. Pat breadcrumb mixture over top. Roast beef 30 minutes longer, or until desired doneness. If liquid in pan evaporates, add more.
4. Meanwhile, in a nonstick saucepan sprayed with cooking spray, heat oil over medium-high; cook onions for 10 minutes, or until golden. Stir in brown sugar, vinegar, and garlic; reduce heat to low and cook 10 minutes longer, or until onions are caramelized and tender.
5. Let roast stand, covered, for 10 minutes. Discard pan drippings. Carve roast. Serve with warm caramelized onions.

Makes 14 servings.

NUTRITIONAL ANALYSIS
PER SERVING
338 calories
19 g protein
23 g fat, total
8.5 g fat, saturated
6.8 g carbohydrates
168 mg sodium
70 mg cholesterol
0.7 g fibre

TIP
I ask my butcher to carve the bone away from the meat, and then refasten with a string; I have no problems cutting the meat. To tell if meat has reached desired doneness, insert a meat thermometer, which will read 135°F (57°C) at medium-rare and 155°F (68.5°C) at medium. Calculate cooking time of 15 to 20 minutes per pound for rare.

Tex-Mex Flank Steak with Corn Salsa

Makes 6 servings.

NUTRITIONAL ANALYSIS
PER SERVING
226 calories
24 g protein
9.6 g fat, total
3.9 g fat, saturated
11 g carbohydrates
416 mg sodium
59 mg cholesterol
0.5 g fibre

TIPS
If I'm making a flank
steak, I find it just as easy
to marinate it the night
before. Leftovers are great
for sandwiches or tossed
into a pasta salad the
next day.

Flank steak is one my favourite cuts of beef, because it is not only tender but extremely low in fat. It has less than half the fat than other cuts of beef with only 4 grams of fat per 3-oz (90 g) serving—almost the same as the white meat of chicken. The only tricks are that you must marinate flank steak for at least 2 hours for it to be tender, and you have to cut it against the grain or the meat will be stringy.

1 cup barbecue sauce 250 mL	**Corn Salsa (optional)**
1/3 cup cider vinegar 75 mL	1 cup drained canned corn 250 mL
2 tbsp molasses 25 mL	1 cup diced sweet red peppers 250 mL
1/4 tsp hot pepper sauce 1 mL	1 cup canned black beans, rinsed and
1-1/2 lb flank steak 750 g	drained 250 mL
	1/3 cup chopped green onions 75 mL
	1/4 cup chopped coriander 50 mL

Preheat grill or grill pan sprayed with vegetable spray.

1. In a bowl, whisk together barbecue sauce, vinegar, molasses, and hot pepper sauce. Place flank steak in a shallow baking dish. Pour marinade over steak. Cover with plastic wrap. Refrigerate for 2 hours or overnight.
2. To make salsa (if using): In a nonstick skillet sprayed with vegetable spray, sauté corn and peppers for 5 minutes, or until corn begins to brown. Add beans, onions, and coriander. Set aside.
3. Remove steak from marinade, reserving marinade.
4. Grill beef over medium-high heat for 5 to 8 minutes per side, or until desired doneness.
5. In a small saucepan, bring reserved marinade to a boil; boil for 5 minutes. Serve steak with marinade and salsa, if using.

Herb-Crusted Rack of Lamb

Rack of lamb has to be one of the most decadent meats—it is higher in fat and calories than other meats. But don't cut it out of your diet. The honey, mustard, and breadcrumb crust makes this irresistible. Serve only 2 ribs per person and have a large salad, vegetable dish, or soup to accompany.

2 racks of lamb, each about 12 oz/375 g
   (New Zealand spring) 2
1 tbsp honey 15 mL
2 tsp Dijon mustard 10 mL
1/3 cup seasoned dry breadcrumbs 75 mL
2 tbsp chopped fresh parsley 25 mL
1-1/2 tbsp finely chopped toasted pecans 22 mL
1/4 cup water 50 mL
1 tbsp olive oil 15 mL
1 tsp minced garlic 5 mL
1/2 tsp Dijon mustard 2 mL
1/2 tsp dried rosemary 2 mL
1/8 tsp each: salt and freshly ground black pepper 0.5 mL

Preheat oven to 400°F (200°C). Spray a baking sheet with vegetable spray.

1. In a large nonstick frying pan sprayed with vegetable spray and set over medium-high heat, cook racks of lamb, turning frequently, for 5 minutes, or until browned on all sides. Transfer to prepared baking sheet.
2. In a small bowl, stir together honey and 2 tsp (10 mL) mustard. Rub over browned lamb. Roast in centre of oven for 15 minutes. Stir together breadcrumbs, parsley, pecans, water, olive oil, garlic, 1/2 tsp (5 mL) mustard, rosemary, salt, and pepper. Press onto lamb. Roast 10 to 15 minutes longer, or until desired doneness (medium-rare is 145°F/63°C and medium is 155°F/68.5°C on a meat thermometer).

Makes 6 servings.

NUTRITIONAL ANALYSIS
PER SERVING
341 calories
20 g protein
19 g fat, total
7.3 g fat, saturated
17 g carbohydrates
564 mg sodium
69 mg cholesterol
1.1 g fibre

TIP
If you decide to enjoy a larger portion, keep your fat intake low during the rest of the day. Consider this meal an extravagance in terms of your regular eating plans.

Leg of Lamb Stuffed with Sun-dried Tomatoes

Makes 12 servings.

NUTRITIONAL ANALYSIS
PER SERVING
258 calories
22 g protein
16 g fat, total
7.3 g fat, saturated
4.5 g carbohydrates
232 mg sodium
110 mg cholesterol
0.9 g fibre

TIP
You can buy your lamb butterflied, or get your butcher to remove the bone, forming a pocket to hold the filling.

This is another one of my favourite cuts of meat. Leg of lamb has only 7 grams of fat per 3-1/2-oz (105 g) serving, which is excellent. Be sure to trim the fat. The stuffing of sun-dried tomatoes, black olives, and goat cheese is out of this world.

3- to 4-lb boneless leg of lamb, butterflied 1.5 to 2 kg
2 tsp vegetable oil 10 mL
2 tsp crushed garlic 10 mL
1/2 cup beef or chicken stock 125 mL
1/2 cup red wine 125 mL
3 oz sun-dried tomatoes 90 g
1/3 cup sliced black olives 75 mL
2 oz goat cheese 60 g
2 tsp olive oil 10 mL
1 tsp crushed garlic 5 mL
1/2 tsp dried basil 2 mL

Preheat oven to 375°F (190°C).

1. Place lamb on rack in a roasting pan. Rub lamb with vegetable oil and 2 tsp (10 mL) garlic. Pour stock and wine in bottom of pan.
2. Soak sun-dried tomatoes in boiling water for 15 minutes, or until soft. Drain.
3. In a food processor, purée sun-dried tomatoes, olives, goat cheese, olive oil, 1 tsp (5 mL) garlic, and basil. Spread half on one side of lamb; fold lamb in half to enclose filling. Place remaining mixture in a bowl to serve later.
4. Roast lamb for 15 to 20 minutes per pound (approximately 45 to 60 minutes for 3 lb/1.5 kg, 60 to 80 minutes for 4 lb/2 kg), or until desired doneness. Lamb temperature should register at 145°F (63°C) on a meat thermometer for medium-rare. If liquid evaporates in pan, add more wine or stock.
5. Let lamb rest for 10 minutes before carving. Serve extra sun-dried tomato stuffing on the side. Discard pan juices.

Moroccan Stew with Pearl Onions and Baby Carrots

A lovely woman by the name of Kate who assists me in my home and cooking school gave me this recipe. I adapted it to a lower fat version and I was so impressed that I had to put it in this book. Enjoy it and thank you Kate! Serve it over couscous or rice.

1 lb boneless lamb leg, cut into 1-inch (2.5 cm) cubes 500 g
2 tbsp all-purpose flour 25 mL
2 tsp vegetable oil 10 mL
1 cup chopped onions 250 mL
2 tsp minced garlic 10 mL
2 cups diced, peeled sweet potatoes 500 mL
2 cups beef or chicken stock 500 mL
1 cup baby carrots 250 mL
1 cup canned chickpeas, rinsed and drained 250 mL
1 cup white wine 250 mL

1 cup pearl onions, peeled 250 mL
3/4 cup raisins 175 mL
1 tbsp finely grated orange rind 15 mL
3 tbsp thawed orange juice concentrate 45 mL
1 tsp cumin 5 mL
1/2 tsp cinnamon 2 mL
1/2 tsp each: salt and freshly ground black pepper 2 mL
2 tsp cornstarch 10 mL
1 tbsp water 15 mL
1/3 cup chopped fresh coriander or parsley, as garnish 75 mL

1. Dust lamb cubes with flour. In a large nonstick saucepan sprayed with cooking spray, heat oil over medium-high heat; cook lamb for 5 minutes, or until browned on all sides. Remove lamb from pan.
2. Respray pan. Cook onions and garlic over medium-high heat for 3 minutes. Stir in sweet potatoes, stock, carrots, chickpeas, wine, pearl onions, raisins, orange rind, orange juice concentrate, cumin, cinnamon, salt, pepper, and browned lamb. Bring to a boil. Reduce heat to simmer; cover and cook for 40 minutes, or until lamb and vegetables are tender.
3. Mix cornstarch and water until smooth. Add to stew and cook for 2 minutes, or until slightly thickened. Serve garnished with coriander.

Makes 4 servings.

NUTRITIONAL ANALYSIS
PER SERVING
475 calories
32 g protein
11 g fat, total
3.1 g fat, saturated
62 g carbohydrates
957 mg sodium
71 mg cholesterol
8 g fibre

TIP
If you don't enjoy lamb, use an inside round cut of beef. I avoid stewing beef because it takes too long to become tender.

Asian Meatballs with Rice Noodles

Makes 4 servings.

NUTRITIONAL ANALYSIS
PER SERVING
391 calories
19 g protein
11 g fat, total
3.1 g fat, saturated
54 g carbohydrates
743 mg sodium
74 mg cholesterol
1 g fibre

TIP
You can substitute another
noodle such as fettuccine,
or even another grain such
as rice, for the rice noodles.

This recipe can be served as a first or main course. It is a wonderful change from meatballs and spaghetti sauce! Be sure to purchase lean or extra-lean beef. Ground chicken is leaner than beef.

8 oz lean ground beef or chicken 250 g
3 tbsp seasoned dry breadcrumbs 45 mL
2 tbsp finely chopped green onions 25 mL
1 tbsp low-sodium soy sauce 15 mL
1 tsp minced garlic 5 mL
1 tsp minced fresh ginger 5 mL
1 egg 1

Sauce
1/2 cup plum sauce 125 mL
1/3 cup beef or chicken stock 75 mL
1-1/2 tbsp rice wine vinegar 22 mL
1-1/2 tbsp low-sodium soy sauce 22 mL
1 tbsp packed brown sugar 15 mL
1 tbsp sesame oil 15 mL
1-1/2 tsp minced garlic 7 mL
1 tsp minced fresh ginger 5 mL

6 oz thick rice noodles 175 g

Garnish
1/4 cup chopped green onions 50 mL
3 tbsp chopped coriander or parsley 45 mL
1 tsp toasted sesame seeds 5 mL

1. Combine beef, breadcrumbs, onions, soy sauce, garlic, ginger, and egg. Form into 24 small meatballs.
2. To make sauce: In a bowl, combine plum sauce, stock, vinegar, soy sauce, brown sugar, sesame oil, garlic, and ginger.
3. In a nonstick frying pan sprayed with cooking spray and set over medium heat, cook meatballs until browned on all sides. Add sauce, cover, and simmer on low heat for 10 minutes.
4. In a pot of boiling water, cook noodles for 5 minutes, or just until tender. Drain. Transfer to serving platter. Pour meatballs and sauce over top. Garnish with green onions, coriander, and sesame seeds.

Greek Feta Burgers

Just by adding some mushrooms, feta cheese, and oregano you have a new burger. I love to serve these over a bed of couscous—and forget the bun.

1 cup chopped mushrooms 250 mL

1/2 cup chopped onions 125 mL

2 oz light feta cheese, crumbled 60 g

1 lb lean ground beef or lamb 500 g

1/4 cup finely chopped fresh chives or green onions 50 mL

3 tbsp chopped fresh oregano (or 1 tsp/5 mL dried) 45 mL

2 tbsp barbecue sauce 25 mL

3 tbsp seasoned dry breadcrumbs 45 mL

2 tsp minced garlic 10 mL

1 egg 1

Preheat grill or grill pan. Spray with cooking spray.

1. In a nonstick frying pan sprayed with cooking spray, cook mushrooms and onions over medium-high heat for 4 minutes, or until softened and browned. Remove from heat. Stir in feta.

2. In a bowl, stir together beef, chives, oregano, barbecue sauce, breadcrumbs, garlic, and egg. Stir in onion mixture. Form into 5 patties.

3. Grill patties over medium-high heat for 3 to 5 minutes per side, or until cooked through. Patties can also be placed on a baking sheet sprayed with cooking spray and baked in centre of preheated 450°F/ (230°C) oven for 10 to 15 minutes, or until cooked through, turning once.

Makes 5 servings.

NUTRITIONAL ANALYSIS
PER PATTY
194 calories
21 g protein
9.6 g fat, total
3.6 g fat, saturated
5.9 g carbohydrates
210 mg sodium
76 mg cholesterol
0.8 g fibre

TIPS
Try to buy a good-quality barbecue sauce without extra flavourings. If serving on a bun, include lettuce, tomatoes, and onions for an extra serving of veggies.

Meatloaf Rolled with Roasted Red Pepper

Makes 6 servings.

NUTRITIONAL ANALYSIS
PER SERVING
196 calories
20 g protein
9.3 g fat, total
3.8 g fat, saturated
8.6 g carbohydrates
478 mg sodium
65 mg cholesterol
0.8 g fibre

TIPS
Use a sharp knife to cut the meatloaf so it doesn't break. I love to serve this on a bed of mashed potatoes.

Toss out the old meatloaves and get trendy with this gorgeous rolled loaf. When it is cut, the green onion, red pepper, and white cheese is exposed. It's easy to roll, so don't be intimidated.

1 lb lean ground beef 500 g
1/3 cup seasoned dry breadcrumbs 75 mL
1-1/2 tsp minced garlic 7 mL
1 egg 1
3 tbsp finely chopped green onions 45 mL
3 tbsp barbecue sauce 45 mL
4 oz roasted red peppers, thinly sliced 125 g
1 oz goat cheese 30 g
1/4 cup chopped green onions 50 mL
1/4 cup barbecue sauce 50 mL

Preheat oven to 350°F (180°C). Spray a 9- x 5-inch (2 L) loaf pan with cooking spray.

1. In a bowl, combine ground beef, breadcrumbs, garlic, egg, the 3 tbsp (45 mL) green onions, and the 3 tbsp (45 mL) barbecue sauce until well mixed.
2. Lay a 12-inch (30 cm) piece of waxed paper on work surface. Spread meat mixture into a rectangle. Lay roasted pepper strips crosswise on top, distributing them evenly. Spread goat cheese evenly. Sprinkle with the 1/4 cup (50 mL) green onions. Using the waxed paper to help you, tightly roll up into a log. Spread out waxed paper and invert prepared pan over meatloaf. With hand under waxed paper, turn over gently so that meatloaf falls into pan. Pour the 1/4 cup (50 mL) barbecue sauce over top.
3. Bake, uncovered, for 45 minutes, or until cooked through. Let stand for 10 minutes. Invert and slice.

Fish and Seafood

Fish Stew with Plum Tomatoes

Makes 4 servings.

NUTRITIONAL ANALYSIS
PER SERVING
133 calories
15 g protein
4.5 g fat, total
0.6 g fat, saturated
8 g carbohydrates
189 mg sodium
55 mg cholesterol
1.7 g fibre

TIPS
Substitute other types of
fish, or omit the shellfish
and substitute fresh fish, if
you like. The key is not to
overcook the fish or it
will dry out. The fish or
shellfish should be just
opaque when cooked and
not tough. If you don't
have fish stock or clam
juice, you can use chicken
stock.

I had a recipe for a traditional fish stew, known as cioppino, that required more work and more ingredients. Not only have I reduced the preparation time, but I have also greatly improved the taste. There's just a hint of curry; you can add more if you like the flavour.

2 tsp vegetable oil 10 mL
1 cup chopped onions 250 mL
2 tsp minced garlic 10 mL
2 cups chopped plum tomatoes (about 3 large) 500 mL
1 cup fish stock or clam juice 250 mL
1/2 tsp curry powder 2 mL
12 oz combination scallops, peeled and deveined shrimp,
   and chunks of skinless halibut fillet 375 g
1/4 cup chopped fresh coriander or parsley 50 mL

1. In a nonstick saucepan sprayed with cooking spray, heat oil over medium-high heat; cook onions and garlic for 3 minutes, or until golden. Stir in tomatoes, fish stock, and curry powder. Bring to a boil. Reduce heat to simmer; cover and cook for 10 minutes.
2. Stir in shellfish and fish; cover and cook for 3 to 5 minutes, or until shellfish and fish are cooked through. Stir in coriander.

Olive-Crusted Fish

The topping for this dish, which combines two types of olives, breadcrumbs, garlic, and lemon juice, is delicious. Olives contain monounsaturated fat, which means they're heart healthy, but you still have to watch the amount you consume since they are high in calories and fat. I use them to highlight this dish.

1/2 cup seasoned dry breadcrumbs 125 mL
3 tbsp sliced black olives 75 mL
3 tbsp sliced green olives 75 mL
1/2 tsp dried oregano 2 mL
1/2 tsp minced garlic 2 mL
2 tsp olive oil 10 mL
1 tbsp fresh lemon juice 15 mL
4 4-oz (125 g) skinless white fish fillet portions such as halibut, tilapia, haddock, or cod 4
Lemon wedges and sprigs fresh parsley, as garnish

Preheat oven to 425°F (220°C). Spray a rimmed baking sheet with cooking spray.

1. In a food processor, combine breadcrumbs, black and green olives, oregano, garlic, oil, and lemon juice. Process until finely chopped.
2. Place fish on prepared baking sheet. Sprinkle with breadcrumb mixture. Bake 10 minutes per inch (2.5 cm) thickness of fish and topping, or until fish flakes easily when prodded with a fork.
3. Serve garnished with lemon wedges and parsley sprigs.

NUTRITIONAL ANALYSIS
PER SERVING
199 calories
25 g protein
6.9 g fat, total
0.8 g fat, saturated
8.1 g carbohydrates
435 mg sodium
36 mg cholesterol
0.5 g fibre

TIPS
Use any thickness of white fish you like; just remember the fish cooking rule of 10 minutes per inch (2.5 cm) at 425°F (220°C). Using a milder fish is recommended since the olives have a distinct flavour. If you like, you can use just one type of olive.

Thai Halibut with Peppers and Coconut Sauce

The light coconut sauce with sautéed bell peppers and onions suits this mild-tasting fish beautifully. The texture of halibut is crab-like, and it has a sweet flavour.

2 tsp vegetable oil 10 mL
1 cup sliced onions 250 mL
1 cup sliced sweet red peppers 250 mL
1/2 cup light coconut milk 125 mL
2 tbsp fresh lime or lemon juice 25 mL
1-1/2 tbsp packed brown sugar 22 mL
1 tbsp fish or oyster sauce 15 mL
1 tsp minced garlic 5 mL
1 tsp minced fresh ginger 5 mL
1/2 tsp hot Asian chili sauce 2 mL
4 4-oz (125 g) skinless halibut fillet portions 4
1/4 cup each: chopped green onions and chopped coriander, as garnish 50 mL

Preheat oven to 425°F (220°C). Spray a rimmed baking sheet with cooking spray.

1. In a nonstick frying pan sprayed with cooking spray, heat oil over medium-high heat; cook onions and peppers for 5 minutes, or until softened. Set aside.
2. In a small saucepan, combine coconut milk, lime juice, brown sugar, fish sauce, garlic, ginger, and hot Asian chili sauce. Bring to a boil. Reduce heat to simmer; cook for 5 minutes, or until slightly thickened. Remove from heat.
3. Place halibut on prepared baking sheet. Spread onions and peppers over fish. Spoon one-quarter of sauce on fish. Bake for 10 minutes per inch (2.5 cm) thickness of fish and topping, or until fish flakes easily when prodded with a fork.
4. Serve sprinkled with green onions and coriander, and with remaining sauce on the side.

Makes 4 servings.

NUTRITIONAL ANALYSIS
PER SERVING
207 calories
25 g protein
6.5 g fat, total
1.9 g fat, saturated
12 g carbohydrates
417 mg sodium
36 mg cholesterol
1.6 g fibre

TIPS
You can make the sauce early in the day; bake just before serving. This fish tastes good the next day served at room temperature. If coriander is not to your taste, substitute dill or fresh Italian parsley.

Hoisin-Glazed Salmon

Whenever I have a corporate group attending my school, I love to prepare this salmon dish because it's easy and delicious. Instead of baking, you can grill the salmon and serve it with the sauce over top. Hoisin sauce is an Asian sauce, found in all supermarkets, made from soybeans and often sweet potatoes.

1/4 cup hoisin sauce 50 mL
2 tsp low-sodium soy sauce 10 mL
2 tsp sesame oil 10 mL
1 tsp honey 5 mL
1 tsp minced garlic 5 mL
1/2 tsp minced fresh ginger 2 mL
4 4-oz (125 g) skinless salmon fillet portions 4
2 tsp sesame seeds 10 mL
Parsley or coriander

Preheat oven to 425°F (220°C). Spray a rimmed baking sheet with cooking spray.

1. In a bowl, stir together hoisin sauce, soy sauce, sesame oil, honey, garlic, and ginger.
2. Place salmon on prepared baking sheet. Spoon half of hoisin mixture over salmon. Sprinkle with sesame seeds. Bake in centre of oven for 10 minutes per inch (2.5 cm) thickness of fish, or until fish flakes easily when prodded with a fork.
3. Serve with remaining sauce. Garnish with parsley or coriander.

Makes 4 servings.

NUTRITIONAL ANALYSIS
PER SERVING
232 calories
24 g protein
11 g fat, total
1.7 g fat, saturated
9.2 g carbohydrates
398 mg sodium
64 mg cholesterol
0.7 g fibre

TIP
This sauce is also wonderful with chicken or pork. I often make a triple batch and keep it either refrigerated or frozen for later use.

Honey Nut–Coated Salmon

Makes 4 servings.

NUTRITIONAL ANALYSIS
PER SERVING
293 calories
23 g protein
13 g fat, total
2.7 g fat, saturated
21 g carbohydrates
87 mg sodium
69 mg cholesterol
0.6 g fibre

TIP
You can grill the fish and
cook the sauce separately
if you like. Bring the sauce
to a boil, then simmer for
3 minutes until slightly
thickened.

The pecan–maple syrup sauce gets thick and sticky—almost candy-like—upon cooling. If you like the sauce looser, heat just before serving. Salmon has a higher fat content than other fish, but it contains good omega-3 fatty acids that help to lower bad cholesterol and help in the prevention of cancer.

3 tbsp chopped pecans 45 mL
3 tbsp honey 45 mL
3 tbsp maple syrup 45 mL
2 tsp butter 10 mL
1/2 tsp Dijon mustard 2 mL
4 4-oz (125 g) skinless salmon fillet portions 4
Chopped fresh coriander or parsley,
    as garnish

Preheat oven to 425°F (200°C). Spray a rimmed baking sheet with cooking spray.

1. In a small nonstick frying pan set over medium-high heat, toast pecans for 3 minutes, or until golden and fragrant. Stir in honey, maple syrup, and butter. Reduce heat to simmer; cook for 3 minutes, or until slightly thickened. Remove from heat; whisk in mustard. Cool slightly.
2. Place salmon on prepared baking sheet. Pour half of pecan mixture evenly over salmon. Bake for 10 minutes per inch (2.5 cm) thickness of fish, or until fish flakes easily when prodded with a fork.
3. Serve fish with remaining pecan mixture and garnish with coriander.

Pesto-Glazed Salmon

Homemade pesto is much lower in fat and calories than the store-bought version. I like to prepare containers of it when basil is in season and freeze them through the winter. I use it over fish, chicken, pizzas, and pasta. The light cream cheese and stock allow me to reduce the oil content.

Pesto

1 cup packed fresh basil leaves 250 g

2 tbsp grated Parmesan cheese 25 mL

1 tbsp toasted pine nuts 15 mL

1 oz light cream cheese 30 g

1 tsp minced garlic 5 mL

3 tbsp chicken or vegetable stock 45 mL

2 tbsp olive oil 25 mL

6 4-oz (125 g) skin-on salmon fillet
   portions 6

2 tbsp pine nuts 25 mL

1 oz light feta cheese, crumbled 30 g

Preheat oven to 425°F (220°C). Spray a rimmed baking sheet with cooking spray.

1. To make pesto: In a food processor, combine basil, Parmesan, pine nuts, cream cheese, and garlic; purée. With machine running, add stock and olive oil through the feed tube. Process until smooth.

2. Place salmon, skin side down, on prepared baking sheet. Spread pesto over salmon. Sprinkle with pine nuts and feta. Bake in centre of oven for 10 minutes per inch (2.5 cm) thickness of fish and topping, or until fish flakes easily when prodded with a fork.

3. Remove fish skin before serving.

Makes 6 servings.

NUTRITIONAL ANALYSIS
PER SERVING
254 calories
26 g protein
16 g fat, total
3.2 g fat, saturated
1.4 g carbohydrates
194 mg sodium
69 mg cholesterol
0.4 g fibre

TIP
Remember that the fat contained in salmon is omega-3 fatty acids, which are considered heart healthy and actually help lower bad cholesterol.

Salmon Parcels Wrapped in Rice Paper

Makes 4 servings.

NUTRITIONAL ANALYSIS
PER SERVING
255 calories
24 g protein
11 g fat, total
2.7 g fat, saturated
15 g carbohydrates
250 mg sodium
64 mg cholesterol
0.6 g fibre

TIP
It's not easy to tell when
the fish is cooked when it's
wrapped in rice paper.
Keep in mind the fish
cooking rule of 10 minutes
per inch (2.5 cm) either
grilled or in a 425°F
(220°C) oven. I always cut
into one piece and peek to
see if it's ready. I like to
serve it still slightly pink
inside.

Rice paper sheets come in different sizes; be sure to buy one that will comfortably fit your salmon portion. The rice paper forms a shell around the salmon and, when sautéed, becomes crisp—a wonderful contrast to the moist salmon inside. The light coconut sauce is perfect with the salmon.

4 large (8-1/2-inch/21 cm) round rice paper
    wrappers 4
1 tbsp hoisin sauce 15 mL
4 4-oz (125 g) skinless salmon fillet
    portions 4
2 tsp vegetable oil 10 mL

Sauce
1/2 cup light coconut milk 125 mL
1 tbsp low-sodium soy sauce 15 mL
1 tbsp packed brown sugar 15 mL
2 tsp fresh lime or lemon juice 10 mL
1/2 tsp minced garlic 2 mL
1/2 tsp minced fresh ginger 2 mL
2 tbsp chopped fresh basil or coriander
    25 mL

1. Fill a shallow baking dish with cold water. Soak rice paper wrappers for 2 minutes, or until softened. Place flat on a clean tea towel.
2. Divide hoisin sauce among fillets, spreading over top. Place one fillet of salmon on each rice wrapper, hoisin side down. Wrap salmon fillets, completely enclosing in rice wrapper.
3. In a large nonstick frying pan sprayed with cooking spray, heat oil over medium heat. Cook salmon parcels for 4 minutes per side, or until rice paper is golden and salmon is cooked through.
4. To make sauce: In a small saucepan, combine coconut milk, soy sauce, brown sugar, lime juice, garlic, and ginger. Bring to a boil. Reduce heat to simmer; cook for 3 minutes, or until slightly thickened. Remove from heat.
5. Place one salmon parcel in middle of each of four dinner plates. Spoon sauce over top and sprinkle with fresh basil.

Salmon Strudel

I rate this as my best-tasting and most elegant fish dish. The wild and white rice, spinach, feta cheese, and salmon packaged in phyllo pastry is well worth the effort.

2 tsp vegetable oil 10 mL
1 cup chopped onions 250 mL
1 tsp minced garlic 5 mL
1/3 cup wild rice 75 mL
2-1/4 cups chicken or fish stock 550 mL
1/3 cup jasmine rice 75 mL
Half 10-oz/300 g pkg frozen chopped spinach, thawed Half
1-1/2 oz light feta cheese, crumbled 45 g
2 tbsp chopped fresh dill 25 mL
1/8 tsp freshly ground black pepper 0.5 mL
6 sheets phyllo pastry 6
4 6-oz (150 g) skinless salmon fillet portions 4

Preheat oven to 400°F (200°C). Spray a baking sheet with cooking spray.

1. In a saucepan sprayed with cooking spray, heat oil over medium heat; cook onion and garlic for 3 minutes, or until softened. Stir in wild rice; cook for 1 minute. Add stock. Bring to a boil. Reduce heat to medium-low; cover and cook for 25 minutes. Stir in jasmine rice; cover and cook for 15 minutes longer, or until liquid is absorbed and rice is tender. Cool.
2. Squeeze excess liquid from spinach. Stir into rice, along with feta, dill, and pepper.
3. Layer two sheets of phyllo, keeping remaining phyllo covered with a cloth to prevent drying out. Spray phyllo with cooking spray. Layer on one more sheet. Cut in half widthwise. Set aside. Repeat with remaining 3 sheets of phyllo.
4. Spoon one-quarter of rice mixture onto centre of each stack of phyllo. Top each stack with a salmon portion. Fold long sides of phyllo up over salmon. Fold short edges over to completely enclose. Place on prepared baking sheet. Spray strudels with cooking spray.
5. Bake in centre of oven for 15 to 20 minutes per inch (2.5 cm) thickness, or until golden. Slice phyllo packets in half.

Makes 8 servings.

NUTRITIONAL ANALYSIS
PER 1/2 STRUDEL
207 calories
16 g protein
7 g fat, total
1.4 g fat, saturated
20 g carbohydrates
374 mg sodium
34 mg cholesterol
1.7 g fibre

TIP
When fish is wrapped in phyllo pastry it's not easy to determine when it is cooked. The best rule is to follow the fish cooking rule of 10 minutes per inch (2.5 cm) at 400°F to 425°F (200°C to 220°C). The additional rice filling in this recipe may add another couple of minutes to the baking time. Carefully cut into the salmon to peek, and cook just until centre is still slightly pink.

Salmon Teriyaki

Makes 4 servings.

NUTRITIONAL ANALYSIS
PER SERVING
250 calories
24 g protein
10 g fat, total
1.6 g fat, saturated
16 g carbohydrates
323 mg sodium
64 mg cholesterol
0.3 g fibre

TIP
You can also grill the
fish and serve the sauce
separately.

The image on the front cover of *Rose Reisman Brings Home Light Cooking* showed this recipe, one of the most delicious in that book. I improved on the recipe, making the sauce more like a glaze. Use the sauce over chicken as well.

1/4 cup packed brown sugar 50 mL
2 tbsp low-sodium soy sauce 25 mL
1 tbsp water 15 mL
2 tbsp rice wine vinegar 25 mL
2 tsp sesame oil 10 mL
2 tsp cornstarch 10 mL
2 tsp minced garlic 10 mL
1-1/2 tsp minced fresh ginger 7 mL
4 4-oz (125 g) skin-on salmon fillet portions 4
2 tsp sesame seeds 10 mL
Parsley, as garnish

Preheat oven to 425°F (220°C). Spray a rimmed baking sheet with cooking spray.

1. In a small saucepan, whisk together brown sugar, soy sauce, water, vinegar, sesame oil, cornstarch, garlic, and ginger. Cook over medium heat until thickened and smooth, approximately 2 minutes. Remove from heat.
2. Place salmon, skin side down, on prepared baking sheet. Spoon half of sauce over salmon. Sprinkle with sesame seeds. Bake in centre of oven for 10 minutes per inch (2.5 cm) thickness of fish, or until fish flakes easily when prodded with a fork.
3. Remove fish skin before serving. Serve with remaining sauce on the side. Garnish with parsley.

Red Snapper with Shrimp, Black Bean, and Corn Salsa

An unusual recipe for fish with a seafood salsa. The salsa could be served over any other fish or even over chicken. I like to sauté the corn because it brings out a charred flavour and texture.

Salsa

1/2 cup drained canned corn 125 mL

4 oz cooked shrimp, chopped 125 g

3/4 cup canned black beans, rinsed and
   drained 175 mL

1/3 cup chopped roasted red peppers, 75 mL

1/4 cup diced onions 50 mL

3 tbsp chopped fresh basil or coriander
   45 mL

3 tbsp finely chopped green onions 45 mL

3 tbsp fresh lemon juice 45 mL

1 tbsp olive oil 15 mL

1/2 tsp minced garlic 2 mL

6 4-oz (125 g) red snapper fillets, or other
   white fish like tilapia or halibut 6

Preheat grill or grill pan sprayed with cooking spray.

1. To make salsa: In a nonstick frying pan sprayed with cooking spray, cook corn over medium heat, stirring often, for 8 minutes, or until slightly charred. In a bowl, stir together corn, shrimp, black beans, red peppers, onions, basil, green onions, lemon juice, olive oil, and garlic.

2. Grill red snapper over medium-high heat for 10 minutes per inch (2.5 cm) thickness of fish, turning once, or until fish flakes easily when prodded with a fork.

3. Serve red snapper with salsa.

Makes 4 to 6 servings.

NUTRITIONAL ANALYSIS
PER 1/6-RECIPE SERVING
120 calories
21 g protein
2.2 g fat, total
0.4 g fat, saturated
9.3 g carbohydrates
254 mg sodium
78 mg cholesterol
2 g fibre

TIPS
The fish and salsa can be served at room temperature or warm. You could substitute imitation crabmeat, or surimi, for the shrimp. Buy bottled roasted red peppers packed in water (not oil) or roast your own.

Swordfish with Mango–Coriander Salsa

Often made with fresh fruit, vegetables, and herbs, salsas are a wonderful alternative to heavy sauces. This mango salsa goes well over fish, chicken, or pork. If mangos aren't in season, try pineapple, pears, or peaches. Mangos contain beta carotene, which helps in the fight against cancer.

1-1/2 lb swordfish fillet, or other white fish
   like tuna, seabass, or halibut 750 g
1 tsp vegetable oil 5 mL

Salsa
1-1/2 cups finely diced mango or peach
   375 mL
3/4 cup finely diced sweet red peppers
   175 mL
1/2 cup finely diced sweet green peppers
   125 mL
1/2 cup finely diced red onions 125 mL
1/4 cup chopped fresh coriander 50 mL
2 tbsp thawed orange juice concentrate
   25 mL
1 tbsp fresh lemon juice 15 mL
2 tsp olive oil 10 mL
1 tsp minced garlic 5 mL
1/2 tsp granulated sugar 2 mL

Preheat grill or grill pan sprayed with cooking spray.

1. Brush swordfish with oil on both sides.
2. Grill swordfish over medium-high heat for 10 minutes per inch (2.5 cm) thickness of fish, turning once, or until fish flakes easily when prodded with a fork. (Or bake in a preheated 425°F/220°C oven for 10 minutes per inch/2.5 cm thickness.)
3. To make salsa: In a bowl, combine mango, red and green peppers, red onions, coriander, orange juice concentrate, lemon juice, olive oil, garlic, and sugar.
4. Serve salsa over fish.

Bruschetta Pasta with Goat Cheese and Fresh Basil, p. 258

Coconut Layer Cake with Italian Meringue Icing, p. 338

Tilapia with Tomato, Olive, and Cheese Topping

You can use any firm white fish with this delicious olive, tomato, and cheese topping. Tilapia is very popular—delicious and affordable!

1 cup chopped plum tomatoes 250 mL
1/2 cup shredded light mozzarella cheese 125 mL
1/4 cup chopped black olives 50 mL
1-1/2 oz goat cheese 45 g
1 tsp minced garlic 5 mL
1 tsp dried basil 5 mL
1 lb tilapia fillets, or other firm white fish like halibut, snapper, or haddock 500 g

Preheat oven to 425°F (220°C). Spray a rimmed baking sheet with cooking spray.

1. In a bowl, stir together tomatoes, mozzarella, black olives, goat cheese, garlic, and basil.
2. Place tilapia on prepared baking sheet. Top with tomato mixture. Bake for 10 minutes per inch (2.5 cm) thickness of fish and topping, or until fish flakes easily when prodded with a fork.

Makes 4 servings.

NUTRITIONAL ANALYSIS PER SERVING
198 calories
27 g protein
8.5 g fat, total
3.6 g fat, saturated
3.3 g carbohydrates
255 mg sodium
60 mg cholesterol
0.5 g fibre

TIPS
The topping can be prepared up to a day in advance. It's best to bake just before serving. When you add a topping to fish, be sure to add it to the thickness measurement when cooking.

Seared Tuna and Udon Noodles

Makes 4 to 6 servings.

NUTRITIONAL ANALYSIS
PER 1/6-RECIPE SERVING
420 calories
39 g protein
6.7 g fat, total
0.8 fat, saturated
55 g carbohydrates
544 mg sodium
54 mg cholesterol
0.6 g fibre

TIP
Udon noodles are long, white, and round with a dense texture. They are found in the produce section of your supermarket where the Asian or soy ingredients are. If you are unable to find them, substitute wide rice noodles.

The combination of seared tuna, sautéed oyster mushrooms, and udon noodles is amazing. If you're not comfortable eating fairly raw fish, cook the fish to your preference, but keep in mind that tuna dries if overcooked. I believe that once you try it seared, you'll never go back.

1 tsp vegetable oil 5 mL
2 cups chopped oyster mushrooms 500 mL
1 tsp chopped garlic 5 mL
1 tsp chopped fresh ginger 5 mL
2 tbsp low-sodium soy sauce 25 mL
2 tbsp rice wine vinegar 25 mL
4 tsp honey 20 mL
1 tbsp sesame oil 15 mL
1 lb fresh udon noodles 500 g
1-1/2 lb fresh skinless tuna steak 750 g
1 tsp vegetable oil 5 mL
2 tsp toasted sesame seeds 10 mL

Sauce
2 tbsp low-sodium soy sauce 25 mL
2 tbsp packed brown sugar 25 mL

1/4 cup chopped green onions, as garnish 50 mL

1. In a nonstick frying pan sprayed with cooking spray, heat oil over medium-high heat; cook mushrooms, garlic, and ginger for 5 minutes, or until mushrooms are browned. Stir in soy sauce, vinegar, honey, and sesame oil; cook for 1 minute. Set aside.
2. In a pot of boiling water, cook udon noodles for 3 minutes, or until tender but firm. Drain. Toss with mushroom mixture.
3. Rub tuna with oil and sprinkle with sesame seeds. In a nonstick frying pan sprayed with cooking spray and set over medium-high heat, cook tuna for 2 minutes per side, or until desired doneness. Do not overcook. Slice thinly.
4. To make sauce: In a small saucepan, combine soy sauce and brown sugar. Bring to a boil. Reduce heat to simmer; cook for 1 minute, or until slightly thickened.
5. Place noodle mixture on a large platter. Arrange tuna on top. Drizzle with sauce. Serve garnished with green onions.

Thai Mussels in Coconut Sauce

The most common mussel is the blue variety. They contain only 2 grams of fat per 3-oz (90 g) serving, with only 70 calories! The light coconut milk and Thai flavours match these shellfish beautifully. Serve with crusty bread.

2 lb mussels 1 kg
3/4 cup light coconut milk 175 mL
1/2 cup thinly sliced sweet red peppers 125 mL
1/3 cup chopped green onions 75 mL
1 tbsp fresh lemon juice 15 mL
4 tsp oyster or fish sauce 20 mL
1-1/2 tsp minced garlic 7 mL
1 tsp minced fresh ginger 5 mL
1/2 tsp hot Asian chili sauce 2 mL
1/4 cup chopped fresh coriander 50 mL

1. Rinse mussels under cold water. Remove any beards. Discard any open mussels that do not close when tapped.
2. In a large saucepan, combine coconut milk, red peppers, green onions, lemon juice, oyster sauce, garlic, ginger, and hot Asian chili sauce. Bring to a boil. Add mussels. Reduce heat to medium-high; cover and cook, shaking pan occasionally, for 3 to 5 minutes, or until mussels open. Discard any mussels that do not open.
3. Serve mussels along with liquid from pan, sprinkled with coriander.

Makes 4 servings.

NUTRITIONAL ANALYSIS
PER SERVING
211 calories
27 g protein
6.5 g fat, total
2.3 g fat, saturated
11 g carbohydrates
653 mg sodium
62 mg cholesterol
0.9 g fibre

TIP
Even with farm-cultivated mussels, which are cleaner than wild, rinse well. If buying them a day before, it's best to keep them on ice to maintain freshness. Toss out any mussels that are cracked or do not open after cooking. Continued cooking will not open mussels; a closed mussel usually means it's no longer alive.

Shrimp in Orange–Black Bean Sauce over Chow Mein Noodles

Whenever I eat this seafood noodle dish I feel as if I'm in an authentic Asian restaurant. Yet the recipe is so simple. You can find fresh chow mein noodles in the produce section of most supermarkets, or in Asian stores. Be sure not to purchase the fried ones.

Makes 4 servings.

NUTRITIONAL ANALYSIS
PER SERVING
315 calories
18 g protein
3.9 g fat, total
0.5 g fat, saturated
52 g carbohydrates
202 mg sodium
86 mg cholesterol
2 g fibre

TIPS
If you don't have chow mein noodles on hand, substitute rice vermicelli. Black bean sauce is also available in the ethnic section of all good supermarkets. Use it sparingly since it is quite salty.

8 oz fresh chow mein noodles 250 g
2 tsp vegetable oil 10 mL
1 cup sliced onions 250 mL
1-1/2 cups thinly sliced sweet red peppers 375 mL
1 cup thinly sliced sweet green peppers 250 mL
1-1/2 tsp minced garlic 7 mL
1 tsp minced fresh ginger 5 mL
8 oz shrimp, peeled and deveined 250 g
1 cup orange juice 250 mL
3 tbsp black bean sauce 45 mL
2 tbsp packed brown sugar 25 mL
1 tbsp cornstarch 15 mL
1/2 cup chopped fresh coriander or parsley 125 mL

1. Place noodles in a bowl; add boiling water to cover. Let stand for 5 minutes, or until soft. Drain.
2. In a nonstick wok or large saucepan sprayed with cooking spray, heat oil over medium-high heat; stir-fry onions for 3 minutes, or until lightly browned. Stir in red and green peppers, garlic, and ginger; stir-fry for 3 minutes. Add shrimp; stir-fry for 2 minutes, or until shrimp are pink.
3. In a bowl, whisk together orange juice, black bean sauce, brown sugar, and cornstarch. Add to wok. Cook for 2 minutes, or until thickened and bubbly.
4. Arrange noodles on a serving platter. Pour shrimp mixture on top. Sprinkle with coriander. Serve immediately.

Mediterranean Squid with Mushrooms and Tomatoes

Squid is known as calamari and inkfish. You should select fresh squid if possible, and it should have a fresh, sweet smell. The meat is actually firm, slightly chewy, and white when cooked. Overcooking makes it tough. I like to serve this dish either as a main or first course.

1 lb cleaned squid 500 g
2 tsp vegetable oil 10 mL
1 cup chopped oyster mushrooms 250 mL
3/4 cup chopped onions 175 mL
1 cup chopped, seeded plum tomatoes 250 mL
3 tbsp chopped black olives 45 mL
1/2 tsp dried oregano 2 mL
3 tbsp fresh lemon juice 45 mL
1-1/2 tbsp olive oil 22 mL
1 tsp minced garlic 5 mL
Chopped fresh parsley or oregano, as garnish

1. Cut squid bodies crosswise into rings 1/2 inch (1 cm) thick. Divide tentacles in half if large.
2. In a nonstick frying pan sprayed with cooking spray, heat 1 tsp (5 mL) oil over medium-high heat; cook mushrooms and onions for 5 minutes, or until softened. Stir in tomatoes, olives, and oregano; cook for 1 minute longer. Remove from heat. Stir in lemon juice, olive oil, and garlic.
3. In another nonstick frying sprayed with cooking spray, heat remaining 1 tsp (5 mL) oil over high heat; cook squid for 2 minutes, or until cooked through but still tender. Transfer to a serving dish. Pour tomato–olive mixture on top of squid. Garnish with fresh parsley.

Makes 4 servings.

NUTRITIONAL ANALYSIS
PER SERVING
210 calories
19 g protein
10 g fat, total
1.3 g fat, saturated
11 g carbohydrates
112 mg sodium
264 mg cholesterol
1.5 g fibre

TIPS
Be sure to remove the transparent cartilage in the body of the squid if it is still there. This dish is also delicious served at room temperature or cold.

Seafood Kebabs with Pineapple and Green Pepper in Apricot Glaze

Makes 4 servings.

TIP
When using a sweet glaze on the barbecue, watch carefully, since the sugar burns quickly. Keep heat down to medium-high. Or you can barbecue the kebabs until they're half-way done, then brush the glaze over top.

Put aside the chicken and beef kebabs and have this delicious and unique seafood kebab. The colour and texture combination is beautiful, with apricots, green pepper, and fresh pineapple. The sauce has a savoury taste with the flavours of apricot jam and Dijon mustard.

16 dried apricots 16
1 lb scallops, peeled and deveined shrimp, and/or firm white fish like halibut or cod cut in 2-inch (5 cm) cubes 500 g
1 sweet green pepper, cut in 16 chunks 1
16 1-inch (2.5 cm) chunks fresh pineapple 16

4 long or 8 short skewers

Glaze
2/3 cup apricot jam 150 mL
1/4 cup fresh lemon juice 50 mL
2 tbsp water 25 mL
2 tbsp chopped fresh coriander or parsley 25 mL
1 tbsp vegetable oil 15 mL
2 tsp Dijon mustard 10 mL
2 tsp minced garlic 10 mL
1 tsp curry powder 5 mL

Preheat grill or grill pan sprayed with cooking spray.

1. Soak apricots in boiling water for 10 minutes; drain. If using wooden skewers, soak in water for 15 minutes. Thread seafood or fish cubes, alternating with apricots, green peppers, and pineapple chunks, onto 4 long or 8 short skewers.
2. To make glaze: In a small bowl, whisk together apricot jam, lemon juice, water, coriander, oil, mustard, garlic, and curry powder. Divide glaze in half. Brush kebabs with half of glaze. Save remaining glaze to serve with cooked kebabs.
3. Grill kebabs over medium-high heat, turning once, for 5 to 8 minutes, or until cooked through. (Or cook in preheated 425°F/220°C oven for 10 minutes.) Serve with reserved glaze.

Desserts

Carrot Cake with Cream Cheese Frosting

Makes 16 servings.

NUTRITIONAL ANALYSIS
PER SERVING
223 calories
4 g protein
5 g fat, total
1 g fat, saturated
41 g carbohydrates
30 mg cholesterol
1 g fibre

TIPS
Very ripe bananas can
be kept frozen for up to
one year. Raisins can be
replaced with chopped,
pitted dates, apricots,
or prunes. Use a food
processor to mix the
batter, but take care not
to overprocess it.

My favourite cake from my first cookbook, *Toronto's Dessert Scene*, was the Carrot Cake by Carole Ogus of Carole's Cheesecake. It is fabulous but loaded with fat and calories. This version greatly reduces the fat by replacing a lot of the oil and butter with pineapple, more carrots, and low-fat yogourt. The icing uses a small amount of light cream cheese and spreads nicely over the cake. People often think carrot cake is healthier than other desserts. Not so! Most of these cakes use a batter made of oil, butter, eggs, and regular sour cream, and an icing based on butter or vegetable shortening. Beware of recipes that sound healthy!

1/3 cup vegetable oil or butter 75 mL
1 cup granulated sugar 250 mL
2 large eggs 2
1 tsp vanilla 5 mL
1 large ripe banana, mashed 1
2 cups grated carrots 500 mL
2/3 cup raisins or dried cranberries 150 mL
1/2 cup drained canned crushed pineapple
   125 mL
1/2 cup low-fat yogourt 125 mL
2 cups all-purpose flour 500 mL
1-1/2 tsp each: baking powder, baking soda,
   and cinnamon 7 mL
1/4 tsp nutmeg 1 mL

Icing
1/3 cup light cream cheese, softened
   75 mL
2/3 cup icing sugar 150 mL
1 tbsp low-fat milk or water 15 mL

Preheat oven to 350°F (175°C). Spray a 9-inch (23 cm) Bundt pan with cooking spray.

1. In a large bowl, mix together oil and sugar until smooth; add eggs and vanilla, and beat well (the mixture may look curdled). Add banana, carrots, raisins, pineapple, and yogourt; stir until everything is well combined.
2. In another bowl, stir together flour, baking powder, baking soda, cinnamon, and nutmeg until combined. Add to carrot mixture; stir just until combined. Pour into prepared pan.
3. Place pan in the centre of the oven and bake for 35 to 40 minutes, or until a tester inserted in the centre comes out clean. Let the pan cool for 10 minutes before inverting the cake onto a serving plate.
4. To make icing: In a bowl or food processor, beat together cream cheese, icing sugar, and milk until smooth; drizzle over top of cake. Decorate with grated carrots if desired.

Date Cake with Coconut Topping

Dates are often used in desserts to lower the fat. They have a buttery taste when puréed and give the cake the moisture that fat would supply. They are also a good source of protein and iron.

12 oz chopped, pitted dried dates
   (2-1/2 cups/625 mL) 375 g
1-3/4 cups water 425 mL
1/4 cup vegetable oil or butter 50 mL
1 cup granulated sugar 250 mL
2 large eggs 2
1-1/2 cups all-purpose flour 375 mL
1-1/2 tsp baking powder 7 mL
1 tsp baking soda 5 mL

Topping
1/3 cup unsweetened coconut 75 mL
1/4 cup packed brown sugar 50 mL
3 tbsp low-fat milk 45 mL
2 tbsp vegetable oil or butter 25 mL

Preheat oven to 350°F (175°C). Spray a 9-inch (23 cm) square cake pan with cooking spray.

1. Place the dates and water in a saucepan; bring to a boil, cover, and reduce the heat to low. Cook, stirring often, for 10 minutes, or until dates are soft and most of the liquid has been absorbed. Set aside to cool for 10 minutes.
2. In a large bowl or food processor, beat together oil and sugar. Add eggs and mix well. Add cooled date mixture and mix everything well.
3. In another bowl, combine flour, baking powder, and baking soda. Stir dry ingredients into date mixture, just until combined. Pour into prepared pan.
4. Place pan in the centre of the oven and bake for 35 to 40 minutes, or until a tester inserted in the centre comes out dry. Let the pan cool on a wire rack.
5. To make topping: In a small saucepan, combine coconut, brown sugar, milk, and oil; cook over medium heat, stirring, for 2 minutes, or until sugar dissolves. Pour topping over cooled cake.

Makes 16 servings.

NUTRITIONAL ANALYSIS
PER SERVING
217 calories
3 g protein
5 g fat, total
2 g fat, saturated
41 g carbohydrates
27 mg cholesterol
2 g fibre

TIPS
To chop dates easily, use kitchen shears. Whole pitted dates can be used; use a food processor to mash them after they are cooked. Try chopped, pitted prunes instead of dates.

Double Chocolate Chip Banana Cake

Makes 16 servings.

NUTRITIONAL ANALYSIS
PER SERVING
270 calories
3.7 g protein
7.5 g fat, total
2.2 g fat, saturated
63 g carbohydrates
30 mg cholesterol
2.2 g fibre

TIPS
The surprise ingredient
here is carrot, which gives
incredible moisture to the
cake. Zucchini works well,
too. Freeze overripe
bananas in their skins for
up to one year. Defrost and
use them mashed in
baking. Try the cake
without the icing—it's
delicious either way.

This has to be the best chocolate cake I've ever baked. The combination of fruit and vegetables keeps it moist, and the cocoa and sprinkling of chocolate chips give it a dense chocolate flavour. Carrots are an extremely low-fat vegetable. Like the banana and pineapple in this recipe, they add moisture without adding fat.

1 cup packed brown sugar 250 mL
1/2 cup granulated sugar 125 mL
1/3 cup vegetable oil 75 mL
1 medium ripe banana, mashed
   (1/3 cup/75 mL) 1
1 tsp vanilla 5 mL
2 large eggs 2
2 cups finely chopped or grated carrots
   500 mL
1/2 cup drained canned crushed pineapple
   125 mL
2 cups all-purpose flour 500 mL
1/3 cup unsweetened cocoa powder 75 mL
1-1/2 tsp baking powder 7 mL
1-1/2 tsp baking soda 7 mL
1/3 cup semi-sweet chocolate chips 75 mL
1/4 cup low-fat sour cream 50 mL

Chocolate Cream Cheese Icing
1/3 cup light cream cheese, softened 75 mL
1 cup icing sugar 250 mL
1 tbsp unsweetened cocoa powder 15 mL
1 tbsp low-fat milk 15 mL

Preheat oven to 350°F (175°C). Spray 9-inch (23 cm) Bundt pan with cooking spray.

1. In a food processor, combine brown sugar, granulated sugar, oil, banana, vanilla, and eggs; process until smooth. Add carrots and pineapple; process just until combined.
2. In a bowl, stir together flour, cocoa, baking powder, and baking soda. Stir wet ingredients into dry ingredients, just until mixed. Stir in chocolate chips and sour cream. Spoon mixture into prepared pan.
3. Place pan in the centre of the oven and bake for 40 to 45 minutes, or until a tester inserted in the centre comes out clean. Let the pan cool on a wire rack.
4. To make icing: With an electric mixer or in a food processor, cream together cream cheese, icing sugar, cocoa, and milk. Spread mixture over cooled cake.

Orange Poppyseed Bundt Cake

This is a dense orange coffee cake with a strong citrus flavour. Light cream cheese is not a low-fat product, so use it carefully.

1-1/3 cups granulated sugar 325 mL

2 large eggs 2

1 cup smooth 5% ricotta cheese 250 mL

2/3 cup low-fat yogourt 150 mL

1/3 cup vegetable oil 75 mL

3 tbsp thawed orange juice concentrate
    45 mL

1 tbsp finely grated orange rind 15 mL

1-1/3 cups all-purpose flour 325 mL

2-1/4 tsp baking powder 11 mL

2 tsp poppyseeds 10 mL

1/2 tsp baking soda 2 mL

Icing

2 oz light cream cheese, softened 60 g

2/3 cup icing sugar 150 mL

1 tbsp thawed orange juice concentrate
    15 mL

Makes 14 servings.

NUTRITIONAL ANALYSIS
PER SERVING
213 calories
4.6 g protein
6.9 g fat, total
1.6 g fat, saturated
32 g carbohydrates
20 mg cholesterol
0.2 g fibre

TIPS
Be sure to beat the ricotta mixture well to get it as smooth as possible. A food processor lets you achieve a good consistency. Don't be concerned if this cake sinks slightly after baking.

Preheat oven to 350°F (175°C). Spray a 9-inch (23 cm) Bundt pan with cooking spray.

1. In a food processor, combine sugar, eggs, ricotta, yogourt, oil, orange juice concentrate, and orange rind; purée until smooth. Transfer to a large bowl.

2. In another bowl, stir together flour, baking powder, poppyseeds, and baking soda. With a wooden spoon, stir dry ingredients into the orange mixture, just until combined. Pour into prepared pan.

3. Place pan in the centre of the oven and bake for 30 to 35 minutes, or until a tester inserted in the centre comes out clean. Let the pan cool on a wire rack.

4. To make icing: Using either a food processor or an electric mixer, beat together cream cheese, icing sugar, and orange juice concentrate until smooth. Drizzle over cake.

Coconut Layer Cake with Italian Meringue Icing

Makes 14 servings.

NUTRITIONAL ANALYSIS
PER SERVING
238 calories
3.2 g protein
7.8 g fat, total
2.2 g fat, saturated
38 g carbohydrates
30 mg cholesterol
0.7 g fibre

TIP
To toast the coconut,
brown it in a frying pan
over high heat for approximately 2 to 3 minutes.

I used to avoid coconut desserts because coconut milk contains saturated fat. Now that light coconut milk, which is 75% reduced in fat, is available, I'm constantly looking for recipes to use it in. Coconut is one of the few fruits that contain saturated fat, so use it sparingly to highlight a dessert.

1-1/4 cups granulated sugar 300 mL	2 large egg whites 2
3/4 cup light coconut milk 175 mL	1/4 tsp cream of tartar 1 mL
1/3 cup vegetable oil 75 mL	
2 large eggs 2	**Icing**
1-1/2 tsp vanilla 7 mL	3 large egg whites 3
1-1/4 cups all-purpose flour 300 mL	3/4 cup granulated sugar 175 mL
1-1/2 tsp baking powder 7 mL	1/4 cup water 50 mL
1/4 tsp salt 1 mL	1/4 tsp cream of tartar 1 mL
2 tbsp toasted coconut 25 mL	3 tbsp toasted coconut 45 mL

Preheat oven to 350°F (175°C). Spray two 9-inch (23 cm) round cake pans with cooking spray.

1. In a large bowl, using a whisk or an electric mixer, beat 1 cup (250 mL) of the sugar, the coconut milk, oil, eggs, and vanilla.

2. In another bowl, stir together flour, baking powder, salt, and coconut. With a wooden spoon, stir dry ingredients into coconut milk mixture, just until combined.

3. In a separate bowl, beat egg whites with cream of tartar until foamy. Gradually add the remaining 1/4 cup (50 mL) sugar, beating until stiff peaks form. Stir one-quarter of egg whites into the cake batter. Gently fold in the remaining egg whites. Divide mixture between the prepared pans.

4. Bake in the centre of the oven for approximately 15 minutes, or until a tester inserted into the centre comes out dry. Let the pans cool on a wire rack.

5. To make icing: In the top of a double boiler, or in a glass or metal bowl over top of a saucepan of simmering water, combine egg whites, sugar, water, and cream of tartar. Place over medium-low heat. With an electric mixer, beat for 6 to 8 minutes, or until thickened and soft peaks form. Remove from heat; beat for 1 minute, or until stiff peaks form. Stir in 2 tbsp (25 mL) of the toasted coconut.

6. Place one cake layer on a cake platter. Spread some icing over top. Place the second cake layer on top of the first and ice the top and sides. Sprinkle with remaining 1 tbsp (15 mL) toasted coconut.

New York–Style Cheesecake with Glazed Strawberry Topping

This is one of my favourite cheesecake recipes. It's light and airy, yet tastes rich and satisfying. Strawberries are an excellent source of vitamin C, and provide potassium and iron. They also play a role in cancer prevention.

Crust

1-3/4 cups vanilla wafer crumbs 425 mL
2 tbsp granulated sugar 25 mL
2 tbsp water 25 mL
1 tbsp vegetable oil or butter 15 mL

Filling

1-1/2 cups smooth 5% ricotta cheese 375 mL
3/4 cup low-fat yogourt 175 mL
4 oz light cream cheese, softened 125 g
2 large eggs, separated 2

1-1/2 tsp vanilla 7 mL
1 cup granulated sugar 250 mL
1/4 cup all-purpose flour 50 mL
1/8 tsp salt 0.5 mL
1/4 tsp cream of tartar 1 mL
2 tbsp granulated sugar 25 mL

Topping

2 cups sliced strawberries 500 mL
2 tbsp red currant or apple jelly 25 mL

Makes 16 servings.

NUTRITIONAL ANALYSIS
PER SERVING
210 calories
5.7 g protein
6.6 g fat, total
2.8 g fat, saturated
32 g carbohydrates
40 mg cholesterol
0.7 g fibre

TIPS
To make wafer crumbs, place whole wafers in the food processor and process until they reach the desired consistency. Then measure out what you need. You can substitute graham crackers.

Preheat oven to 350°F (175°C). Spray a 9-inch (23 cm) springform pan with cooking spray.

1. To make crust: In a bowl, stir together wafer crumbs, sugar, water, and oil until mixture holds together. Pat onto the bottom and up the sides of prepared pan.
2. To make filling: In a food processor, combine ricotta, yogourt, cream cheese, egg yolks, vanilla, the 1 cup (250 mL) sugar, flour, and salt; purée until smooth. Transfer to a large bowl.
3. In another bowl, using a whisk or an electric mixer, beat egg whites with cream of tartar until foamy. Gradually add the 2 tbsp (25 mL) sugar, continuing to beat until stiff peaks form. Gently fold egg whites into the cheese mixture, just until incorporated. Pour into prepared crust.
4. Place a pan of hot water on the bottom rack of the oven. (This retains the moisture.) Bake cheesecake in the centre of the oven for 55 to 60 minutes, or until slightly loose at the centre.
5. Run a knife around edge of cake. Let cake cool on a wire rack.
6. To make topping: Arrange strawberries on top of the cheesecake. In a microwave or on the stovetop, heat jelly until melted. Brush over the berries. Chill before serving.

Sour Cream Brownie Cheesecake

Chill before serving.

This cake is sinfully delicious—a thick layer of brownie topped with a creamy cheesecake layer make it irresistible to kids and adults alike. Usually cheesecakes contain high-fat cream cheese, which has 35% MF, and regular sour cream, which has 14% MF, as well as many eggs. But this recipe uses low-fat sour cream, ricotta cheese, and light cream cheese to reduce calories and fat.

Brownie Layer
2/3 cup granulated sugar 150 mL
1/4 cup vegetable oil 50 mL
1 large egg 1
1 tsp vanilla 5 mL
1/3 cup all-purpose flour 75 mL
1/3 cup unsweetened cocoa powder 75 mL
1 tsp baking powder 5 mL
1/4 cup low-fat sour cream 50 mL

Cheesecake Layer
1 cup smooth 5% ricotta cheese 250 mL
1/2 cup granulated sugar 125 mL
1/3 cup light cream cheese 75 mL

1/4 cup low-fat sour cream 50 mL
1 large egg 1
2 tbsp all-purpose flour
 25 mL
1 tsp vanilla 5 mL
2 tbsp semi-sweet chocolate chips 25 mL

Topping
1 cup low-fat sour cream 250 mL
2 tbsp granulated sugar 25 mL
1 tsp vanilla 5 mL

1 tbsp semi-sweet chocolate chips 15 mL

Preheat oven to 350°F (175°C). Spray an 8-1/2-inch (22 cm) springform pan with cooking spray.

1. To make brownie layer: In a bowl, beat together sugar, oil, egg, and vanilla. In another bowl, stir together flour, cocoa, and baking powder. Stir wet ingredients into the dry ingredients, just until combined. Stir in sour cream. Pour into prepared pan.
2. To make cheesecake layer: In a food processor, combine ricotta, sugar, cream cheese, sour cream, egg, flour, and vanilla; purée until smooth. Stir in chocolate chips. Pour cheese mixture on top of the brownie layer.
3. Place a pan of hot water on the bottom rack of the oven (this helps to retain moisture). Bake cheesecake in the centre of the oven for 40 minutes. The brownie layer may rise slightly around the edges.
4. To make topping: In a small bowl, stir together sour cream, sugar, and vanilla.
5. When the cake layers have baked, pour topping mixture carefully over top, smoothing it with the back of a spoon; sprinkle chocolate chips over top. Bake 10 more minutes. Let the pan cool on a wire rack.

Rocky Mountain Miniature Cheesecakes

I find that individual cheesecakes are elegant to serve, especially these ones, which are almost mousse-like in texture. Light cream cheese is 25% reduced in fat, compared to regular cream cheese. When combined with light ricotta, it tastes like full-fat cream cheese.

1-3/4 cups smooth 5% ricotta cheese 425 mL
3 oz light cream cheese, softened 90 g
1/2 cup low-fat sour cream 125 mL
1 large egg 1
3/4 cup granulated sugar 175 mL
3 tbsp unsweetened cocoa powder 45 mL
1-1/2 tbsp all-purpose flour 22 mL
1/3 cup miniature marshmallows 75 mL
3 tbsp semi-sweet chocolate chips 45 mL

Preheat oven to 350°F (175°C). Line a 12-cup muffin tin with paper muffin liners.

1. In a food processor, combine ricotta, cream cheese, sour cream, egg, sugar, cocoa, and flour; purée until smooth. Divide among prepared muffin cups.
2. Set the muffin tin in a larger pan. Pour enough hot water into the pan to come halfway up the sides of the muffin cups. (This keeps the cheesecakes moist.)
3. Bake in the centre of the oven for 20 minutes. Sprinkle marshmallows and chocolate chips evenly over cheesecakes. Bake for 5 minutes longer, or until marshmallows and chocolate chips begin to melt.
4. Remove the muffin tin from its water bath. Let the tin cool on a wire rack. Chill before serving.

Makes 12 servings.

NUTRITIONAL ANALYSIS
PER SERVING
161 calories
6.2 g protein
6.2 g fat, total
3.8 g fat, saturated
20 g carbohydrates
36 mg cholesterol
0.6 g fibre

TIPS
If you have only large marshmallows, use scissors to cut them into small pieces. You can replace the ricotta with 2% cottage cheese; just be sure to process it well for a smooth batter. These cheesecakes freeze beautifully.

Chocolate Chip Crumb Cake

Makes 16 servings.

NUTRITIONAL ANALYSIS
PER SERVING
226 calories
5 g protein
7 g fat, total
4 g fat, saturated
36 g carbohydrates
42 mg cholesterol
2 g fibre

TIP
A 9-inch (23 cm)
springform pan can be
used instead of a Bundt
pan; check the cake at
30 to 40 minutes to see if
it needs to bake a few
minutes longer. This cake
freezes beautifully.

If I had to rate my number one dessert of all time, this crumb cake would be it. I created it for *Enlightened Home Cooking,* and even today I whip it up all the time. My children can now bake it blindfolded! I adapted it from a recipe from the Silver Palate bakery in New York City. By using cocoa, light ricotta, and yogourt, I reduced the amount of fat and calories to make a heart-healthy version of this delicious cake. Even though chocolate is higher in fat and cholesterol than cocoa, 1/2 cup (125 mL) of chocolate chips spread over 16 slices is acceptable. Here's proof you don't have to eliminate chocolate when you eat light!

8 oz smooth 5% ricotta cheese 250 g
1/3 cup vegetable oil or butter 75 mL
1-1/4 cups granulated sugar 300 mL
2 large eggs 2
2 tsp vanilla 10 mL
1-1/2 cups all-purpose flour 375 mL
2 tsp baking powder 10 mL
1/2 tsp baking soda 2 mL
3/4 cup low-fat yogourt 175 mL
1/2 cup semi-sweet chocolate chips 125 mL

Filling
1/2 cup packed brown sugar 125 mL
4 tsp unsweetened cocoa powder 20 mL
1/2 tsp cinnamon 2 mL

Preheat oven to 350°F (175°C). Spray a 9-inch (23 cm) Bundt pan with cooking spray.

1. In a large bowl or in a food processor, beat together ricotta, oil, and sugar, mixing well. Add eggs and vanilla; mix well.
2. In another bowl, combine flour, baking powder, and baking soda; add to ricotta mixture in batches, alternating with the yogourt, mixing just until incorporated. Stir in chocolate chips. Pour half the batter into prepared pan.
3. To make filling: In a small bowl, combine brown sugar, cocoa, and cinnamon. Sprinkle half over the batter in the pan. Add remaining batter and top with remaining filling.
4. Place pan in the centre of the oven and bake for 35 to 40 minutes, or until a tester inserted in the centre comes out dry.
5. Let the pan cool on a wire rack. After cake has cooled, sprinkle with icing sugar, if desired.

Banana Chocolate Chip Pound Cake with Streusel Topping

This banana cake beats all the others. It is moist from the bananas and yogourt, and it has a delicious crunchy topping, with a few chocolate chips thrown in. Grape-Nuts is a low-fat breakfast cereal made from toasted wheat and barley. Its nutty texture is delicious not only for breakfast, but also for use in baking without adding excess fat or calories.

3/4 cup granulated sugar 175 mL
1 large ripe banana, mashed
    (1/2 cup/125 mL) 1
1/4 cup vegetable oil 50 mL
1 large egg 1
1 large egg white 1
2 tsp vanilla 10 mL
1 cup low-fat yogourt 250 mL
1-2/3 cups all-purpose flour 400 mL
1-1/2 tsp baking powder 7 mL
1/2 tsp baking soda 2 mL
1/3 cup semi-sweet chocolate chips 75 mL

Topping
1/3 cup Grape-Nuts cereal 75 mL
1/4 cup packed brown sugar 50 mL
1 tbsp all-purpose flour 15 mL
1-1/2 tsp vegetable oil 7 mL
1 tsp water 5 mL

Preheat oven to 350°F (175°C). Spray a 9- x 5-inch (23 x 12 cm) loaf pan with cooking spray.

1. In a large bowl, using a whisk or an electric mixer, combine sugar, banana, oil, egg, egg white, vanilla, and yogourt.
2. In another bowl, stir together flour, baking powder, baking soda, and chocolate chips. With a wooden spoon, stir dry ingredients into the banana mixture, just until combined. Pour into prepared pan.
3. To make topping: In a bowl, stir together cereal, brown sugar, flour, oil, and water until combined. Sprinkle topping evenly over batter.
4. Place pan in the centre of the oven and bake for 40 to 45 minutes, or until a tester comes out dry. Let the pan cool on a wire rack.

Makes 16 half slices.

NUTRITIONAL ANALYSIS
PER SERVING
194 calories
3 g protein
6.4 g fat, total
1.8 g fat, saturated
31 g carbohydrates
18 mg cholesterol
1 g fibre

TIP
For best results, use the ripest bananas you can find. In fact, keep overripe bananas in the freezer so they're handy for baking; just defrost and mash them. The intensity of the flavour is superb.

Orange–Apple Sour Cream Cake

Makes 16 servings.

NUTRITIONAL ANALYSIS
PER SERVING
248 calories
3.5 g protein
7.8 g fat, total
0.8 g fat, saturated
42 g carbohydrates
31 mg cholesterol
1.2 g fibre

TIPS
Try chopped pears or
peaches instead of apples.
To increase fibre in your
diet, use 2/3 cup (150 mL)
whole-wheat flour and
1 cup (250 mL) all-purpose.

Coffee cakes are simple and delicious to have any time of day, but this one puts coffee cakes in a different league completely. I like to serve it when I'm entertaining. Many people don't think traditional coffee cakes are high in fat. But beware! Most contain loads of butter, regular sour cream, and lots of eggs.

Topping
1/3 cup packed brown sugar 75 mL
3 tbsp chopped pecans 45 mL
1-1/2 tbsp all-purpose flour 22 mL
2 tsp vegetable oil or butter 10 mL
1/2 tsp cinnamon 2 mL

Filling
2 cups chopped, peeled apples
   (approx. 2 apples) 500 mL
1/2 cup raisins 125 mL
1 tbsp granulated sugar 15 mL
1 tsp cinnamon 5 mL

Cake
2/3 cup packed brown sugar 150 mL
1/2 cup granulated sugar 125 mL
1/3 cup vegetable oil 75 mL
2 large eggs 2
1 tbsp grated orange rind 15 mL
2 tsp vanilla 10 mL
1-2/3 cups all-purpose flour 400 mL
2 tsp baking powder 10 mL
1 tsp baking soda 5 mL
1/2 cup orange juice 125 mL
1/2 cup low-fat sour cream 125 mL

Preheat oven to 350°F (175°C). Spray a 10-inch (25 cm) springform pan with cooking spray.

1. To make topping: In a small bowl, combine brown sugar, pecans, flour, oil, and cinnamon until crumbly. Set aside.
2. To make filling: In a bowl, mix together apples, raisins, sugar, and cinnamon. Set aside.
3. To make cake: In a large bowl, using a whisk or an electric mixer, beat together brown sugar, granulated sugar, and oil. Add eggs one at a time, beating well after each addition. Mix in orange rind and vanilla.
4. In a separate bowl, stir together flour, baking powder, and baking soda. In another bowl, stir together orange juice and sour cream. Add flour mixture to beaten sugar mixture in batches, alternating with sour cream mixture, mixing just until blended. Fold in apple mixture; pour into prepared pan; sprinkle with reserved topping.
5. Place pan in the centre of the oven and bake for 40 to 45 minutes, or until a tester inserted in the centre comes out clean. Let the pan cool on a wire rack.

Pecan Cream Cheese Pie

The combination of cheesecake and pecans is too good for words. I like to serve this pie either at room temperature or chilled. Pecans are a good source of protein and a healthy polyunsaturated fat. But nuts are high in calories and fat, so eat them in moderation, or as an alternative source of protein in your diet.

Crust

1-1/2 cups vanilla wafer
 crumbs 375 mL
2 tbsp granulated sugar
 25 mL
2 tbsp water 25 mL
1 tbsp vegetable oil 15 mL

Cheesecake Filling

3/4 cup smooth 5% ricotta
 cheese 175 mL
1/3 cup granulated sugar
 75 mL
1/3 cup light cream cheese
 75 mL
1/4 cup light sour cream
 50 mL
1 large egg 1
1 tbsp all-purpose flour
 15 mL
1 tsp vanilla 5 mL

Pecan Filling

2/3 cup packed brown
 sugar 150 mL
1/2 cup chopped pecans
 125 mL
1 large egg 1
2 large egg whites 2
1/2 cup corn syrup
 125 mL
1 tbsp molasses 15 mL

Preheat oven to 375°F (190°C). Spray a 9-inch (23 cm) pie plate with cooking spray.

1. To make crust: In a bowl, stir together wafer crumbs, sugar, water, and oil until mixture holds together. Pat onto the bottom and up the sides of prepared pie plate.
2. To make cheesecake filling: In a food processor, combine ricotta, sugar, cream cheese, sour cream, egg, flour, and vanilla; purée until smooth. Pour into pie crust.
3. To make pecan filling: In a bowl, whisk together brown sugar, pecans, egg, egg whites, corn syrup, and molasses. Pour carefully over cheesecake layer.
4. Place pie plate in the centre of the oven and bake for approximately 30 to 35 minutes, or until the filling is almost set. It may rise up around the edges or even through the middle of the pecan filling. Let the plate cool on a wire rack.

Makes 12 servings.

NUTRITIONAL ANALYSIS
PER SERVING
290 calories
5.1 g protein
10 g fat, total
2.9 g fat, saturated
46 g carbohydrates
48 mg cholesterol
0.7 g fibre

TIPS
Be sure to process the cheesecake batter well to make as it as smooth as possible. Pay attention when pouring the pecan layer on top of the cheesecake so that they don't mix. Crust may stick to the pan when cutting; use a sharp knife.

Peanut Butter Mousse Pie

I never thought I could have a peanut butter mousse with a chocolate wafer crust and still call it low fat. You must try this dessert—it's sensational! Peanuts are a source of monounsaturated fat, which has been proven to help lower blood cholesterol. But they should be eaten in moderation because they are high in calories and fat.

Crust
1-3/4 cups chocolate wafer crumbs 400 mL
2 tbsp granulated sugar 25 mL
2 tbsp water 25 mL
1 tbsp vegetable oil 15 mL

Mousse
3/4 cup smooth 5% ricotta cheese 75 mL
2 oz light cream cheese, softened 60 g
1 cup granulated sugar 250 mL
1/3 cup smooth peanut butter 75 mL
1/2 cup low-fat yogourt 125 mL
2 tsp unflavoured gelatin powder 10 mL
3 tbsp cold water 45 mL
3 large egg whites 3
1/4 tsp cream of tartar 1 mL

Spray a 9-inch (23 cm) pie plate with cooking spray.

1. To make crust: In a bowl, stir together wafer crumbs, sugar, water, and oil until mixture holds together. Set aside
   1 tbsp (15 mL) of the crumb mixture and pat remainder onto the bottom and up the sides of prepared pie plate.
2. To make mousse: In a food processor, combine ricotta, cream cheese, 2/3 cup (150 mL) of the sugar, peanut butter, and yogourt; purée until smooth.
3. In a small microwavable bowl, combine gelatin and water, and let sit for 2 minutes; microwave on High for 20 seconds. Stir the mixture until it is dissolved. With the food processor running, add gelatin to ricotta mixture through the feed tube. Transfer to a large bowl.
4. In another bowl, beat egg whites with cream of tartar until foamy. Gradually add remaining 1/3 cup (75 mL) of the sugar, beating until stiff peaks form. Stir one-quarter of the egg whites into ricotta mixture. Gently fold in remaining egg whites, just until blended. Pour into prepared crust. Sprinkle reserved 1 tbsp (15 mL) crumb mixture over top of filling. Chill for 2 hours, or until filling is set firm.

Lemon Tiramisù

In *Enlightened Home Cooking*, I created a Chocolate Coffee Tiramisù that was luscious. You'd never know it didn't contain mascarpone cheese. I adapted it to a Lemon Tiramisù that I think may be even better. Thanks to ricotta cheese and light cream cheese, there is little fat in this wonderful traditional dessert.

1-3/4 cups smooth 5% ricotta cheese 425 mL
4 oz light cream cheese, softened 125 g
1/2 cup granulated sugar 125 mL
1 tbsp finely grated lemon rind 15 mL
1/3 cup fresh lemon juice 75 mL
1 large egg yolk 1
3 large egg whites 3
1/4 tsp cream of tartar 1 mL
1/3 cup granulated sugar 75 mL
1/2 cup boiling water 125 mL
3 tbsp fresh lemon juice 45 mL
3 tbsp granulated sugar 45 mL
20 3-inch/8 cm ladyfinger cookies 20

Spray a 9-inch (23 cm) square cake pan or decorative serving dish with cooking spray.

1. In a food processor, combine ricotta, cream cheese, the 1/2 cup (125 mL) sugar, lemon rind, the 1/3 cup (75 mL) lemon juice, and egg yolk; purée until smooth. Transfer to a large bowl.

2. In another bowl, beat egg whites with cream of tartar until foamy. Gradually add the 1/3 (75 mL) cup sugar, beating until stiff peaks form. Stir one-quarter of the egg whites into ricotta mixture. Gently fold in remaining egg whites, just until blended.

3. In a bowl, whisk together water, the 3 tbsp (45 mL) lemon juice, and the 3 tbsp (45 mL) sugar, until sugar dissolves. Dip each ladyfinger in lemon juice mixture just enough to moisten it; place 10 dipped ladyfingers in bottom of the prepared pan. Pour half of ricotta mixture over ladyfingers. Repeat layers. Chill at least 2 hours. Garnish with a lemon twist or grated lemon rind.

Makes 12 servings.

NUTRITIONAL ANALYSIS
PER SERVING
204 calories
7.8 g protein
6.3 g fat, total
3.4 g fat, saturated
29 g carbohydrates
88 mg cholesterol
0.2 g fibre

TIPS
Process the cheeses well until the batter is no longer grainy. Be sure to beat the egg whites and sugar well until all the granules are dissolved. Use only fresh lemon juice.

Notes

The State of the (Fat) Nation

1. University of California at Berkeley, *The New Wellness Encyclopedia*, Houghton Mifflin Company: 1995, page 46.

2. University of California at Berkeley, *The New Wellness Encyclopedia*, Houghton Mifflin Company: 1995, page 55.

3. University of California at Berkeley, *The New Wellness Encyclopedia*, Houghton Mifflin Company: 1995, page 56.

4. "News about Diabetes" University of California at Berkeley, *Wellness Letter*, Volume 18, Issue 2, November 2001, page 1.

Diets: The Good, the Bad, and the So-So

1. Atkins, Dr., *New Diet Revolution*, Avon Books, New York: 1999.

2. Sears, Barry, *Enter the Zone*, Regan Books, HarperCollins, New York: 2001.

3. Steward, H. Leighton, et al., *Sugar Busters*, Ballantine Books, New York: 1998.

4. Heller, Dr. Rachael, and Heller, Dr. Richard, *The Carbohydrate Addict's Healthy Heart Program*, Ballantine Books, New York: 1999.

5. Diamond, Harvey, and Diamond, Marilyn, *Fit for Life*, Twin Streams Kensington Publishing, New York: 2000.

6. Somers, Suzanne, *Eat Great, Lose Weight*, Crown Publishers, New York: 1996.

7. D'Adamo, Dr. Peter, and Whitney, Catherine, *Eat Right for (4) Your Type*, G.P. Putnam and Sons, New York: 1996.

8. Montignac, Michel, *Eat Yourself Slim*, Michel-Ange Publishing, 1999.

9. Ornish, Dr. Dean, *Dr. Dean Ornish – Program for Reversing Heart Disease*, Ivy Books, New York: 1996.

10. Cooper, Jay, *Body Code – Green Valley Spa*, Simon and Schuster, New York: 1999.

11. Willcox, Dr. Bradley, and Suzuki, Dr. M., *The Okinawa Program*, Three Rivers Press, New York: 2001.

The New Nutrition

1. *Canada's Food Guide*, Minister of Public Works and Government Services Canada: 1997.

2. *Nutrition Recommendations for Canadians*, Health Canada, 1990.

3. Among others, Beck, Leslie, and Bauer, Joy, *The Complete Idiot's Guide to Total Nutrition for Canadians*, Prentice Hall Canada, Toronto: 2002, page 15.

4. Atkins, Dr., *New Diet Revolution*, Avon Books, New York: 1999.

5. Null, Gary, *The Complete Guide to Health and Nutrition*, Dell Publishing, New York: 1984.

6. Weil, Andrew, *Natural Health, Natural Medicine*, Houghton Mifflin Company, Boston, Massachusetts: 1990.

7. University of California at Berkeley, *Wellness Letter*, May 1999.

8. Among others, see Nelson, Miriam E., *Strong Women Eat Well*, Putnam and Sons, New York: 2001; and University of California at Berkeley, *Wellness Letter*.

9. University of California at Berkeley, *The New Wellness Encyclopedia*, Houghton Mifflin Company: 1995, page 125.

Don't Go to the Supermarket without Me

1. As discussed in Powter, Susan, *Food*, Simon and Schuster, New York: 1995.

The Light Kitchen

1. University of Toronto Faculty of Medicine, *Health News*, Volume 18, No. 6, December 2000/January 2001, page 1.

Bibliography

Atkins, Dr., *New Diet Revolution*, Avon Books, New York: 1999

Beck, Leslie, *Leslie Beck's Nutrition Encyclopedia*, Prentice Hall Canada, Toronto: 2001

Beck, Leslie, *Managing Menopause*, Prentice Hall Canada, Toronto: 2000

Beck, Leslie, and Bauer, Joy, *The Complete Idiot's Guide to Total Nutrition for Canadians*, Prentice Hall Canada, Toronto: 2002

Benard, Dr. Melvin, *Food Additives Dictionary*, Simon and Schuster, New York: 1981

Bender, Arnold, and Bender, David, *The Oxford Dictionary of Food and Nutrition*, Oxford University Press, New York: 1995

Bohme, Karine, *The Silent Thief*, Prentice Hall Canada, Toronto: 2001

Buckland, Wendy, and Nicoll, Barb, *Armed and Dangerous*, Key Porter Books, Toronto: 1996

Canada's Food Guide, Minister of Public Works and Government Services Canada: 1997.

Casselmans, Barbie, *Good for You Cooking*, Random House, Toronto: 1993

Chuey RD, Patricia, *The 101 Most Asked Nutrition Questions*, Eating for Energy, Vancouver: 1999

Cooper, Jay, *Body Code – Green Valley Spa*, Simon and Schuster, New York: 1999

D'Adamo, Dr. Peter, and Whitney, Catherine, *Eat Right for (4) Your Type*, G.P. Putnam and Sons, New York: 1996

Diamond, Harvey, and Diamond, Marilyn, *Fit for Life*, Twin Streams Kensington Publishing, New York: 2000

Douglas, Ann, *The Incredible Shrinking Woman*, Prentice Hall Canada, Toronto: 2000

Gottlieb RD, Sharon, *Seeing the Light*, The Nutrition Institute, Toronto: 1999

Greene, Bob, and Winfrey, Oprah, *Making the Connection*, Hyperion, New York: 1996

Health Canada, *Nutrition Recommendations for Canadians*, 1990.

Heller, Dr. Rachael, and Heller, Dr. Richard, *The Carbohydrate Addict's Healthy Heart Program*, Ballantine Books, New York: 1999

Henner, Marilu, *Healthy Kids*, Regan Books, HarperCollins, New York: 2001

In the Kitchen with Heloise, Berkeley Publishing Group, New York: 2000

Josephson RDN, Ramona, *The HeartSmart Shopper*, Douglas and McIntyre, Vancouver: 1997

Levy, Linda, and Grabowski, Francine, *Low Fat Living for Real People*, Lake Isle Press, New York: 1998

Margen MD, Sheldon, and the University of California at Berkeley Wellness Letter, *The Wellness Nutrition Counter*, Rebus, New York: 1997

The Meat and Seafood Answer Book, Try Foods, Florida: 1999

Montignac, Michel, *Eat Yourself Slim*, Michel-Ange Publishing, 1999

Natow, Annette, and Heslin, Jo-Ann, *Eating Out Food Counter*, Simon and Schuster, New York: 1998

Nelson, Miriam E., *Strong Women Eat Well*, Putnam and Sons, New York: 2001

Null, Gary, *The Complete Guide to Health and Nutrition*, Dell Publishing, New York: 1984.

Ornish, Dr. Dean, *Dr. Dean Ornish – Program for Reversing Heart Disease*, Ivy Books, New York: 1996

Powter, Susan, *Food*, Simon and Schuster, New York: 1995

Pressman, Alan, *The Complete Idiot's Guide to Vitamins and Minerals*, Macmillan: 2000

Prevention: 1001 Best Health Tips, Rodale Press: 2001

Rosenberg, Monda, *Chatelaine Wonder Foods*, Prentice Hall Canada, Toronto: 2001

Sarah, the Duchess of York, and Weight Watchers, *Dieting with the Duchess*, Fireside, New York: 1998

Sarah, the Duchess of York, and Weight Watchers, *Win the Weight Game*, Simon and Schuster, New York: 2000

Sears, Barry, *Enter the Zone*, Regan Books, HarperCollins, New York: 2001

Shoppers Guide to Fresh Produce, Try Foods Canada: 1997

Somers, Suzanne, *Eat Great, Lose Weight*, Crown Publishers, New York: 1996

Steel, Pamela, and Binns, Brigit, *Low Fat Cooking Canadian Style*, Prentice Hall Canada, Toronto: 2000

Steward, H. Leighton, et al., *Sugar Busters*, Ballantine Books, New York: 1998

Toews, Judy, and Parton, Nicole, *Never Say Diet*, Key Porter, Toronto: 1998

Tufts University, *Health and Nutrition Letter*, newsletters, 1999–2002

Twigg, Stephen, *Love Food Lose Weight*, A Plume Book: 1997

University of California at Berkeley, *The New Wellness Encyclopedia*, Houghton Mifflin Company: 1995

University of California at Berkeley, *Wellness Letter*, newsletters, 1998–2002

University of Toronto Faculty of Medicine, *Health News*, newsletters, 1999–2002

Weight Watchers Coach Approach, Macmillan, New York: 1997

Weil, Andrew, Natural Health, *Natural Medicine*, Houghton Mifflin Company, Boston, Massachusetts: 1990.

Willcox, Dr. Bradley, and Suzuki, Dr. M., *The Okinawa Program*, Three Rivers Press, New York: 2001

Index